AN INDIAN WOMAN DRESSED OUT IN HER JEWELS

ISLAM IN INDIA

OR THE

QĀNŪN–I–ISLĀM

The Customs of the Musalmāns of India

COMPRISING A FULL AND EXACT ACCOUNT OF THEIR VARIOUS RITES AND CEREMONIES FROM THE MOMENT OF BIRTH TO THE HOUR OF DEATH

BY

JA'FAR SHARIF

A NATIVE OF THE DECCAN

COMPOSED UNDER THE DIRECTION OF, AND TRANSLATED BY

G.A. HERKLOTS, M.D.

Surgeon on the Madras Establishment

WITH TWENTY ILLUSTRATIONS

NEW EDITION, REVISED AND REARRANGED, WITH ADDITIONS

BY

WILLIAM CROOKE, C.I.E., Hon. D.Sc. Oxon., Hon. Litt. D. Dublin

FELLOW OF THE ROYAL ANTHROPOLOGICAL INSTITUTE; LATE OF THE INDIAN CIVIL SERVICE

ATLANTIC PUBLISHERS AND DISTRIBUTORS

Published by
ATLANTIC PUBLISHERS AND DISTRIBUTORS
B-2, Vishal Enclave, New Delhi-110 027
Phones 5413460, 5429987

Sales Office
4346/4C, Ansari Road, Darya Ganj,
New Delhi-110 002
Phones 3273880, 3285873, 3280451
Fax 91-11-3285873
e-mail : gupta.atlantc@axcess.net.in

ISBN 81-7156-806-8

Typeset at
APD Computer Graphics, Delhi

Printed in India at
Tarun Offset Press, Delhi

Dedication of the First Edition

TO

THE HONOURABLE

THE CHAIRMAN, DEPUTY CHAIRMAN

AND

COURT OF DIRECTORS

OF THE

UNITED EAST-INDIA COMPANY

THIS WORK

PUBLISHED UNDER THEIR KIND AND LIBERAL PATRONAGE

RELATING TO

AN IMPORTANT AND INTERESTING CLASS OF BRITISH SUBJECTS

UNDER THEIR GOVERNMENT

IS, WITH PERMISSION

MOST RESPECTFULLY DEDICATED

BY

THEIR VERY OBEDIENT AND HUMBLE SERVANT

G. A. HERKLOTS

THE AUTHOR'S PREFACE

Lord, Prosper Work with	In the name of God, the Merciful and Compassionate!	and finish this Thy blessing!

Glory be to that God who has, out of a drop of fluid, created such a variety of creatures, rational and irrational![1] Adored be that Creator, who has established such a variety of forms, statures, and vocal sounds among them, though their origin is the same pure, liquid, and genuine spirit!

In praise of the Prophet, Muhammad. A thousand salutations and benedictions to his Sublime Holiness Muhammad Mustafā, the Chosen,—The Blessing and Peace of God be with him! *Salla-l-lāhu 'alaihi*—through whose grace the sacred Korān descended from the Most High![2] How inadequate is man justly to praise and eulogize Him! Salutation and blessing also to His Companions and posterity!

My object in composing the present work is this: I Ja'far Sharīf, alias Lālā Miyān, son of 'Alī Sharīf, who has received the mercy of the Lord[3]—of the Quraish[4] tribe born at Nāgor[5]—may God illuminate his tomb!—pardon his iniquities and sanctify his soul!—a native of Uppu

[1] *Korān*, xcvi. 1–2. [2] *Ibid.*, xxvi. 193–6, liii. 4–6.

[3] *Marhūm*, a euphemistic term, meaning 'deceased', 'one who has received mercy from God.'

[4] The Arab tribe to which the Prophet belonged.

[5] Nāgor, village of the serpent tribe (*nāga-ur*), now included in Negapatam (Nāgapathanam, 'town of the Nāgas'), in the Tanjore District, Madras (*I.G.I.*, xix. 3).

Ellore[1], have for a considerable time been in attendance upon English gentlemen of high rank and noble mind—May their good fortune ever continue!—and under the shadow of their wings have nourished both my soul and body: or, in other words, my office has been that of a teacher of languages.

Gentlemen of penetration used often to observe to me with the deepest interest, that if a concise book were written in a familiar style, and in the genuine Dakkhinī language,[2] containing a full account of all the necessary rites, customs, and usages observed by Musalmāns, Europeans would not only read it with pleasure, but would derive much useful knowledge from its perusal. However, hitherto owing to want of leisure this humble individual has not been able to undertake anything of the kind. But, in the present instance, at the kind request of a possessor of favour and kindness, a man of great learning and magnanimity, a mine of humanity, a fountain of generosity, a just appreciator of the worth of both high and low, well versed in the mysteries of philosophy, a Plato of the age, in medicine a second Galen, nay, the Hippocrates of the day, Dr. Herklots, a man of virtue, an ocean of liberality, May his good fortune ever continue and his age increase![3] I have endeavoured, to the extent of my poor

[1] Telugu Uppuēlūru, 'salt village of rule', the modern Ellore, in Kistna District, Madras (*ibid.*, xii. 23, *Madras Manual of Administration*, iii. 614).

[2] Dakkhinī or Deccan Hindostānī 'differs somewhat from the modern standard of Delhi and Lucknow, and retains several archaic features which have disappeared in the north' (*I. G. I.*, i. 366).

[3] Dr. Herklots adds the following note: 'At the very earnest solicitation of the Author, the translator has been prevailed on (very much against his own inclination) to allow the above hyperbolical eulogiums to remain, though conscious of his being little entitled to them. He has been induced to accede to the Author's wish more particularly to show the remarkable proneness of this class of people to flattery.'

abilities, to arrange this work under different heads, and entitled it 'Qānūn-i-Islām', i. e. 'The Customs of the Musalmāns'.[1]

Although various Hindostānī authors have occasionally adverted to similar subjects, yet no work extant contains so full an account of them as has been given here. I have also included in it local customs which have been super-added to the laws prescribed by the sacred Korān and Hadīs,[2] observed by Musalmāns, in order that the liberal-minded Englishman should not continue ignorant of, or remain in the dark as to any rite or ceremony observed by Musalmāns.

Although this Author, who deems himself no wiser than a teacher of the A B C, be somewhat acquainted with the science of divinity, i. e. the knowledge of the interpretation of the Korān and the Hadīs, or precepts of Muhammad, as well as with law and medicine, he has confined himself merely to a narration of the established and indispensable customs commonly observed by the Musalmāns in the Dakkhin, and to an idiom of language calculated to be understood by even the illiterate. Of him who can judge of the state of the pulse of the pen, i. e. estimate the beauty of composition, and is likewise erudite, I have this request to make, that should he observe any errors in it, he would kindly consign them to oblivion by erasing them with his quill.

This work was completed Anno Hijrae 1243, corresponding with Anno Domini 1832.[3]

[1] *Qānūn*, Greek κανών,—'canon, ordinance, regulation.'

[2] *Hadīs*, plural *Ahādīs*, 'a saying, revelations delivered to the Prophet in addition to those contained in the *Korān*, and held to be authoritative on moral, ceremonial, or doctrinal questions' (Hughes, 639).

[3] The Muhammadan era of the Hijra, or 'Flight', is dated from the first day of the month preceding the flight of Muhammad from Mecca to Medīna, i. e. Thursday, 15 July, A.D. 622, and it commenced on the day following. For the rules used in converting these dates into those of the Christian era, see *EB*. iv. 1001.

THE PREFACE OF THE TRANSLATOR, DR. HERKLOTS

THE manners, customs, social habits, and religious rites of nations have ever been esteemed an object of rational and interesting inquiry ; hence, with this view, travellers have explored the remotest regions and antiquarians pushed their researches into the farthest verge of recorded history. The toils of the journey, the uncongeniality of climate, the savage character of the inhabitants have not been able to deter the progress of the former ; the labour of solitary study, the scantiness of the materials, or the dark mists of antiquity have failed to damp the ardour of the latter. The adventurous foot of man has penetrated the dark forests of America, crossed the burning deserts of Africa, and ascended the lofty snow-clad summits of the Himalaya ; his ships have swept the ocean and visited the most sequestered shores, from the dreary abodes of the torpid Esquimaux to the tepid isles of cheerful Otaheite and the inhospitable coast of the cannibals of New Zealand : and though nature, inanimate and irrational, has not escaped his notice, yet his own species under every variety of form has chiefly attracted his attention and engrossed his reflections ; feeling, in the words of the poet, that 'The proper study of mankind is man.'

If the manners and customs of other tribes of men be worthy of our study, certainly not less so are those of the Muhammadan natives of India. They are the immediate descendants of the race of conquerors who exercised supreme dominion over the greater part of that vast country for so many centuries, until it fell into British hands. As their successors in Indian rule, we must naturally feel a curiosity regarding the character and habits of our predecessors in power, now our subjects. And it is not a topic of philosophical speculation merely, but a matter of real practical utility, to understand thoroughly a people with whom we have constant transactions and daily intercourse, in the relations of public officers, soldiers, and subjects, in administering the government of the country.

The utility of a work directed to this object is so obvious that it appears to me a matter of no small surprise something of the kind has not hitherto been undertaken. On the History, Religion, Manners, Customs, &c., of the Hindus, ample information may be obtained from valuable works already before the public, such as Mill's *History of British India*, Moor's *Hindoo Pantheon*, Ward's *History, Literature, Mythology, Manners, and Customs of the Hindoos*, Coleman's *Mythology*, the Abbé Dubois on the *Manners and Customs of the Hindoos*, and others. But, as far as my knowledge extends, no similar work exists giving a methodical account of the Muhammadan branch of the Indian population which embraces the various subjects comprehended in this, or which treats of them individually with sufficient precision and accuracy. From the comparative simplicity of the Muhammadan system of religion, its followers are less accessible to the influence of conversion, and may have therefore attracted less attention from Christian missionaries, who are the closest observers of a people among whom they pursue their pious labours, while few Europeans could have acquired the minute and curious information necessary for composing such a work; and learned natives did not think of describing to their own countrymen matters which they knew from daily observation and practice.

But whatever may have been the cause of the almost total neglect of this interesting field of inquiry, I shall proceed to explain the object of the following sheets. It is to give a detailed account of the customs adopted and observed in India, more particularly in the Dakkhin, vulgarly written Deccan, i. e. the Peninsula or southern part of India, by the followers of the Arabian Prophet, in addition to the duties inculcated on them in the Korān and Hadīs. Among the customs described, not a few will be discovered to have been borrowed from the Hindus; and although the work professes to treat on the customs of the Musalmāns, it will be found interspersed also with observations on their manners.

To guard against misconception on the part of those who have a partial knowledge of India, it may be remarked that many of the customs described in this work are peculiar to the Dakkhin, and some of them are observed only at certain places, not throughout every part of that division of India, far less in remote quarters of the country, such as Bombay, Bengal, and Upper Hindostān. Yet a very general resemblance will be found in the manners and customs of the Muhammadan inhabitants in all parts of it.

The following is the plan which the Author has followed in describing his countrymen. He traces an individual from the period of birth, and even before it, through all the forms and ceremonies which religion, superstition, and custom have imposed on the Indian Musalmān. The account begins with the ceremonies at the seventh month of the mother's pregnancy, details the various rites performed by the parents during the several periods of the lives of their children as they grow to maturity, and the almost endless ceremonies of matrimony. Then follow the fasts, festivals, &c., which occur in the different months of the year. These are succeeded by an account of vows, oblations, and many minor subjects, such as the pretended science of necromancy, exorcism or the casting out of devils, detecting thieves, determining the most auspicious times for undertaking journeys or other enterprises, all of which are matters of almost daily occurrence: and the whole concludes with an account of their sepulchral rites and the visiting of the grave at stated periods during the first year after death. For a fuller view of the extent and variety of the subjects discussed and the order of arrangement I must refer to the Table of Contents.

The persons to whom I conceive the work will prove most acceptable are, in the first place, gentlemen in the service of the Honourable East India Company generally; and, in particular, all military officers serving in India, more especially those on the Madras Establishment. For example, how often during the year do we find Musalmāns of a native regiment apply for leave or exemption from duty to celebrate some feast or other, when the commandant to whom such request is submitted, being unacquainted, as frequently happens, with either the nature of the feast or the necessity of attending it, cannot be certain that in granting the application he is doing justice to the service, or that in refusing it he would not infringe upon the religious feelings of his troops. If an officer be more endowed than others with a spirit of inquiry, he may ask after the nature of the feast for which the holiday is solicited. The only reply he obtains is some strange name which, though to a native it may be very expressive and quite explicit, is to him as a foreigner altogether unintelligible. Should he inquire further, his want of sufficient knowledge of the language prevents him from understanding the explanations offered, and these are often rendered still more dark by the ignorance of the informers themselves, of whom few even know the origin and nature of the feast they are about to celebrate. This want of knowledge the present work is intended to supply, and how far the Author has succeeded I leave to the judgement of the reader.

Having myself felt the want of such a work ever since my arrival in India, I set about collecting all the intelligence procurable relative to the various subjects comprised in these pages. To accomplish this object, it must be admitted, was no easy task in a country where the natives, as is well known, are very reluctant to impart information respecting their religious rites, ceremonies, &c. This arises perhaps from an unwillingness to expose themselves to the ridicule of persons of totally different national customs and religious faith, or from a wish simply to keep Europeans in the dark, under a vague apprehension that frankness would ultimately prove to their own detriment. I had succeeded, notwithstanding, in accumulating a pretty extensive stock of the requisite materials, when I accidentally became acquainted with the liberal-minded Author of these sheets. At my particular request he composed in the Dakkhinī language the treatise now presented to the public, while I acted merely as a reviser, and occasionally suggested subjects which had escaped his memory.

Though the enlightened English reader will smile at some of the notions gravely propounded by an Oriental writer, yet I must do my Author the justice to say that in all my intercourse with natives of India I have seldom met with a man who had so much of the European mode of thinking and acting, or who was so indefatigable in the pursuit of knowledge. He was penetrating and quick of comprehension, and, according to my professional judgement, a skilful and scientific physician.

I have made the translation as literal as the different idioms of the two languages would admit of, bearing in mind that though a free translation has often more ease and elegance, a close version is more characteristic of the original. And I considered this the more important as I have some intention of publishing hereafter the Oriental version of this work,[1] and conceive that the close correspondence between the two will be of great advantage to the young Oriental student.

As my object has been to give a complete and precise idea of the things described, I have by a full and minute description avoided the obscurity which often arises from vagueness of language and brevity of expression. During the progress of the work and researches connected with it, a large quantity of useful miscellaneous information has come into my hands. Part of this I have comprised in an Appendix under the heads of Relationship, Weights and Measures, Dresses of Men and Women, Female Ornaments, Muhammadan Cookery, Musical Instruments, Fireworks, Games, and Children's Plays.

[Here follows an account of the system of transliteration adopted by the translator.]

For the sake of the European reader and those unacquainted with the native language of India I have subjoined a copious Glossary of all Oriental words occurring and which have not been already explained in the body of the work or in the Index, in which it was found more convenient to insert the Oriental terms expressive of such subjects as are particularly treated of in the work. All the Oriental words are put in italics, and this will serve as an intimation that every word so distinguished will be found explained in the Glossary or Index.

Since this work was prepared for press I have had an opportunity of consulting two recent publications which throw considerable light on the subject: viz, the correct and interesting *Observations on the Mussulmauns of India*, by Mrs. Meer Hassan Ali, 1832,[2] and the learned and

[1] The Hindostānī version was not published, and has been lost.
[2] Republished, Oxford. 1916.

curious *Mémoires sur les Particularités de la Religion Mussulmane dans l'Inde* (Paris 1831), by that ingenious and profound Orientalist the Professor of Hindostānī to the French Government, Monsieur Garcin de Tassy. I have carefully compared their labours with the following sheets, and whenever I found anything of interest and importance in them which had been omitted or otherwise stated by my Author, I have supplied the omission, or marked the difference in notes and a few addenda, so as to render this work, as far as possible, complete. I may now therefore, I think, venture to say that it embraces an account of all the peculiarities of the Musalmāns worthy of note in *every part* of India.

I would remark that any one at all conversant with the Muhammadans or their faith will instantly perceive that the first work above alluded to embraces the opinions of a Shī'a and that of my Author of a Sunnī or orthodox Musalmān. The two works thus develop the conflicting opinions of the two great sects who entertain the most inveterate hatred towards each other, and, combined, afford as complete an insight into the national character of that race as can reasonably be desired or expected. Barring the difference of their religious notions, the general description given of their manners, customs, &c., accord so entirely that so far from one at all detracting from the merits of the other, the statements of the English lady and the Indian Musalmān will be found to afford each other mutual support and illustration.

G. A. HERKLOTS

LONDON, 1*st September* 1832.

INTRODUCTION TO THE PRESENT EDITION

SINCE the publication of the English version of this work in 1832 it has maintained its reputation as one of the most authoritative accounts of the beliefs and practices of the Musalmāns of India. Sir R. Burton, an eminent authority on such questions, writes: 'I know no work upon the subject of the south Indian Hindis that better deserves a reprint, with notes and corrections'; and in his version of *The Book of the Thousand Nights and a Night* he speaks of it as 'an excellent work', praising in particular the chapters on the use of astrology as a means of prognosticating events.[1] It has been the source from which later writers on Islām in India have derived much information. For the anthropologist the chapters on the various forms of Magic, domestic rites, and the many festivals of the Musalmāns will provide much novel and interesting detail.

The original edition gives little or no information about the author and the translator. Inquiries kindly made at the India Office by Mr. W. Foster, C.I.E., Registrar and Superintendent of Records, and by Mr. A. G. Ellis, Assistant Librarian; in India by the British Resident at the Court of H.H. The Nizām of Hyderābād; at Madras by Mr. F. J. Richards, I.C.S., have elicited some facts of importance. The Resident at Hyderābād merely states that the author, Ja'far Sharīf, 'was a man of low origin and of no account in his own country', and that no information about his career is now procurable. He was, as appears from his own statement, a Munshī or tutor,

[1] *Sind Revisited*, i. 308: *AN*, i. 195.

employed in teaching Arabic, Persian, and Urdū to officers in the service of the Madras Government. In the course of these duties he gained the patronage of Mr. G. A. Herklots, M.D., a Surgeon on the Madras establishment, by whose encouragement he was induced to compile the *Qānūn-i-Islām*, the rules of religious and social life in force among his co-religionists, the Musalmāns of southern India. He was also a skilful physician, following the established methods of Muhammadan medicine. Further than this we know nothing of his personal history, except that he was possibly a resident of the municipal town Ellore in the Kistna District, Madras Presidency, where he finished the work.

He was an orthodox Musalmān of the Sunnī sect, but he shows little intolerance towards the beliefs of the rival sect of Shī'as, which gained considerable influence in southern India owing to patronage at the Court of Bījāpur, where half the members of the 'Adil Shāhī dynasty (A. D. 1490–1626) were Sunnīs and half Shī'as. From their rather precarious position as strangers in a foreign land, rulers of a people mostly of Dravidian origin, the 'Adil Shāhīs were forced to adopt a policy of toleration towards Musalmān sectaries as well as Christians and Hindus. Like all men of his class, he believed in Magic and sorcery, but his association with Europeans seems to have checked his credulity, and he sometimes writes about these questions in a deprecatory, half apologetic tone. He was learned in the history and literature of the Faith, and he obviously describes it in a spirit of honest belief, but with candour and discrimination.

We know more of the career of Dr. G. A. Herklots, the editor and translator of the book. He belonged to a family of Dutch origin settled in the town of Chinsura in Bengal, now included in the Hooghly municipality. The Dutch established themselves there in the early part of the seventeenth century and held the place till 1825, when it was ceded by the Netherlands to Great Britain in part exchange for the British possessions in Sumatra. The *Bengal Obituary*[1] among burials at Chinsura records that of 'Mevrouw C. G. Kloppenburg Weduioee (*sic*) van Wylen den Heere Gregorius Herklots, in leeven opperhoof te Kassimbazaar, obit (*sic*) 9th October 1820, oud 73 Jaaren'

Another notice in the *Bengal Obituary*[2] mentions the death of Mrs. C. C. Herklots on 9 June 1846, aged 72 years, 3 months. In the same tomb had previously been interred five of her children and four grandchildren belonging to the families of Betts, Lacroix, and Herklots. She is described on her monument as the wife of Gregory Herklots Esq., Fiscal of Chinsura. 'She was born and educated in this country and rose above all the real or imaginary disadvantages of a whole life spent in India. By the grace of God, her naturally buoyant and lively temper was constrained for the service of Christ, which rendered her at once a cheerful and instructive companion. She was the mother of sixteen living children, the whole of whom were in a great measure reared under her roof; these, together with the parties connected with her family by alliance and their descendants, amounted to not less than 105 souls.' The inscription ends by recording her merits as a true Christian, devoted to good works, even when at the close of her life she became nearly blind.

These two ladies and their husbands, both named Gregorius or Gregóry Herklots, seem to have been respectively the grand-parents and parents of the translator, Gerhard Andreas Herklots.

The only information procurable about G. A. Herklots

[1] p. 336. C. R. Wilson (*Tombs in Bengal*, 1896) records this inscription in the Dutch cemetery at Chinsura, but reads 'Weduwe', and gives 72 as her age.

[2] p. 353.

is furnished by M. Garcin de Tassy.[1] It appears from an affidavit made by him at the time of his appointment as Surgeon on the Madras establishment, that he was born at Chinsura on 28 February 1790, the son of Gregory Herklots of Bremen, capital of the Free State of that name, and of Caroline Catherine, his wife, who was born at Middelburg, the ancient capital of the province of Zeeland in Holland. His father went to India about 1788 and held an appointment under the Dutch Government until Chinsura was surrendered in 1825 to the British, when, as his son believed, he was appointed assistant to Mr. Gordon Forbes, the East India Company's Commissioner. He was sent to England to study medicine, and on 31 March 1818 Mr. William Dick certified that he was qualified in physic to hold the post of Assistant Surgeon in the service of the East India Company. He was appointed on the following day and posted to the Madras establishment, his commission as Assistant Surgeon being dated 18 July 1818. He arrived at Madras on 7 June 1819, and in January 1822 he was attached to the 1st Battalion of the 19th Madras Native Infantry, and later to the 10th Native Infantry, in which he served in the first Burmese war which ended by the treaty of Yandaboo in February 1826. On his return from active service he probably induced Ja'far Sharīf to compile this work, the English translation of which was in progress about the time when he went on furlough to England, the preface being dated London, 1 September 1832. The whole or part of the funds spent on publishing the book were supplied by the East India Company. He returned to India and died at Wālājābād on 8 July 1834. This place, situated in the Chingleput District, Madras, became a military cantonment about 1786, and was occupied by European and Native Regiments. But it was found to be very unhealthy, and the

[1] *Histoire de la Litterature Hindoue*, Paris, 1870, vol. ii. p. 61.

mortality among the troops was so great that it was called 'the grave of Europeans'. The cantonment was abandoned and the last occupants, a veteran battalion, were removed in 1860. The tomb of Dr. Herklots at Wālājābād is mentioned in Mr. J. J. Cotton's *List of Inscriptions on Tombs or Monuments in Madras.* There is no record of his marriage in the lists preserved at the India Office.

It is a remarkable coincidence that the *Qānūn-i-Islām* was published three years before E. W. Lane's classical account of *The Manners and Customs of the Modern Egyptians.* It is possible that a copy of Herklots' book may have reached Lane in Cairo, but there is little resemblance between the two monographs, and I have not traced any reference by Lane to the book; he certainly does not mention it in his preface to the first edition dated from Cairo in 1835.

It appears that the original work of Ja'far Sharīf was chiefly confined to the account of Musalmān beliefs and practices which form the greater part of the book. To this Dr. Herklots attached a long appendix containing articles on relationships, weights and measures, dress, jewellery, cooking, games, children's plays, and fireworks, to which was added a glossary containing particulars of many matters referred to in the body of the book and of others here discussed for the first time. This inconvenient arrangement obviously lessened the value of the book, since much of the information was scattered in various places, and even with the aid of an index was not easily accessible.

The work is not a classic in the sense that Tod's *Annals of Rajasthan* and Sleeman's *Rambles and Recollections*, both republished in this series, are classics, the works of learned, accomplished men writing in their own language, which deserved to be reprinted as they came from the hands of the authors. This is merely a translation, and rather a rude translation, of a lost original in Hindostānī. It was, therefore, believed that if the work in its new form was to be made more useful to students of the Musalmāns of India, it was necessary to rearrange and partially rewrite it; to separate those chapters relating to domestic life from those describing religious beliefs and usages; and to transfer into the body of the book from the appendix and glossary anything which appeared to be of permanent value. Some of this scattered material has been brought together into separate chapters, such as those dealing with food, intoxicants and stimulants, and the like. Many of the articles in the original appendix consist merely of lists of names, in Urdū or some south Indian language, of articles of food, clothing, jewels, musical instruments, and so on. In many cases the explanations and descriptions of these things were so inadequate that it would serve no useful purpose to reprint them. Many of these words in the course of time have been transferred from this book into later dictionaries, such as the *Dictionary of Urdū, Classical Hindī, and English*, published by Mr. J. T. Platts in 1884, where they find their fitting place. Even if it were within my powers to extend these vocabularies so as to make them representative of Musalmān India as a whole, it would have added largely to the size of the book without rendering it more practically useful. I have, however, retained in the body of the book a large number of technical terms which can easily be traced through the Index. In this rearrangement and condensation I trust that I have omitted nothing of real importance, and that I have as far as possible retained the original oriental atmosphere of the book. The space thus gained has been utilized for the inclusion of much new information which is, I believe, of much more value than anything which I have been forced to discard.

Another matter deserving attention is the scope of the

work. As originally compiled by a Musalmān of southern India, it was devoted mainly to the beliefs and customs prevailing in that part of the country. But in order to include an account of Indian Islām as a whole, Dr. Herklots, while preparing the book for the press, embodied some information derived from Mrs. Meer Hassan Ali's *Observations on the Mussulmans of India*, which has been republished in this series, and from M. Garcin de Tassy's *Mémoires sur les Particularités de la Religion Mussulmane dans l'Inde*. He stated that thus extended 'it embraces an account of all the peculiarities of the Musalmāns worthy of note in every part of India'. The authorities which he quoted are of high value, but it is hardly necessary to say that while Ja'far Sharīf's book furnishes an admirable account of the Musalmāns of southern India, it cannot pretend, even with the additions made in a hasty way by Dr. Herklots, to embody all or most of the information regarding this people throughout the Indian Empire. Thus the statement of the editor-translator is likely to cause some misapprehension. Since this book was published for the first time, an immense amount of information, some of which I have included in this edition, has become available. The extent of these fresh materials may be gathered from the selected bibliography which I have added. For example, in the original work there is little information regarding the Musalmāns of northern, central, eastern, and western India, except that collected from Mrs. Meer Hassan Ali's account of the Shī'as of Lucknow. Nothing is said about the Musalmāns of the Panjāb and that most interesting group of tribes on the north-west frontier, in Sind and Balūchistān, where Islām has produced little effect upon the indigenous Animistic beliefs and practices. No account of Islām as it exists in India can be regarded as satisfactory which ignores these and other tribes and castes which more or less conform to the orthodox faith. The inclusion of facts beyond the scope of the original work necessarily gives an appearance of scrappiness to the present edition, in which it was impossible, from consideration of space, to present this new information in any but a condensed form. I hope, however, that the additions which I have made, combined with a careful citation of the original authorities, will make the book more useful to students of Islām. I have also, particularly in the case of southern India, given references to the Hindu sources from which certain dogmas and ritual have been derived ; or rather it would be preferable to say that these beliefs and usages are part of the original heritage of these people who have assimilated Islām only in an imperfect way.

I have not, as a rule, aimed at considering the principles which underlie much of this local Musalmān ritual, but I have occasionally given references to standard anthropological works in which these subjects are discussed. As regards quotations from the Korān, I have substituted the version of Rodwell for that of Sale. The transliteration has been corrected throughout according to the system generally current in India and that used in well-known works of authority like the *Dictionary* of Mr. Platts and the valuable *Dictionary of Islām* by Mr. Hughes.

The facts thus collected, I believe in a large measure for the first time, may help to remove a current misconception. While the beliefs and customs of the Hindu tribes and castes have been carefully examined, much less attention has been devoted to those of the Indian Musalmāns, because it has been supposed that the recognition by them of an authoritative body of Scriptures, the Korān with the later Traditions of the teaching of the Prophet, has imposed a well-defined, uniform system of belief and ritual which permits little or no variation. On the contrary, Islām in India has no pretensions to be regarded as a well-organized system of dogma and practice, and throughout the Empire the variations are often startling. This is due to the clash or contact of the new faith with the old. From this point of view it presents many features of interest to the student of comparative religion, and it deserves more attention than it has hitherto received. In the chapter on Ethnography I have given a brief survey which is essential for the study of the account of religion and sociology which follows.

W. CROOKE.

CONTENTS

CHAPTER V

CIRCUMCISION

CHAPTER VI

GROWTH AND EDUCATION

CHAPTER VII

THE COMING OF AGE OF A GIRL AND A BOY

CHAPTER VIII

MARRIAGE

CHAPTER IX

DEATH

CHAPTER X

THE FOUNDATIONS OF ISLĀM

CHAPTER XI

PRAYER

CHAPTER XII

VOWS AND OBLATIONS ; SOME INDO-MUSALMĀN SAINTS

CHAPTER XIII

RELIGIOUS BUILDINGS AND APPLIANCES FOR WORSHIP

CHAPTER XIV

THE MUHARRAM FESTIVAL

CHAPTER XV

THE TERAH TEZĪ AND ĀKHIRĪ CHĀRSHAMBA FESTIVALS

CHAPTER XVI

THE BĀRAH WAFĀT; NEW YEAR AND SPRING FESTIVALS

CHAPTER XVII

THE FESTIVAL OF THE SAINT PĪR-I-DASTAGĪR

CHAPTER XVIII

THE FESTIVAL OF THE SAINT ZINDA SHĀH MADĀR

CHAPTER XIX

THE FESTIVAL OF THE SAINT QĀDIRWALĪ SĀHIB

CHAPTER XX

CHAPTER XXI

THE SHAB-I-BARĀT FESTIVAL

CHAPTER XXII

THE RAMAZĀN FESTIVAL

CHAPTER XXIII

THE FESTIVAL OF THE SAINT BANDA NAWĀZ, GESŪ DARĀZ

CHAPTER XXIV

THE 'ĪDU-L-FITR FESTIVAL

CHAPTER XXV

THE BAQAR 'ĪD FESTIVAL

CHAPTER XXVI

MAGIC

CHAPTER XXVII

AMULETS AND CHARMS

CHAPTER XXVIII

MAGICAL METHODS

CHAPTER XXIX

THE MAGICAL DETECTION OF THIEVES

CHAPTER XXX

TRAVELLING, LUCKY AND UNLUCKY DAYS

CHAPTER XXXI

SŪFĪ MYSTICISM

CHAPTER XXXII

DRESS, THE TOILET

CHAPTER XXXIII

JEWELLERY

CHAPTER XXXIV

FOOD AND DRINK

CHAPTER XXXV

INTOXICANTS, STIMULANTS

CHAPTER XXXVI

GAMES

LIST OF ILLUSTRATIONS

PUBLISHER'S NOTE

In this new impression the half-tone illustrations of monuments facing pp 67, 102, 104, 142, 146 and 148 have been omitted for technical reasons. This in no way diminishes the value of the work since they did not form part of the original Herklots' edition but were a later addition.

BIBLIOGRAPHY

With some abbreviated titles of Works quoted in the notes.

Āīn. Abū-l-Fazl Allāmī. The *Āīn-i-Akbarī*, translated and edited by H. Blochmann and H. S. Jarrett. 3 vols. Calcutta, 1873–94.

Aitken, E. A. *The Gazetteer of Sind*. Karachi, 1907.

Albiruni. *Chronology of the Ancient Nations*, trans. C. E. Sachau. London, 1879.

Anantha Krishna Iyer, L. K. *Cochin Tribes and Castes*. 2 vols. Madras, 1909–12.

Arnold, T. W. *The Preaching of Islam*. Westminster, 1896.

Atkinson, E. T. *The Himalayan Districts of the North-West Provinces of India*. 3 vols. Allahabad, 1882–86.

Atkinson, J. *Customs and Manners of the Women of Persia and their Domestic Superstitions*. London, 1832.

Baillie, N. B. E. *A Digest of Moohummudan Law*. 2nd ed. London, 1875.

Balfour, E. *Cyclopaedia of India*, 3rd ed. 3 vols. London, 1885.

Benjamin, S. G. W. *Persia and the Persians*. London, 1887.

Bernier, F. *Travels in the Mogul Empire*, ed. A Constable, V. A. Smith. Oxford, 1914.

BG. *Gazetteer of the Bombay Presidency*, ed. Sir J. Campbell. 27 vols. Bombay, 1874–1904.

Bilgrami, Syed Hosain, Willmott, C. *Historical and Descriptive Sketch of H. H. the Nizam's Dominions*. 2 vols. Bombay, 1883.

Brand, J. *Observations on Popular Antiquities*. 3 vols. London, 1848.

Bray, Denys. *The Life History of a Brāhūī*. London, 1913.

Browne, E. G. *A Year Amongst the Persians*. London, 1893.

Burnes, Sir A. *Cabool*, 1836–8. London, 1842.

Burton, Sir R. *A. N. The Book of a Thousand Nights and a Night*. 12 vols. London, 1893.

—— *Sindh and the Races that inhabit the Valley of the Indus*. London, 1851.

—— *Sind Revisited*. 2 vols. London, 1877.

—— *A Personal Narrative of a Pilgrimage to Al-Madinah and Mecca*. 2 vols. London, 1893.

Chevers, N. *Manual of Medical Jurisprudence for India*. Calcutta, 1870.

Cousens, H. *Bījāpur and its Antiquities*. Bombay, 1916.

C.R. *Census Reports*; Baluchistan. 1901, 1911; Baroda, 1901, 1911; Bengal, 1901, 1911; Berar, 1881; Central Provinces, 1911; Central India, 1901; Kashmir, 1911; Punjab, 1881, 1901, 1911; United Provinces, 1911.

Crawley, E. *The Mystic Rose, a Study of Primitive Marriage.* London, 1902.

Crooke, W. *Tribes and Castes of the North-West Provinces and Oudh.* 4 vols. Calcutta, 1896.

—— *Popular Religion and Folklore of Northern India.* 2 vols. Westminster, 1896.

—— *Things Indian.* London, 1906.

Dabistan, or School of Manners, trans. D. Shea, A Troyer. 3 vols. Paris, 1843.

Deutsch, E. *Literary Remains.* London, 1874.

E.B. Encyclopaedia Britannica. 28 vols. 11th ed. Cambridge, 1911.

ERE. Encyclopaedia of Religion and Ethics, ed. J. Hastings. 10 vols. Edinburgh, 1908–18, in progress.

Erman, E. *Life in Ancient Egypt.* London, 1894.

Fanshawe, H. C. *Delhi Past and Present.* London, 1902.

Farnell, L. R. *Greece and Babylon.* Edinburgh, 1911.

Forbes, A. *Ras Mālā, or Hindoo Annals of the Province of Goozerat,* new ed. London, 1878.

Frazer, *G.B.*, Frazer, Sir J. G. *The Golden Bough,* 3rd ed. 12 vols. London, 1907–12.

—— *Lectures on the Early History of the Kingship.* London, 1905.

—— *Psyche's Task,* 2nd ed. London, 1913.

Greeven, R. *The Heroes Five.* Allahabad, 1898.

Gummere, F. B. *Germanic Origins, a study in Primitive Culture.* New York, 1892.

Hartland, E. S. *Primitive Paternity.* 2 vols. London, 1909.

Haug, A. *Essays on the Sacred Language, Writings, and Religion of the Parsis,* London, 1878.

Hoey, W. *Monograph on the Trade and Manufactures of Northern India.* Lucknow, 1880.

Hughes, T. P. *A Dictionary of Islam.* London, 1885.

IGI. Imperial Gazetteer of India. 26 vols. Oxford, 1908.

Jastrow, M. *The Civilization of Babylonia and Assyria.* Philadelphia, 1915.

JRAI. Journal of the Royal Anthropological Institute.

Koran, trans. G. Sale. London, 1844; trans. J. M. Rodwell, Everyman's Library. London, n.d.

Lane, E. W. *The Thousand and One Nights.* 3 vols. London, 1877

—— *ME. An Account of the Modern Egyptians,* 5th ed. 2 vols. London, 1871.

Layard, Sir A. H. *Discoveries in the ruins of Nineveh and Babylon.* London, 1853.

Leeder, S. H. *Veiled Mysteries of Egypt and the Religion of Islam.* London, 1912.

Lenormant, F. *Chaldean Magic.* London, 1877.

Macdonald, D. B. *The Development of Muslim Theology, Jurisprudence and Constitutional Theory.* London, 1915.

Malcolm, Sir J. *The History of Persia from the most Early Period to the Present Day.* 2nd ed. 2 vols. London, 1829.

Malik Muhammad Din. *The Gazetteer of the Bahawalpur State.* Lahore, 1904.
Manucci, N. *Storia do Magor*, ed. W. Irvine. 4 vols. London, 1907–8.
Margoliouth, D. S. *Mohammed and the Rise of Islam.* London, 1905.
Meer Hassan Ali, Mrs. *Observations on the Mussulmauns of India.* 2nd ed., Oxford, 1916.
Mishkāt. *Mishcat-ul-Masabih* trans. A. N. Matthews. Calcutta, 1809.
Monier-Williams, Sir M. *Brahmanism and Hinduism*, 4th ed. London, 1891.
Morier, J. *A Journey through Persia, Armenia and Asia Minor, to Constantinople, between the years 1808 and 1809.* London, 1812.
—— *A Second Journey through Persia, Armenia and Asia Minor between the Years 1810 and 1816.* London, 1818.
—— *Hajji Baba.* London, 1831.
Muir, Sir W. *The Caliphate, its Rise, Decline and Fall.* London, 1891.
—— *The Life of Mahomet*, 3rd ed. London, 1894.
—— *Annals of the Early Caliphate.* London, 1883.
NINQ. *North Indian Notes and Queries.* Allahabad, 1891–6.
Nicholson, R. A. *A Literary History of the Arabs.* London, 1907.
Osborn, A. D. *Islam and the Khalifs of Baghdad.* London, 1878.
Palgrave, W. G. *A Personal Narrative of a Year's Journey through Central and Eastern Arabia.* London, 1879.
Parks, F. *Wanderings of a Pilgrim in Search of the Picturesque.* 2 vols. London, 1850.
PNQ. *Panjab Notes and Queries.* 5 vols. Allahabad, 1883–7.
Pelly, Sir L. *The Miracle Play of Ḥasan and Husain.* 2 vols. London, 1879.
Redhouse, J. W. *The Mesnevi of Jelalu-d-din.* London, 1881.
Rice, B. L. *A Gazetteer of Mysore*, 2nd ed. 2 vols. London, 1897.
—— *Mysore and Coorg from the Inscriptions.* London, 1909.
Risley, H. H. *The Castes and Tribes of Bengal.* 2 vols. Calcutta, 1891.
Rose, H. A. *A Glossary of the Tribes and Castes of the Punjab and North-West Frontier Province.* 3 vols. Lahore, 1911–19.
Russell, R. V. *The Tribes and Castes of the Central Provinces.* 4 vols. London, 1916.
Rydberg, A. V. *Teutonic Mythology.* London, 1899.
Sell, E. *The Faith of Islam.* Madras, 1880.
Skeat, W. W. *Malay Magic.* London, 1900.
Sleeman, Sir W. *Rambles and Recollections of an Indian Official*, ed. V. A. Smith, Oxford, 1915.
Smith, V. A. *The Oxford History of India.* Oxford, 1919.
—— *Akbar, the Great Mogul.* Oxford, 1917.
Smith, W. Robertson. *Lectures on the Religion of the Semites*, 2nd ed. London, 1894.
—— *Kinship and Marriage in Early Arabia.* Cambridge, 1883.
Syad Muhammad Latif. *Agra Historical and Descriptive.* Calcutta, 1896.
Sykes, P. H. *The Glory of the Shia World.* London, 1910.
Tavernier, J B. *Travels in India*, ed. V. Ball. 2 vols. London, 1889.

Temple, Sir R. C. *A Dissertation on the Proper Names of Panjabis.* Bombay, 1883.
—— *The Legends of the Panjab.* 3 vols. Bombay, 1884-86.
Thorburn, S. S. *Bannu, or our Afghan Frontier.* London, 1876.
Thurston, E. *Ethnographic Notes in Southern India.* Madras, 1906.
—— *Castes and Tribes of Southern India.* 7 vols. Madras 1909.
Tod, J. *Annals and Antiquities of Rajasthan*, ed. W. Crooke. 3 vols. Oxford, 1920.
Tupper, C. L. *Punjab Customary Law.* 3 vols. Calcutta, 1881.
Waddell, L. A. *The Buddhism of Tibet or Lamaism.* London, 1895.
Ward, W. *A View of the History, Literature, and Mythology of the Hindoos*, 2nd ed. Serampore, 1818.
Watson, C. C. *Gazetteer, Ajmer–Merwara.* Ajmer, 1904.
Watt, *Econ. Dict.* Watt, Sir G. *A Dictionary of the Economic Products of India.* 6 vols. Calcutta, 1889-93.
—— *Com. Prod.* *The Commercial Products of India.* London, 1908.
Westermarck, E. *The History of Human Marriage.* London, 1895.
—— *Origin and Development of the Moral Ideas.* 2 vols. London, 1906.
—— *Marriage Ceremonies in Morocco.* London, 1914.
Wigram, W. L. and E. T. A. *The Cradle of Mankind, Eastern Turkistan.* London, 1914.
Wilkins, W. J. *Hindu Mythology.* Calcutta, 1885.
Wilks, M. *Historical Sketches of the South of India*, 2nd ed. Madras, 1869.
Wills, C. J. *In the Land of the Lion and the Sun, or Modern Persia.* London, 1891.
Wilson, J. *Indian Caste.* 2 vols. Bombay, 1877.
Wise, J. *Notes on the Races, Castes and Trades of Eastern Bengal.* London, 1883.
Yule, Sir H., Burnell, A. C. *Hobson-Jobson, a Glossary of Colloquial Anglo-Indian Words and Phrases.* 2nd ed. London, 1903.
Zwemer, S. M. *Arabia, the Cradle of Islam.* Edinburgh, 1900.

CHAPTER I

ETHNOGRAPHY

THE Musalmāns of India, according to the Census of 1911, numbered 66 millions, or more than one-fifth of the population of the empire. The total number of adherents of Islām being estimated at about 220 millions, India contains nearly one-third, and Great Britain is thus, from the point of numbers, the greatest Muhammadan power in the world. In the north-west frontier Province the population, except a small minority, is Musalmān ; in the Panjāb and Bengal the proportion is about one half ; one in five in Bombay ; one in seven in the United Provinces of Agra and Oudh ; while in the Central Provinces, Madras, and Burma their numbers are comparatively inconsiderable. Thus the present distribution of Islām has followed the course of the Muhammadan conquests from the north and west, and they are strongest in proportion to their vicinity to the head-quarters of the Faith in western Asia. The most remarkable exception to this general rule is the strength and increasing influence of Islām in eastern Bengal. In this part of the country Musalmāns 'are found chiefly in the eastern and northern districts. In this tract there was a vigorous and highly successful propaganda in the days of the Pathān kings of Bengal [A.D. 1338–1539]. The inhabitants had never been fully Hinduized, and at the time of the first Muhammadan invasions most of them probably preferred a debased form of Buddhism. They were spurned by the high class Hindus as unclean, and so listened readily to the preaching of the Mullās, who proclaimed the doctrine that all men were equal in the sight of Allāh, backed, as it often was, by a varying amount of compulsion '.[1] Bengal now contributes 24 millions, or 36 per cent., to the total number of Musalmāns in India.

In southern India the process of conquest was begun by

[1] *Census Reports*, India, 1911, i. 128 ; Bengal, 1901, i. 156 f. ; 1911, i. 202 ff.

Alāu-d-dīn in the beginning of the fourteenth century, but the rulers at Delhi were unable to control this vast region situated at an immense distance from the seat of their power, and five independent Musalmān States were created. The first serious attempt to re-assert Mughal supremacy was made by Akbar (1596–1600). This policy of advance continued under Shāhjahān, and it was actively prosecuted by Aurangzeb, with the result that the local Muhammadan dynasties were overthrown. But Mughal control did not last long, and it finally gave way before the rising power of the Marāthas early in the eighteenth century. It is important to note that these Musalmān kingdoms of the south were merely outposts of the Faith amidst a dense Hindu population. Being in a numerical minority, the Musalmāns were here compelled to adopt, as a rule, a policy of toleration and conciliation towards their Hindu subjects. At the present day the Nizām of Hyderābād, the only important Musalmān state in southern India, rules a population of which 86 per cent. are Hindu and 10 per cent. Musalmān. In the Madras Presidency the proportion of Musalmāns falls to 6 per cent. The customs recorded in this book, in its original form, show how much of the original Animism, demonolatry, and magic still survives among the Musalmāns of southern India.

The increase of Islām, as compared with Hinduism, has been slow but continuous during the period for which trustworthy statistics are available.[1] In the early days of Muhammadan rule, compulsion and the pressure of special taxation, particularly the Jizya or poll tax on non-believers during the reign of Aurangzeb, were used to enforce conversion. In the more recent period, direct propaganda seems to have been infrequent. The increase of Islām largely depends upon other causes. In part, it may be attributed to the higher vitality of the Musalmān as compared with that of the Hindu, the result of his connexion with the more virile races of central Asia and of his more nutritious diet, which generally includes

[1] The proportion which Musalmāns bore to the total population was 213 per million in 1911, as compared with 197 in 1881, the increase in the period 1901–11 being 6·7 per cent., as compared with 5 per cent. in the case of Hindus (*Census Report*, India, 1911, i. 128 f.).

meat in some form. But the chief reason seems to be that his social customs are more favourable to a higher birth-rate than those of the Hindu. He is generally a town-dweller, and he is thus less exposed to the danger of famine than the Hindu peasant. He is subject to fewer restrictions on marriage. Early or infant marriage is less common, and widows are freely allowed to marry. There is thus a larger proportion of wives of the child-bearing age among Musalmāns than among Hindus.

Musalmāns are not found in excessive numbers in the vicinity of the great Imperial cities like Delhi or Agra, because in these parts of the country the invaders encountered powerful Hindu tribes, like the Jāts and Rājputs, intensely conservative and controlled by a strong Brāhman hierarchy, which resisted proselytism. In Bengal, however, they are more numerous in north Bihār, the seat of Hindu and Brāhman domination, than round the old Muhammadan centres in south Bihār, Patna, and Monghyr. In Oudh we find many Musalmān communities which owe their origin to grants of waste or confiscated lands conferred by their Musalmān rulers on some successful soldier, or on some Pīr or holy man who attracted a body of disciples. In southern India a large proportion of the Musalmāns are converts drawn from the animistic castes or tribes in ancient or modern times.

Although there has been little organized propaganda for the spread of the Faith, within recent years the fervour of Musalmān life has been stimulated by preachers, by the publication and distribution of religious books, and by the establishment of schools and colleges. It is only perhaps in the case of the Wahhābīs, the Puritans of Islām, that an active propaganda has been organized, but the militant section among them seems to have considerably lost its force. The Wahhābīs in Bengal now reject this title, 'and assume one or another of two names, Ahl-i-hadīs, or 'the people of the Traditions', so called because they claim a right to interpret for themselves the Hadīs, the traditional sayings of Muhammad not found in the Korān, or Ghair-muqallid, meaning 'nonconformists' or 'dissenters', as they do not follow the doctrines of any of the four Imāms of the Sunnī sect. The designation Rafi'yādain is also sometimes applied to them, because they raise both hands in prayers before genuflection and prostration and fold them at the breast and not at the navel like Sunnīs; the name means, literally, 'raising both hands at the time of prayer'. The Ahl-i-hadīs 'are so strongly in opposition to orthodox Musalmāns as to regard them as little more than infidels and their mosques as little better than Hindu temples. They regard it as their duty to take possession of the latter if possible, and have at times had recourse to the civil courts to assert a right to worship in them. In their prayers they pronounce the word Amen in a loud voice; the use of music and the beating of drums at marriage festivities—according to some their use renders the marriage illegal—the offering of sweetmeats &c. to the spirits of deceased ancestors, and visits to the tombs of Saints are all forbidden. Even a pilgrimage to the grave of the Prophet at Medina is looked on with disfavour, and some have been known to return from their Haj pilgrimage after visiting Mecca only'.[1] Conversions certainly occur in the Musalmān community, but they are largely due to social causes. The outcast groups of Hindus, popularly known as the 'Untouchables', have begun to realize that as objects of contempt to all who follow the strict rule of Brahmanism, their position is intolerable. To such people Islām offers full franchise after conversion, and the number of converts is increased by those who, on account of the breach of Hindu social observances, such as the eating of forbidden food, association with people considered to be impure, violation of some rule of marriage or sexual connexion, have been expelled from the community, or to use the popular phrase, have been deprived of the right of smoking tobacco or drinking water with their co-religionists. For these persons the choice lies between accepting Christianity or Islām. This tendency has led to attempts by the more liberal-minded Hindus to adopt measures for the ameliorization of these wretched classes, but up to the present this movement seems to have produced little effect.

The first contact of militant Islām with India occurred in the Khilāfat of Walīd, when in A.D. 712, Muhammad, son of Qāsim,

[1] *Census Report*, Bengal, 1911, i. 248.

son-in-law of Hajāj, governor of Persia, invaded Sind.[1] But the force of this Arab movement on the western frontier was exhausted when it reached the Indus valley, and the first effective step towards the conquest of India for the new Faith was taken by a dynasty founded by a Turkish slave at Ghaznī between Kābul and Kandahār. The greatest of these princes, Mahmūd, between 999 and his death in 1050, made a series of raids with the object of plunder and the destruction of the temples and idols of the Hindus. It was not the intention of Mahmūd to occupy the country, and the real task of conquest was undertaken by Muhammad Ghorī, ruler of a petty kingdom between Ghaznī and Herāt, who, after some preliminary attempts, invaded India in 1191, and though he was at first checked by Prithivīrājā, the Chauhān Rājput king of Ajmer, defeated and slew the Hindu leader in the following year. The conquests of Muhammad Ghorī were extended by his lieutenant, Qutbu-d-dīn, and by 1206 the Muhammadans had mastered northern India from Peshāwar to the Bay of Bengal. From that time until 1526 thirty-four kings reigned at Delhi, Slave kings, Khaljīs, Tughlaqshāhīs, Sayyids, and Lodīs. But their hold over northern India was precarious, and the country was repeatedly raided by bands of fierce Mongols from central Asia. The Tughlaqshāhīs fell before Taimūr the Lame, who occupied and sacked Delhi in 1398. The Sayyids and Lodīs succeeded to a kingdom ruined by the foreign invaders and convulsed by the struggles of rival claimants. The time was ripe for the coming of a stronger ruler, when in 1526 Bābur, king of Kābul, defeated Ibrāhīm Lodī on the historical field of Pānīpat in the Karnāl District of the eastern Panjāb, and founded the Mughal Empire.

His son, Humāyūn, a gallant soldier, but addicted to opium-eating and possessed of less energy and enterprise than his father, was obliged to take refuge in Persia while his Indian dominions were occupied by Sher Shāh, an Afghān officer in Bihār, who led the Hindostānī Musalmāns against the Mughals. After his death Humāyūn recovered his kingdom in 1555, and on his death, the result of an accident, his eldest son Akbar (1556–1605) succeeded to the throne.

[1] V. A. Smith, *Oxford History of India*, 190 ff.; IGI, ii. 350 ff.

It is unnecessary here to describe in any detail the foundation, extension, and ultimate decay of the Mughal Empire. Four Emperors, Akbar, Jahāngīr, Shāhjahān, and Aurangzeb, reigned between 1556 and 1707. The policy of Akbar, known as the Great Mogul, was devoted to conquest, consolidation, fiscal and social reorganization. He practically discarded orthodox Islām, and aimed at establishing a new, eclectic religion, known as the Divine Faith, while his sympathies led him to conciliate his Hindu subjects and to repress Musalmān bigotry.[1] During the rule of his successors, Jahāngīr and Shāhjahān, the empire retained its magnificence, the Court ceremonies were conducted with splendour, splendid buildings were erected, but the administration was less efficient, and though persecution of the Hindus occurred, the rapprochement with the faith of the masses of the subject races was encouraged by royal marriages with Rājput princesses. Thus the loss of constant streams of fresh recruits from Kābul and central Asia was compensated by the devotion to the Mughal throne of the Rājputs, the most virile of the Hindu tribes. Under Aurangzeb, a fanatical Sunnī Musalmān, the policy of toleration was abandoned, and the destruction of Hindu temples and idols and the imposition of the Jizya or poll-tax on unbelievers alienated the Rājputs and led to the rise of the Marāthā power in the Deccan. Between the death of Aurangzeb in 1707 and the establishment of British supremacy in Bengal after the battle of Plassey in 1757, the empire gradually fell into decay.

This rapid historical summary of events will help to explain the present position of Islām in India. Its influence largely depends on the fact that its adherents retain the tradition that their ancestors were once the rulers of the land, and their capacity for administration increases their efficiency as officers of the British Government. As now constituted, the Musalmāns represent groups drawn from the indigenous races more or less leavened by a strain of foreign blood derived from successive bodies of invaders or emigrants from the regions beyond the north-western frontier. Even in the case of the

[1] V. A. Smith, *Akbar the Great Mogul*, chap. viii. For the Rājputs see J. Tod, *Annals of Rajasthan*, ed. 1920; Index, *s.v.* 'Rājput'.

earlier invaders their racial purity was gradually lost by intermarriage or concubinage with Hindus, and though a few families claim to have resisted this intermixture of blood, the majority of the Musalmān population, particularly in Bengal and southern India, are by race practically Hindus pure and simple.

The result of this continuous amalgamation of the foreign with the indigenous elements in the Musalmān population is shown in the south Indian customs recorded in this book, which differ in many important respects from the orthodox system prevailing among the Musalmāns of Persia, Arabia, or Egypt. Local magical practices have been largely engrafted on the system prescribed in the Korān, the Shar, or Way of Life, laid down by the Prophet and the legists who succeeded him, and the Sunnat or Rule inherited from the Hadīs or Traditions. Thus, in northern India tribes like the Rājputs and Jāts, or other castes which have accepted Islām, have both a Hindu and a Musalmān branch, and members of the latter often supplement the orthodox ritual of Islām by Hindu marriage or death rites, follow Hindu rules of succession to real and personal property, and, particularly in time of trouble, reverence the local village deities. Even on the north-west frontier and in Balūchistān, where Hindu influence is practically absent, Islām has in a large measure failed to supersede the primitive animism. 'Brāhūīs, Baloch and Afghāns are equally ignorant of everything connected with their religion beyond the most elementary doctrines. In matters of faith the tribesman confines himself to the belief that there is a God, a Prophet, a Resurrection, and a Day of Judgement. He knows that there is a Qorān, but in the absence of knowledge of Arabic and of qualified teachers who can expound its meaning, he is ignorant of its contents. He believes that everything happens by inevitable necessity, but how far this is connected in his mind with predestination on the part of the Creator it is difficult to say. His practice is, to say the least, un-Islāmic. Though he repeats every day that there is one God only who is worthy of worship, he almost invariably prefers to worship some Saint or tomb. The Saints or Pīrs, in fact, are invested with all the attributes of God. It is the Saint who can avert calamity, cure disease, procure children for the childless, bless the efforts of the hunter, or even improve the circumstances of the dead. The underlying feeling seems to be that man is too sinful to approach God direct, and therefore the intervention of some one more worthy must be sought. Any one visiting a shrine will observe stones, carved pieces of wood, bunches of hair tied to trees, remnants of clothes, horns of wild animals, bells and various articles of trifling value. They are placed at the shrines by devotees in performance of vows. The mother who is blessed with a child will bring it to the shrine, where she will shave it and offer the hair and the baby's clothes in performance of vows made during the course of pregnancy. The object is that the local Saint may be induced to interest himself or herself—for the Saints are of both sexes—in the welfare of the little one. The hunter brings the horns of the deer which he has killed in the hope of further good sport, while those who are suffering from disease pass the stones or pieces of carved wood over the part affected, trusting that by this means the ill from which they are suffering will be removed '.[1]

In Bengal, before the recent crusade against idolatry, it was the practice of low-class Musalmāns to join in the Durgā Pūjā and other Hindu festivals. They are very careful about omens and auspicious days, and dates for weddings and other rites are fixed after consulting Hindu Pandits. Hindu deities, like Sītalā who controls small-pox, and Rakshyā Kālī who protects her votaries from cholera, are worshipped during epidemics. In Bihār Musalmāns join in the worship of the sun, and some of them visit Hindu temples. But the most important deviation from the standard rules of Islām is the widespread worship of Pīrs and Saints.[2] Facts of the same kind are reported from other parts of the country. In the Central Provinces Musalmān Ahīrs or cowherds perform their marriages in Hindu fashion, and at the end call in a Qāzī who repeats the Musalmān prayers and records the amount of the dowry and settlement.[3] Kurmīs, Hindu peasants in Bihār, keep the Musalmān feast of the Muharram and fast at Ramazān.[4] The Lambādī carriers in

[1] *Census Report*, Balūchistān, 1901, i. 39.

[2] *Census Report*, India, 1911, i. 176 ff.

[3] Russell, ii. 288.

[4] Risley, *Tribes and Castes of Bengal*, i. 534.

Madras combine the Musalmān rite of marriage with the original tribal ritual.[1] The shrine of Qādirwalī Sāhib in the Tanjore District, Madras, is visited by crowds of Hindu women, and the Hindu princesses send large gifts to the Nāgor mosque from the Palace.[2] Particularly in the north, the Saint Sālār Mas'ūd, otherwise known as Ghāzī Miyān, is worshipped by crowds, the majority of whom are Hindus, and in many places Hindus share in the procession of the Ta'ziyas or Tābūts, the cenotaphs of the martyrs Hasan and Husain, at the Muharram festival. Much of this fusion of beliefs and rites is, of course, due to the eclectic character of Hinduism, which readily accepts the worship of any Saint or even of a martyr because he was slain in battle with the Hindus, whose advocacy with the Higher Powers is supposed to be effectual. But it also points to the close association of Hinduism and Islām among the lower-class votaries of both religions, a union based upon the ethnical identity of the two bodies.

Islām, in its orthodox type, does not permit the differentiation of its followers into castes. In theory, at least, all Musalmāns are brethren and can eat together, and though endogamy is the rule among certain tribes and castes, particularly in the case of those families which claim Arabic or Persian lineage, there is nothing to prevent intermarriage with strangers. But among the class of Musalmān converts from Hinduism the laws of endogamy and exogamy still have force, and the rules which prohibit eating or drinking with strangers to the group are observed.[3]

Musalmāns in India are popularly divided into four groups: Sayyid, Shaikh, Mughal, Pathān.

The Sayyids, a term meaning 'lord', also known as Pīrzāda, 'descendants of a Saint', or Mashāikh, 'venerable', claim descent from Fātima, daughter of the Prophet, and as religious teachers, soldiers, and adventurers, flocked into India with the Muhammadan armies. They tell a tale that the Angel Jabrāīl or Gabriel, when he came down from heaven with the divine

[1] Thurston, *Castes and Tribes*, iv. 231 f. [2] Sell, 263.

[3] Particularly in Bengal, the distinction between those who claim Arab or other foreign descent, known as 'noble' (*ashrāf*), and local converts, or artisans, the 'common folk' (*ajlāf*), is carefully recognized.

revelation, held a sheet over the Panjtan-i-pāk, the Five Holy Ones, Muhammad, 'Alī, Fātima, Hasan, and Husain, and exclaimed, 'O Muhammad! The Almighty showers his blessings upon thee, and ordains that thou and the offspring of the four who sit with thee shall henceforth be Sayyids'. It is difficult to say how many of the present Sayyids belong to the true foreign stock, but probably their number is small. The saying runs, 'Last year I was a Julāhā or weaver, this year I am a Shaikh, next year, if prices rise, I shall be a Sayyid'. As cultivators the Sayyids are idle and thriftless, qualities which they ascribe to Tawakkul, or resignation to the Divine will, a development of the Sūfī belief which some authorities suppose to be derived from Christianity. Many of them occupy a quasi-religious position as Pīrs or spiritual guides in wealthy families, and support themselves on alms and gifts. The men take the title of Sayyid or Mīr, that is Amīr, 'leader', before their names, or Shāh, 'prince' after them, while the women add the title Begam, 'lady'. At the census of 1911 the Sayyids numbered about 1½ millions, generally distributed except in Burma.[1]

Shaikh, 'venerable leader', is a term which should properly include only those of pure Arab descent, and the name is specially applied to three branches of the Quraish tribe from which the Prophet sprang: the Siddīqī, claiming descent from Abū Bakr, the first Khalīfa, known as Siddīq, 'the veracious'; Fārūqī, from 'Umar-al-fārūq, 'the discriminator between truth and falsehood', the second Khalīfa; 'Abbāsī, from 'Abbās, paternal uncle of Muhammad. But the term Shaikh has now become little more than a title of courtesy, and it is generally assumed by Hindu converts to Islām. At the census of 1911 Shaikhs numbered 32 millions, thus including the majority of Musalmāns.

The term Mughal is a form of the name Mongol, the race which invaded India after the campaigns of Chengiz Khān, and it is now generally applied to the followers of Bābur or those who were attracted to India by his successors. They are generally divided into two groups, Persian and Chagatāī, the Turkish tribe to which Bābur belonged. Bernier[2] explains

[1] Rose, iii. 390 ff.; *BG.* ix, part 2, 7 f. [2] p. 209.

that in the time of Aurangzeb the name was applied to 'white men, foreigners and Mahometans'. Many of the Panjāb Mughals are probably of Central Asian descent, with intermixture from other sources, but, like Shaikh, the name has been assumed by certain agricultural tribes and recent converts. In Gujarāt most of them belong to the Shī'a sect, and the Persian Mughals form a distinct community, having their own places of worship and marrying only amongst themselves.[1] They have adopted Hindu usages less than other Gujarāt Musalmāns. Mughals prefix to their names the title Mīrzā, Amīrzāda, 'leader-born', and the women use the title Khānam 'lady'. They numbered at the census of 1911 350,000, and they are found throughout the peninsula.

The name Pathān, a corrupted form of Pashtānā or Pakhtānā, speakers of Pashto, a language current beyond the north-west frontier and within British territories in the trans-Indus Districts as far south as Derā Ismāīl Khān, is a name popularly applied to certain tribes on the north-west borderland.[2] It is synonymous with Rohillā or Rohelā, an inhabitant of the Roh or mountain tracts. The term has been erroneously applied to the Sultāns of Delhi from 1206 to 1450. In reality, Bahlol Lodī (1450–89) was the first Pathān or Afghān Sultān, and the only other Pathān rulers at Delhi were the Sūr family of Sher Shāh, already mentioned as the opponent of the Emperor Humāyūn.[3] The theory that the Afghāns, especially the Durrānī branch, are of Hebrew descent is of purely literary origin, and it may be traced in the *Makhzan-i-Afghānī*, compiled by Khānjahān Lodī in the reign of the Emperor Jahāngīr (1605–27).[4] At the present time gangs of traders, known under the name Pathān, continue the custom which has prevailed from time immemorial of flocking into the Indian plains with their Powindās (*pavanda*, 'nomads') or in caravans when the passes are open.[5]

Among the less important Musalmān groups the following

[1] Rose, iii. 130 f.; *BG*. ix, part 2, 9 f.
[2] *Census Report*, India, 1901, i. 293 ff.
[3] Smith, *Oxford History of India*, 253.
[4] *Encyclopaedia of Islām*, i. 151.
[5] *Census Report*, Balūchistān, 1911, 44, 154 ff.; Rose, iii. 205 ff.

deserve mention. The term Navāyat has been supposed to mean 'new-comers', but it is more probably derived from Nāīt, a branch of the Arabian Quraish tribe, who are said to have been driven from 'Irāq or Mesopotamia in the eighth century A.D., and to have migrated to southern India. Those on the west coast have preserved the purity of their blood by avoiding intermarriages with Indians, and for a time they refused to ally themselves even with the highest local Musalmān families.[1]

The term Labbai is said to be a corruption of 'Arabī or Arab, and designates a class of traders and growers of the betel vine in the Tanjore and Madura Districts, Madras. They are converted Hindus or Dravidians with some intermixture of Arab blood. They claim a common origin with the Navāyat, but the latter affirm that the Labbai are descended from their domestic slaves.[2]

The name Moplah is properly Māppillā, said to be an honorific title meaning 'great children'. On the western coast they are a hybrid race, the numbers of which are constantly recruited by the conversion of the slave tribes of Malabar. They have both a Shī'a and a Sunnī branch, and they are notorious for occasional outbreaks of sullen fanaticism, in the course of which they have attacked their Hindu neighbours and have dared even to encounter British troops.[3]

The Bohrā traders of Gujarāt and other parts of central and western India are representatives of the Ismāīliya Shī'a sect, the members of which believe that Ismāīl ibn Ja'far, and not Mūsa-as-sādiq, was the true Imām, and they refuse to associate with the Deity the qualities of existence or non-existence, intelligence or non-intelligence, power or helplessness, because they believe God to be the Maker of all things, even of names and attributes.[4] At present the Bohrās have both a Sunnī and a Shī'a branch, the former including most of the city traders, the latter the rural agriculturists. The Shī'a branch owes its origin to a body of missionaries who were kindly

[1] Thurston, *Castes*, v. 272 f.; *BG.* x. 133, xv, part 1, 400 ff.; Wilks, i. 150; Yule–Burnell, *Hobson-Jobson*, 620.

[2] Thurston, *Castes*, iv. 198 ff.; Yule–Burnell, 523; Wilks, i. 150.

[3] Thurston, *Castes*, iv. 455 ff.; L. K. Anantha Krishna Iyer, ii. 459 ff.

[4] Edwardes, i. 180 f.; Hughes, 220.

received by the kings of Anhilwārā in Gujarāt in the eleventh century, while the Sunnī section was established by the influence of the local Musalmān kings. Their leader, H.H. the Āghā Khān, who commands much respect among Musalmāns, especially in western India, and who performed notable service for the empire in the great war, is the successor of Āghā Shāh Hasan 'Alī, who came from Persia to India in 1845, and was recognized as the head of the community.[1]

The Khwājā or Khojā caste, the term meaning 'honourable converts', who also acknowledge the leadership of the Āghā Khān, are said to be descended from the so-called Assassins, Hashāshīn, 'drinkers of hashish or hemp', founded under the title of Fidāī or Fidāwī, 'devoted ones', by Hasan ibn as-sabbāh, who died in 1124 at Alamūt, the 'Falcon's Nest', in northern Persia. Their grand-master, under the title of 'The Old Man of the Mountain', was the subject of many legends in the Middle Ages.[2]

The Molēsalām are said to derive their name from Maulā-i-Islām, 'lords in Islām', and are Rājputs converted to Islām in the reign of the famous Mahmūd Begadā or Bīgarhā of Ahmadābād (1459–1513). They intermarry with the higher class Musalmāns, but it is said that the son of a chief may take a Rājput bride. They employ Musalmān Qāzīs and Maulavīs as well as Brāhman priests and bards drawn from the Bhāt and Chāraṇ tribes.[3]

The Momnā take their name from Mūmin, 'believer', and are orthodox Shī'a Musalmāns, originally Hindus of Gujarāt converted by the Ismāīliya missionaries, but those resident in Ahmadābād sometimes use Hindu names, call in a Brāhman as well as a Qāzī to perform the marriage rites, and their women, after a death in the family, wail and beat their breasts like Hindus.

[1] *BG.* ix, part 2, 41; xiii, part 1, 239 f.; *Census Report*, Baroda, 1911, i. 320 f.; Forbes, *Rās Mālā*, 264 f. They are known in the Panjāb as Maulāī, Rose, iii. 73 f.

[2] Macdonald, 49; *BG.* ix, part 2, 239 ff.; Thurston, *Castes*, iii. 288 ff.; Yule, *Marco Polo*, 1st ed., i. 132 f.; Edwardes, i. 181 f. In the Panjāb the word Khwājā means a eunuch, a scavenger converted to Islām, and a Musalmān trader, Rose, i. 536.

[3] Forbes, *Rās Mālā*, 264; *BG.* ix, part 2, 68.

Musalmāns are divided into two main sects, the Sunnī and the Shī'a, the former term meaning 'one of the Path, a traditionalist', the latter 'a follower', that is to say, of 'Alī, cousin-german of the Prophet and husband of his daughter Fātima. The Shī'as maintain that 'Alī was the first legitimate Imām, divinely illuminated and preserved (*ma'sūm*) from sin, and they accordingly reject the first three Khalīfas recognized by the Sunnīs, Abū Bakr, 'Umar and 'Usmān. Hence the Sunnīs are called Chāryārī, 'those who follow the four', the Shī'as Tīnyārī, 'those who follow the three Khalīfas'. Shī'as are also known as Imāmiyā, the Imām being the rightful leader of the faithful, while the Sunnīs call them Rāfizī or 'forsakers of the truth'. The list of the twelve Shī'a Imāms begins with 'Alī and ends with Muhammad al-askarī, the Imām Mahdī, who has for the present withdrawn from the world, but, it is believed, will appear again in the last days. The religious life of the Shī'a centres round a body of traditions, beliefs, and observances which have their source in 'Alī, Fātima, and their sons Hasan and Husain who, with the Prophet, make up the venerated Panjtan-i-pāk, the Five Holy Ones. 'Alī is revered as the vicar or even as the incarnation of Allāh. The differences between these two sects are partly religious, partly social. The Sunnī makes pilgrimage to the holy cities, Mecca and Medīna, the Shī'a to Karbalā, or Mashshadu-l-Husain, the scene of the martyrdom, about fifty miles south-west of Baghdād and six miles west of the river Euphrates. Shī'as recognize the Mujtahid, or 'learned doctors', the highest order of Musalmān divines, while the Sunnīs say that in the present condition of Islām they cannot be appointed. Shī'as observe the Muharram festival, in which only the less strict Sunnīs join. Some sects of Shī'as include among the Ahlu-l-kitāb, or 'men of the Book', the Majūsī or Magi fire-worshippers in addition to Jews and Christians. Shī'as admit the principle of Taqīya, 'guarding oneself', that is that they are justified in minimizing or denying the peculiarities of their religious beliefs in order to avoid persecution.[1] Among

[1] In support of this they quote the passage in the Korān (iii. 27), as usually interpreted: 'Whether ye hide what is in your breasts, or whether ye publish it abroad, God knoweth it.'

differences in the forms of prayer it may be noted that Shī'as add to the Azān or Bāng, the call to prayer, the words 'Come to the best of works! Come to the best of works!', and repeat the last sentence, 'There is no God but Allāh', twice instead of once, as the Sunnīs do. During the Qiyām or standing posture in prayer the Shī'as keep their hands on either side of the body, not on the navel or breast. They also usually omit the Subhān or 'blessing', and at the Takbīr-i-rukū', or bending of the body, they add 'And with His praise!'. In the Creed they add ''Alī is the Prophet of Allāh'.[1]

In upper India, as a whole, the relations of Sunnīs and Shī'as are marked, if not by friendliness, at least by mutual toleration. The Muharram processions of the Shī'as are generally conducted without opposition, and Sunnīs sometimes take a part, even if it be subordinate, in these celebrations. But elsewhere instances of tension, and occasionally of active opposition, have occurred. In 1709 there were serious disturbances at Lahore in consequence of an order that in the Khutba or bidding prayer the Shī'a form ''Alī is the Saint of God and heir (*wasī*) of the Prophet of God', should be added.[2] In 1872 there were serious riots between the followers of the rival sects in the city of Bombay, and again during the Muharram of 1904 which culminated in a refusal to bring out and immerse the cenotaphs.[3] The Ghair-i-Mahdī sect and the Sunnīs have come into conflict in southern India.

Among the Sunnīs there are four orthodox schools ot Law interpretation: 1. Hanafī or Hanīfī, founded by Abū Hanīfa, which is followed in Turkey, central Asia, and north India. It is distinguished by the latitude allowed to private judgement in the interpretation of the Law. It has been called 'the high and dry party of Church and State, a system of casuistry, an attempt to build up on scientific principles a set of rules which would answer every conceivable question of Law';[4] 2. Shāfi'ī, founded by Imām Muhammad ibn Idrīs as-Shāfi'ī, born in 767,

[1] For Shī'a beliefs in the Panjāb hills, Rose, i. 574 ff. For the practices of the Mulāhida, 'infidels', or Chirāghkush, Elias–Ross, 218 f.

[2] Elliot–Dowson, vii. 420, 427. There is much enmity between the two sects on the north-west frontier, Rose, ii. 279.

[3] Edwardes, ii. 105, 179.

[4] *Census Report*, Panjāb, 1891, i. 189; Macdonald, 95.

'one of the greatest figures in the history of Law';[1] 3. Mālikī, founded by Imām Mālik, mostly confined to north Africa, with few adherents in India;[2] 4. Hanbalī, followers of Ibn Hanbal (780–855), little known in India, but favoured by the Arabian Wahhābīs.[3]

While by the possession of its Scriptures, traditions, and decisions of jurists Islām presents the outward characteristics of a well-organized system, there are throughout India great differences of dogma, ritual, and social practices which have arisen partly from the isolation of many of its groups from the centres of Muslim belief and usage, and partly because many of its adherents have carried with them into their new faith principles and practices which grew up in their original environment. Such differences are possible in the type of Islām prevailing in India because, like Hinduism, it possesses no Pope, holds no Councils or Convocations, and has no great local centre like Cairo or the sacred cities of Arabia for western Islām, such as Rome or Canterbury are in Christianity. Fervour in belief and practice is usually confined to special classes of devotees and to special occasions. The village Musalmān seldom attends any but the Friday prayers, and even for this purpose, in regions where Hinduism is dominant, mosques are often absent. The Muharram is to Shī'as a season of solemn grief and self-denial, when religious enthusiasm is vigorously stimulated. The Ramazān is generally a time of fasting, and the Tarāwih, or special night prayers are recited with special devotion. Among some of the higher classes the habit of appointing Pīrs or Murshids, teachers and religious guides, is common, and though some of these, like the Hindu Gurūs, do not always practise what they preach, the system tends to promote a more careful observance of the Law and a deeper tone of religious life. The organization of these family chaplains is fully described in this book.

[1] Macdonald, 144.
[2] Ibid., 99; *ERE*. viii. 372.
[3] *ERE*. vii. 69 f.

CHAPTER II

BIRTH

THOUGH the desire for male offspring does not influence Musalmāns to the same extent as Hindus, who believe that it is only a son who can perform the funeral rites which admit the spirit of his father into the company of his sainted ancestors, still among Musalmāns the craving for a male heir is often intense. Among the Brāhūīs, 'in the wide world there is naught man and wife set their hearts on more than the birth of a son. For who would be content to quit this world and leave no son behind? As for a daughter, a daughter is little more than a gift to your neighbour'.[1] Hence many devices are employed to relieve barrenness. In Gujarāt, 'some 'Āmils or exorcists give their applicants cardamoms, or cloves, or pieces of candied sugar, on which the mystic and powerful Names of God being blown, they are supposed to possess the virtue of casting out the spirit of barrenness, since, as a rule, barrenness is due to spirit-possession. Others direct strands of thread to be worn round the abdomen or the neck; others, again, simply write or trace some name or charm of words with the tip of the finger over the womb of the woman or the loins of the man. An exorcist or 'Āmil has also to help after conception with the object that the issue may be male. He gives charms to be washed in water for a monthly bath. Some dead Saints have a reputation as child-givers. To tie knots on bits of string or ribbon to a post or pillar supporting the canopy over a Saint's tomb is considered by barren women one of the surest

[1] Bray, 1. The Arabs objected to the birth of a girl. 'And they ascribe daughters unto God. Glory be to Him! But they desire them not for themselves' (*Korān*, xvi. 59). There is, however, no evidence of infanticide among them, a common custom among certain Hindu castes (*Census Report*, India, 1911, i. 215 ff.). The custom among the Gakkhars of the Panjāb hills seems to be sporadic or of foreign origin (Ferishta, i. 183).

means of obtaining issue '.[1] The tomb of Shaikh Salīm Chishtī at Fathpur Sīkrī, by whose intercession Akbar believed that he had been blessed with a son, is even at the present day visited by childless Hindu and Musalmān women who tie threads or rags on the lovely screen which surrounds it.[2] A tree in the enclosure of the Saint Shaikh 'Ālam at Ahmadābād yields a peculiar acorn-like fruit which is much valued by childless women. If the birth of a child follows the eating of the fruit, the man or woman who used it should for a term of years at every anniversary of the death of the Saint come and water the roots of the tree with milk. The leaves of a tree near the grave of Mīrān Sāhib at Ānjhā have the same effect. The Baloch, when a woman desires a child, hold a staff against a wall and make the woman pass three times beneath it, or she is sent to visit shrines, particularly that of Shāh Wasāwā, where she embraces a tree which overhangs his tomb.[3] Other approved methods are: to give the woman a charm or magic diagram which is either washed in rose-water and drunk, or worn round the neck; to bathe in water drawn from seven wells on the night of the Dīvālī or Hindu Feast of Lights, when spirits are abroad; to scare the evil spirit which besets the woman by abusing her; to castigate her with a charmed chain; to write on a piece of bread a series of numbers which make up seventy-three, and give it to a black dog; to burn down the hut of a neighbour to remove the taboo.[4] The Brāhūī with the same object circumcise the woman, but if the fault is supposed to lie with her husband and a physician fails to remedy it, a Mullā provides a charm or amulet, and if this fails the blame is laid on the Jinn.[5]

[1] *BG.* ix, part 2, 147 f. Such tombs are known in the Panjāb as *Khānaqāh*, the original meaning of which is 'a convent' (Rose, i. 519). On magic by means of knots see *ERE.* vii. 747 ff.

[2] Smith, *Akbar the Great Mogul*, 104 ff. Miniature cradles are often hung at shrines as a charm for children, a Bedouin practice. A. H. Layard, *Discoveries in the Ruins of Nineveh and Babylon*, 309.

[3] *Census Report*, Balūchistān, 1911, p. 83. For trees at Saints' tombs, see Frazer, *Folklore of the O.T.*, iii. 41.

[4] *Census Report*, Baroda, 1911, i. 177; Crooke, *Popular Religion*, i. 50, 68, 87, 100, 160, 226; *JAS.*, Bombay, iv. 63. On hut-burning in Indian ritual, see W. Crooke, *Man*, xix. 18 ff.

[5] Bray, 1 ff.; Hartland, *Primitive Paternity*, i. 30 ff.

When conception is announced, the expectant mother is subjected to various taboos, and she takes various precautions to avoid the attacks of evil spirits. All her cravings for food must be indulged, such as that for eating earth, which is supposed to check vomiting.[1] If such things are denied to her, the result will be a miscarriage. In Gujarāt she wears silk threads round her waist, each thread bearing a knot for each month of her pregnancy. At the ninth month these are unwound, incense is burned over them, and they are thrown into water.[2] The Dīvālī or Hindu feast of lights is a specially dangerous time, because evil spirits are likely to be about. She must not enter a shed used at marriage or other festivities; she must not be present at death or other family rites. She, her husband, and her relatives must not eat anything during an eclipse, because these are supposed to be caused by evil spirits attacking the sun or moon. If anything folded, like betel, is cut at this time, the child will be born with folded ears or will suffer from hare-lip, and if any one smokes, the child will have a weak chest which causes gurgling like that of a tobacco pipe. During an eclipse the friends should pray and read the Korān, lay grain on a bed and give it to friends. During pregnancy the woman should not wear new clothes or ornaments, use eye collyrium, stain her hands or feet with henna, or colour her teeth, because such things attract the Evil Eye. She must not touch a coco-nut or any underground root because such things resist the gatherer, must be dug up with force, and thus delivery may be impeded. Many of these taboos are identical with those of the Hindus or have been borrowed from them.[3]

The sex of the expected child may be foretold by an examination of the woman by a committee of midwives. Among the Baloch a house snake is killed and the woman steps over its body, and then it is thrown in the air in the hope that it will

[1] On earth-eating see *Memoirs ASB.* 1908, p. 249 ff.; Russell, iii. 197; iv. 69; Thurston, *Notes*, 552 ff.; Mrs. L. Milne, *The Shans at Home*, 181. On pregnancy rites in general, *ERE*. x. 242 f.; *JRAI*. xxxv. 271 ff.; 279 ff.; *Folk-lore*, xiii. 279; Rose, i. 759 f.

[2] *BG*. ix, part 1, 149.

[3] Russell, iv. 68 f., 551; Crooke, *Popular Religion*, i. 18

fall on its back, but if it falls on its belly the birth of a daughter is certain.[1] In Baroda a few drops of milk are squeezed from the woman's breasts, and if the milk is thin the birth of a boy is anticipated.[2]

In the Deccan before the announcement of the first pregnancy the woman's lap and that of her husband are filled with fruits of various kinds, her mother sends clothes and the friends are feasted. The Satmāsā, Satwānsā or Satwāsā, the rite in the seventh month which has been borrowed from the Hindus, is the most important. The woman is invited by her parents, who give her new clothes, perfume her with rose-water and sandalwood, invite a few friends to a party, sit up with her all night, and scare evil spirits by music and festivity. They press a little of her milk on a yellow cloth, and if a white stain is left they expect a girl, if it leaves a yellow mark a boy. At the Naumāsā, or ninth month, the friends assemble, and the woman is allowed to wear the new clothes and jewellery which up to this time she has discarded. Then comes the Sahnak or pot rite of Bībī Fātima. Food is cooked in little pots, over which the Fātiha[3] or first chapter of the Korān is read in the name of Fātima, daughter of the Prophet, and the food is given to some women who are selected on account of their virtue. Vigil, as before, is kept with rejoicings. In Gujarāt slaked lime is served with the food as a sort of ordeal, because it is supposed not to burn the mouth of a chaste woman.[4] The glance of no male, not even that of a boy, must fall on the food thus served. In north India such rites are done four months and five days after the announcement of pregnancy, usually only in the case of the first child, and also at the ninth month.

[1] *Census Report*, Balūchistān, 1911, p. 83 f.

[2] *Census Report*, 1911, i. 178. Cf. Russell, ii. 27; A. L. K. Anantha Krishna Iyer, ii. 372.

[3] Fātiha, 'the opener', the Paternoster prefixed to the Korān, was probably composed late in the Prophet's career, as it contains polemical references to Jews and Christians ('those who have incurred anger and go astray'), because his hostility to the Jews did not begin till after his migration, and that towards Christians some years later. Birth in the eighth month is unlucky, and it is attributed to a cat entering her room. Hence eight is never used in counting a child's age, being called *anginnat*, 'uncounted' (Rose, i. 738 f.).

[4] *BG.* ix, part 2, 151 f.

The woman's nails are cut and the parings are put in a silver box which is given to the barber's wife. The woman who dresses her must be one who enjoys the fullest married happiness.[1] Among the Brāhūīs, on the new moon of the seventh month seven kinds of grain are cooked and distributed among the kin, who must send a gift in return. After the rite they keep vigil.[2]

It is a general custom that the first child should be born at the house of the mother's parents.[3] A separate room is arranged, and a fire is kept burning in it to defend the mother and child from the Jinn and the Evil Eye.[4] As among Hindus, many charms are used to aid delivery. A line of boys fetch water from the well, and the speed with which the vessel is passed from hand to hand helps delivery, or a lump of clay from a potter's wheel, which has thus acquired the quality of swiftness, is mixed with water and given to her to drink.[5] A square rupee of Akbar, which bears the Emperor's name with that of the four Companions of the Prophet, is dipped in water which is given to her, but no British or other secular coin can be used in this way.[6] By way of sympathetic magic, delivery is aided by giving the schoolboys a holiday, or the girdle of some holy man is dipped in water which she drinks. In the act of delivery she lies on a quilt spread on the ground, with her head north and her feet south, for in case she dies in childbirth this is the position in which Musalmāns are buried, with the face towards Mecca. Or she squats on the ground holding a bed while the midwife rubs her back and presses a broom against her abdomen. Among the Brāhūī she lies on sand, and they say that a boy is born with his head towards the ground, a girl facing her mother.[7] In labour she is assisted by a

[1] *NINQ*. iii. 186 ff. [2] Bray, 7.

[3] This is also a Hindu rule (Dubois, *Hindu Manners*, 338; *BG*. xix. 85; Thurston, *Castes*, vi. 101; Russell, ii. 434). On the special powers of first-born children, Rose, i. 742 f.

[4] This is also an Arab custom (Burton, *AN*. ix. 184) and common among Hindus.

[5] Russell, ii. 27, iii. 563; Crooke, *Popular Religion*, i. 116. Water in which a brick from the Chakravyāhu, a labyrinthine fort of the Mahābhārata war, is given to her to drink (Crooke, *op. cit.* i. 116).

[6] *PNQ*. iii. 8, iv. 10. For Musulmān coins used as amulets, *ERE*. iii. 708. [7] *JRAI*. xxxvii. 237; Bray, 9; Russell, iv. 222.

midwife, known as Dāī, Janāī or Chamārin, who is so ignorant and careless about sanitary precautions that any but an ordinary presentation is fatal to the mother.[1] In cases of protracted labour, alms are given to the poor, prayers are said, an amulet is hung on the thigh of the patient, water in which the beard of some holy man has been dipped is administered to her, a charmed potsherd is laid on her abdomen. Among the Pathāns the midwife brings water to the husband, who washes his hands and feet, and the water is given to the woman to drink.[2]

Immediately after delivery she is made to swallow a small copper coin or a bit of copper to help to expel the placenta. The midwife calls for a piece of sharpened silver, which she claims as her perquisite after she has severed the cord with it. She then puts the cord into a pot with a copper coin and betel leaf, and buries it in a corner of the room or in a cool place where the water-pots are kept, so that the cool damp may cause it to grow and so benefit the child. If a knife is used to cut the cord it must not be put to any other purpose, but it is left near the patient till the fortieth day, when Kājal or lampblack is collected on it and applied to the eyes of the child. In the Panjāb the pot containing the cord is buried inside the house, and betel leaf, silver, turmeric, and charcoal are thrown on it to repel evil spirits, while a fire is lighted over it for six days till it is supposed to be consumed.[3] The Brāhūī bury the cord in a place where no dog can find it, for if it chances to be eaten by a dog the baby grows restless and becomes a squaller.[4] The Baloch think that if a dog or cat gets hold of the cord the mother's milk will dry up, so they bury it in the house and cover it with rice and molasses, a precaution which leads to a second pregnancy.[5] In the Imperial household they used to sever the cord with a thread and put it in a small bag which was kept under the child's pillow 'with certain superstitious writings'.[6]

[1] Wise, 50 ff; Burton, *Sindh*, 147.
[2] Burton, *Sindh*, 147; Bray, 9; *BG*. ix, part 2, 155; Rose, iii. 225.
[3] *JRAI*. xxxvii. 237.
[4] Bray, 10.
[5] *Census Report*, 1911, p. 184. Cf. Russell, iii. 197, 396; *BG*. ix, part 2, 157, xix. 91, xxii. 74; Crawley, 118.
[6] Manucci, ii. 346.

As soon as the placenta is expelled, they give the woman some asafoetida to prevent her from catching cold. A handkerchief is tied on her head, a roller bound round her abdomen, and she is laid on a bed or on a sheet spread on the ground, in a warm room, which in rich families is enclosed with curtains, while beside the bed are laid a lemon, leaves of the Nīm tree (*melia azadirachta*), a Katār or dirk, a knife or other weapon to keep off evil. They then give her a packet of betel leaves with some myrrh (*bol*) to chew. In Gujarāt, when the child is born, the midwife, in order to deceive the spirits, if it is a boy, says that it is a girl or blind of an eye, but if it is a girl the fact is stated because a girl does not provoke jealousy and the Evil Eye.[1] In north India, if it is a boy, the midwife cries 'A son, may you be lucky!'; if a girl 'May she be a blessing!' In the case of a son the father discharges a gun from the housetop, as it is said to announce the birth, but really to scare evil spirits, and with the same object he strikes an iron griddle-plate three times with a stick. The midwife washes the baby in water mixed with Chanā or gram flour, and the friends throw coins into the pot as her fee, while she also gets the clothes and bedding used by the patient.[2] In the Panjāb the midwife washes the mother's breasts with water, using, as the Hindus do, some blades of holy grass as a brush, and this washing is done a second time by the baby's sister or some other woman of the family. Next day the midwife fastens a charm made of green leaves on the house door and the child is suckled.[3]

In south India the drink given to the mother for forty days is water boiled in which a red hot horseshoe or other piece of iron has been slaked. In some places, as in Persia, she gets nothing to eat or drink for the first three days.[4] Some give Achhwānī or Achwānī, a caudle, so called because it consists of dill (*ajwain, ligusticum ajowan*), sugar and flour. This is followed by vegetables and wheaten flour, sugar and butter boiled into a paste, and then a wheaten dumpling (*thalī, thulī*). Many people give her Sathaurā or Sonthaurā, so called because it is made of dry ginger (*sonth*), boiled with soft sugar and butter.

[1] *BG.* ix, part 2, 154.
[2] *NINQ.* iii. 188.
[3] *JRAI.* xxxvii. 232.
[4] J. Atkinson, 49.

After this she is allowed old rice seasoned with black pepper. By the tenth or twelfth day she resumes her ordinary food. In the Panjāb she is fed with pieces of bread soaked in butter and sugar, which is said to promote the flow of milk and is used as long as she is suckling.[1] Soon after birth the midwife gives the baby Ghuttī, 'a gulp or draught', a cleansing medicine made of aloes, spices, and borax, or honey water is given and next day an infusion of dill, beans, and a light sweetmeat. In Gujarāt the Ghuttī consists of aniseed, myrobolans, dried rose leaves, senna, and droppings of mice or goats.[2]

Whenever the child is bathed or taken out of the house the knife used to cut the cord is taken with it as a protective, and when the child is brought back the knife is replaced beside the mother, and it is used on the Chilla or fortieth day in sacrificing a sheep or a cock. In some families the mother does not oil or comb her hair for forty days after her delivery, but wears a handkerchief on her head, and some people during that time do not allow her to leave her room except to bathe on the Chhathī or sixth day and on the Chilla or fortieth, or for the purpose of counting the stars as described later on. During this time when a stranger enters the house he or she throws some Sipand or Ispand (*peganum harmala*) on the fire to disperse any evil that may have come with them. Some place an iron plate on which lampblack is collected and a broom beside the door until the fortieth day.[3] Great care is taken that no dog or cat enters, and even the name of a cat is not mentioned. But Muhammad said 'Cats are not impure; they keep watch around us'.[4]

After the child is washed and swaddled he is presented to the friends. The Azān or Bāng, the call to prayer, is uttered into his right ear and the Kalima or Creed in his left. This is generally done by the preacher or Khatīb, or by a boy who gets a reward for saying 'Allāhu akbar!' 'God is very great!'

[1] *PNQ.* i. 86; cf. Risley, *Tribes*, i. 211; *Census Report*, Baroda, 1911, i. 179; Anantha Krishna Iyer, i. 297, ii. 314, 468; Russell, ii. 413, iv. 293; *JRAI.* xxxvii. 242.

[2] Rose, iii. 226; *NINQ.* iii. 128; *JRAI.* xxxvii. 2[illegible], *BG.* ix. part 2, 155.

[3] On the broom in magic, *Folklore*, xxx. 169 ff.

[4] Hughes, 49.

Among rich people a Mashāikh, or venerable man, or the Murshid, or family guide, dips his finger in honey or chews a date or a grape and puts it into the child's mouth before he is put to the breast, in order that the wisdom of the sage may be imparted to him. The Fātiha is then said, and sugar and betel are distributed. When the friends hear of the birth they come to the house each of them carrying a blade or two of green grass, which the leader sticks in the father's hair. In return for congratulations he gives them a Got or present which is spent on an entertainment in one of their houses or in a neighbouring garden.

The custom of moulding the child's head prevails on the north-west frontier.[1] The Brāhūī shape by pressure the head and features of the child, measure the mouth, and if it is bigger than the space of a finger joint they press it into shape with a ring, rub the lips to make them thin and press the nose. In the case of a girl they press back any Bhaunrī or lock of hair which projects in front, and at the same time the body and feet are anointed and brought into the proper shape.[2] In the Bahāwalpur State they mould the head in a deep cup-shaped earthen pot in order to make the back of the skull round.[3]

There are four kinds of Dāī or nurses: the midwife, Dāī, Dāījanāī, or Chamārin, wife of a man of the Chamār caste, workers in leather; Dāī-dūdh-pilāī or Annā, a wet nurse; Dāī-khilāī, Chhochhā, the dry nurse or nursery-maid; Dāī-asīl, Māmā, Āyā, a ladies' maid. The Mughal name for a nurse or foster-mother was Anaga or Anka, for a foster-father Koka or Kukaltash, a nurse's husband and her male relations Atka.[4] The poorer orders usually take nurses from the lower orders. Musalmān children are generally nursed till they are two and a half years old, which according to the Law is the time during which the nurse is treated as a foster-mother;

[1] It is mentioned by the Buddhist pilgrims (Beal, *Si-yu-ki*, i. 19, ii. 306; Watters, *On Yuan Chwang*, i. 59, ii. 292).

[2] Bray, 18 ff.; Thorburn, 145 f.; *Man*, ii. 3, 40; *Census Report*, Balūchistān, 1911, 182 f.; *Census Report*, Andaman Islands, 1911, 199; *JRAI*. xviii. 367, xxiii. 238; Frazer, *Lectures on the History of the Kingship*, 260.

[3] Malik Muhammad Din, *Bahāwalpur Gazetteer*, 96.

[4] Elliot–Dowson, v. 231; Smith, *Akbar*, 20; *Āīn*, i. 323.

but if the child is nursed by another woman during that time she is not regarded as his proper foster-mother, and it is not unusual to see children three and four years old hanging about their mother's breasts.[1] Ladies scarcely ever nurse their own children, as they consider nursing to be weakening and injurious to the figure.

The child is bathed morning and evening and fumigated with the smoke of Ispand (*paganum harmala*) and lignum aloes, and they tie round its neck patchouli leaves (*pogostemon heyneanus*) and asafoetida to prevent the shadow of strangers falling upon it.[2] Whenever the child is bathed they take some red or yellow dye made of quicklime and turmeric and add to it a few bits of charcoal, all of which the nurse waves three times over the child and then throws it away, or she merely takes some water in a vessel, waves it over the child, and then pours it on her own feet, signifying 'May all the child's misfortunes fall on me!' So people say 'All the child's troubles have beset the midwife'.

The naming of children is often done on the day of birth or on that day week.[3] Generally the former day is chosen because until the child is named the mother in some families does not receive even a drink of water, much less betel, perfumes, or other luxuries. After the naming the Fātiha is said over sweetmeats and these are sent accompanied by music to absent friends. This is the business of the midwife, who receives gifts in return. In Gujarāt the mother, according to Hindu custom, is led to a window and made to count seven stars.[4]

The children of Musalmāns belong to the tribe of the father, and consequently if the boy be a Sayyid's son the first word of his name will be Sayyid or Mīr, as Sayyid 'Alī or Mīr Ahmad.

[1] Crooke, *Things Indian*, 99; Lane, *ME.* i. 68.

[2] On danger from the shadow, Frazer, *GB.*, Taboo and Perils of the Soul, 255. In the Panjāb women go on Sundays to the shrine of Bībī Purānīwālī to get relief from the shadow (*parchhāwān*) of a demon or apparition (Rose, i. 593).

[3] On the importance of names see Frazer, *GB.*, Taboo and Perils of the Soul, 308 ff.; Fowler, *Religious Experiences of the Roman People*, 29; Hartland, *Primitive Paternity*, i. 222 ff.

[4] *BG.* ix. part 2, 392; Monier-Williams, *Brahmanism and Hinduism*, 4th ed., 344.

But these honorific titles are often dropped in after life, and so it becomes necessary to ask the tribe to which a man belongs. The original rule of the Law runs 'Call your children after the Prophet': and the names God loves best are 'Abdu-l-lāh, 'servant of God', 'Abdu-l-rahmān, 'servant of the Compassionate', Harith or 'husbandman', Humām, 'diligent'; while the worst are Harb, 'war', and Murra, 'bitterness'.[1] But these rules do not apply to modern Indo-Musalmāns.

If he be the son of a Shaikh, then at the beginning or end of his name is added one of the following designations: Khwāja, 'lord', Ghulām, 'servant', Muhammad, the Prophet, Dīn, 'religion', 'Alī, son-in-law of the Prophet, Bakhsh, 'given', 'Abd, 'servant'; as Khwāja Yūsuf, Ghulām Nabī, Muhammad Husain, Shamsu-d-dīn, Hasan Bakhsh, Razā 'Alī, Shaikh Muhammad, 'Abdu-l-qādir. These names, however, do not always indicate a Shaikh, since Sayyids often use the same names.

If he be the son of a Mughal, his name begins or ends with the titles Mirzā, Mīrzā, Amīrzāda, 'son of an Amīr or lord', or Āgā, Āghā, 'chief', as for instance, Mīrzā Ahmad, Ismāīl Beg, Āgā or Āghā Ja'far. In the royal family of Persia the title Mīrzā is placed after the name instead of before it.[2] The title Mīrzā seems to have been adopted because the mother was a Sayyid, the males of which group have the title Mīr even if the father was a Mughal. In the case of Pathāns the title Khān, 'lord, master', or Khān Sāhib is invariably used at the end of the name, as Bahādur Khān, 'valiant lord'. We frequently however, find Shaikhs and Sayyids with the title Khān attached to their names, as Ghulām Ahmad Khān; but in such cases it is bestowed upon them by their masters as an honorary title.

The following are exceptions to these rules. Should the father be a Shaikh and the mother a Sayyid the word Sharīf, 'eminent', is usually added to the beginning or end of the child's name, as Ja'far Sharīf or Sharīf Ja'far. It is customary with some people to add this appellation to all the names of the family, as Ja'far Sharīf, son of 'Alī Sharīf, son of Sharīf Hamīd.

[1] *Mishkāt*, ii. 421. On Arabic names see *ERE*. ix. 137 ff.
[2] J. Morier, *Journey through Persia in 1808-9*, 234.

In most cases, however, when the mother is a Sayyidānī and the father a Shaikh, they leave out the word Sharīf, call themselves Shaikh Ahmad, or some equivalent name, and belong to the Shaikh group. In other places, again, they add the word Khwāja, 'nobleman'. When the father is a Mughal and the mother a Sayyidānī their offspring get the name of Khwājazāda, 'son of a nobleman', and the title Khwāja is often given to spiritual guides, like the Pīr or Murshid. Others, again, of all the four groups add to their names the titles Sāhib, 'master', Miyān, 'sir', Jān, 'life' as, for example, Dāūd Sāhib, 'Ammū Jān. This, however, is not the established practice in any group, but parents are accustomed to call their children by these familiar names out of affection, so that when they grow to manhood these names become established and the real names are often forgotten.

The following names are added to the beginning or end of the full titles of girls. Among Sayyids women are called Begam, 'lady', Bī, Bībī, 'mistress', Nissa, 'woman', Shāh, 'queen'. To the names of Shaikh girls they add only the titles Mā, 'mother', Bī or Bībī, except in the case of children of rank who get the title Begam. This is also the rule with Mughals and Pathāns. Mughal women use the title Khānam, 'lady', added to the end of their names, but illegitimate daughters receive the title Bāī, 'lady'. Rich people sometimes adopt the daughters of other people who are called Gāyan, 'singers', and the word Bāī is added to their names, but when they make favourites of such girls they are called Begam. In the old days, slave girls with whom their masters cohabited were first called Bībī, then Bāī, Khānam or Begam. There are two kinds of Musalmān dancing-girls, Natnī and Kanchanī, the latter being usually a Hindu, while Kasbī or Harjāī is the usual term for a prostitute. The former sometimes receive the titles Bāī or Kunwar, the latter Bakhsh.

It is not customary among Musalmāns to give their own names to their children. The modes of naming are as follows: First the child is named after some member of the family, as the grandfather on either side, or after the tutelary Saint of the family. In north India the name should never be that of an ancestor within two or three generations; indeed it is contrary to rule to give the child the name of a relation or member of the family.[1] We must also distinguish the 'Alam, or individual name ; Kunyat, that of relationship ; Laqab, honorary ; the 'Alāmat, or royal title ; the 'Anwān, that of honour ; Ansab, that implying denomination, and Takhallus, the nom de plume. Secondly, at an auspicious time which is fixed from the table given below, eight or ten learned men meet and fix upon the first letter of any page of the Korān opened at random (*fāl*) as that which should begin the name.[2] The name is often fixed by astrological considerations. Thus Akbar was named immediately after his birth Badru-d-dīn ' full moon of religion ', because he was born on the full moon of the month Sha'bān. But his relations, with the object of protecting him from Black Magic, and to frustrate the calculations of hostile astrologers, selected a new official birthday, the fifth of the month Rajab. His former name being thus inappropriate, he was renamed Jalālu-d-dīn ' the splendour of religion '.[3] Thirdly, a few tickets on which different names are inscribed are rolled up, laid on a plate or put into a cup which is covered with a handkerchief, and the contents are shaken about and scattered on the floor. Any little child present is desired to pick up one of them and the name inscribed on it is selected. Fourthly, some people choose a name from among those which begin with the letter found at the beginning or end of the name of the planet under which the child was born. The following are the rules : The planets, seven in number, Shams, the Sun, Qamar, the Moon, Zuhal, Kaiwān, Saturn, Zohra, Venus, 'Utārid, Mercury, Mirrīkh, Mars, Mushtarī, Jupiter, are supposed to preside over the twenty-four hours of day and night.

[1] *NINQ*. i. 116. Among Syrian Musulmāns to call a child after a relative is equivalent to saying, ' May you soon die, and this child prove to be your heir ' (*Folk-lore*, ix. 14 f.).

[2] This is also known as *istikhāra*, and it is practised at the tomb of Hāfiz, at Shīrāz, by consulting the works of the poet (Wills, 277).

[3] Smith, *Akbar*, 18 f.

GENETHLIACAL SCHEME

Day of Saturday or Night of Wednesday.	*Day of Friday or Night of Tuesday.*	*Day of Thursday or Night of Monday.*	*Day of Wednesday or Night of Sunday.*	*Day of Tuesday or Night of Saturday.*	*Day of Monday or Night of Friday.*	*Day of Sunday or Night of Thursday.*
Saturn 6 to 7 a.m.	Venus 6 to 7 a.m.	Jupiter 6 to 7 a.m.	Mercury 6 to 7 a.m.	Mars 6 to 7 a.m.	Moon 6 to 7 a.m.	Sun 6 to 7 a.m.
Jupiter 7 to 8 a.m.	Mercury 7 to 8 a.m.	Mars 7 to 8 a.m.	Moon 7 to 8 a.m.	Sun 7 to 8 a.m.	Saturn 7 to 8 a.m.	Venus 7 to 8 a.m.
Mars 8 to 9 a.m.	Moon 8 to 9 a.m.	Sun 8 to 9 a.m.	Saturn 8 to 9 a.m.	Venus 8 to 9 a.m.	Jupiter 8 to 9 a.m.	Mercury 8 to 9 a.m.
Sun 9 to 10 a.m.	Saturn 9 to 10 a.m.	Venus 9 to 10 a.m.	Jupiter 9 to 10 a.m.	Mercury 9 to 10 a.m.	Mars 9 to 10 a.m.	Moon 9 to 10 a.m.
Venus 10 to 11 a.m.	Jupiter 10 to 11 a.m.	Mercury 10 to 11 a.m.	Mars 10 to 11 a.m.	Moon 10 to 11 a.m.	Sun 10 to 11 a.m.	Saturn 10 to 11 a.m.
Mercury 11 to 12 a.m.	Mars 11 to 12 a.m.	Moon 11 to 12 a.m.	Sun 11 to 12 a.m.	Saturn 11 to 12 a.m.	Venus 11 to 12 a.m.	Jupiter 11 to 12 a.m.
Moon 12 to 1 p.m.	Sun 12 to 1 p.m.	Saturn 12 to 1 p.m.	Venus 12 to 1 p.m.	Jupiter 12 to 1 p.m.	Mercury 12 to 1 p.m.	Mars 12 to 1 p.m.
Saturn 1 to 2 p.m.	Venus 1 to 2 p.m.	Jupiter 1 to 2 p.m.	Mercury 1 to 2 p.m.	Mars 1 to 2 p.m.	Moon 1 to 2 p.m.	Sun 1 to 2 p.m.
Jupiter 2 to 3 p.m.	Mercury 2 to 3 p.m.	Mars 2 to 3 p.m.	Moon 2 to 3 p.m.	Sun 2 to 3 p.m.	Saturn 2 to 3 p.m.	Venus 2 to 3 p.m.
Mars 3 to 4 p.m.	Moon 3 to 4 p.m.	Sun 3 to 4 p.m.	Saturn 3 to 4 p.m.	Venus 3 to 4 p.m.	Jupiter 3 to 4 p.m.	Mercury 3 to 4 p.m.
Sun 4 to 5 p.m.	Saturn 4 to 5 p.m.	Venus 4 to 5 p.m.	Jupiter 4 to 5 p.m.	Mercury 4 to 5 p.m.	Mars 4 to 5 p.m.	Moon 4 to 5 p.m.
Venus 5 to 6 p.m.	Jupiter 5 to 6 p.m.	Mercury 5 to 6 p.m.	Mars 5 to 6 p.m.	Moon 5 to 6 p.m.	Sun 5 to 6 p.m.	Saturn 5 to 6 p.m.

For example, if the child be born on Sunday between 6 and 7 a. m., on reference to the table we find that Shams, the Sun, is dominant at that time. Consequently the name should begin with *sh* ; or the last letter of Shams being *s* the name may begin with that letter.

This table, or genethliacal scheme, may be used in three ways ; first, in the selection of names as just described ; secondly, in ascertaining what day or hour is propitious or the reverse for doing any particular business. For example, during the time that Saturn rules no good work must be undertaken, as Saturn being the celestial eunuch is unpropitious; Sun, the cook, indifferent ; Venus, the prostitute, propitious ; Mercury, the teacher, propitious ; Moon, the messenger, indifferent ; Mars, the executioner, unpropitious ; Jupiter, the judge, propitious.[1] Thirdly, having ascertained from the table under the dominance of which planet the child was born, they cast his nativity and hereby predict his future destiny. For instance, if a person is born on Sunday at 12.30 or 12.45 a.m., which according to the Musalmān calendar would be Sunday night—as they calculate the day from 6 p.m. to 6 a.m., or roughly speaking from sunset to sunrise—the planet dominant at that time being Venus, her influence will be exerted on him, and he will be fond of music and singing, of dress and perfumes.

The planets exercise many influences, favourable and unfavourable, on the human race, of which a few examples may be given. The Dispositions of the Sun : One born under the dominance of the Sun, male or female, will be wealthy, sensible, passionate, easily irritated, generous, he will acquire much property, his word will be much respected, he will prefer black

[1] An astrologer told Rāī Dāhir that victory would rest with his Arab opponents because Venus is behind them and before you. So Dāhir had a golden image of Venus fastened to his saddle straps, so that the planet might be behind him, and give him victory. But Dāhir was defeated and slain (Elliot–Dowson, i. 171). Before the battle of Kanwāhā or Sīkrī, in A. D. 1527, in which Bābur defeated the Rājputs under Rānā Sangā, the astrologer told Bābur that as Mars was seen every evening in the west, whoever marched in that direction would be defeated. When the prediction proved false the emperor rewarded the astrologer, but compelled him to leave the kingdom (Ferishta, ii. 54 f., 59).

and red clothes, be amorous, addicted to drinking, a scoffer, little famed for pious works, annually indisposed, his birth will be inauspicious to his parents, he will live long and outlive them both. The Dispositions of Venus : he will be fond of music and singing, and still more of dress and sweets, partial to sweet and dainty dishes, amorous, beautiful, accomplished, amiable, endeavouring to appear neat and well dressed, constantly trying to enrich himself at the expense of others, unwilling to disclose his own secrets, never without perfumes, harmonious in voice and a good singer, a pleasant speaker, of agreeable conversation, eloquent and charming to many, and he will support not only his parents but also his brothers and sisters. The Dispositions of Mercury : a man of wisdom and learning, a good scribe, versed in many sciences, a clever painter, blessed with a good memory, nay even a Hāfiz, who knows the whole Korān by rote,[1] a poet, wealthy, master of arts, his society and friendship profitable to many, never solitary, but surrounded by people obedient to his will, an arithmetician, of uncommon penetration, useful to any one to whom he is well disposed, but if he dislikes a person he will avoid even the sight of him. The Dispositions of the Moon : he will be a gambler, good-looking, a drunkard, a great traveller, addicted to falsehood, a gabbler, famous in the assemblies of the great, subject every half year to diseases due to debility and cold, dreading water, in danger of his life while travelling, a blessing to his parents and friends. The Dispositions of Saturn : of a swarthy, dark complexion, long lived, of thin habit of body, black eyes, a flatterer, of a bilious temperament, loud voiced, courageous and a brave soldier, good looking, of a hasty disposition, perverse, tyrannical, fond of chastising, unkind, liberal, capricious, detesting flattery, pure in mind, without malice, very forgetful. The Dispositions of Jupiter : his daily food will be ever abundant ; he will be good-looking, a Hāfiz, a man of science, a judge, learned, a governor, a monarch, a Nawwāb, distinguished in science and politics ; he will have many enemies, but will always overcome them ; none will be able to injure him ; in handicraft, drawing and penmanship he

[1] Aurangzeb and some ladies of the Mughal royal family knew the whole Korān by heart (Jadunath Sarkar, *Life of Aurangzīb*, i. 8)

will be unrivalled; sensible, a counsellor, charitable, firm in mind, of a delicate constitution, high-spirited, and extremely persevering in all undertakings. The Dispositions of Mars: he will be tyrannical, of a ruddy complexion, a quick talker, kind, easily irritated, fond of white dress and perfumes, skilled in many arts and sciences, earnest in the search of knowledge, inclined to deprive another of his money and to hoard it himself, most ambitious.

The name of the child is selected from the following list. If a boy is born on the day or night of Sunday he is named Ibrāhīm, Abraham, Sulaimān, Solomon, Dāūd, David, Mūsā, Moses, 'Ayūb, Job, Hāshim, 'bread-breaker', Imrān, 'long-lived'. If it be a girl she is called Halīma, 'gentle', Habība, 'friend', Zainab, 'fragrance', Khadīja, 'aborter'. If on a Monday, a boy is named Muhammad, 'greatly praised', Ahmad, 'most praised', Mahmūd, 'praised', Qāsim, 'divided', Qādir, 'powerful'. If it be a girl she is called Fātima, 'weaner', Ammā, 'security', Hamīda, 'praised', Rafī'a, 'exalted', Ruqīa, 'enchanting', Zarīna, 'golden'. If on a Tuesday, a boy is named Ismā'īl, Ishmael, Ishāq, Isaac, Abū Bakr, 'father of the maiden', Iliās, Elias, Yāsīn, Pharaoh, while a girl is called Hanīfa, 'a sincere Muslim', 'Āyīsha, 'life', wife of the Prophet, Sharīfa, 'praised', Sakīna, Hebrew Shekinah, 'that which dwells'. If on a Wednesday, a boy is named 'Usmān, 'serpent', 'Alī, 'exalted', Hārūn, Aaron, Hasan, 'beautiful', Husain, 'little beauty', 'Umar, 'bought'. If a girl Rabī'ī, 'vernal', 'Azīza, 'excellent', Jamīla, 'beautiful', Fāzila, 'excellent', Najm, 'star', Khurshed, 'sun', Sitārā, 'star'. If on Thursday, a son is called Yūsuf, Joseph, Hamīd, 'praised', Mustafā, Murtazā, 'the chosen', Sajjād, 'bowing in adoration', Bāqir, 'learned', 'Askarī, 'soldier', Razā, 'content', Ja'far, 'a stream', Muhammad Ghaus, 'an ardent Saint'. If a girl, Maryam, Mary, Asya, 'running water', Zulaikha', 'she that slipped', the wife of Potiphar, Khairan, 'happy', Wājida, 'finder', Wāsila, 'beloved', Ghafūr, 'forgiving', Ma'rūf, 'celebrated'. If on a Friday, a son 'Īsa, Jesus, Anwar, 'resplendent', Nūr, 'bright', Haidar, 'lion', Akram, 'honour', Adam, Ādam, Sultān, 'monarch', Habību-llāh, 'a friend of God', Hāfizu-llāh, 'protected by God',

Karīmu-llāh, 'blessed of God' Rahmatu-llāh, 'mercy of God', 'Alīmu-llāh, 'learned in God', Qudratu-llāh, 'power of God', 'Abdu-llāh, 'servant of God'. If a girl, Māh, 'beloved', Zohra, Venus, Mahbūba, 'beloved', Amīra, 'princess', Ratan, 'jewel', Bānū, 'lady', Khātūn, 'lady', Nissa, 'woman', Hawwā', 'Eve', 'Ārifa, 'pious', Māmā, 'mother'. If born on a Saturday, a boy is named 'Ābdu-l-qādir, 'servant of the Almighty', 'Abdu-l-karīm, 'servant of the All Gracious', 'Abdu-l-razzāq, 'servant of the Bread Giver', 'Abdu-l-wahhāb, 'servant of the All Bountiful', 'Abdu-l-shakūr, 'servant of the Rewarder', 'Abdu-l-latīf, 'servant of the All Gracious', Shamsu-d-dīn, 'Sun of the Faith', Nizāmu-d-dīn, 'ruler of the Faith', Sirāju-d-dīn, 'Sun of the Faith', Muharram, 'the tabooed, honoured', Siddīq, 'he who speaks the truth'. If it is a girl, she is called Nāzuk, 'delicate', Ma'mūla, 'customary', Latīfa, 'the gentle', Bilqīs, Queen of Sheba.[1]

Opprobrious names, implying degradation, disgust, impurity, are often given by low-class Musalmāns to their children as a means of baffling the Evil Eye or the danger from exaggerated praise. Such are Nathū, 'nose-bored', Dukhī, 'afflicted', Gharīb, 'poor', Bhikhī, 'beggar', Kākī, 'crow', Kubrā, 'hunchback',

[1] The interpretation of some of these names is uncertain. The lists in Sir R. Temple, *Proper Names of Panjābīs*, have generally been followed.

CHAPTER III

RITES AFTER BIRTH

Paṭṭī, the parting of the mother's hair on both sides of the head, performed on the third day after the birth, a line being left in the middle, is probably a magical method of freeing the woman from any internal obstruction.[1] The women assemble, perform the rite, dress mother and child in red, tie a handkerchief over the woman's head, hold a red canopy over their heads and apply lampblack and soot to the eyes of mother and child. They fill the mother's lap with cakes spiced with ginger (*sonthānā*) and with betel. The guests apply turmeric to the mother's face, deposit their parting gifts (*raktanī*, *rukhsatāna*) and depart. Among the Shī'as of Lucknow on the fourth day the friends are invited to share in the family joy and there is a noisy feast.[2]

From the birth till the sixth day there is as much festivity as the family can afford. Chhathī, or the sixth day rite, should be done on that day, but it takes place more generally on the seventh or ninth. When many deaths have occurred in the house, in order to change the luck, they perform it on the third. The selection of the sixth is due to the fact that the occurrence of puerperal fever in the mother and tetanus in the child, the latter being due to infection during the sloughing of the navel-cord and the lack of sanitary precautions, is generally noticed on the sixth or seventh day, and these maladies are naturally attributed to the dangerous spirit of the sixth, Chhathī or Satvāī. The midwife smears the house floor with yellow or white clay or cowdung, and the women friends, men taking no part in the rite, send to the mother

[1] The parting of the hair of a pregnant woman is probably intended to secure easy delivery, but in other cases it may be a fertility charm, on the analogy of the plough passing through the furrow. It may be compared with the Hindu rite of Sīmantonnayana (*ERE*. iii. 471, ii. 650; Monier-Williams, *Brahmanism and Hinduism*, 4th ed., 357).

[2] Mrs. Meer Hassan Ali, 212.

D 2

soap-pods (*sikākāī, rīthā, acacia concinna*), used for cleansing the hair, gingeli or sesamum oil used in anointing the body before the Chiksā or perfumed powder is applied, with some lampblack, betel, and caudle. After the child has been bathed, a shirt (*kurtā*) made of any old article of dress worn by some ancient worthy is put on the child, in place of the pinafore worn up to that time, in order that he may reach old age. Should the midwife be an old woman she makes the shirt out of her own clothes. The first clothes of Akbar were made out of the garments of the holy man, Sayyid 'Alī Shīrāzī. On that day it is the custom to wear borrowed (*prada, parad*) clothes, which are provided by the washerman.

Then the mother sits on a bed and she is bathed with a decoction of aromatic herbs and leaves, a gift is given to the midwife, the liver (*kalejī*) of a sheep is served with rice and pulse, a portion is sent to absent friends, and the night is spent in amusement. This rite is done for all children, not for the first alone. From the evening meal a plateful is laid aside with the object that when the child grows up he may not covet every kind of food he sees. Should he prove to be greedy, people say that his dish (*bhāndā*) was not properly filled. In the centre of the dish a four-wicked lamp made of flour paste is sometimes lighted, friends drop a coin or two into it, and it is kept burning all night. This food is called 'the dish of the sixth' (*chhathī kā bhāndā*) or 'the vigil' (*ratjagā*), or by the vulgar 'Mother Sixth' (*Chhathī Mā*), because they suppose that Mother Sixth, the spirit which writes the fate of people, comes on that night and writes the child's destiny. Lower-class people keep the Chhathī rite, but the higher classes substitute the 'Aqīqa for it.

In north India on the Chhathī day female friends assemble, the mother bathes in warm water, and presents (*chhūchak*, a term also applied to the gifts which she receives after she visits her parents when the impurity period ends) are sent by her relations. When mother and child are dressed they come out of the delivery room (*zachhā* or *zachā-khāna*), she holding a Korān in her hands and keeping her eyes shut. When she comes out she opens her eyes and looks seven times at the sky. While she is out of the room a little boy is made to sit on her bed for a moment, a magical device to secure another boy, and before he goes out he demands a present. Then food made of seven kinds of grain (*satnajā*), often used in magic, is laid before the mother, but before she eats, seven women whose husbands are alive each take a mouthful from the dish. The wives of the family barber and gardener make wreaths of green leaves, which are hung on the houses of relations who give them a present.[1] In the Panjāb during the first six days after the delivery the mother is never left alone. This, it is said, is done to prevent her from overlaying the child, but more probably to protect her from evil spirits, and a lamp is kept burning for the same reason all the time. Behmātā or Bidhīmātā, 'Mother Fate', is here the goddess who records the child's destiny at birth. It is a deadly sin to refuse fire to her when she asks for it, and a story is told of a Faqīr who did so and was turned into a glow-worm, which ever carries fire behind it in its tail.[2] The Brāhūī, as soon as a child is born, paint a mark in indigo on all the four walls of the house, so that no spirit may enter, while some strew leaves of the *pīpal* or sacred fig tree about the house to keep off witches, and thrust a knife into the ground near the child's head. This must remain there for forty days, and if the mother happens during that time to go out of doors she must carry it with her as a protective.[3]

As among the Semites, the impurity of the mother lasts for forty days.[4] During that time she is not allowed to pray, touch the Korān, or enter a mosque. These taboos originally lasted as long as any issue of blood continued. In the Panjāb she sits while she nurses her child, lest its nose may become deformed by pressing against her breasts.[5] In south India on the fortieth as well as on the sixth, twelfth, and thirteenth days her friends bring gifts for the child, in particular amulets (*ta'wīz*) of gold or silver with verses of the Korān engraved on them which are hung over one shoulder, crossing the back and chest and reaching below the hip on the other side. This gift-giving

[1] *NINQ*. iii. 189.

[2] *JRAI*. xxxvii. 240. This is also a Jain belief, S. Stevenson, *The Heart of Jainism*, 193 f.

[3] Bray, 16.

[4] Frazer, *GB.*, Taboo and the Perils of the Soul, 147 ff.; Lev. xii. 1 ff.; Exod. xxiv. 15; xxxiv. 26, &c.

[5] *Man*, ii. 40 f.

in north India is usually done on the sixth day. In the Panjāb, among people who do not seclude their women, when the child is one month and ten days old, the mother bathes, is dressed in new clothes, puts on her head a couple of jars filled with boiled grain, goes to the well and offers the food to the water Saint, Khwāja Khizr, after which she fills the jars with water and goes home.[1] In Gujarāt little boats made of grass are taken to the nearest water and set afloat in the name of the Saint.[2] In south India the fortieth day is spent in amusements. Hijrās or eunuchs are paid to sing and dance, and they go about the town shouting 'Where is a son born?'. If the child is a daughter they get little or nothing. If they are not paid they load the father with curses.[3] In the evening male friends are feasted. The Fātiha is said over food in the name of Muhammad Mustafā the Chosen One—on whom be the Peace!—and it is then served to the guests. Some people take the mother and baby into the open air and make her count a few stars, after which a couple of arrows used to be shot into the air.

According to the Traditions the birth sacrifice is combined with the first shaving, the hair being left on the child's head till the seventh, fourteenth, twenty-first, twenty-eighth, or thirty-fifth day after birth, when it is shaved and its weight in silver is given in alms, as the Prophet did when a son was born to him in his old age.[4] In south India either on the sixth, fortieth, or other convenient day the 'Aqīqa [5] rite is done, two he-goats for a boy and one for a girl being sacrificed. The victim must be above a year old, perfect and without blemish (*sahīhu-l-ā'zā*), not blind of one or both eyes, or lame, and it must be so carefully skinned that no flesh remains on the hide, and the meat must be so cut up that no bone is broken.[6] As it is difficult to separate the flesh from the smaller bones, they are boiled and dressed with the flesh, the guests are enjoined to

[1] Rose, i. 565. This is a recognized Hindu practice.

[2] *BG.* ix, part 2, 158.

[3] The same custom prevails in north India, Rose, ii. 333.

[4] *Mishkāt*, ii. 515; Muir, *Life*, 412.

[5] '*Aqīqa* properly means the hair of the new-born infant, but the term is applied by Metonymy to the shaving sacrifice. On tonsure see *ERE*. vi. 538.

[6] Compare the Hebrew Passover rite, Exod. xii. 1-13.

chew and swallow the smaller bones, and the meat is carefully removed from the larger bones without injuring them. The meat is well boiled, and served with various kinds of bread. With the offering the benediction is said : ' O Almighty God ! I offer in the stead of my son, life for life, blood for blood, head for head, bone for bone, hair for hair, and skin for skin. In the name of God I sacrifice this he-goat '. It is held meritorious to distribute the meat to friends, but the person on whose account the offering is being made, his parents and his grandparents, are forbidden to eat it. The bones, boiled or unboiled, skin, feet, and head are buried in the earth, and no one is allowed to use them. In Gujarāt the 'Aqīqa is done on the seventh, fourteenth, or twenty-first day after birth, and the rite consists of two parts, the shaving of the child's head and the offering of the goats. The barber passes his razor over the child's head and draws a knife across the goats' throats with the invocation as recorded above. The parings of the child's hair and nails are laid on a flat half-baked cake and are thrown into a river. The bones are buried, the flesh and skin divided into three parts, one given in charity, one to friends, while the rest is eaten by the relatives, the parents and grand-parents being forbidden to share in it.[1]

In south India the Mūndan or shaving follows the 'Aqīqa on some day after. Though most people combine these two rites, the poor observe only the latter, and the very poor combine the shaving with the ceremonies on the sixth and fortieth days. Those who can afford it have the shaving done with a silver-mounted razor and use a silver cup to hold the water, both being the perquisite of the barber, who receives other gifts. After the head is shaved, the rich rub it with saffron, the poor with sandalwood. The weight of the hair in silver is given to Faqīrs, and the hair is tied up in cloth, buried or thrown into water. The rich, when disposing of the hair, make an offering to Khwāja Khizr and let the hair float away in a stream. Some leave a lock (*chonti*) uncut in the name of a Saint, and great care is taken that nothing pollutes it. Some postpone

[1] *BG*. ix, part 2, 158. On the 'Aqīqa rite see *Encyclopaedia Islām*, i. 239; R. Smith, *Religion of Semites*, 239; Lane, *AN*. i. 277, *ME*. i. 67; *NINQ*. ii. 49; iii. 189 f.; Rose, iii. 227; *JRAI*. xxxvii. 243.

the shaving till it can be done at the Dargāh or shrine of the Saint. In Sind when the hair is shaved it is put with the bones of the victim offered at the 'Aqīqa rite and buried in a cemetery or at the threshold of the house, the common belief being that at the Day of Resurrection the contents of the skin will rise in the form of a horse and will carry the soul of the child over the bridge of death, Al-Sirāt, into Paradise.[1] The Baloch perform the first tonsure prior to circumcision at the shrine of the Saint Sakhī Sarwar, the weight of the hair in silver being given to the Mujāwir or attendants of the shrine.[2]

On the fortieth day, or before, the child is rocked in a swinging cradle (*gahwārā*), a piece of magic to make the child grow taller as the swing goes higher.[3] This is done in the evening, and women friends rub the legs of the cradle with sandalwood and decorate them with red thread. They put a coco-nut at each corner of the cradle with some gram cakes and betel laid on the ground, and while they sing a lullaby they scramble for the food. Then they sit up all night and amuse themselves with singing and dancing.

When the child is about four months old it often claps its hands, and it is said to be making sweetmeat balls (*laddū bāndhnā*). These are provided, relations are invited, the Fātiha is said over them in the name of the Prophet—on whom be the Peace !—and the party eat them.

When the child is seven months old, friends are invited, the Fātiha is said over a hasty pudding (*firnī*) in the name of Muhammad Murtazā—on whom be the Peace ! They take with the forefinger a little pudding, rub it on the child's tongue and make him taste it. This may be regarded as the weaning, but according to the Traditions the child should be suckled for two and a half years, a period often extended to three or four. In Gujarāt this rite is known as Botan (*botā*, ' a bit of meat ') or Namakchashī, ' salt-tasting ', for the father gives the child some rice and milk on a rupee and a bit of meat to suck. The Brāhūī wean a boy after a year and a half, a girl after two. They put seven dates in a pot and bid the child take as many

[1] Burton, *Sindh*, 259. [2] Rose, ii. 51 ; Bray, 25 f.
[3] Frazer, *GB.*, The Dying God, 277 ff.

as it pleases, the number marking the number of days it will trouble its mother for milk.[1]

The teething is called Dānt nikalnā, or Dānt ghūngnī, because when the first tooth appears they make a mess of stirabout (*ghūngnī*) of grain boiled with sugar. After saying the Fātiha over this it is distributed. In north India the fate of the child is supposed to be bound up with that of its maternal uncle who officiates at the rite. A child who first shows a tooth in the upper jaw is unlucky. To avoid trouble, rice, copper coins, a piece of cloth, and four iron nails are put on a tray which is carried outside the limits of the village. The uncle drives the nails into the ground in the form of a square, and touching the child's tooth with the tray, leaves it within the square. The child is carried by his aunt, sister of his maternal uncle, who sits veiled and is not allowed to see what her brother is doing, while after the rite he goes home in silence.[2]

A rite is done when the child begins to close its fists (*mutthī bāndhnā*) and to crawl (*rengnā*). Parched rice (*murmurā*) is made into balls which are given to friends, and the night is spent in singing and dancing. Among the Brāhūī, when a child begins to toddle they throw a little loaf among the assembled friends, and the child is told to pick it up. When he does this a bit of it is given to each guest, and there is a feast.[3] In the case of Akbar the Turkī custom was observed, that when a child begins to crawl, the father, grandfather, or whoever represents him takes off his turban and strikes the child with it so as to make him fall. This is said to be as good as the herb of grace (*ispand*, *sipand*, *Lawsonia inermis*) to protect him from the Evil Eye.[4]

When a girl is a year or two old her ears are bored. This is done by the goldsmith or barber, into whose lap two coco-nut kernels (*khoprā*) are put, and his neck is smeared with sandal-wood. By degrees other holes are bored along the whole edge

[1] Bray, 24 f. On the ceremonial feeding of the child see R. Smith, *Kinship*, 154; Crawley, 136. Compare the Hindu rite of Annaprāsana, Monier-Williams, *Brahmanism and Hinduism*, 4th ed., 358 f.

[2] *Man*, ii. 60. For similar Hindu rites at teething see Thurston, *Castes*, vii. 73; *BG*. xv, part 1, 218; Russell, iii. 300.

[3] Bray, 24.

[4] Smith, *Akbar*, 21.

of the ear, and even in the centre part, till by the time the girl is two or three years old she has thirteen holes in the right and twelve in the left. Some people bore a hole in each lobe, in the part projecting over the orifice, one above it and a few others here and there, but in the Deccan most people think it vulgar to bore holes uniformly all round the edge, as that is the custom of the lower castes.[1]

[1] On the protective influence of ear-boring see Frazer, *Folklore OT.*, iii. 165 ff. For the Hindu rite, Dubois, 159: *Census Report*, 1911, Bengal, i. 448; Kashmīr, i. 144; Central Provinces, i. 157.

CHAPTER IV

INITIATION, BIRTHDAYS

THE rite of initiation, Bi'smillāh, 'pronouncing the name of God',[1] is observed when a boy or girl has reached the age of four years four months and four days. In the case of girls the plaiting of the side locks (*palgūndhan, pahlūgūndhan*) is done for the first time at this rite. Strings of black silk are plaited into the long hair, the braids or plaits must be uneven in number, and women swear by them as men do by their beards.[2] During two or three days before the rite, the child is dressed from head to foot in yellow clothes, Chiksā or scented powder is rubbed on his body by women whose husbands are alive (*suhāgan*), and he is seated in a room with a canopy over his head, and coloured clothes hung round to resemble a throne. Every morning and evening while he is being massaged, musicians play and the child is not allowed to walk about. This part of the rite is called in south India 'sitting in state' (*manjā, manjhā baithnā*).[3] The day before the ceremony the lady guests are invited by sending round cardamoms to their houses, and other friends by letter in the following form : 'To such a one, the obliger of friends, greeting ! At this poor man's house his son (or daughter, as the case may be) is this evening to be taught to repeat the name of God (*Bi'smillāh-khwānī*). I beg that you by joining the party will grace the assembly with your presence and joyfully partake of something. For by so doing you will afford me peculiar pleasure'. Then the men and women meet apart. The child having been well bathed in the afternoon, and all the perfumed paste removed from his body, his yellow dress is exchanged for better garments, red or white, made of various kinds of brocade or other stuffs. Gold or silver amulets, which some of the friends may have

[1] *ERE.* ii. 666 ff.

[2] Burton, *AN.* iii. 93 ; Lane, *ME.* i. 55.

[3] *Manjā, manjhā*, a large couch, is used by the Sikhs as a technical term for a diocese allotted by Gurū Amar Dās to his disciples, Rose, i. 681.

given, are hung on his neck, and he is perfumed. Garlands of flowers are hung round his neck and wrists and a wreath made of gold wire (*seharā*, *sehrā*) over his forehead. Thus bedecked, he is seated in the presence of his family tutor or some Mashāikh or venerable personage. Near them are placed trays with sweetmeats, two of the largest balls having gold or silver paper pasted over them, with other gifts including a small gold or silver plate and a pen and inkstand intended as gifts for the tutor. He, after reciting the Fātiha over the food in the name of the Prophet—on whom be the Peace !—writes on a plate with his pen dipped in sandalwood the words ' In the name of God, the Merciful, the Compassionate ! ' and orders the child to lick it off. He lays the two ornamented sweet balls in the child's hands to tempt him to perform his task. It is also the rule to write the first chapter of the Korān on red paper, but those who can afford it write this on a gold or silver plate, and giving it to the boy or girl require him or her to repeat first the words ' In the name of God, the Merciful, the Compassionate ! ' and afterwards from the ninety-sixth chapter the opening words : ' Recite thou in the name of the Lord who created, created man from clots of blood ! Recite thou ! For thy Lord is most beneficent, who has taught the use of the pen, hath taught that thou knowest not ! ' This being the first sentence of the Korān revealed to the Prophet—on whom be the Blessing !—it is considered of high value, and is taught to children. In north India the words of the blessing are engraved on a small silver tablet which the child, after repeating the words, hands to the old man after whom he has said them.[1] Presents are then made to the tutor, and the child rises from his seat, salutes his tutor, and the friends present who give him presents. Then the sweets over which the Fātiha has been said are placed on the Dastarkhwān or dining cloth, and with other food are served to the guests. Next day the lady guests are sent home in litters after the host has given them presents. After this the boy is sent to school. In Gujarāt the boy is sent to visit the shrine of the family Saint, and when he returns the women surround him and each strives to be the first to take his troubles upon herself

[1] *NINQ.* iii. 192.

(*balāēn lenā*) by passing her hands over him from head to foot, and then pressing against his temples her knuckles and finger-tips till they crack.[1]

The mode of sending invitations to guests to attend family rites is of great importance. In the Deccan and south India female guests receive invitations (*da'wat*) to attend these and other rites by the sending of cardamoms (*ilāchī*), while men are generally invited by letter. When ladies are invited, some woman who is in the habit of going about the bazars and lanes of the town or city is employed as a messenger. She is decked in her best clothes, and, accompanied by musicians, she starts with a plate in her hand containing sandalwood, packets of betel-leaf and areca nut, with sugar candy and cardamoms wrapped in red paper, a packet for each guest. She approaches the lady with much respect, and making a salutation she delivers the message in these terms: 'Such and such a lady (naming her) sends her best compliments and embraces to you, and informs you that tomorrow there will be a little gaiety at her house. She wishes all her lady friends by their presence to grace and ornament with their feet the house of this poor person, and thereby to make it a garden of roses. So you must certainly come, and by remaining a couple of hours honour her humble abode by your company'. Should the lady accept the invitation, the bearer of the cardamoms rubs a little sandalwood paste on her neck, breast, and back, and puts her share of the sugar candy and cardamoms into her mouth, or these things are handed to her with the packet of betel-leaves. If the lady declines the invitation, sandalwood alone is applied, and a packet of betel without any of the cardamoms and sugar candy is handed to her. When the messenger has finished the round of visits and announced the names of those who have

[1] *BG.* ix, part 2, 160. Among the Bannūchī some old women wave three red chillies several times round the head of a person troubled by evil spirits, each time saying, 'Herewith I draw off the eye, be it man's, woman's, or spirits.' Then each pepper-pod is put into the fire (Thorburn, 161). Cf. *ERE.* iii. 447. Compare the Hindu Ārtī, or waving rite (Manucci, iii. 340). When the Emperor Shāhjahān was sick, his daughter liberated several slaves, made them walk round her father, and then sent them away to carry his infirmities with them (Ibid. i. 217. Mrs. Meer Hassan Ali, 215).

accepted the invitation of her employer, next day a litter (*dolī*), accompanied by a maid-servant, is sent to fetch each guest. If the lady of the house be poor, she merely sends her own maid-servant to escort the guests to her house a little before daybreak.

When they arrive the hostess advances to the gate to welcome them, takes them by the hand, and leading them into the house seats them on the carpet. On other less important occasions invitations are sent by a messenger, but she is not attended with music and does not carry sugar candy, cardamoms, or betel-leaf.

When guests attend such rites they are expected to bring presents (*neotā, manjā*) with them proportionate in value to the nature of the rite and their own means. At the Chhathī and Chilla rites, already described, the gifts consist generally of a necklace (*hanslī*), ankle-rings (*karā*), a cap (*topī*), a sheet (*sārī*), a bodice (*cholī*), betel-leaves, areca nut, flowers, and sandalwood. At the Bi'smillāh rite for children they bring a small gold or silver plate weighing eight annas, or half a rupee (a rupee = 1 *tolā*, 179 grains), hung on a red thread together with sufficient velvet to make a bodice, betel, flowers, sandalwood, and sweetmeats. For a wedding the gift consists of a shawl, a piece of muslin, a sheet, a turban, a bodice, betel, some choice delicacy, cakes (*malīdā*), sweetmeats, or merely betel with plantains, and coco-nuts. The guests bring these things in person, or in the case of great people they are brought by the men guests with great pomp and state. Poor people give at least a velvet bodice, sweetmeats, betel, flowers, and sandalwood, according to their means. If they have brought no gift in kind they are expected to put a rupee or two or less into the hand of the child or of the mistress of the house.

The anniversary of the birthday is celebrated with great rejoicing, relatives being entertained, and the Fātiha said over the food in the name of the Prophet and Father Nūh or Noah—on whom be the Peace !—so that the child may attain the age of the patriarch. Then some old woman ties a knot in a red or yellow thread, known as the Sālgirāh or 'year knot', or by converts from Hinduism Janamgānth or 'birth knot'. The mother keeps the string and produces it at each of the boy's birthdays. A girl's years are counted by a silver loop or ring being added yearly to her Gardanī or silver neck-ring. The occasion is marked by feasting and rejoicings. The practice is believed to have been borrowed from the Hindus, and Akbar is said to have adopted it from the Hindu ladies of his Zanāna. On his birthday Akbar was weighed against gold and other valuables, the proceeds of which were given to the poor, while in the time of Aurangzeb a yellow cord was used for princes and princesses.[1] The Author, Ja'far Sharīf, remarks that on such occasions in southern India drinking is not uncommon; 'though in public women, as well as men, drink only water, sherbet, or milk, it is not uncommon for them in private to take strong drink, although it is prohibited in the Korān, excusing themselves by saying that there is no harm in the use of the juice of a fruit, meaning the grape '.[2]

[1] *Āīn*, i. 267; Elliot–Dowson, v. 307; Manucci, ii. 346.
[2] On this distinction see Lane, *ME.* i. 118.

CHAPTER V

CIRCUMCISION

CIRCUMCISION (*khatna*, *sunnat*, in Sind *sathra*, *tohāru*) should be performed between the ages of seven and twelve or fourteen, but it is lawful to do it seven days after birth.[1] Akbar prohibited the rite before the age of twelve, and it was then to be optional with the boy.[2]

On the appointed day friends are invited and entertained. For a few days before the rite the boy is rubbed with Haldī or turmeric and made to sit in state (known in south India as *manjā baithnā*). He is dressed in red or yellow clothes, decorated with flowers, and Missī or dentifrice is rubbed on his teeth, this being the only occasion on which males use it. He is then carried in procession round the town. Others postpone the dinner and the procession till after the operation. The boy is seated on a large new earthen pot inverted, or on a chair with a red handkerchief spread over it. A couple of hours before he has been dosed with the electuary known as Ma'jūn, made from hemp and used as an anodyne. Some friends hold the boy firmly and the barber performs the operation with a sharp razor. When it is over the boy is told to call out three times 'Dīn', 'The Faith'. To divert his attention he is made to slap the operator for causing him so much pain. One of the relatives chews betel and squirts the red spittle on the wound to make him believe that there has been no flow of blood. While the operation is in progress the Brāhūī mother puts a handmill on her head, a kinswoman a Korān, and they stand facing west and praying till all is over ; in the Marī

[1] The meaning of the rite is still obscure. For various explanations see Frazer, *GB.*, The Magic Art, i. 96 ; *Folklore OT*. ii. 330 ; *ERE*. iii. 659 ; ix. 826 ; Hastings, *Dict. Bible*, v. 622 ; Crawley, 138, 309. On mock circumcision, Thurston, *Castes*, ii. 120 ; *Man*, xv. 65. On the Musalmān ritual, *ERE*. iii. 677 ff. ; Burton, *AN*. iv. 163 ; *BG* ix, part 2, 160 f.

[2] *Āīn*, i. 207.

tribe the mother stands in the centre of a group of singing women having in her hands an upper millstone over which are sprinkled red earth and rice, and on these an iron ring, a green bead, and a piece of red cloth, all tied together with a red string apparently symbolical of virility.[1] In Sind, while the mother holds a stone on her head, a male relation pours water upon it, and sometimes instead of the mother, the father stands with his feet in water and holds a Korān on his head.[2] Care is taken of the severed foreskin, lest a witch may work evil magic by means of it. Pathāns on the north-west frontier bury it in a damp part of the house where the water jars are kept, possibly in the hope that it may grow and increase the virility of the boy. In other parts of the Panjāb it is buried, thrown on the house roof, or attached to it by a straw; in Delhi it is tied with a peacock's feather to the boy's left foot, so that no evil shadow may fall upon him and injure him. Some Brāhūīs bury it under a green tree so that the lad may be fruitful in generation, or they bury it in damp earth, thinking to cool the burning pain of the wound.[3]

After the operation the barber applies a dressing, and the wound heals in the course of a week or so. While the rite is being done, some rice and other gifts are laid close by which are given to the barber, but if the boy was seated on a chair this is not given away. In Sind the father places the fee under the lad's right foot and the friends wave money, which the barber receives, over the boy's head, or he puts his brass saucer in the room and people drop money into it.[4]

Some people never have a boy circumcised alone, but always with another to make the number equal, because the operation involves taboo. Hence when they have one or three boys to undergo the rite, they get some poor woman's son to be circumcised with them. If they fail to find such a boy they substitute for him a Badhnā, or water-pot with a spout, in the mouth of which a packet of betel is placed and cut by the barber. They think it favourable if the boy during the operation makes water, as this clears the urethra. They guard the boy against

[1] *Census Report*, Balūchistān, 1911, i. 60 f. [2] Aitken, 209.
[3] *JRAI*. xxxvii. 255; Bray, 30; Rose, i. 778 ff.; iii. 228.
[4] Aitken, 209; *NINQ*. iii. 192.

contact with dogs or cats and from other defilements, such as that of a woman in her courses. Ants are kept away by spreading ashes round the bed, or by placing the legs of it in stone pots filled with water. They tie a peacock's feather, a copper ring (*chhallā*) with a blue thread to the wrist, neck, or ankle of the lad, and they burn Ispand or herb of grace as a protective.

Female circumcision, or clitorodectomy, prevails among some tribes in the Panjāb and on the north-west frontier and probably extends more widely, but from the nature of the case, it is difficult to procure evidence. Some Musalmān Jāts remove the tip of the clitoris, not with the idea of promoting chastity, but as a religious act.[1] The Brāhūī circumcise a woman to remove the curse of barrenness, and the custom prevails in the Bahāwalpur State and among the Marī of Balūchistān.[2] The authenticity of a tradition allowing it has been disputed. The custom seems to have spread eastwards from Egypt and the Sudan.[3]

[1] *PNQ.* i. 86. On this rite see Lane, *ME.* i. 73; Burton, *AN.* iv. 228, *Pilgrimage*, ii. 20; *Man*, xiii. 137 ff.; xv. 66; in Africa, *JRAI.* xxxii. 309; xxxiii. 351; xxxiv. 169, 265; *ERE.* ii. 223; iii. 667 ff.

[2] Bra[illegible] *Census Report*, Balūchistān, 1911, i. 61, 107. The Kehal t[illegible]njāb circumcise a young wife if she does not conceive wi[illegible]s after marriage, Rose, ii. 487.

[3] [illegible] ff.

CHAPTER VI

GROWTH AND EDUCATION

In Balūchistān a boy is given trousers at the age of three, a girl between two and four. On the falling of the first tooth the child's mouth is washed with salt and bitter oil, that the new tooth may be white and shapely. He is made to jump out of doors, shouting 'O crow! Thy teeth are black! Look, mine are bright! O crow! Thy teeth are crooked, mine aright!'[1]

After a boy or girl has finished the reading of the Korān from end to end, a propitious day is fixed, according to the system used in selecting names, for the purpose of making gifts to the tutor and exhibiting the child's skill in reading. The friends are invited, and the boy now able to read the Korān (*qur'ān-khwān*), dressed in his best, is seated in the men's hall with the Korān in his hands. A robe of honour (*khil'at*) and other gifts are set out for the tutor, and the boy is made to read the first, part of the second, the thirty-sixth, and the fifty-fifth chapters. The tutor then recites the Fātiha over the food in the name of the Prophet—the Blessing!—and makes the boy breathe on it. After the blessing he says 'I forgive all the trouble I have undergone in teaching the sacred Korān, and I freely bestow on thee the knowledge which I have taught thee!' Then the food which has become sacred by having the whole contents of the Korān blown upon it is distributed, and the gifts are given to the tutor.[2]

Besides this ceremony, at every feast, marriage, or dinner the tutor receives his dues. He is honoured, says Ja'far Sharīf, as a father, because a man is said to have four fathers: his

[1] Bray, 31 f. Hindus, when a child's teeth fall out, throw them on the house roof, which is infested by rats and mice, in the hope that the new teeth will be as white and shapely as those possessed by these animals.

[2] When Humāyūn was about to invade India, he sent for his son Akbar, read some verses of the Korān, and at the end of each verse blew upon the boy (Smith, *Akbar*, 28). For Christian examples of blowing upon a person as a means of communicating afflatus, see *EB.* vi. 976.

natural father, his tutor, his father-in-law, and his Murshid or spiritual guide. Besides this, the Prophet has assured us that if any person in his daily prayers says the Du'ā-i-ma'sūr, or prayer for the remission of sins, for his parents and his tutor, the Almighty will hear and answer. For children who go to school the master usually writes the 'Īdī or 'feast verse', or a blessing on the child, on paper sprinkled with gold dust (*zar-i-fishān*), and desires him to read it to his parents, who send an 'Īdī, or feast gift, in return. Such presents are made at four festivals, the Ākhirī-chār-shamba, the Shab-i-barāt, the Ramazān, and the Baqar 'Īd. In Musalmān schools in north India the pupils on the eve of the Friday holiday bring lamp-money (*charāghī, chirāghī*) for the teacher, a term also used for money spent in lighting a lamp on a Saint's tomb, or the percentage taken by the owner of a gambling-house.[1]

There are thirty sections (*juz, sipāra*) in the Korān, and at the beginning and end of each of these it is usual to give a present to the tutor, this gift being known as Hadīya. Of these there are four principal occasions: at the end of a quarter, half, three quarters, or the whole Korān, of which the last is most important. Besides this, when a boy begins a new book it is usual to give a present, sweetmeats, betel, and money. The tutor recites the Fātiha over these, rubs sandalwood on the boy's neck and sometimes on his own, or taking them in his hand smells them, repeats the Durūd or blessing, hears the lessons and then gives a half-holiday. If the number of boys be great, and so it would be necessary to give a half-holiday for each, he puts off the Fātiha till a Thursday, the usual half-holiday, and deals with the gifts of two or more boys at the same time.

In short, every opportunity is taken to compliment the tutor, for a blessing from his auspicious lips is as good as the reading of a hundred books, and if his curse rests on any one the reading of a hundred books will be of little profit; nay, he is equal to, if not greater than one's father or mother, inasmuch as he teaches the Law and the writings of God and His Messenger, and explains the doctrines of the Faith. While his natural parents nourish the body of their son with temporal food, he provides that which is spiritual.

[1] *NINQ*. v. 178.

CHAPTER VII

THE COMING OF AGE OF A GIRL AND A BOY

WHEN a girl menstruates for the first time she is said to be 'grown up' (*bāligh honā*), 'to have her head dirty for the first time' (*pahlē sir mailā honā*), owing to the prohibition against bathing during this period, or 'to mix with those who are grown up' (*baron men milnā*). The illness at the lunar periods is expressed by 'the approach of the menses' (*haiz ānā*), 'the arrival of the season for bathing' (*nihānī ānā*), 'the head becoming dirty' (*sir mailā honā*), 'becoming unfit for prayers' (*benamāzī ānā*), or 'to become unclean' (*nāpāk honā*). Among Musalmān girls the time of puberty is from ten to fourteen, generally about twelve, and the function continues till the fortieth, or in some cases the forty-fifth year.[1] Among women in south Gujarāt a ceremony known as 'donning the scarf' (*orhnī urānā*) is performed secretly when a girl reaches womanhood.[2] Baloch mothers press their daughters' breasts and rub them with ashes and salt to prevent them from swelling or holding milk, and when menstruation occurs for the first time the mother takes three small stones, arranges them on the ground in the form of a triangle, and bids the girl leap over them thrice, in order that the menses may not last more than three days, the furthest limit being five or six days.[3] At a girl's first menstruation in the Deccan seven or nine married women of the house and neighbourhood meet in the afternoon and each of them rubs a little perfumed powder (*chiksā*) on the girl's body, puts a couple of garlands of flowers round her neck and anoints her with fragrant oil (*phulel kā tel*). After this she is confined in a private room and the women go home after spending a little time in music. For seven days the girl is kept shut up in this room, she is not allowed to go out, to do any

[1] Mrs. Meer Hassan Ali, 185; N. Cheevers, *Medical Jurisprudence in India*, 671.

[2] *BG.* ix, part 2, 162.

[3] Bray, 32 f.

sort of work, or to bathe. During this time her diet consists of rice boiled with pulse (*khicharī*), fish, flesh, salt, and acid foods being prohibited. On the seventh day she is bathed. The married women, as before, assemble in the morning, hold a red cloth over her head as a canopy, take a small water vessel with a spout (*badhnī*), either plain or decorated with paint, fasten a packet of betel-leaves with a red thread to the neck of the pot, drop into it four or five fruits of the two kinds of myrobalan, and each woman pours water from it twice over the girl's head. Before the women do this their laps are filled with cakes and betel, and sandalwood is rubbed on their necks. On that evening a feast is given, and the girl is adorned with glass bangles and dressed in her best. They keep vigil during the night to guard against evil spirits. If the girl be already married and consummation has not yet taken place, which is more than probable as Musalmāns object to infant marriage, her husband, leaving the party to enjoy themselves, takes his bride home and consummates the marriage. On this occasion he is usually given a present of clothes, and the pair are wreathed with flowers. But it is only the lower classes who make this public, and more respectable people do not announce the event.

When a boy on arriving at his twelfth, thirteenth, fourteenth, or fifteenth year, or as some say, at the age of eighteen, experiences a pollutio nocturna,[1] he must conform to the duties of his religion as regards prayer, fasting, almsgiving, and pilgrimage. This is also the rule for girls. Previous to this period, that is, during childhood, all their good and evil deeds are laid to the charge of their parents, but after this they are responsible for their own actions. When the youth is overtaken with pollutio in somno he must perform the Ghusl or major ablution by bathing on the following morning, for until he has purified himself in this way it is unlawful for him to eat, pray, touch the Korān, or go to the mosque. These rules also extend to other ablutions, of which there are four: after pollutio nocturna (*ihtilām*), which was abrogated by Akbar;[2] after coitus (*jimā'*);[3] after menses (*haiz*); after puerperium (*nifās*). The period to which the first and second bathing may be

[1] Cf. Deut. xxiii. 10–11. [2] *Āīn*, i. 194. [3] Burton, *AN*. iii. 359.

deferred is nine or ten next morning ; the last should be deferred till the discharge has ceased, but some ignorant women have fixed it for the fortieth day after childbed. The bathing is done thus : After slightly wetting the body and reciting some short prayers appointed for this purpose, the boy gargles his throat three times, then he bathes, thoroughly wetting his whole body and uttering the following sentences in Arabic : 'I desire by the ablution to purify my body for prayer and to remove all inward filth and corruption '. Some ignorant or vulgar people first throw three pots of water on the head, then three on the right shoulder, then three on the left, and having taken a little water in the hand, either after or without reciting the Durūd or blessing, they sprinkle it on the clothes which are thus purified. In the complete ablution the water must be pure and not less than a certain quantity, and it must touch every part of the skin beginning with the right side of the person and ending with the left. Hence among Arabs a plunge bath is generally preferred.[1]

[1] Ibid. iv. 153. Properly speaking, it should be done in running water, and hence Musulmāns use a vessel with a spout (*badhnā*) for the purpose.

CHAPTER VIII

MARRIAGE

MARRIAGE is enjoined on every Musalmān, and celibacy was condemned by the Prophet, but it is often enforced by poverty or other causes. The proportions of the married and unmarried among Musalmāns differ from those of the Hindus. Among Musalmāns 'the proportion of the unmarried is larger and that of the married and widowed smaller. Of every 100 males 53 are unmarried, 43 married, and 4 widowed, while of the same number of females 38 are unmarried, 47 married, and 15 widowed. The difference is most notable amongst the young of both sexes. Under the age of 5 the proportion of Muhammadan girls who are married is not much more than a quarter of the corresponding figure for Hindus, and between 5 and 10 it is only a half. It is not till the age period 15–20 that an equality between the proportions is reached, while above that age the relative number of females who are married is greater amongst Muhammadans than amongst Hindus. The Muhammadans have fewer widows at all ages, but the difference is most marked in the prime of life. This is owing to the fact that women who lose their first husbands while still capable of bearing children have less difficulty than their Hindu sisters in marrying a second time. A prejudice against widow marriage exists, however, amongst many classes of Muhammadans, especially those who are descended from local converts '.[1]

The prohibited degrees include: consanguinity—mother, grandmother, sister, niece, aunt, &c.; affinity—mother-in-law, step-daughters, grand-daughters, &c.; fosterage; with the wife's sister during the lifetime of the wife, unless she is divorced; of the wife of another until the period of probation (*'iddat*) has expired, three months after divorce, four months ten days after widowhood; with polytheists, who do not include Jews or Christians.[2]

[1] *Census Report*, India, 1911, i. 266.
[2] See *ERE*. vii. 866; Lane, *ME*. i. 123.

'It is considered desirable that a man should take as his first wife a virgin bride of the same social standing as himself, and preferably of the same division or tribe. As regards subsequent wives there is no restriction whatever. There are no exogamous groups; the marriage of persons more nearly related is forbidden, but that of first cousins, whether the children of brothers or sisters, is considered very suitable; failing them, an alliance is preferred with some family with which there have already been marriage relations; it is sometimes said that the object of cousin marriage is to keep the family as free as possible from foreign blood, and to retain in the family the property inherited by the young couple'.[1]

Marriage is usually by dower or settlement (*mahr*, *sadqa*, *nuhl*), the latter 'not the exchange or consideration given by the man to the woman for entering into the contract, but imposed by law on the husband as a token of respect for its subject, the woman'.[2] Marriage by purchase is not common, but Khojās in Gujarāt practise the custom, the father of the bridegroom paying 5¼ rupees to the father of the bride, the amount being given over to the Jamā'atkhāna or assembly lodge of the caste, and it is the rule among the Arabs.[3] In some cases, as among the Brāhūī, the wives of two brothers being pregnant promise to wed son to daughter, if such be born.[4] Temporary marriages (*muta'*, *sīgha*, *nikāh-i-muwaqqat*), contracted for a limited period, are recognized by Shī'as, a practice which has done much to demoralize the community. They were forbidden, but subsequently in part sanctioned by the Prophet.[5] The term marriage by capture has sometimes been

[1] *Census Report*, India, 1911, i. 252; Burton, *Pilgrimage*, ii. 84. The rules depend not on biological, but on social considerations, *ERE*. iv. 30; viii. 425 f. On cross-cousin marriage see Rivers, *JRAS*. 1897, pp. 64 ff.; Frazer, *Folklore in OT*. ii. 99 ff.

[2] Baillie, 91; *ERE*. v. 743; vii. 865 f.

[3] *BG*. ix, part 2, 45; Burton, *Pilgrimage*, ii. 111.

[4] Bray, 11; *Census Report*, Balūchistān, 1911, i. 103.

[5] *Korān*, iv. 28; *Mishkāt*, ii. 88, 90; *Āīn*, i. 174; Sell, 84; Browne, *A Year*, 462; Ibn Khallīkān, iv. 37; Hartland, *Primitive Paternity*, ii. 6; *ERE*. iii. 815. Fīroz Shāh Bahmanī (A.D. 1397–1422) raised a controversy on the subject, the Sunnī divines denying its legality, the Shī'as maintaining that it was allowed in the time of the Prophet and of his first Khalīfa, and that, though it was abrogated by the second

rather loosely applied to those cases where a real or pretended opposition is made by the friends of the bride when the bridegroom comes to fetch her home. Instances of this practice are found among Pathāns, Khattaks, and Wazīrīs; among the last named tribe swords are brandished and injury occasionally results, and in the Delhi royal family it was the rule to make a mock resistance when the bridegroom came to take his bride home.[1] The custom seems to be occasionally based upon the belief that a mock fight is a means of repelling evil spirits.[2]

When a man wishes to marry, he sends for three or four women who act as go-betweens, whom he deputes to search for a bride, beautiful, eligible, clever, accomplished, rich; and he promises a reward in case they are successful. Special regard is paid to birth, position, and individual eligibility. Widows are to be avoided, and four points are to be sought: her stature should be less than that of her husband; she should be younger; possess less property; be inferior in rank and station. The best complexion is dark with black hair, indicating modesty and virtue; a red pallid skin is to be avoided as it indicates a choleric, sensual temperament.[3] These matchmakers go about selling trifles and gossiping in families, by which means they come to know the girls and are able to report about them. If the girl belongs to the family of a friend or acquaintance go-betweens are not required, the negotiations being conducted by the senior ladies of both houses.

According to the Law a boy should be married at puberty, a girl at the age of twelve. In Sind it is fixed at fifteen for males and twelve for girls; in Gujarāt between sixteen and twenty-two for men, ten to fifteen for girls; in north India eighteen for youths, thirteen or fourteen for girls.[4] Akbar forbade boys under sixteen and girls under fourteen to marry.[5]

When the family connexions, pedigree, religion, and customs

Khalīfa, it was still legal. The king accepted the reasoning of the Shī'as, and received into his harem three hundred women in one day (Ferishta, ii. 364 f.).

[1] Rose, ii. 531; iii. 228; [F. Parks], *Wanderings of a Pilgrim*, i. 436 f.

[2] E. Westermarck, *History of Human Marriage*, 383 ff.; Crawley, 290 ff.

[3] Burton, *Sindh*, 159 f.

[4] *Mishkāt*, ii. 86; Lane, *AN*. i. 281; Burton, *Sindh*, 260; *BG*. ix, part 2, 162; Mrs. Meer Hassan Ali, 184.

[5] *Āīn*, i. 195.

are found to correspond, and the parties consent to the union, astrologers are consulted to predict their destiny, good or bad. For this purpose a few persons in company with astrologers and Mullās, or men of understanding, meet and have the horoscopes of the pair cast. For instance, if a person's name begins with any of the following seven letters of the Arabic alphabet, the elements of his temperament will be as follows: Earth, *bē, wāw, yē, swād, tē, zwād, nūn*; Water, *zāl, hē, lām, 'ain, rē, khē, ghain*; Air, *jīm, zē, qāf, sē, zāē*; Fire, *alif, hē, toē, sīn, dāl*. Other astrologers refer to the following table to ascertain by the initial of the person's name his constitutional peculiarities.

THE SIGNS OF THE ZODIAC AND PLANETS INFLUENCING MARRIAGE

Signs of the Zodiac.			*The Planets.*	*Genders.*	*The Twenty-eight Letters of the Arabic Alphabet.*	*The Four Elements.*
Arabic.	*Hindostānī.*	*Telugu.*				
Hamal Ram	Mesh	Meshamu	Mirrīkh Mars	Male	Alif, Lām, 'Ain, Yē	Fire
Saur Bull	Sānr	Vrisha- bhamu	Zohra Venus	Female	Bē, Wāw	Earth
Jauzā Twins	Mithun, Hamzād	Mithunamu	'Utārid Mercury	Male	Qāf, Kāf	Air
Saratān Crab	Kekrā	Karkāta- kumu	Qamar Moon	Female	Hē, Hā	Water
Asad Lion	Singh, Sher	Simhamu	Shams Sun	Male	Mīm	Fire
Sumbula Virgin	Kanyā	Kanya	'Utārid Mercury	Female	Ghain	Earth
Mīzān Scales	Tarāzū Tulā	Tula	Zohra Venus	Male	Rē, Tē, Toē	Air
'Aqrab Scorpion	Bichhū	Vrischi- kamu	Mirrīkh Mars	Female	Zāl, Zoē, Nūn, Zē, Zwād	Water
Qaus Archer	Kamān- dār	Dhanussu	Mushtarī Jupiter	Male	Fē	Fire
Jadī He Goat	Mendā	Makaramu	Zuhal Saturn	Female	Khē, Jīm	Earth
Dalv Waterpot	Kumbhā Dol	Kumbhamu	Zuhal Saturn	Male	Swād, Sē, Sīn, Shīn	Air
Hūt Fish	Mīn Machhlī	Minamu	Mushtarī Jupiter	Female	Dāl	Water

In order to ascertain the fate of the couple, the following plan is adopted: In the first place, it must be ascertained by reference to this table to which of the elements, Fire, Air, Earth, Water, the initials of the parties correspond, and if these elements agree it is concluded they will harmonize. Thus, if a man's name be Ja'far, his initial being *J*, and his temperament Earth, and the girl's name be Bānū Bībī, her initial being *B* and her temperament also Earth, these agreeing, it is held that they will live happily together. In detail, if the temperament of both be Earth, they will for the most part agree, but not always. If it be Water, they will agree for a time, but their love will soon decrease. If it be Air, they will be inclined to quarrel, but will be ready to make up their differences. If Fire, though quarrels will occur between them, they will not last long. If the temperament of a husband be Earth, and that of his wife Water they will agree and live amicably, the women being obedient to her lord. If the husband's be Water, and that of his wife Earth, they will agree, but the wife will rule the house. If the man's be Earth, and that of the girl Air, they will often quarrel, but they will settle their differences, and the wife will rule her husband. If the man's be Earth, and the girl's Fire, there will be little love between them, and the wife will rule her husband. If the man's be Fire, and the girl's Air, they will not be very affectionate, but if they are they will be very happy, and the man will be subject to his wife. If the man's be Air, and the girl's Water, the result will be the same, but the husband will rule his wife. If the man's be Water, and the girl's Fire, it will be difficult for them to agree, and the husband will rule his wife. If the man's be Air, and the girl's Fire, the result will be the same, but the wife will rule her husband. If the man's be Fire, and the girl's Air, they will love each other, and the husband will rule, but he will treat her kindly.

Omens by consultation of a verse taken by random from the Korān or the works of the poet Hāfiz, known as Fāl, and Istikhāra, or attempts to ascertain the will of the Deity by praying for a dream, are also used. The father of the youth, when a proposal is made by the friends of a girl will write 'To be' and 'Not to be' on several slips of paper, which he puts under his prayer-carpet, and after prayers he takes out one of them by random and then a second. If both are favourable the offer will be accepted.[1]

In the Deccan and south India when the astrologer reports that the prospects are good, some women of the youth's family visit the girl's house and say that they are come to eat sweet stew (*mīthā pulāo*) and sugared rice (*shakar-bhāt*). If the other side are well disposed they give a pleasant answer, if not the matter comes to an end. The women never settle the business at the first interview, but after a few visits, if all goes well, a date is fixed for the 'distribution of betel standing' (*kharē pān*), the 'sugar bringing' (*shakarānā*) or the 'asking' (*mangnī*). These three customs are not always done. The first being less expensive is preferred by the poor, the second by the middle classes, while the last is the most expensive because valuable presents must be given. It is the custom not to offer any food or drink, betel, tobacco, or even water to connexions on the other side until they have eaten something sweet, which they do on the 'sugar-bringing' day, or afterwards at a special entertainment, the sweets being supposed to bring affection and good luck.

Many observances are included in the betrothal. In the Deccan there is, first, the rite of 'distributing betel standing'. Some friends of the youth go to the bride's house and distribute packets of betel-leaves, each receiving one in return. No presents are given, and the women call this rite the 'taking up of the betel' (*pān uthānā*). Betel is supposed to possess mystic powers, swearing on it is equivalent to an oath on the Korān, and Rājputs were in the habit of eating betel as a solemn pledge of loyalty before a battle.[2] This, however, is not a part of the Law, but an innovation introduced by Indian Musalmāns. The violation of such an agreement often leads to a quarrel, but if anything is found objectionable in the

[1] Mrs. Meer Hassan Ali, 187 f., and see above, p. 29; the practice is common in the East (*EB.* vii. 812; cf. Halliday, *Greek Divination*, 217 f.). Fīroz Shāh never transacted any business without referring to the Korān for an augury (Elliot-Dowson, iii. 329); on Aurangzeb taking omens from the writings of Hāfiz, see Manucci, ii. 148.

[2] J. Tod, *Annals of Rajasthān*, ed. 1920, i. 346, 381, 481, 552, 570, 69, 1040; Russell, ii. 197 f.

pedigree or character of one of the couple, the Qāzī or law-officer may pronounce the betrothal void.

In the 'sugar-bringing' rite the youth sends to the girl certain articles of dress, bangles, perfumes, and flowers. The first relation of the girl who meets the party receives the 'contract betel' (*qaul bīrā*), and then her friends make the following announcement: 'A son of B is betrothed to C daughter of D. Declare before the friends whether you do or do not agree to the marriage'. He replies 'I assent', and the question and answer are repeated three times. Then they recite the 'prayer of good will' (*nīyat khair kā Fātiha*); that is the first chapter of the Korān followed by the one hundred and tenth: 'When the help of God and the victory arrive and thou seest men entering the religion of God in troops, then utter the praise of thy Lord, for He loveth to turn in mercy'. These rites are performed by the Qāzī or law-officer, the Khatīb or preacher, the Nāib-i-Qāzī, or assistant law-officer, by a Mashāikh, or reverend man, or by a Mullā or Maulavī, doctors of the Law. In some cases the engagement by giving betel is dispensed with, and only the Fātiha is said, he who recites it naming the couple and saying 'Hereby I betroth you'. The betel and sugar are then divided and the gifts sent by the bridegroom are given to the bride, who sits modestly, her head bent to the ground, her eyes closed and her face covered. Then the lady friends of the bridegroom anoint her head with perfumed oil, tie up her hair with a red string sent by the bridegroom, and adorn her with the jewels. An old woman of the family puts one hand behind her neck and the other under her chin and holds up her face to view. Each lady takes a look at her, and gives her a ring or some money, at the same time drawing her own hands over her head and cracking her fingers on her own temples so as to take away any ill luck on her own head (*balāēn lenā, tasadduq*). This rite is known as the 'sugar-eating' (*shakarkhorī*), the 'betrothal' (*nisbat*), the 'asking' (*mangnī*), the 'sherbet-drinking' (*sharbatkhorī*), and the 'green creeper' (*harī bel*).

In some places, however, the 'asking' forms a special rite, when presents (*charhauwā, charhāwā*) are given to the bride. The youth goes to her house with music and carries on trays various gifts. This procession starts in the afternoon and halts every now and then while the dancing-girls sing. If he lives at a distance the gifts are sent in his absence with the same ceremony. When the party arrives at the house they rest for a while and the 'betel of the contract' (*qaul bīrā*) is distributed. The trays with the gifts are sent to the bride's room and the guests add something as they are being sent. If the bridegroom is present he receives a gift of clothes of the marriage colours, yellow, red, or green, for black symbolizes mourning and white that of the burial shroud. In Gujarāt on the betrothal day the kindred on both sides meet, gifts are carried in procession, and sherbet is served at the bride's house.[1] In north India this interchange of gifts between bride and bridegroom is called Sāchaq.[2]

Some ten or fifteen days after the 'asking', the bride's people return the trays or pots in which the bridegroom's gifts were sent, filled with cakes which he shares with his friends.

In the Deccan the rite of 'threshold treading' (*dahlīz khundlānā*) follows. This is done in case after the betrothal it is necessary to postpone the wedding. The bridegroom sends cooked food to the bride accompanied with music, and he receives the 'salutation gift' (*salāmī*), after which he salutes his mother-in-law. The reason of this custom is that it is unusual for the bridegroom to go to the bride's house or eat there until after the consummation of the marriage, but after this rite he becomes a member of the family and may eat any dish seasoned with salt at the house of his betrothed.

In some places a day or two after the betrothal the bridegroom sends food and a betel-box (*pāndān*) to the bride, who returns the compliment a day or two after. This is called the 'salt-tasting' (*namakchashī*). After this he may dispense with the rule to eat only sweets at her house, and he may eat food seasoned with salt or acid condiments. Various other gifts are also sent by the betrothed man to his fiancée. Thus at the Muharram festival he sends a necklace (*ānṭī*) of coloured thread, perfumed powder (*abīr*), a conserve (*sukhmukh*) made of betel nut, melon seeds, fine-cut coco-nut kernels, coffee, and

[1] *BG.* ix, part 2, 162. [2] Mrs. Meer Hassan Ali, 197 ff.

cardamoms. At the Ākhirī-chār-shamba he sends cakes and sweets; at Sha'bān food and fireworks; at Ramazān vermicelli (*siwaiyān*) and sweets; at the 'Īd-i-qurbānī a sheep and some money. During an eclipse the girl sends to him offerings of intercession (*sadqa*) with a goat or kid, which must be tied to the leg of his bed till the eclipse is over.

Among respectable people the betrothed couple are kept apart till marriage. But among some Musalmāns on the north and west frontier betrothal is deemed to be equivalent to marriage and the pair cohabit. In Sind 'after betrothal the prudent parents do all they can to prevent the parties meeting; both, however, are permitted to visit one another's relations of the same sex. Among the upper classes any *pregustatio matrimonii* is considered disgraceful. It is not, however, difficult here, as elsewhere, to persuade the betrothed female to grant favours which, under other circumstances, she would refuse; consequently accidents are not of rare occurrence. It is the same in Afghānistān and other parts of Central Asia, where the mother of the betrothed not infrequently connives at what is called 'the game of the betrothed' (*nāmzadbāzī*), or visiting the future bride unknown to her father. In Sind the lower classes, such as the Mohānā and others, think they have a right to intrigue with their future brides; some of them will go so far as to consider the mother-in-law a substitute for the daughter until the latter is of age to be married'.[1] In Bannū the betrothed youth secretly visits his fiancée, and if he is detected he is detained for three days, and each night the unmarried girls pull him about till he is glad to escape.[2]

Marriage is known as Byāh, Shādī being the rejoicings accompanying the rite; Nikāh, the marriage service, but in north India this term is applied to a left-handed or informal marriage, as when the bride is a widow.

In north India the marriage celebrations are supposed to begin with the reciprocal sending of gifts or Sāchaq, and from that day the pair are called bride and bridegroom, Dulhā, Dulhin. The second day is known as Menhdī or Hinnabandī,

[1] Burton, *Sindh*, 261 f.; C. Masson, *Narrative of Various Journeys in Balochistan, Afghanistan, and the Panjab*, iii. 287 f.

[2] Thorburn, 154.

'the henna day', because both are anointed with the plant *Lawsonia alba*. With this is usually combined the rubbing with Haldī or turmeric when the pair sit in state (*manjā, manjhā baithnā*). This rubbing with henna, saffron, or turmeric seems to be, partly a form of initiation, partly protective and stimulating or fertilizing, and when the condiment used by one of the pair is sent to be used in anointing the other it is a charm to promote union. It is a common rite among the Hindus from whom it was probably borrowed by the Indo-Musalmāns.[1] Hence a taboo is attached to these plants. In the Central Provinces some people will not grow saffron because it is a 'sacred' plant.[2] Turmeric is believed to be a protective against the Evil Eye and evil spirits. Saffron, perhaps on account of its colour, is also connected with fertility. In the Deccan before the bridegroom is anointed, the lap of the bride is filled with cakes and betel as a fertility charm. The first anointing, known as the 'thief' (*chor haldī*), or secret rubbing, is done by the women of the family, who rub her with fragrant powder (*chiksā*). After the bridegroom has been anointed they rub the bride with what is called the 'public' (*sāhū, sāū*) turmeric, about which there is no secrecy. Guests are invited and feasted, the laps of the ladies are filled with cakes and betel, the bride is seated on a chair with a red cloth canopy over her, and a red handkerchief is spread on a red carpet before her. Then they sing and do the rite of 'filling the square' (*chauk bharnā*),[3] in which a square is made with raw rice, and a log of sandalwood bound round with red thread is placed near the seat of the pair on which they rest their feet, as it is held unlucky to tread on the square. The bride's younger sister stands behind her covered with a red veil (*dāmanī, dāwanī*) and takes hold of her by the ears. Two dry coco-nut kernels are filled with dry dates and poppy seed and rolled up

[1] L. A. Anantha Krishna Iyer, i. 201; ii. 193; Russell, iii. 70, 540; iv. 63; Thurston, *Castes*, i. 260, 265; Rose, i. 816, 837; ii. 261; Dubois, 222, 229. On anointing as a magical rite see *ERE*. viii. 318; R. Smith, *Religion of the Semites*, 383; Crawley, 325 f.

[2] Russell, ii. 463.

[3] In the Panjāb, when women have made vows to a Saint and their desires are accomplished they repair to his shrine, and sit there for a day and a night, a rite known as *chaukī bharnā* (Rose, i. 643).

with a bit of sandalwood. This bundle, called the 'lap' (*god*), is placed in the bride's lap as a charm for fertility. Then some happy married woman (*sohāgan*) rubs a little turmeric on her face, body, and dress, and thus communicates fertility to her. Singing and dancing follow. The anointing of the bridegroom is done in the same way except that the fragrant powder is rubbed on him by the family barber.

After the turmeric has been rubbed on the bride she is made to sit in state in a separate room. She is not allowed to do any work, eats only rice and pulse, bread and sugar, and she is rubbed with a preparation of lignum aloes (*'ūd*). This, with frankincense, is used to perfume her, and the powder makes her skin soft and fragrant.

Many people take a pomegranate branch, cover it with red cloth, bend it to represent the way a modest bride sits, deck it with flowers or a silver necklace, fix it in a lump of rice and put it in an earthen pot round which they lay food and fruits. They sit up all night with music, and singing songs recording the exploits of the Saint Ghāzī Sālār Masa'ūd. Some hang up a curtain on which are painted scenes of his battles and martyrdom. Next morning the bridegroom carries the pot on his shoulder, accompanied by Faqīrs, to the water edge, where, after the Fātiha is recited, it is set adrift to take bad luck away with it. On that evening the bridegroom is again anointed, and a sort of ship (*jahāz*) is made with a wooden framework like a stool, and to each of the four legs an earthen pot or pumpkin is tied. Or it is made of straw and bamboos, in the shape of a boat, so that it cannot sink, and flowers are hung on it. Then it is filled with flowers and fruits, covered with a cloth dyed with saffron, and on the top is put a lamp made of flour, and lighted. Food is taken to the water edge and the Fātiha is said over it in the name of the Saint Khwāja Khizr—on whom be Peace!—The shipwright takes the food and distributes it among the poor, the lamp is replaced and the structure is set afloat. Friends are feasted and the bridegroom is again anointed.

The 'storehouse' or 'share' (*bhandārā, chhāndā*) of the Saint Shāh Madār is then displayed. They take a cow and some wheat flour, sacrifice the animal, and ask some Madārī Faqīrs to make out of the meat a stew (*chakolī, sutrī*). When the Fātiha has been recited over the food in the name of the Saint, the Faqīrs scramble for it. On this occasion the bridegroom wears a pink or yellow dress.

After being anointed the bridegroom submits to certain taboos. He does not go to the bazar to do shopping, lest he may be the victim of the Evil Eye or Black Magic. Every day food of various kinds, sherbet in a copper or brass pot (*tanbālū, tambālū*), with a red thread tied round the neck, and spattered over with pounded sandalwood, with a tooth-twig (*miswāk*), are sent to him from the bride. The first day some sweet stew is sent as a form of *confarreatio*, that by eating this the pair may live happily together. The women who bring the food see that he washes his face, eats his breakfast, and chews betel before they return. The customs thus described are those current in the Deccan.

In Sind the barber's wife attends daily to wash the bride with sweet oil and flour (*pithī*) made of wheat or beans, and her body hair is ṛemoved by depilatories and vellication. Her hands, feet, and hair are stained with henna, her lips with walnut bark, her cheeks rubbed with rouge (*surkhī*) made of lac, and her eyes with lampblack (*kājal*). The hair, twisted from the front, is allowed to hang behind in one or two plaits, and the 'salt' or brilliancy of her complexion is heightened with silver leaf or talc applied with a pledget of cotton. The girl is trained to handle a bit of musk enclosed in an embroidered cloth, and moles (*khāl, tirā*) are drawn on her face with needles dipped in antimony or some other colouring matter.[1] The Bangash Pathāns, three days before the wedding, strip the bride of all her ornaments and shut her up in a room by herself. Next night the women unplait her hair through fear of 'trammelling or impeding the action in hand, whatever it may be'.[2] Among the Pathāns of the Panjāb, for seven days before the wedding, the bride and bridegroom rest, do no work, and their bodies are rubbed with perfumed powder.[3] In the United Provinces the pair, when they sit in state, wear dirty clothes, probably to avoid the Evil Eye.[4]

[1] Burton, *Sindh*, 266.
[2] Rose, ii. 58; Frazer, *GB.*, Taboo and Perils of the Soul, 310 f.
[3] Rose, iii. 228.
[4] *PNQ.* ii. 182.

It is a general custom, perhaps borrowed from the Hindus, that the condiments used in the anointing are exchanged between the bride and bridegroom, a magical device to promote the union of the pair.

The measuring for the wedding dress, known as 'foot service', or 'feet exalting' (*pānw minnat, pānw mez*), is a formal act. Each of the pair provides the dress of the other, and the measurement is made by a tailor who attends at their houses, or by some old lady of the family, each of whom receives a gift.

In the Deccan before the wedding begins, a shed (*mandwā, pandal*), as in the case of the Hindus, is set up at both houses, and in it six or seven water pots (*kalas kā māt, jhol kā gharā*) are placed, as is the Hindu rule.[1] These pots are smeared with sandalwood paste and they are placed in the shed pointing towards the right side of the house. Grain is also scattered there, probably as a fertility charm. The pots are not filled with water but with curdled milk (*dahī*) and large cakes, the tops being covered with a red cloth. Four happy married women, known as 'ladies of the marriage shed', do the smearing with sandalwood, and when they have put into them a little perfumed powder they cover them with a wheaten cake. At both houses food is prepared, and over it the Fātiha is said in the names of the Prophet, the Saints, deceased ancestors, and women of the house who died before their husbands. The food is then given to ladies of rank who are noted for their virtue. These are called 'partakers of the dish of the Lady Fātima', the model of all wifely virtues. This food is given only to these selected ladies, who have fasted all day, and what is left, over which the Fātiha has not been recited, is distributed among the others. Some place among the things over which the Fātiha is recited a red earthen cup filled with slaked lime, and the specially selected ladies dip their fingers once or

[1] The pots placed at a Hindu wedding are intended to be the abodes of the benign spirits which attend to bless the marriage (Thurston, *Castes*, i. 13; *BG.* ix. part 1, 161; xv, part 1, 248). The installation of the goddess in a jar (*gharā*) is part of the ritual at the Hindu festival, the Durgā Pūjā (Pratapachandra Ghosha, *Durga Puja, with notes and Illustrations*, 22 ff.) They are not used in Jain marriages (Mrs. S. Stevenson, *The Heart of Jainism*, 198).

twice in the lime, suck them and then eat the other food. This is regarded as a chastity test. When the 'shed of the ladies' is erected, either before or after the Fātiha has been said, they spread a red cloth on the carpet, tie a red string round the top and handle of a flour stone mill (*chakkī*), mark it all round with sandalwood, place it on the carpet, when seven happy married women in the shed of the bridegroom, and nine in that of the bride, sing 'the song of the mill', which is usually sung at weddings. Then the mill is set going and the perfumed powder (*chiksā*) used at the wedding is ground in it. When this is ready they tie up some of the powder in a corner of the veil of each woman, put a little in the water pots, as already described, and rub the rest on bride and bridegroom. This powder rite is called the 'renown of the mill' (*chakkī ṅāwarī, nāmāwarī*).[1] Some of these south Indian rites do not seem to be practised in north India or in other Musalmān countries. They have possibly been borrowed from the Hindus, and they are peculiar to women, who regard them as of greater importance than the Korān and the Traditions.

Gifts (*barī, sāchaq*), consisting of food, articles of dress, and ornaments, are sent to the bride. They are carried to her house by a party of the bridegroom's friends, accompanied by music, while the ladies follow the procession in litters. When the presents arrive they are handed to the friends of the bride, and rich people give a dinner. Some people combine with this the sending of the dowry, the 'rice of chastity' and the 'lifting of the oil pots'. In the evening, food, known as 'coloured gifts' (*rangbarī*), is sent by the bride to the bridegroom.

The bridal paraphernalia (*jahez, dahez*) consists, first, of a wedding dress provided by the friends of the bride for the bridegroom, a quantity of the bride's clothes which have been worn, a box (*sohāgpurā, sohāgpitārā*) containing nutmeg, mace, clothes, catechu, poppy seed, and a silver coin, enclosed in a piece of folded paper tied with a bit of mica and a red

[1] A similar rite, analogous to that practised by Hindus (*BG.* ix, part 1, 163), is done by Musalmāns at Lucknow, by tying the string (*nārā*) to the pestle (*mūsal*) used in grinding the condiment with which bride and bridegroom are anointed. It is probably a fertility charm (Mrs. Meer Hassan Ali, 207).

thread. Secondly, there is a selection of jewellery for the bride, a canopy, wall hangings, a prayer-carpet (*jānamāz*), beds and bedding, cooking utensils, a spittoon (*pīkdān*, *ugāldān*), a palanquin (*pālkī*), cattle, and in old days a female slave. Among the Brāhūī 'Jhalawāns of estate will stand out for a couple of handmaids, all kinds of ornaments, and a set of furniture for the house, a set of vessels and ever so much more. And there's often a deal of heart-burning in the matter'.[1] These articles provided by the bride's family as her dowry are gifts intended by her family to procure for their daughter a husband of equal or higher rank than their own. The dowry remains the property of the bride as long as she lives, if she dies childless her nearest relatives can reclaim it, but if she leaves children they take it. It must be distinguished from the settlement (*mahr*) made by husband on his wife. Among Shī'as it is a common act of piety among ladies who, after a life of longing, have induced their husbands to bring them on a pilgrimage to the holy places, to forgo their claim to a settlement on first catching a glimpse of the sacred shrine.[2]

On the afternoon of the bridegroom's night procession (*shabgasht*) his sister is decked in new clothes and she performs the rite of 'rending the pot covers' (*jhol phornā*). This consists in forcibly tearing the cloth tied on the mouth of the pots and taking out some of the contents. She tastes a little of the curds and gives the remainder to friends. The same rite is performed by the bride's sister at her house and the pots are left unwashed.[3]

When the invitations have been issued for the procession of the bridegroom the men are feasted apart and the ladies in the women's apartments. After dinner the women go to the bride's house and do the rite of 'winnowing the rice of chastity' (*pat kā chāwal charhānā, charwānā*). They put a couple of pounds of raw rice in a red handkerchief, and with a heavy wooden pestle (*mūsal*), to which a packet of betel leaves is attached, they get the women, including the bride, to make a pretence of husking it while they sing the usual songs.

[1] Bray, 39. [2] Sykes, *Glory of the Shī'a World*, 229.

[3] This rite seems to be confined to the Deccan, and is apparently a magical aid for the defloration of the bride.

After this the rite of the 'oil pot offering' (*tel charhānā*) is done at the bridegroom's house. Seven empty oil pots, decorated by the women with the sign of an arrow, to which a packet of betel and a cake (*suhālī*) are fastened by a red thread, are put into a basket, and sugar candy and dentifrice (*missī*) with some sweet oil are put out in cups. The women rub some dentifrice on the youth's teeth, make him chew a little sugar candy, apply oil to his forehead, and then they lay the oil pots on trays with the dentifrice and take them with music to the bride. The bride is brought out and seated in the wedding shed with a red handkerchief held over her to scare evil spirits. First, some happy married woman rubs dentifrice on her teeth and makes her rinse her mouth, in the hope that she may be as old and as happy as the woman who applies it, and that by sharing the dentifrice with the bridegroom she may also share his love. All the other women then rub the oil on her body with the tip of an arrow, and lay the pots, four on the right and three on the left of the girl. Women then hand the pots to each other across the bride to shield her from harm. This is done three times while the women sing songs. During this time the girl holds between her lips the bit of sugar candy which the bridegroom has already sucked, as a mark of union, and then she gives it to some child who is present. Dentifrice is held in high estimation because it was sanctified for use in the toilet by Fātima, and in Gujarāt women in their courses do not use it.[1] It is customary for a boy or girl not to use dentifrice until after marriage. Boys, however, apply it once after circumcision, but girls never use it till their wedding day. Hence the black mark on the teeth shows that she is a married woman. Among women of some castes the rites of the 'virgin rice' and that of the oil pots are held to be so important that no bride at whose wedding they have been omitted is considered to be in south India a fit member of society.

The procession of the bridegroom known as 'noctural' (*shabgasht*), or 'dawn of day procession' (*sargasht*, *sargarū*, the last a Sind term) leads up to the actual wedding. After the oil pot rite the youth is shaved and bathed, and if he

[1] *BG.* ix, part 1, 52.

wears his hair long he has it perfumed with aloewood (*'ūd*). When he is tying on his turban, if any old man of the family whose wife is alive happens to be present, he is asked to twist the end of it two or three times round his own head, signifying that bride and bridegroom, like himself and his wife, may enjoy a long and happy married life. The old man gives back the turban and the youth ties it on with his own hands. He is decked in the wedding dress provided by the friends of the bride, puts collyrium (*surmā*) on his eyes, dentifrice on his teeth, chews betel, pastes strips of silver-leaf or tinsel (*afshān*) on his cheeks, hangs flowers round his neck, ties the gold and flowered veil (*sihrā*) on his head, and over it the outer veil (*miqna'*) to protect himself from the Evil Eye. Then he mounts his horse or is seated in a litter (*ambārī*), and makes a tour of the town. Artificial trees made of coloured paper, the pith of the sholā tree (*bhend*)[1] and wax, decorated with mica (*talk, talq*), and gold leaf (*zarwaraq*) are carried with him. They let off fireworks, carry lights fixed horizontally on ladders, and halt occasionally to watch the performance of the dancing-girls. Thus he goes to the mosque, says the two-bow prayers and the thanksgiving (*shukrīyā*), and thence to the bride's house, an umbrella made of flowers or paper, ornamented with mica, being twirled round his head.

In the Deccan, before he alights from his horse, the bride's brother gives him hot milk or sherbet, so that his married life may be sweet. A coco-nut is dashed on the ground before him and lemons are cut and thrown over his head to the four quarters to scare evil spirits. When he alights there is a general scramble for the decorations (*arāish*), which are kept as charms to ensure a happy wedding for their possessors. Sometimes the carriers of these things resist and keep them for the 'bracelet' day, on which they must be handed over to the crowd, unless they are borrowed, in which case they must be preserved. During the scramble there is much confusion, and this is followed by mock resistance to the entry of the bridegroom, which is done by the bride's brother or other near

[1] *Aeschynomene aspera*, out of which the Solā or 'Solar' Topī, or hat, worn by Europeans to protect the head from the sun, is made (Watt, *Comm. Prod.*, 28 ff.).

relation holding up a bamboo screen across the gate until he receives a forfeit (*dhaingānā*, 'teasing, worrying'). The fee is usually placed in a small cup (*matkī*) which is carried by the resisters. As they resist, the friends of the bridegroom call out 'Who are you who dare to obstruct the King's cavalcade ?' To this the other party reply, 'So many thieves are about at night, perhaps you are some of them'. Besides this badinage there is often some horse-play in which a man or two are hurt. Finally the bridegroom gives the fee and he is helped to dismount and is carried in on some-one's back, probably as a mark of respect to the threshold. In Gujarāt the bride drops rice over him from a window as he enters.[1] In other places the bride is brought out and she is given flowers, sugar, and raw rice which she is told to throw three times over the bridegroom from behind a screen. When this is done the bridegroom joins his friends in the men's room.

The general name of the marriage service is Nikāh, which in north India means an informal marriage. Another term used is Bārāt, which properly means the coming of the bridegroom to fetch his bride.

In the Deccan, if the hour at which he reaches the house is auspicious, the Nikāh is done at once, otherwise it is deferred to the fourth or other lucky hour after. In the latter case the guests go home, and are recalled at the fixed hour. Up to this point, if the bridegroom has reason for objecting to the match, it may be dissolved.

The Qāzī or law-officer or his deputy usually attends, and some of the youth's lady friends are brought in litters. The Qāzī appoints two men of full age as witnesses (*wakīl*) on the part of the bridegroom, and orders them to go to the bride's friends and ask them to give orders for the Nikāh, and to state the amount of the Mahr or marriage settlement required. When these men have given their message a Wakīl, or agent, returns with them to negotiate on the part of the bride's

[1] The object of throwing rice at weddings is uncertain. It may be done in order to detain the soul of the bridegroom, which is ready to fly away at this crisis, or it may be a fertility charm, rice being a sacred and prolific grain (Frazer, *GB.*, Taboo and the Perils of the Soul, 33 ff.; Crawley, 325).

relations. Some jokes are played by the bride's friends, such as giving them a packet of betel leaves in which the leaf of some other plant has been enclosed, or the bride's brother gives the Wakīl a blow on the back with a leather strap, saying that this is the punishment for giving false evidence. The bride's agent says in a jocular way, 'The settlement is so great that the bridegroom can never pay it. But first hand over as earnest money twelve ships laden with silk, ten camel loads of needles, a couple of vessels laden with garlic and onion peel, fifty white elephants and a million gold mohurs. Then I will tell you the amount of the settlement'. The Qāzī in reply asks if this is correct, or if he has been bribed to speak in this way on the part of the bride. The witnesses carry on the joke, 'He did go behind the screen and had a consultation, but we cannot say that he was bribed'.

According to the Law the Mahr or settlement consists of two parts: Muajjal, 'prompt', demandable on entering into the contract; Muwajjal, 'deferred', payable on dissolution of the contract. The former is not usually paid at marriage, but it is a guarantee of the good conduct of the bridegroom, as he must pay it in the case of divorce due to his fault. Both the Prophet and Kings, like Akbar,[1] disapproved of high settlements, for they are rarely if ever paid, but they prevent rash divorces. At this time also it is usually settled whether the presents of jewellery made before marriage are to be the property of husband or wife in the event of separation or divorce. Among the Brāhūī the customary rate of dower is that current of old in the bride's family, but usually the bridegroom has to pay the 'milk share' (*shīrpailī*) to the bride's mother and Lab or bride-price to her father.[2] Among Pathāns the bride's parents generally accept money to defray expenses, including the girl's ornaments and clothes, but poor parents now-a-days accept money as the price of the girl.[3]

When the amount of the settlement is fixed the Qāzī informs the bridegroom and asks whether he accepts the terms. When he agrees, the Qāzī having taken the veils (*ṃiqna'*, *siharā*)

[1] *Āīn*, i. 278.

[2] Bray, 68; *Census Report*, Balūchistān, 1911, i. 100 f.

[3] Rose, iii. 228, 410, 499, 505.

from his face, up to which time they must be worn, makes him gargle his throat three times with water, and seating him with his face towards the Qibla or Mecca, makes him repeat, first, the deprecation (*astaghfāru-llāh*) 'I ask forgiveness of God', secondly, the four Quls, i. e. the four chapters of the Korān beginning with the word 'Say' (109, 112, 113, 114), which have nothing to say to marriage, but seem to be selected only on account of their brevity; the five clauses of the Kalima or Creed, the articles of belief (*sifat-i-īmān*)—belief in God, in His Angels, in the Scriptures, in the Prophet, in the Resurrection and Day of Judgement, in the absolute decree and predestination of good and evil— and the 'prayer of praise' (*du'ā-i-qunūt*). If he is illiterate these are explained to him in Hindostānī. Then having made him repeat the marriage contract (*nikāh kā sīgha, 'aqd-i-nikāh*) in Arabic, and having explained its meaning, he desires the Wakīl of the bride and bridegroom to join hands together, and directs the former to say to the latter 'So and so's daughter, so and so, by the agency of her representative and the testimony of two witnesses, has, in her marriage with you, had such a settlement made upon her. Do you consent to it?' The bridegroom replies, 'With my whole heart and soul, to my marriage with this lady, as well as to the already mentioned settlement made upon her, I do consent, consent, consent'.[1] In the Panjāb among Musalmāns who are converts from Hinduism, the Hindu rite of Gānth jorā, the tying of the sheets of the pair, is followed, and the bride, who is often a mere child, keeps her marriage sheet as long as she is a virgin.[2] The Bannūchīs tie together the sheets of the bridegroom and of the girl who acts as proxy for the bride, the pair walk to a stream, the bridegroom lets a few drops of water fall three times into a pitcher, he does the same with a sword, the water from which falls three times into the pitcher, after which the knots are untied and the proxy withdraws.[3] During the performance of the Nikāh a tray is placed before the Qāzī containing sugar candy, dried dates, almonds, and betel. In some places a couple of pounds of raw rice and sandalwood paste are put in a cup, with a necklace

[1] Compare the account in Lane, *ME.* i. 202 ff.

[2] Temple, *Legends*, ii. 160.

[3] Thorburn, 156.

of two strings of black beads (*pot kā lachhā*) in it, and in the tray is laid the Qāzī's fee, 2¼ rupees, with clothes and other gifts. In Gujarāt he receives 5 rupees and a shawl, and 1¼ rupees are paid to the warden of the mosque in the street where the bride lives.[1]

Under Muhammadan rule the Qāzī acted as civil and criminal judge. At present, save that he often leads the prayers at the Ramazān and Baqar 'Īd feasts, he is little more than a marriage registrar. He has no right to demand a fee for the marriage service, because this is a solemn rite enjoined by the Law. Gifts and grants of land (*in'ām, jāgīr*) and salaries were conferred upon Qāzīs by the former kings, which the East India Company and the British Government—may its good fortune be perpetual!—have continued to them, solely for the discharge of the following functions: to perform the Nikāh, to train children in the knowledge of Islām, to bury the helpless poor, to act as Imām or prayer-leader daily at the five times of worship in the mosque, to appoint the Mutawalī or superintendent of the mosque and the Khatīb or preacher, to deliver the Khutba, the bidding prayer or sermon, on feast days and at the Friday services, to appoint the Muazzin or caller to prayer, the Mujāwir or Khidmatī to sweep the mosque and provide water for ablution—all which charges the Qāzī should defray from his own purse, or from contributions collected from the congregation. If the Qāzī neglects these duties the ruler may dismiss him and appoint another in his stead, for the object of his office is to give relief to the servants of God, and this is frustrated if the poor are required to pay exorbitant marriage fees. But in Musalmān states the mosque officials are generally appointed by the ruler, and as they receive pay from him they are not in the Qāzī's service, and he, therefore, naturally demands marriage fees. Qāzīs are appointed for the advantage of the ignorant, and learned men have no occasion for their services because they can perform the marriage, funeral, and other rites themselves, a practice against which there is no prohibition either by God or by His Prophet.

After the Nikāh the Qāzī offers up a prayer on behalf of the bride and bridegroom: 'O Great God! Grant that mutual

[1] *BG.* ix, part 2, 166.

love may reign between this couple, as between Adam and Hawwā', or Eve, Ibrāhīm, or Abraham, and Sarah, between Yūsuf, Joseph, and Zulaikhā, wife of Potiphar, Moses and Safūrā or Zipporah, His Highness Muhammad Mustafā and 'Ayīshā, between 'Alīu-l-Murtazā and Fātimatu-z-zuhrā!' He then takes the contents of the tray and handing the sugar candy and beads to the bridegroom's mother or some other lady, he tells her to take them to the bride and inform her that from this day she must consider herself married to so and so, son of so and so, that such and such a jointure has been settled upon her, that she is to wear this necklace as a sign of wedlock and eat the sugar candy as an emblem of the sweets of married life. On hearing this the bride weeps, or is supposed to weep. In the men's room the bridegroom falls upon the necks of his friends, kisses their hands and receives congratulations. Even were he a slave, on this occasion he would be allowed to embrace the men present. On the departure of the Qāzī the musicians strike up a loud, discordant peal in order to scare evil spirits, and the friends of the bridegroom are feasted.

The bridegroom accompanied by his blood and marriage relations, to whom the bride's friends offer sandalwood paste, enters the room, a red cloth being spread on the floor for him to walk on and a red cloth canopy is held over their heads as they walk in. As a joke, their mouths are smeared with some sandalwood and the guests enjoy a laugh at their expense. Betel is handed round and they are seated on the carpet. By way of a joke some bits of leather or potsherds are put under the carpet. A basin (*chilamchī*) and an ewer (*āftāba*) are brought, a red cloth is hung over them, a little sherbet is poured over their hands, and they are given water to wash. Betel and sherbet are handed round. As each partakes of the sherbet he drops a rupee or other coin into the bowl, and some do the same as they wash. Sometimes, as a joke, a decoction of gram is given instead of the sherbet, and when a man has drunk some one rubs his mouth with a starched towel till his lips bleed. Then the table-cloth (*dastarkhwān*) is spread, and boiled rice (*bhāt*) with sweet stew (*mītha pulāo*) is served. The hands of the bridegroom are washed by his brother-in-law, who puts handfuls of the food into his mouth, after which the bridegroom eats with his own hands. The money dropped into the cups is taken by the servants, but sometimes it is given to the master of the house. When the meal is over, betel nuts, flowers, and rose water (*'itr*) are handed round, and then the guests take their leave, only his near relations remaining with the bridegroom.

According to the Korān and the Traditions marriage depends on three facts : the assent of the parties, the evidence of two witnesses, the marriage settlement. If any of these are wanting, the marriage is void. Men of wealth usually pay the whole or one-third of the settlement at the time of marriage, the poor by instalments. As it is fixed by divine command, they must pay it partly in jewels, clothes, or in some other way, or induce the friends of the bride to remit a portion. Should the bridegroom not have received this immunity or has not caused the demand to be cancelled, he is responsible, and should he die his father or son is obliged to discharge it. Should the wife die, her relations can demand it, or recover it by law. But if a woman of her own accord leaves her husband she forfeits the settlement, and if her husband turns her out of doors he must first pay it.

Before the bridegroom leaves the men's room and enters that of the women, her friends adorn the bride to receive her husband. This is the 'displaying' (*jalwa, jilwa*) of the bride. In southern India after the Nikāh is over, the bride's veil (*siharā*) is sent from the bridegroom's house to that of the bride with a procession of women and music. These women are feasted. At the displaying of the bride, her relations attend on the bride. In the afternoon a tire-woman (*mashshāta*) fastens the veil on the bride's head, brings her in and seats her on a bed. The bridegroom is made to sit opposite to her with a red screen hung between the pair. The tire-woman holding a piece of red string puts it with some raw rice in the bride's hand, and helps her to throw it over the curtain on her husband's head. The bridegroom's sister ties a ring to the end of the thread and putting it with some rice in her brother's hand makes him throw these over the curtain on the bride. The ring is thrown backwards and forwards three times, a marriage song (*hajūluhā*) being sung all the time, and then the tire-woman tells the husband to remove the curtain. The pair sit on the bed side by side while the tire-woman makes jokes. When the sister or mother of the bridegroom asks her to show his wife's face to him she says, 'The bride eclipses the moon in beauty! Were I to allow him to have a single glance, the poor fellow would go mad!'

In southern India about dawn the bride's brother calls the husband to the women's room. He goes in by himself and finds all unveiled except the bride, because women need not be veiled before a king or a bridegroom, both known as Shāh. While a Dom singer woman sings, the pair are seated on a bed separated by a red curtain. Rice and a red thread are thrown backwards and forwards over it, and at last the Dom woman asks the husband to pull down the curtain and his wife's face is shown to him for the first time in a mirror. As he looks on her face he recites from an open Korān the first verse on which his eyes happen to fall.[1] Some time is spent before he sees her face. The tire-woman puts a bit of sugar candy on the bride's head and tells her husband to take it up with his lips. This is repeated on her shoulders, knees, and feet. At the last time, instead of taking the sugar in his mouth, he tries to do it with his left hand, the use of which is not allowed as it is employed for purposes of ablution, but his mother and sister insist that he should be allowed to do as he pleases, and finally he has to take it with his right hand. The tire-woman taking hold of the bride's head moves it backwards and forwards two or three times, and she does the same to the bridegroom. Finally she holds a mirror between and he gets a peep at her, while a Korān is shown to him. All this time the girl does not open her eyes. A cup of milk is given to the bridegroom who drinks and touches the bride's lips with what is left, hoping to increase their mutual love. In the Deccan when the pair descend from the bed, a large vessel of red water is placed before them. A ring from the bride's hand is dropped into the water, and the pair try which of them can pick it out first. Whoever succeeds will rule the house. The bride is helped in the search by a sister or friend, and she is generally allowed to

[1] *BG.* xviii, part I, 487.

win.[1] In the Deccan four round switches covered with flowers are given, two to the husband and two to the wife, and they are told to beat each other with them. When the sticks are broken the women present throw slippers and brinjals (the egg plant, *solanum melongena*) at the bridegroom, the mock beating and pelting being probably intended to scare evil spirits and promote fertility.[2] After this the pair are led into the cook-room, where the bride is made to knead some wheat flour and her husband to bake it, while the women jeer at him. Then they return to the women's room, where the bride is displayed to such male relatives as are allowed to see her. They bless her and present gifts. Then the bride's mother puts the bride's hand in that of her husband, saying, 'Hitherto this girl's modesty and reputation have been in our hands, and we now entrust them to you'. She is assured that her daughter will be well cared for. After this the bridegroom makes his salutation (*taslīm*) to the relatives of his wife, and the ladies present gifts to him.

When the husband goes away with his wife he rides, as he did when he came to fetch her, and she is seated in a litter (*miyānā*).[3] At his door he lifts her out and carries her inside in his arms, so that she may not touch the threshold. Here his sister meets him and demands that she shall have the first daughter born as the wife of her son, to which he replies that she may have the first daughter of his bond-maid or of his cat. After a little opposition he promises to give his daughter. A fowl or a sheep is sacrificed in the name of the couple, and the meat is given to the poor. The pair are then made to embrace each other and perform two prostrations (*sijda*). After this the bride washes her husband's feet in sandalwood and water,

[1] This is also a Panjāb custom (Rose, i. 815). It is common among Hindus (Thurston, *Castes*, i. 143, 243; A. K. L. Anantha Krishna Iyer, ii. 193 (catching fish); Russell, ii. 5, 533; *BG.* ix, part 1, 92; *Census Report*, Balūchistān, 1911, i. 108 ff.

[2] *BG.* xviii, part 1, 487.

[3] In Egypt the lucky days are the eve of Friday or Monday, the latter being preferred (Lane, *ME.* i. 205). Precise Musalmāns in the Panjāb send the bride to her husband's house mounted on a mare, not in a litter (*dolī*) (Rose, i. 822).

and he does the same for her.[1] Then they retire to the nuptial chamber. The best time for entering it is said to be between midnight and day dawn. In Sind, before consummating the marriage, the bridegroom is directed to wash the bride's feet and to throw the water into the four corners of the room, as it brings good luck and disperses the evil spirits which impede consummation. The husband takes hold of his wife's front hair and repeats the prayer, 'O Lord! Bless me and my wife! O Lord! Give to her and mine their daily bread! O Lord! cause the fruit of this woman's womb to be an honest man, a good Muslim, and not a companion of devils!'[2] At sunrise the bride's mother warns the sleepers that it is time to bathe and dress. After coitus (*jimā'*) the body is impure (*junūb*) and the greater ablution (*ghusl*) is required.

Among the Brāhūī the two mothers with other ladies of the kin keep watch and ward at the chamber door till they are called. If there be unreasonable delay the groom calls for water blessed by the priest.[3] The inspection of the wedding sheet to confirm the fact of the bride's virginity is a well-known Semitic practice.[4] It is a purely domestic rite confined to women, and it is seldom mentioned, particularly if the result be unfavourable to the girl's virtue. It is well known among the Brāhūī and Baloch, the bride's mother exhibiting with triumph the proof of her daughter's virginity.[5]

On the third or fourth day after the wedding the marriage bracelet is untied (*kangan kholnā*), the rite on the third day being called Bahorā, on the fourth Chauthī in southern India. The bracelet consists of a few pearls, some grains of raw rice,

[1] The custom of going to the public bath before consummation, an important part of the rite in other Musalmān countries (Westermarck, *Marriage Customs in Morocco*, 136), does not prevail in India, where the use of the Turkish bath is uncommon.

[2] Burton, *Sindh*, 160. Among some classes consummation is deferred, as in the case of the Three Nights of Tobias (*ERE*. ii. 51; iii. 502; Rose, iii. 507).

[3] Bray, 71.

[4] Deut. xxii. 13 ff.; Burton, *AN*. i. 373; *Pilgrimage*, ii. 111; Westermarck, *Marriage Ceremonies in Morocco*, 159, 228 f., 236, 240. In case of failure the blood of a pigeon or other bird is used to disguise the fact (*JRAI*. xlv. 37; Burton, *AN*. i. 373).

[5] *Census Report*, Balūchistān, 1911; i. 105 f.; Bray, 72.

flowers, and a quarter rupee piece tied up in red cloth and fastened by a red thread to the right wrist of bride and bridegroom on the night of the procession. On this occasion the relatives are invited, and when the brother of the bride arrives at the house of the married pair he is presented with a sheet or handkerchief and assisted to dismount. His wife is received with respect, and a mantle, bodice, and bangles are given to her. There is much festivity, men and women wearing dresses soaked in red or yellow dye, and bespattering each other with pitchers of coloured water and pelting each other with egg-shells or thin balls made of sealing-wax filled with red powder.[1] This is followed by a dinner. The pair are seated in the marriage shed, and water, vegetables, sandalwood paste, and lemons are set out in a large flat dish (*sīnī*). The tire-woman takes the bangles from the wrists of the pair and throwing them into the dish calls out ‘Which of you will first take them out?’ The bride, sitting modestly with her eyes shut, has her hands held by the tire-woman or some other lady present, and dipping them into the dish takes out the bracelets. Should the bridegroom be the first to take them out he is assailed on all sides. The bride's sister and other relations strike him with flower wands, pelt him with sweetmeats, fruits, and cakes, and his sister-in-law rubs his ears and cheeks smartly. If he wins the game he makes the bride humbly beg for the bracelets, saying ‘I am your wife and slave’. If she wins she makes him do the same. This is done three times and the bracelets are put back into the dish.[2] After this they braid the side-locks (*mihrī*, *zulf*) of the bride, arrange her back hair in a plait, and make the bridegroom undo one of her side-locks with one hand.[3] If he uses both hands he is roughly treated by her sister. After this the friends of the bridegroom receive a dress of honour (*khil'at*)[4] from the bride's friends. It is not customary

[1] A well-known fertility rite practised at the Hindu Holī, or spring festival (*Folk-lore*, xxv. 80).

[2] For these auguries see p. 80 above, and compare *BG.* xviii, part 1, 397; *Mysore Ethnographical Survey*, vii. 10; Russell, ii. 533.

[3] A charm to promote coition (Frazer, *GB.*, Taboo and Perils of the Soul, 293 ff.).

[4] *Khil'at*, ‘what one strips from his person’, the used garments conveying the qualities of his donor to him to whom they are presented

to offer money on this occasion, nor if it were offered would it be accepted. Then the pair are escorted home; in fact, it is usual only in some families that the husband has the pleasure of leading his wife home (*zifāf*). In Sind the husband passes seven days and nights in his father-in-law's house.[1] When the Brāhūī brings his wife home 'as soon as they reach the dwelling a sheep is sacrificed on the threshold, and the bride is made to step on the blood that is sprinkled in such wise that one of the heels of her shoes is marked therewith. A little of the blood is caught in a cup and the mother of the bride stains the bride's forehead with the blood as she steps over the threshold. And the cup is taken to a running stream, and the green grass and the blood are then flung out; or if there be no running stream close by, they pour the blood underneath a green tree, and there they leave the green grass. But now-a-days among fine folk who have learned more of the ways of the Faith, the bride's forehead is not stained with the blood. The groom's mother hands her a cup of milk with a bunch of green grass in it, and the bride dips her little finger in the milk, and the milk and the green grass are then thrown into a stream or flung under a green tree'.[2]

The rite of 'resumption of the use of the hands' (*hāth bartānā*) takes place in southern India three or four days after the removal of the marriage bracelets. Sometimes it is deferred to the Juma'gī, the fifth or last Friday of the honeymoon, and until this is done the pair are not allowed to do any work. On the day appointed the pair with all their relatives and friends are invited by sending round cardamom seeds or in some other way, as already described. The bride's relatives bring with them to the husband's house food, betel, flowers, a handkerchief, and a ring. As a matter of form, they make the pair cook a couple of butter cakes (*pūrī*) and afterwards do some light work, such as lifting a pot of water, swinging a net (*chhīnkā*) in which food is kept out of the reach of cats or

(Burton, *AN*. i. 179; Manucci, ii. 464; Morier, *First Journey*, 121, 215 Yule-Burnett, *Hobson-Jobson*, 2nd ed. 483).

[1] Burton, *Sindh*, 272.

[2] Bray, 76 f. Compare a similar rite among the Kachins (Scott-Hardiman, *Gazetteer, Upper Burma and the Shan States*, part 1, vol. i 407; Crawley, 362; Abbott, *Macedonian Folklore*, 176).

rats, stirring the stew with a skimmer, picking vegetables, or locking and unlocking a trunk in which they put some rupees. Before the cake-making the husband is obliged to unwind a thread twisted round some of the cakes. If he is sharp he does this easily, but if he delays his brother-in-law or his sister-in-law pelts him. After this the pair are made to break some flour balls, some of which they eat out of each other's hands, and give the rest to the ladies present.[1] A feast follows at which the friends of the bridegroom give dresses to the bride's father, mother, and sister.

Feasts are given on the Juma'gī or five Fridays of the honeymoon, on the first at the bride's house, on the three following there or at the house of some near relative, on the fifth at the husband's house. But practice varies, and in Gujarāt on the four Fridays after the wedding the pair dine with the bride's relations.[2] Much is thought of these Friday dinners, and if they are not given a man seldom visits his father-in-law. In north India for a year after the consummation of the marriage the bride has to visit her parents. Half the months of Sha'bān, Muharram, and Safar should be spent with them, and sometimes Rabi'u-l-awwal and Shawwāl. She must come to see them at the Musalmān festivals of Muharram and Shab-i-barāt, and at the Hindu feasts of Holī and Dīvālī, and she ought to pass the whole of Ramazān with them. She should pass the Baqar 'Īd half with her parents and half with her husband. These rules apply only to the first year of married life. At her parents' house she wears a veil (*ghūnghat*) in the presence of males of the family. For two or three years she must not address her husband in the presence of the house elders.[3]

According to the precepts of the Prophet—on whom be the Peace!—Musalmāns are allowed by the Korān and the Traditions to have four wives.[4] 'One quarrels with you, two are sure to involve you in their quarrels; when you have three factions are formed against her you love best; but four find society and occupation among themselves, leaving the

[1] As before, magical fertility rites.
[2] *BG.* ix, part 2, 167.
[3] *NINQ.* v. 205.
[4] *Korān*, iv. 3.

husband in peace'.[1] 'Wives there be four: there's Bed-fellow, Muckheap, Gadabout, and Queen o' women. The more's the pity that the last is one in a hundred'.[2] 'A man should marry four wives: a Persian to have some one to talk to; a Khurāsānī woman for his housework; a Hindu for nursing his children; a woman from Māwarāu-n-nahr, or Transoxiana, to have some one to whip as a warning to the other three'.[3] Most men. however, have only one wife, a few two or three, scarcely any four. 'In practice, except among wealthy Muhammadans, a second wife is very rarely taken unless the first one is barren or suffers from some incurable disease'.[4] In the Panjāb polygamy is more general among rich Musalmāns than in other parts of the country.[5]

There are three forms of divorce[6] (*talāq*): revocable (*talāq-i-bāin*) within three menstrual periods, the husband saying only once to his wife 'I have divorced you'; irrevocable (*talāq-i-raja'ī*) unless a second marriage between the parties is performed, the husband repeating the same words twice; absolute (*talāq-i-mutlaqa*) three similar repetitions. If a man divorces his wife by the revocable form he may within three menstrual periods take her back, but not afterwards. If he has given her the irrevocable form of words he may, if both agree, either maintain her within doors, or after paying her settlement send her away. In the former case, should the woman be unwilling to remain, she may resign half or a quarter of her settlement and depart with the rest. It is unlawful for him to take her back unless he marry her a second time. When a woman is divorced by the absolute form it is unlawful to cohabit with her until she has married another man and has been divorced by him. Such a person is called 'one who makes lawful' (*mustahal*, *mustahil*), and the practice is generally held to be disgraceful.[7] If a woman desires divorce and the husband is ready to grant it, he begins by refusing, but finally makes the condition that if she insists upon it he

[1] Burton, *Sindh Revisited*, i. 340. Cf. Lane, *AN*. ii. 210.
[2] Bray, 81.
[3] *Āin*, i. 327.
[4] *Census Report*, India, 1901, i. 447.
[5] Ibid. 1911, i. 246.
[6] *ERE*. vii. 868 f.; Hughes, 86 ff.; Lane, *ME*. i. 124 ff.
[7] *Mishkāt*, ii. 122 f.; Burton, *AN*. iii. 175; Lane, *AN*. ii. 287 f.; *ME*. i. 124, 229; Muir, *Life*, 325 f.; Sale, *Korān*, 27.

will agree, but that she must abandon her settlement. As she has no alternative she generally agrees. After the irrevocable form a man may not cohabit with a slave girl as in the case of a free woman, and she needs to wait only two menstrual periods instead of three. In divorcing a wife a man must wait till the menstrual period has ended, and then without touching her announce the divorce. Should she be in child he must wait till she is delivered, and if he pleases, the mother must nurse the infant for two years. After arranging the settlement, that is after the Nikāh rite but previous to consummation, if a man wishes to divorce his wife, he must pay her half her settlement, but if he pay the whole it is more commendable. The above statement represents the practice of Sunnīs in south India, but there is great diversity of custom. The Shī'a divorce law is more rigid than that of the Sunnīs: the husband must be an adult of understanding, the divorce must be express and repeated in Arabic in the presence of at least two witnesses. According to the Korān [1] a period of probation (*'iddat*) must be observed by the divorced wife before marrying again—three months after divorce, and in the case of a widow, four months and ten days after the death of her husband. But many women prefer a life of widowhood, and when they do remarry their status is often that of a second rank wife (*dolā*), when the service (*nikāh*) only is read and there are no rejoicings (*shādī*), which are only allowed in the case of a virgin bride. Among the hill Baloch divorce is effected by casting a stone seven or three times and dismissing the wife.[2] Afghāns cast in succession three stones on the ground, saying 'once divorce, twice divorce, thrice divorce' (*yak talāq, do talāq, sih talāq*).[3] Among the Shirannī Pathāns divorce is usually a repurchase of the wife by her father or guardian, who repays, as a rule, not more than half the set sum, less dowry, received for her, and if the parent or guardian declines to take back the woman the husband divorces her and turns her out of the house. This means that she is expelled from the tribe. If any one else marries her he must pay compensation to her parents or guardian, and also pay the husband what he

[1] lxv. 4; ii. 234.
[2] Rose, ii. 51.
[3] C. Masson, *Narrative of Various Journeys*, iii. 8.

would have received if the parent or guardian repurchased her. The form of divorce is throwing three clods of earth after the woman.[1]

In south India people of rank continue the rite of anointing with turmeric for six months, during which time music and feasting go on daily. The other rites are performed every month or fortnight, and so the marriage is completed within a year. Among the middle classes the rites are finished within eleven days or less, as follows : on the first three days the turmeric-rubbing or sitting in state ; on the fourth the sending of henna from the bridegroom to the bride, and on the fifth from bride to bridegroom ; on the sixth the measuring of the bride for her wedding dress ; on the seventh that of the bridegroom ; on the eighth the pot rites, the 'ladies of the marriage shed', the sending of presents ; on the eleventh the Nikāh and the exhibition of the bride ; after two or three days the unloosing of the wedding bracelets and resumption of the use of the hands, usually done on the fifth Juma'gī or Friday. Among the poor all these rites occupy three days : first, the turmeric-rubbing and measuring for the wedding dress ; on the second the sending of gifts and paraphernalia ; on the third the Nikāh and the exhibition of the bride. But if they be much pressed for time, all these take place on one day, a rite being performed every hour or so. In north India the marriage ceremonies usually last for three days : first the procession with gifts ; second the henna rite ; third the procession of the bridegroom to fetch the bride.[2] In Gujarāt the rites extend over a longer period, but last for a much shorter time than in southern India.[3]

[1] Rose, iii. 411.
[2] Mrs. Meer Hassan Ali, 197 ff.
[3] *BG.* ix, part 1, 162 ff.

CHAPTER IX

DEATH[1]

Generally about four or five days before the approach of death the sick man executes a written agreement (*wasīqa*) or a will (*wasīyat-nāma*), in which he disposes of his property and appoints an executor (*wasīy*), only one being required. It is not necessary that the will should be in writing, but it must be certified by two male witnesses, or by one male and two females.[2]

When he is about to expire, a learned reader of the Korān is summoned and asked to recite in a loud voice the Yāsīn chapter of the Korān (xxxvi), which the Prophet called 'the heart of the Korān' (*qalbu-l-qur'ān*), in order that, as Musalmāns believe, the living principles of his whole system should be concentrated in his head,[3] the result of which is death. It is said that when the spirit was commanded to enter the body of Adam, 'the Chosen One of God' (*safīyu-llāh*) —on whom be the Peace !—the soul looking into it once said 'This is an evil, dark place, and unworthy of me; it is impossible that I can occupy it'. Then the Just and Holy God illuminated the body of Adam with 'lamps of light', and commanded the spirit again to enter it. It went a second time, beheld the light, and seeing its future dwelling said 'There is no pleasing sound here to which I can listen'. Oriental mystics say that this was the reason why the Almighty created music. The spirit, delighted with the music, then entered Adam's body.[4] Commentators on the Korān, expositors of the

[1] See the account of Musulmān death rites in *ERE.* iv. 500 ff.

[2] For the law of wills, ibid. vii. 877; Baillie, 623 ff.

[3] Frazer, *GB.*, Taboo and Perils of the Soul, 252; Hindus believe that, at death, the soul departs through a suture (*brahmarandhra*) in the skull (Monier-Williams, *Brahmanism and Hinduism*, 4th ed., 291).

[4] For other legends about the creation of Adam, see Sale, *Preliminary Discourse*, *Korān*, 4, 228.

Hadīs or Traditions, and divines state that the melody thus produced resembled that of the Sūra Yāsīn, and hence this chapter is recited at death to tranquillize the soul. The 'comfortable words' (*kalimatu-t-taiyib*) and the 'word of testimony' (*kalimatu-sh-shahādat*) are also recited with an audible voice to those present. The patient is not required to repeat the Kalima or Creed himself, because he usually lies insensible and cannot speak. But the pious retain their faculties and power of converse till the very last. It is an important rule that if any one desires the patient to repeat the Creed, and he expires without being able to do so, his faith is held to be doubtful, but the man who so directed him incurs guilt. It is, therefore, preferable that those present should recite the words, in the hope that the dying man by hearing them may recall them to his recollection, and repeat them either aloud or mentally. In general, when a person is dying they pour sherbet down his throat to facilitate the exit of the soul, but some, though rarely, substitute water from the holy well Zamzam. 'The death agony is supposed to be the final temptation of the arch-fiend, who greets the thirsty soul as it leaves the body with a cup of sweets. If the soul falls into the snare the cup is dashed aside and the tempter disappears'.[1] 'The Recording Angels, Kirāmu-l-kātibīn, sit one on a man's right shoulder, noting down good deeds, and the other on the left taking note of evil deeds. Every night, as the man sleeps, they fly up to Heaven, and record on his leaf in the tree of life, called Tūbā', his acts of the day. Each person has a leaf to himself, and when the end approaches the leaf drops off the tree, and the Recording Angels carry it to 'Azrāīl or 'Izrāīl, the Angel of Death, who forthwith dispatches them and a third Angel back to earth, to show the dying man his life account. On reading it, according as the balance is struck for or against him, he dies happily or in torments'.[2]

The moment the spirit has fled the mouth is shut because, if left open, it would present a disagreeable spectacle,[3] and the eyes are closed with a pledget of cotton, held in its place by

[1] *BG.* ix, part 2, 168. [2] Thorburn, 167; *ERE.* x. 606.

[3] The real reason is probably to prevent a demon from entering the corpse (Frazer, *GB.*, Taboo and Perils of the Soul, 125).

a cloth wound round the temples. The two great toes are brought into contact and fastened together with a thin strip of cloth to prevent the legs from remaining apart.[1] In northern India Shī'as put pomegranate or honey syrup in the mouth of the dead.[2] In Gujarāt leaves of marjoram, a plant held sacred by Musalmāns, are rubbed on the face, and pastilles of aloe wood (*'ūd battī*) are burnt close by.[3]

Certain euphemisms are employed to denote the fact of death. Thus we read of the Emperor Bābur that he 'departed from this fleeting world for his everlasting abode in Paradise'.[4] To die is 'to make a transference' (*intiqāl karnā, farmānā*); 'to make a departure' (*rahlat karnā, farmānā*); a person is dead, 'on whom God has shown mercy' (*marhūm*).

If death occurs in the evening the shrouding and burial take place before midnight; if at a later hour and the articles required are not immediately procurable, the corpse is buried early next morning. Despite the risk of vivisepulture, immediate burial is the Semitic rule.[5] According to the Traditions Muhammad said, 'Be quick in raising up the bier, for if the dead man have been a good man it is right to bear him to the grave without delay, and if bad, it is frowardness ye put from your necks. When any of you dieth, you may not keep him in the house but bear him quickly to the grave'.[6] The popular belief is that if a good man be quickly buried the sooner he will reach Paradise. If he was a bad man he should be speedily buried in order that his unhappy lot may not fall upon others. It is well that the relatives should not weep over-much or go without food.

There are professional washers of the dead (*ghassāl ghāsil, murdashū*), who wash and shroud the dead for payment. Sometimes, however, the relatives perform the duty themselves. A hole is dug in the ground to receive the water used in the washing, because some people think it dangerous to

[1] The object is probably to prevent the ghost from 'walking' (Frazer, *JRAI*. xv. 66; Thurston, *Castes*, iv. 494; Lane, *AN*. ii. 337).

[2] *NINQ*. ii. 139.

[3] Enthoven, *Folklore Notes, Gujarāt*, 137.

[4] Elliot-Dowson, v. 187.

[5] Gen. xxiii. 1–4; Burton, *AN*. iv. 145; Lane, *ME*. ii. 253.

[6] *Mishkāt*, i. 387.

tread on such water, and some women will not venture near the place during the washing.[1] The corpse is placed on a bed, plank, or straw, stripped and laid on the back with the head to the east and the feet west, the face pointing to the Ka'ba. It is covered with a covering cloth (*satrposh*), reaching in the case of a man from the navel to the calves of the legs, for a woman from the chest to the feet. Sunnīs, unlike Shī'as, use warm water, and in the water the leaves of the jujube tree (*ber, zizyphus jujuba*) are boiled. According to the Traditions the corpse should be washed in pure water in which the leaves of the Lote tree (*sidr, rhamnus spina christi*, or *r. nabeca*) are mixed. At the last washing a little camphor is used ; hence Persians dislike camphor because it is used in disinfecting the dead.[2] The washer draws a cotton bag, used like a glove, over his hand, and with a clod of earth begins the purification. He rubs the abdomen four or five times and then pours plenty of water and completes the cleansing with soap (*sābun*), soap pods (*sikākāī, acacia concinna*), and soap-nut (*rīthā, sapindus mukorosi*). More than one bag is used in the operation. Then the rest of the body is washed, but this is done gently because, though life has departed, the body is still warm and is thought to be sensible to pain. This is the greater ablution (*ghusl*), and it is followed by the lesser (*wuzū'*), purifying the mouth and nostrils and washing the arms up to the elbows. They never put warm water into the mouth or nostrils, but clean them with pledgets of cloth. Bits of the same material are used to stop up the mouth and nose, and the whole of the face is washed, the hair and beard being cleansed with fuller's earth, mainly consisting of silica and known as *Multāni mittī*, in Sind *met*, in Persia *gil-i-sar-shūī*, ' head-cleansing clay '.[3]

Water mixed with jujube leaves and camphor in a large new pot is poured over the corpse from a water pot with a spout (*badhnī*) three times, first from the head to the feet, then from the right, and finally from the left shoulder to the feet. Every time the water is poured the washer or some one present recites the 'word of testimony' (*kalimatu-sh-shahādat*) :

[1] Cf. *ERE*. iv. 417.
[2] *Mishkāt*, i. 370 ; Burton, *AN*. ii. 399 ; xi. 68 ; Rose, i. 876 f.
[3] Watt, *mm. Prod.* 329 f.

'I bear witness that there is no God but God, Who is One and has no co-equal; and I bear witness that Muhammad is His servant and is sent from Him!' The body is then wiped dry with a piece of new cloth, or a clean white sheet is thrown over it and rubbed so that the remaining moisture dries up. Among the Shī'as of Lucknow the corpse is washed in a tent or behind a screen (*qanāt*), pitched near the tomb or in a place where water is procurable.[1] Pounded camphor is rubbed on the hands, feet, knees, and forehead, these parts having been rubbed in the daily acts of prostration during prayer. The Brāhūī 'in the old days would anoint with henna, as though for a bridal, the hands and feet of women cut off in their prime, in token that death had come upon them before the fullness of their days, or ever they had drunk deep of the sweet joys of the world. But the custom is on the wane, and it is only in noble houses and among the well-to-do that you will now see the like'.[2] The Brāhūī also lay an iron bar on the belly of the dead to keep down the swelling, and place a pot of rice or other grain by the head, which is the fee of the washer.[3] In southern India poor people pay the corpse washer a fee of four annas, others from fifty to a hundred rupees, and the author has seen them obtain in this way a pair of shawls, brocades, and other valuables. These people desire the death of some great man so that they may receive money and clothes. Many wealthy, ignorant people have a horror of a corpse, and refuse to touch the clothes and furniture used by the deceased before death. These things are, therefore, given away in charity to the washers, who dispose of them in the bazars.

The shroud (*kafan*) consists of three pieces of cloth for a man, five for a woman.[4] Those of a man are, first the cloth (*izār*, *lūng*) reaching from the navel down to the knees or ankle-joints. This is torn in the middle to the extent of two-thirds,

[1] Mrs. Meer Hassan Ali, 73; cf. Lane, *ME.* ii. 253 f.

[2] Bray, 121 f.

[3] Ibid. 122. This is intended to repell the Jinn (Lane, *AN.* ii. 337; Burton, *AN.* ix. 21). In parts of England a plate of salt is laid on the corpse for the purpose, it is said, of checking decay (J. Brand, *Observations on Popular Antiquities*, 1848, ii. 234).

[4] At Sātāra in the Deccan the shroud is seventy-five feet long for a man, ninety feet long for a woman (*BG.* xix. 133 f.).

the two divisions covering the legs being tucked under them on both sides, the upper part left entire covering the fore part of the pelvis, the sides tucked under to left and right, and the ends tied behind. Secondly, the shirt (*qamīs*, *kurtā*, *alfā*, *pairāhan*), reaching from the neck to the knees or ankles, having a slit made in the middle through which the head is passed, and drawn down before and behind. Thirdly, a sheet or envelope (*lifāfa*), reaching from the head to below the feet. Women have two additional pieces: a breast-band (*sīnaband*) extending from the arm-pits to above the ankle-joints, and a veil (*dāmanī*), which encircles the head once and has its two ends hanging on either side. The first or chief cloth is called the shroud (*kafan*), and religious sentences should be traced with the clay of Mecca on the part which covers the breast. Various perfumes, such as rose water (*gulāb*), otto of roses (*'itr*) and powder (*abīr*), are sprinkled over the body, which is then covered with a sheet, the skirts of which are tied together at both ends to that on which the body lies. Finally, a shawl or some such covering is thrown over the upper sheet, a Korān belonging to the Mullā is placed at the head of the bier, and the body is ready for interment. There are, of course, differences of practice according to the wealth of the family. Though there may be plenty of cloth in the house it must not be used for the shroud, and the materials must be bought lest another death should follow. The practice of pilgrims dipping the shroud which is intended for their burial in the water of the well Zamzam at Mecca is now confined to people like the Sudanese, Indians, and some Algerians.[1]

In the Deccan the manner of shrouding is as follows. Having placed the shroud clothes on a new mat and fumigated them with the smoke of benzoin or benjamin, and sprinkled them with perfumed powder, essence of roses, or rose water, the sheet is first spread on the mat, then the loin-cloth, above that

[1] Leeder, 218. The shroud was sometimes assumed by persons in danger of death, as in the case of the rebel, Malik Qāsim Barīd, who presented himself before Sultān Qulī Qutb Shāh of Golkonda (1512–43) wearing a shroud, and with a sword slung round his neck, imploring pardon (Ferishta, iii. 347). White and green are the usual colours of the shroud, or any colour save blue, but white alone in India (*ERE*. iv. 501).

the body-cloth, and on the top the breast-cloth. In the case of a woman the head-cloth is kept separate and tied on afterwards. The corpse is carefully brought from the washing-place and laid on the shroud-cloths. Antimony (*surmā*) is applied to the eyes with a tent made of rolled-up paper, with a ring (*chhallā*), or with a copper coin. Camphor is rubbed on seven places: the forehead including the nose, the palms of the hands, the knees, and great toes. After this the shroud-cloths are put on in the order in which they lie. The shroud must be white, no other colour being allowed. It is, however, admissible to spread a coloured cloth over the bier (*janāza*, *tābūt*), or on the coffin (*sandūq*, *ṣundūq*), because after the funeral, or after the recitation of the Fātiha on the fortieth day, this is made over to the Faqīr who is in charge of the cemetery, or it is given in charity. The coffin is a square box the length of the corpse, but when the latter is removed the coffin is brought home. Among the poor a coffin is sometimes not used. In the case of a man his turban is often laid on the coffin.[1]

After shrouding the body they tie one band across the head, a second below the feet, and a third about the chest, leaving about six or seven fingers' breadth of cloth above the head and below the feet to admit of the ends being fastened. Should the widow be present they undo the head-cloth and show her the face of the dead. She is asked to remit the settlement which he had made on her, but it is preferable that she should do this while her husband is alive. If the widow be absent she should remit it when she receives news of his death. If his mother be present she says 'The milk with which I nursed thee I freely bestow on thee'. This is done because a person is considered to be under an obligation to his mother, and this debt she remits in this way. But this is merely a custom of the country and not prescribed by the Law of Islām. Over the corpse a flower-sheet (*phūl kā chādar*) is laid, or merely wreaths of flowers with some perfumed powder. In Gujarāt the widow breaks her glass bangles at the death of her husband according to the Hindu practice, but among the Mochī or cobbler caste she continues to wear a red handkerchief.[2] Then the Fātiha is

[1] Manucci, iii. 153.

[2] *BG.* ix, part 2, 78.

recited with the Qul texts:[1] 'Say, God is One! Say, I seek the protection of the Lord of the Daybreak! Say, I seek the protection of the Lord of Men!' This recital confers on the dead the rewards attached to these texts. When this is done the body is raised with the mat on which it lay and placed on a bed, and a sort of bier (*dolā*) is made by constructing an upper framework of bamboos, or, if they can afford it, it is placed in a coffin. In the United Provinces Shī'as cover the coffin with a cloth and place a canopy over it, the coffin being usually thrown away after the funeral. In Gujarāt a shawl is laid over the bier, of green or other dark colours for men, red for women.[2] It is a common custom, in order to baffle the ghost and prevent it from returning, to remove the corpse, not through the house door, but through an opening in the wall, as was done at the burial of the Emperors Akbar and Shāhjahān.[3]

Four or five relations or friends carry the bier on their shoulders, being every now and then relieved by an equal number of bearers, some touching it with their hands and repeating the Creed or the Benediction. The funeral procession moves at a rapid pace to avoid the evil spirits which beset the soul until the interment.[4] It is highly meritorious to follow the bier and that on foot, this being one of the imperative obligations (*farz kifāī*);[5] but if one out of eight or ten persons present perform this duty it is held to be sufficient. People who meet a funeral should rise and follow for at least forty yards. No one, however, should walk in front of the corpse, as this space is left for the angels who precede it. The service is generally performed in a mosque in preference to a grave-yard, which is held to be polluted. The service should be recited by the 'owner' of the corpse, that is, the nearest relative, but if he is not present or is illiterate any other person

[1] *Qul* means 'say'. The texts are chapters 112, 113, 114 of the *Korān*.

[2] *BG.* ix, part 2, 169.

[3] Smith, *Akbar*, 327; Manucci, ii. 126; iv. 431; Frazer, *The Belief in Immortality*, i. 452 f.; Crooke, *Popular Religion*, ii. 56.

[4] It may also be intended to puzzle the ghost and prevent its return (*ERE.* iv. 426). The Jews hasten the funeral to avoid the Shēdīm, or evil spirits (Hastings, *Dict. Bible*, i. 332).

[5] *Mishkāt*, ii. 413.

present at the request of the relatives performs the duty. The Qāzī or his assistant is appointed to bury the friendless poor.

The form of the service is as follows. First, some one calls out, as they do at the summons to daily prayer, 'Here begin the prayers for the dead (*as-salātu-l-janāza*)'. On this summons all persons within hearing should go to the spot. Those present stand in three rows, the Imām or leader in front, opposite the head of the corpse, if it be that of a man, and in line with the waist in case of a woman. The service consists of four recitals of the Takbīr or Creed, 'God is very Great!', the Durūd or supplication, and the Du'ā or prayer for forgiveness. The Imām recites the 'Intention' (*nīyat*), the notice that he intends to begin the rite. Placing his thumbs on the lobes of his ears he calls out 'God is Great!' Then he lays his right hand over the left a little below the navel, the congregation doing the same. Without removing his hands he says the prayer (*du'ā*), the blessing or ejaculation (*subhān*), reads the second Creed and in like manner the third and fourth. After which he calls out again the words 'God is Great!' Then turning his face over the right shoulder so that the congregation may be able to see him, he repeats the same words, adding 'The Peace be upon you and the Mercy of God!' Those present repeat the Creed and the Salutation (*salām*) with the Imām. After that the 'owner' of the corpse calls out 'All have permission to depart!' (*rukhsat-i-'āmm*), meaning that all except relatives and close friends may leave.

The Fātiha for the dead is again recited, and the bier is raised and taken to the grave. One or two persons, relatives or others, descend into the grave to lay the body down, while two take the sheet that covered the body, twist it round, and lifting up the body put it under the waist. Then standing, one on each side of the grave, they hold on by the two ends, and with the help of two or three at the head and as many at the feet, they hand the corpse to the men who have descended into the grave. They lay the body on the back with the head to the north and the feet to the south, turning the face to the westward towards Mecca, the Qibla. Some turn the head in that direction, others the right side including the head.[1] Each

[1] Burton, *AN*. ix. 27.

person present takes up a little earth and recites mentally or in a whisper the words 'Say He is God alone, God the Eternal! He begetteth not and He is not begotten, and there is none like unto Him!' Or this verse 'From it [the earth] we have created you, and unto it we will return you, and out of it we will bring you forth a second time!'[1] The earth is then gently replaced in the grave, or arranged by those who have descended into it.

It is sometimes the habit to place messages or prayers with the dead. At the funeral of a Bohrā a prayer for pity on his soul and body addressed to the Archangels Michael, Gabriel, or 'Azrāīl is placed in the dead man's hand.[2] Fīroz Shāh of Delhi writes: 'Under the guidance of the Almighty I arranged that the heirs of those persons who had been executed in the reign of my late lord Muhammad Shāh, and those who had been deprived of a limb, nose, eye, hand, or foot, should be reconciled to the late Sultān and be appeased with gifts, so that they executed deeds declaring their satisfaction, duly attested by witnesses. These deeds were put into a chest which was placed in the Dāru-l-amān [the house of peace] at the head of the tomb of the late Sultān, in the hope that God, in His great clemency, would show mercy on my late friend and patron, and make these persons feel reconciled to him'.[3]

The grave, which is usually dug beforehand, is about four cubits square, with a hole in the centre as nearly as possible the size of the body.[4] In some cases a small wall of brick or clay, about a cubit and a half high, is erected, leaving sufficient room for the corpse. Over this, to prevent the earth from pressing upon the body, planks, slabs of stone, or large earthen pots are placed resting on the grave wall, and upon these the

[1] *Korān*, cxii; xx. 57.

[2] *BG.* ix, part 2, 31.

[3] Elliot-Dowson, iii. 385 f.; Ferishta, i. 464. Compare the Egyptian custom of placing copies of the Book of the Dead with the corpse (A. Erman, *Life in Ancient Egypt*, 315 f.; *ERE.* iv. 462). Hindus do the same in the case of a Lingāyat priest (*BG.* xxi. 209; xxiv. 132), and cf. Skeat-Blagden, *Pagan Races of the Malay Peninsula*, i. 410; ii. 93.

[4] Musalmāns always inter the dead. A curious Hindu case is reported of the Darshaniyā sect in the time of Akbar, who used to tie uncooked grain and a burnt brick round the neck of the corpse, fling it into water, take it out and burn it at a place where there was no water (*Āīn*, i. 207).

earth is filled in, the surface is smoothed with water, and it is formed in the shape of a tomb. After the body has been placed in the grave some people lay planks obliquely over it, one of their ends resting on the right, the other on the left side, and over these mats are spread to prevent the earth from falling into the recess containing the body. A more elaborate arrangement to prevent the pressure of the earth upon the body is to make a side chamber (*baghlī*, *lahd*) on the east side of the grave, level with its bottom and the length of the body. When the corpse is placed in this side-chamber, the entrance of it is closed with mats or wood, and the grave is filled up.[1]

Some people during their lives select a suitable spot and have a grave made lined with bricks and mortar, which is a violation of a precept of the Prophet. Like those of the Greeks and Romans,[2] the tomb is often built on the side of a road because the dead long to be near the sound of busy human life. Others have a mausoleum (*maqbara*) built over it, or merely surround it with a wall in the form of a square, or they fill up the grave with sand or some kind of grain, generally wheat or rice, a south Indian custom which does not seem to prevail in the north, and is possibly a survival of the rite of feeding the dead. When the owner dies they bury him in it and make a structure (*ta'wīz*) over it with square stones.

The rule for digging a grave is that if it be intended for a woman the depth should be the height of a man's chest, for a man the height of the waist. The reason for this assigned by the Brāhūī is, 'that the nature of a woman being so restless, without a large proportion of earth upon her she would not remain quiet, even in the grave'.[3] In general, grave-diggers dig the grave without measuring the length of the corpse, allowing four, or four and a half, cubits for its length and one and a half for its breadth. If it is intended for a particularly tall person or for a child they measure the body.

[1] The side-chamber grave, probably a survival of cave burial, is used by the Hindu Lingāyats (Thurston, *Castes*, iv. 286). For its affinity to the Egyptian form see A. Erman, *Life in Ancient Egypt*, 310 ff.; Sir G. Wilkinson, *The Ancient Egyptians*, 1878, iii. 436; Lane, *ME*. ii. 265.

[2] W. Smith, *Dict. Antiquities*, ii. 644, 647; *ERE*. ii. 29; iv. 506.

[3] C. Masson, *Narrative of Journey to Kalat*, 433 f.

When laying the body in the grave, should the space prove to be too small the ignorant consider the dead person to have been a great sinner and think the circumstance very unlucky. The grave-diggers receive as their fee from eight annas to five rupees, according to the means of the family, but wealthy people give much more by way of a present. It is customary for the grave-digger, without any further remuneration, to plaster and smooth the surface of the grave-mound, which he does before the visitation (*ziyārat*) on the third day. The Faqīr who lives in the cemetery, except in the case of the graves of the friendless dead, never allows a grave to be dug without claiming a fee of from one to a hundred rupees from the relatives. This forms his means of living. The cloth which was spread on the bier becomes his perquisite, but he spreads it on every visitation day up to the fortieth, when he appropriates it. Some people, besides this cloth, have coloured sheets constantly spread on the grave. Poor people who cannot afford to raise a tomb simply smooth the surface of the grave. In northern India [1] they make graves of earth, broad at one end and narrow at the other, in the shape of a cow's tail or the back of a fish, and pour water on it in three longitudinal lines, so that it leaves a mark something in this form :

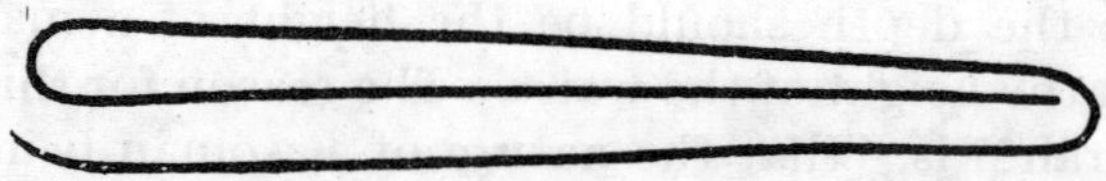

In pouring the water they begin at the feet and end at the head, where they leave the water-vessel inverted, and stick a twig of the sweet basil (*ocymum basilicum*), or pomegranate tree, near it in the earth. In Arabia and other Musalmān countries it is not customary to pour water on the grave, but if a hurricane blows they sprinkle some water over it to prevent the dust from blowing about. The Baloch, probably to prevent damage to the corpse by animals like jackals, heap dry brushwood on the grave, which is removed after six months, and then the grave is marked out with white stones.[2]

[1] The author does not state the part of northern India where this custom prevails.

[2] Rose, ii. 52.

After the burial the **Fātiha** is recited in the name of the dead. As they return home, when about forty paces from the grave, they recite the **Fātiha** in the joint names of all the dead in the cemetery, this being known as the **Dā'ira** or 'cemetery' **Fātiha**. At this juncture two Angels, Munkar and Nakīr, 'The Unknown and the Repudiator', examine the dead man, make him sit up, and inquire who are his God and his Prophet, and to what religion he belongs. If he has been a good man he replies to these questions, but if he was a bad man he becomes bewildered and sits mute, or he mumbles out some incoherent words. In the latter case the Angels severely torment him and beat him with a spiked club (*gurz*). According to some Musalmāns, at the present day Munkar and Nakīr visit the graves of infidels and non-Muslims, while Bashshir, 'news-bringer', and Mubashir, 'giver of good news', come to those of Musalmāns.[1] When the Angels make the interrogatory (*suāl*), if the dead man has been a Kāfir or infidel, a Munāfiq or hypocrite, or one of the wicked, he is attacked by ninety-nine snakes, and he sees Hell through a hole in the side of the grave. The next torture is the 'squeezing of the tomb' (*fashār-i-qabr*), when both sides of the grave press upon the sides of the dead man. Finally, the Rūh or soul is taken from the body and cast into the dungeon (*sijn*) reserved for reprobates. Those who die in the odour of sanctity are merely sleeping, not liable to death or decay like ordinary sinners.[2] In the case of a good man 'Azrāīl, the Angel of Death, sits at the head of the grave and says, 'O pure soul! Come out to God's pardon and pleasure!'[3] After the rites at the cemetery every one, according to his means, distributes grain, salt, bread, and money to beggars and Faqīrs in the name of the dead. Those who have attended the final

[1] Burton, *AN.* viii. 44. The Bannūchīs place a few inches in front of the corpse a stone tablet on which the creed is engraved, because when Munkar and Nakīr arrive fright often causes the memory to fail (Thorburn, 169).

[2] Burton, *Sindh*, 275, 391; Hughes, 27 f. On the state of the soul between death and the judgement, see Sale, *Preliminary Discourse*, sect. iv, Korān; *ERE*. v. 376. Musalmāns in the Panjāb object to beat a brass tray as it is supposed to disturb the dead, who believe that the Day of Judgement has come (*NINQ*. i. 16).

[3] *Mishkāt*, i. 365.

rites accompany the friends of the deceased to their houses, where they recite the prayer of good intent (*Fātiha nīyat khair*) in the name of, and for the benefit of, the family, and console the master of the house, recommending to him patience and comfort, and then depart. Sometimes before they leave they are offered some drink, such as curds or buttermilk. Sometimes relatives and friends send food from their houses, because it is not usual to cook anything in the house till the third day after a death.[1]

Tombs are generally made of clay, stone, or brick and mortar, or sometimes a single stone is hewn into the shape of a tomb, forming three oblong or square platforms (*ta'wīz*), one or one and a half cubits in height or somewhat less. Above that, if for a man, they make a platform about a cubit or more in height, resembling the hump on a camel's back or the back of a fish, in breadth one or one and a half spans. Royal tombs, of course, are built on a more magnificent pattern. For instance, that of Akbar has at the bottom a plinth, above this a platform with leaf ornament, above that a smaller plain plinth, while above this is, again, a projecting platform with leaf decoration, and the upper surface is enclosed by a low screen of marble tracery.[2] If the tomb is that of a woman the length and breadth of the tomb are the same as for a man, but in height it is less, being from four fingers to a span, and flat in shape. The platform (*ta'wīz*) of a boy is of the same type as that of a man, but in height it is less, and that of a girl like that of a woman, only smaller in size. Some people erect a lamp-holder (*chirāghdān, charāghdān*) at the head of the tomb, on which lamps are lighted on Thursday or Friday evenings. In northern India tombs of men are distinguished by a segment of a cylinder called a ' pen-box ' (*qalamdān*), raised on the flat upper surface, while those of women have a flat upper surface in shape like the wooden boards (*takhtī*) on which children are taught to write. Many stone tombs have an oblong hollow on the top which is often filled with earth, or in the case of saintly women devotees sometimes fill the hollow with the sediment of pounded

[1] Possibly through fear that the ghost may be eaten with the food (Frazer, *JRAI.* xv. 91 ff.).

[2] Syad Muhammad Latif, *Agra, Historical and Descriptive*, 168 ff.

sandalwood.[1] On the tomb of Jahānārā Begam (1645–80), daughter of Shāhjahān, and a disciple of the Saint Miyān Mīr, which is situated in Old Delhi, a recess is sunk in the upper side of the marble block, in which grass is planted. On it is inscribed the verse, 'Let green grass only conceal my grave; grass is the best covering of the grave of the meek'.[2] In the Ibrāhīm Rauza at Bījāpur the men's tombs are distinguished from those of the ladies by the arched ridge-stones along the top, the ladies' tombs being quite flat, the ridge-stones being said to represent the pen-box indicating a learned person, and hence in the seventeenth century a man.[3] In south India Shī'as make tombs for men in the same shape as Sunnīs do for women, and for women like those of the Sunnī tombs for men, but with a hollow or basin in the centre of the upper part. Some have a stone erected inscribed with the name of the deceased, either alone or in conjunction with that of his father, together with the date, year, month, week, day, on which he died. Some have this inscribed in verse or prose on the four walls of the tomb. A few have the name and date of death engraved on a square stone tablet fixed over the entrance door of the mausoleum, or they write it in ink over the door. In Afghanistān on Shī'a graves stones with engravings of shields, swords, or lances marking the profession of the deceased are found, and in Kurdistān the figure of a warrior is painted on a wooden memorial.[4] Among the tribes on the north-west frontier the Orakzai Pathāns place over the grave a tombstone, carved or plain, according to the means of the family. Occasionally a piece of wood, two feet long by six inches broad, is substituted for a tombstone, and in some cases these are rudely carved and decorated with figures of birds. A man's grave has only two tombstones, one over the head and the other over the knees. The graves of Mullās have a white flag on a stick at the head and a waterpot (*kūza*) in the middle, while those of a martyr (*shahīd*) also have a flag.[5] The Indo-Musalmān

[1] *PNQ.* i. 38, 121.

[2] Fanshawe, *Delhi Past and Present*, 239; Jadunath Sarkar, *Life of Aurangzīb*, iii. 158 f.

[3] H. Cousens, *Bījāpur and its Antiquities*, 71.

[4] Masson, op. cit., ii. 275.

[5] Rose, iii. 182 f.

cemeteries are, as a rule, carelessly protected, and the graves are left in a ruinous condition, trespass by people of other religions and by animals not being prevented.

The Prophet is said to have reproved a woman for lamenting over a grave, and he at one time forbade, at another permitted, the visiting of graves, especially by women.[1] Sikandar Lodī of Delhi (1489–1517) forbade women to go abroad or to make offerings at Musalmān shrines.[2] Aurangzeb issued orders against the roofing of buildings containing tombs, the white-washing of sepulchres, and the visits of women to cemeteries, while Fīroz Shāh (1351–88) prevented women from visiting tombs on the ground that it led to immorality.[3] But natural feeling has made the custom general in India. Some believe that the ghost remains near the tomb, with liberty, however, of going where it pleases, a belief which they support by the Prophet's custom of saluting graves, and his affirmation that the dead heard these salutations. Hence arose the custom, common among Musalmāns, of visiting the tombs of their relations.[4]

On the third day after the burial, the rites known as those of the third day (*tījā*), the visitation (*ziyārat*), the flower offering (*phūl charhānā*) are performed. On the second day they take fruit, food, betel, a sheet made of flowers, sweetmeats, perfumed powder (*argajā*) and benzoin pastilles (*'ūd battī*) [5] and lay them on the spot where the death occurred. On the third day early in the morning the male relations and Mullās take these things to the grave and have a recital of the whole Korān (*khatm-i-qur'ān*) done by the Mullā, once, twice, or oftener, in order to transfer the benefit to the soul of the dead. This is done by distributing four or five sections, of which there are thirty, to each of the readers, who thus get

[1] *Mishkāt*, i 391, 401, 403; Lane, *ME.* ii. 271. The Prophet himself used to visit graves, and the practice is recommended by Muslim theologians as a religious exercise (*ERE.* iii. 734).

[2] Ferishta, i. 587.

[3] Jadunath Sarkar, *Life of Aurangzīb*, iii. 101; Elliot-Dowson, iii. 380.

[4] Sale, *Korān, Preliminary Discourse*, 55.

[5] These are made of benzoin, wood aloes, sandalwood, rock lichen, patchouli, rose malloes, leaves of *talispatri* (*flacourtia cataphracta*), mastic, sugar candy, or gum (*EB.* xiv. 350).

through the work rapidly.[1] Rich people employ fifty or more Mullās for this purpose. When this is done they spread a white, red, or other coloured sheet on the grave, lay the flower sheet over that, and burn pastilles of benzoin or aloeswood. Each man throws a few flowers into the perfumed water, and with prayers for the remission of the dead man's sins they rub the powder on the grave over the place where the head and breast of the corpse rest. The Fātiha is recited, and the food is distributed to the Hāfiz, or those who know the Korān by rote, the Mullās, Faqīrs, and the poor. Grain, salt, and money are also given in alms. Then having recited the prayer for all the dead who rest in the cemetery (*dā'ira fātiha*) they return home. In Gujarāt friends and relations meet at the mosque, where each of them from small books reads a chapter of the Korān, praying that the merit of the act may pass to the soul of the dead. A Maulavī or learned doctor preaches a sermon (*wa'z*), after which a tray full of flowers and perfumed powder and oil is handed to the guests. Each one as it passes picks out a flower, dips it into the oil, and the whole is poured on the grave. Before leaving the mosque, and again on arriving at the house of the deceased, prayers are offered for his soul and a dinner is sometimes provided. Visits of condolence (*'azā*) are paid about this time to the bereaved family.[2]

For nine days after a death most people cannot eat or drink at the house of the deceased, nor invite the members of it to feasts. Brāhūī widows neglect washing and care of their persons for fifteen days after their husbands' deaths, and at the end of that period their friends bring them the powdered leaves of a plant with which they wash their heads and cease mourning.[3] Musalmān mourners do not eat meat, fish, or savoury food, a local custom not prescribed by the Law. On the ninth day at noon the mourners prepare bread and sweetmeats, and after reciting the Fātiha, eat and send some to their neighbours. In the evening there is a dinner, part of the food being given to the Faqīr of the burial-ground and to

[1] In Persia sheets of the Korān are distributed, so that the recital may be quickly done (Morier, *Hajji Baba*, 303).

[2] *BG.* ix, part 2, 189. For the custom on the North-west Frontier see Thorburn, 148 f.

[3] Masson, *Journey to Kalat*, 434.

other Faqīrs. It is a custom of the vulgar never to eat any food cooked in their own houses after partaking of the funeral feast, and when they receive a share of it they do not allow it to be brought within doors, as they say that it deprives them of the power of speech, but this, says Ja'far Sharīf, is merely fancy. The visitation (*ziyārat*) at the grave on the tenth day differs little from that of the third. Some people prepare food and distribute what remains. This is done also on the nineteenth day when, after reciting the Fātiha, they take a flower-sheet to the grave, spread the sheet on it, and rub sandalwood on the sheet. Among Shī'as in northern India similar rites are done on the third (*tījā*), the tenth (*daswīn*), the twentieth (*bīswīn*), and the thirtieth (*tīswān*) days.

Dark blue is the mourning colour, black that of the 'Abbasside Khalīfas. Mourning dress, however, is not favoured, and when it is worn it is by women, not by men.[1] Widows observe the period of seclusion (*'iddat*) for four months and ten days after the death of their husbands, during which they never leave the house nor join in amusements. In Gujarāt other customs have been borrowed from Hindus, such as the breaking of the bangles of the widow and mother of the deceased. The mother may get new bangles, but, except when they are of gold or silver, the widow when she marries again can never wear bracelets or a nose-ring. When a woman friend visits a widow for the first time she breaks into a wail and the widow joins in the lamentation until she is soothed. This is known as ' the face hiding ' (*munh dhānknā*).[2]

Prayers for the dead are not universal, but the Prophet is said to have recognized the practice. If they are said there is no prostration (*sijda*), but there are recitations of the Korān.[3] Wahhābīs strongly object to prayer for the dead.[4]

On the thirty-ninth day food such as the deceased was in the habit of eating during his life is cooked and placed with perfumed powder (*argajā*), antimony (*surmā*), lampblack (*kājal*), betel, and some clothes and jewellery of the deceased

[1] Burton, *AN*. i. 140 ; ix. 113 ; *Pilgrimage*, ii. 16 ; Lane, *AN*. i. 118 *ME*. ii. 271.
[2] *BG*. ix, part 2, 170.
[3] Burton, *AN*. i. 337 ; ix. 193 ; Hughes, 471 ; Lane, *AN*. i. 382.
[4] Sell, 109.

on the spot where the death occurred, and over them a flower garland is hung from the ceiling. This rite is known as 'filling the side chamber of the grave' (*lahd bharnā*). Some silly women believe that on the fortieth day the ghost leaves the house, if it has not done so previously, and that if it has left it returns on that day, notices the things which have been laid out, eats of such of them as it fancies, swings on the flower wreath, smells the sandalwood, and then departs.[1] On that day they keep vigil (*ratjagā*), and if any reciters of the Korān or of dirges are present these are recited. But these ideas about the return of the soul and eating food are contrary to the Law of Islām. During the forty days a cup (*ābkhorā*) of water and bread are laid out on the place where the death occurred. The water is left there all night, and next morning it is poured out at the root of a green tree, the bread and the cup being given to some Faqīr. A lamp is generally lighted at the place of death, where the body was washed, and sometimes on the grave for three, ten, or forty nights, this being a Hindu practice.[2] Every evening a cup of water and some food are sent to the mosque, and any one, after saying the Fātiha in the name of the dead, may eat of this food. On the morning of the fortieth day a visitation (*ziyārat*) is made to the grave. In Sind the higher classes usually employ a reverend teacher, the Ākhūn or Ākhūnd, to read the Korān at the grave for forty days, and even the poorest people try to do this for a week or a fortnight. Among the literary classes it is common for a man to recite the Korān in the presence of the dead for many years after his decease.[3]

On the third, sixth, ninth, and twelfth month after a death —women generally observing these rites a few days before the expiry of these periods—it is usual to cook food, to eat it after the Fātiha has been said, and to distribute the remainder. Well-to-do people in the name of the dead give charity in money and clothes, and lay a flower-sheet on the grave. Women sometimes visit the grave, and it is meritorious for men to recite the Fātiha there every Friday, but most

[1] On food for the dead, see *ERE*. vi. 65 ff.

[2] Frazer, *GB*., Adonis, Attis, Osiris, ii. 65; Crooke, *Popular Religion*, ii. 55.

[3] Burton, *Sindh*, 280.

people do this on Thursday. After the first year the dead man is numbered with the sainted dead of the family, and the Fātiha is said conjointly for them at the Shab-i-barāt or on the 'Arafa or vigil of the Baqar 'Īd festivals. In Egypt the tomb is visited on the 'Īdu-l fitr and palm branches are laid on it.[1]

The following is the time usually occupied for the performance of religious and social rites, for which leave is generally given to Musalmān sepoys: (*a*) Domestic rites—Chhathī, Chilla, 'Aqīqa, Mūndan, Sālgirah, Bi'smillāh, Khatn, Korān kā hadīya, Bāligh honā, Jahāz kī nazr, Murīd honā—not more than a day and a half; Shādī, or marriage, ten days, but if time presses, five days are sufficient; Juma'gī, one day; on the death of a relation three days, i.e. until the first visitation (*ziyārat*).

(*b*) Religious rites. Muharram, thirteen days, but if pressed for time ten days; Ākhirī-chār-shamba, a day and a half; Bārah-wafāt, a day and a half; Dastgīr kī gyārahwīn, one day; Zinda Shāh Madār kā 'urs, a day and a half; Qādir ka 'urs, a day and a half, but only one day to those at a distance from his shrine, who merely perform the rite of lamp-lighting (*chirāghan*, *charāghan*) in his name; Maulā 'Ali kā 'urs, a day and a half; Sha'bān kī 'Īd, two and a half days; Ramazān kī 'Īd, in the month Shawwāl, deserves no leave; Bandā Nawāz kā Chirāghan, one day; Baqar 'Īd, two days.

[1] Lane, *ME*. ii. 211.

CHAPTER X

THE FOUNDATIONS OF ISLĀM

ISLĀM, 'resignation to the will of God', denotes the religion taught by Muhammad, the Prophet. In it is included the observance of five primary duties (*'ibādat*): bearing witness that there is but one God; reciting daily prayers in His honour; giving the legal alms; observing the feast of Ramazān; making the pilgrimage to the holy places at least once in the lifetime of the worshipper. Other definitions of these duties include: the recital of the Kalima or Creed; Namāz or prayer; Roza or fasting; Zakāt or almsgiving; Hajj or pilgrimage.[1] In Persia they are understood to include six obligations incumbent on every believer: Salāt [2] or prayer; Sā'im or fasting; Hajj or pilgrimage; Khams, tithes, literally 'a fifth part'; Zakāt or alms; and, under certain circumstances, the necessity of the Jihād or war against the infidels.[3] Imān or belief includes six principles: belief in God, in His angels, in His books, in His apostles, in the Last Day, in predestination by God. 'Amal or practice includes: recital of the Creed; prayer at the five stated periods during the day; the observance of the Ramazān feast; the pilgrimage; the legal alms. An Indian Musalmān writer states that the chief articles of the Faith are: belief in the Unity of God; in His angels; in His books, these including with the Muhammadan the Christian and Jewish scriptures, the followers of the two latter religions being known as Ahlu-l-kitāb, 'believers in the books'; in His prophets; in His government of the

[1] The lesser pilgrimage (*'umra*), contrasted with the greater pilgrimage (*hajj*), is confined to the special rites at Mecca, which are meritorious, but not equal to the Hajj. Hajj means 'a festival, visit to a shrine' (*ERE*. i. 668).

[2] The word *salāt* was borrowed from Jewish or Christian sources (Margoliouth, *Mohammed*, 102).

[3] Browne, *A Year amongst the Persians*, 464. On the obligation of the Jihād see Hughes, 243 ff.; *ERE*. vii. 880 f.

world; in good and evil as coming from Him; in the Day of Resurrection.[1] Dīn, another important term, has a wide range of meanings which may be summed up as 'practical religion'.

The Musalmān Creed (*Kalimatu-sh-shahādat*) runs: Lā ilāha illā 'illāhu: Muhammadan Rasūlu 'llāh, 'There is no God but Allāh: Muhammad is the Apostle of God.'

Sunnīs generally offer prayer in a mosque (*masjid*), usually under the guidance of an Imām[2] or leader, if such a person can be procured. Shī'as usually offer their prayers alone. The presence of a learned man is highly desirable, but if they cannot find one they pray alone. Almost every Shī'a keeps a piece of the sacred earth of Karbalā (*khāk-i-Karbalā*), a city in Al-'Irāq, the scene of the martyrdom of Husain, upon which they place their foreheads when they offer prayer.

Sunnīs observe the prescribed forms of prayer, as described below. The Shī'a prays three times: Fajr before sunrise; at noon when he repeats the Zuhr and 'Asr prayers, and at sunset when he says the Maghrib and 'Ishā prayers. Some of them also say the Tahajjud or midnight prayer. Bohrās 'in prayer differ from both Sunnīs and Shī'as, in that they follow their Mullā, praying aloud after him, but without much regularity of posture. The times for commencing their devotions are about five minutes later than those observed by Sunnīs. After the midday and sunset supplications they allow a short interval to elapse, remaining in the mosque meanwhile. They then commence the afternoon and evening prayers, and thus run four services into one.'[3] A clear distinction is marked between Du'ā, or private supplication, and the Salāt, or liturgical mosque service. According to some authorities prayer should not be said in a bath, as it is the resort of the Jinn. It is, however, usually the custom to recite the Ruku'tain or 'two-bow' prayer after religious ablution in the hot weather, but this is improper (*makrūh*), without being sinful, to the members of the Hanafī sect.[4]

[1] *BG.* ix, part 2, 126; Sale, *Korān, Preliminary Discourse*, 50 f.

[2] The Imām is the Khalīfa, or substitute for the Prophet, or for Allāh (*ERE.* vii. 878 f.).

[3] *Census Report*, Berar, 1881, p. 70 f.

[4] Burton, *Pilgrimage*, i. 70.

The Farz or obligatory prayers may be said in any place however impure, but the Sunnat or traditionary and the Nafl or supererogatory prayers are improper, though not actually unlawful, if said in certain places. The terms imposing duties are: 'forbidden' (*harām*); 'required' (*farz, wājib*); 'recommended' (*mandūb, mustahabb*); 'indifferent' (*mubāh*); 'disliked' (*makrūh*).

The following are the times of prayer: i. Fajr kī namāz, Salātu-l-fajr, or morning prayer, is said from 5 a.m. to sunrise. Should this hour unavoidably pass without prayer having been offered, the same prayers should be said at any other convenient time; and although the same blessing will not attend a prayer that has been omitted at the proper time, it should nevertheless be said, and not altogether neglected. ii. Zuhr kī namāz, Salātu-z-zuhr, Namāz-i-peshīn, or midday prayer, between 1 and 3 p.m. iii. 'Asr kī namāz, Salātu-l-'asr, Namāz-i-dīgar, or afternoon prayer, from 4 to 4.30 p.m., or till sunset. iv. Maghrib kī namāz, Salātu-l-maghrib, Namāz-i-shām, or sunset prayer, at 6 p.m. or immediately after sunset. This is of special importance, and it should not be delayed beyond that time. v. 'Ishā kī namāz, Salātu-l-'ishā, Namāz-i-khuftan, or prayer when night has closed, at bed-time, between 8 p.m. and midnight. Should a person, however, be unavoidably kept awake by business or amusement beyond that period, he may say the prayers any time before daybreak. Members of the Hanafī sect wait till the whiteness and red gleams of the west have totally disappeared, and the other three orthodox sects wait only till the ruddy light has waned.[1]

The above five times of prayer are obligatory (*farz*). Besides these there are others known as 'traditional' (*sunnat*) and 'supererogatory' (*nafl*), which are observed by more religious and devout persons: Salātu-l-'ishrāq, Namāz-i-'ishrāq, 'Ishrāq kī namāz, about 7.30 a.m.; Salātu-z-zuhā, Namāz-i-chasht, Zuhā kī namāz, before noon, from 9 to 11 a.m., or, if there be not leisure, at any time before sunset; Salātu-t-tahajjud, Namāz-i-tahajjud, Tahajjud kī namāz, at midnight or at any time before daybreak; Namāz-i-tarāwīh, prayers of

[1] Burton, *AN*. xi. 99.

rest, sometimes applied to the prayer said daily at 8 a.m., but more particularly to prayer, usually of twenty bows, recited at night during the month Ramazān. It is so called because the congregation sit down and rest after every four genuflections and every second Salutation or Salām.[1]

Many are the blessings promised to those who fast during Ramazān, the ninth month. Among others the Prophet, Muhammad Mustafā, 'The Chosen',—on whom be the Peace!—has said that only those who fast will be privileged at the Last Day to enter Raiyān, 'one whose thirst is quenched', one of the eight doors of Paradise, and that the effluvium proceeding from the mouth of him that fasts is more grateful to God than the odour of roses, ambergris, or musk. During the fast eating, drinking, and sexual congress are forbidden, as well as the use of betel leaves, tobacco, or snuff. If, however, the observance of any of these rules be inadvertently neglected, the fast still holds good. But if neglected intentionally the offender must expiate his guilt by the manumission of one male slave (*ghulām*) for every day that he broke the fast. This rule is now obsolete since the abolition of slavery in British India.[2] If he cannot afford to do this he must feed sixty beggars, and if that likewise be beyond his means he must, independently of fasting during the month Ramazān, fast for sixty days together, any time after, for every day that he has broken the fast. And he must add one day for the day he broke it; then and then only will he receive the reward of the fast.

Those who observe this fast breakfast between the hours of 2 and 4 a.m., this meal being called Sahār, Sahārgāhī, 'daybreak', and take food in the evening immediately after evening prayer. During the time appointed for this fast, kettledrums (*naqqāra*) are beaten in the mosque, and in large cities the royal band (*naubat*) plays to give warning to those who fast that they should rise and eat. During that time

[1] *Mishkāt*, i. 277 ff.; Hughes, 628.

[2] Slavery, as far as established by law, was abolished in India by Act V, 1843, but the final blow was dealt on January 1, 1862, when the sections of the Indian Penal Code dealing with the question came into operation (Sleeman, *Rambles*, 282; Balfour, *Cyclopaedia of India*, iii. 672 ff.).

some Faqīrs come to Musalmān houses, beg and recite verses of admonition and advice to wake people from their sleep. When the house people rise they give them something to eat, and at the hearing of the Friday sermon or bidding prayer (*khutba*) they give them, according to their means, a rupee or two and some clothes. On the first day of Shawwāl, the tenth month, comes the Ramazān kī 'Īd, or Ramazān celebration, when every one who fasts before going to the place of prayer (*'īdgāh*) should make the customary fast offering (*roza kī fitrat*), which consists in distributing among a few Faqīrs some 5 lb. of wheat or other grain, dates, and fruit. For until a man has distributed these gifts or the equivalent in money, the Almighty will keep his fasting suspended between Heaven and Earth. These gifts must be given by the head of the house for himself and each member of his family, slaves not excepted, but not for his wife or grown-up sons, since the former should give them out of her marriage portion, and the latter from their own earnings. It is the divine command to give alms (*zakāt*),[1] a word meaning 'purification', annually of five things: money, cattle, grain, fruit, merchandise, provided these things have been in the possession of the giver for a complete year. The duty is not incumbent on a man who owes debts equal to or exceeding the whole amount of his property, nor is it due on the necessaries of life, such as dwelling-houses, clothes, furniture, cattle kept for daily use, slaves employed as servants, armour or weapons for present use, books of science or theology, or tools used by craftsmen.[2]

The rates are as follows: The Sāhib-i-nisāb, or owner of an estate of Rs. 80, pays 1 in 40, or 2½ per cent.; an owner of cattle, such as sheep or goats, need give no alms till they number 40; from 40 to 120 inclusive, one sheep or goat; 121 to 200, two animals; above that a sheep or goat for every 100. Alms on cattle are: from 5 to 25, one sheep or goat; 26 to 35, a yearling female camel; 36 to 45, a two-year-old ditto; 46 to 60, a three-year-old ditto; 61 to 75, a four-year-

[1] See Hughes, 699; Baillie, 555.

[2] Alms were given from the earliest period in Islām, but the yearly tribute was prescribed when the State was organized (Margoliouth, *Mohammed*, 413).

old ditto ; 76 to 90, a two-year-old ditto ; 91 to 120, a three-year-old ditto ; 121 and upwards, a two-year-old female camel for every 40, or a three-year-old female for every 50. In the case of cows and bullocks : if he possesses 30 cows, a one-year-old calf ; 40, a two-year-old ditto ; and so on, a one-year-old beast for every 10. Should he possess 1,000 cows, taking their average term of life at 14 or 15 years, as many cows are to be given as will, by their combined ages, make up 100 years. The alms for buffaloes, male or female, are the same as that for sheep. For horses the rate is like that for camels, or instead of that the Traditions direct that a dīnār, or denarius, which should be worth about half-a-sovereign, but varies in value and does not now represent any current coin,[1] is to be given for every horse the value of which exceeds Rs. 100. No alms need be given for riding-horses or for beasts of burden. For grain and fruits planted in land watered only by the rain, one-tenth part ; if irrigated from a tank or well, one-twentieth part. For articles of merchandise, provided the owner is Sāhib-i-nisāb, or well-to-do, the rate on capital and profits is 1 in 40 ; for gold bullion half a misqāl, the Roman aureus and gold dīnār of 73 grains,[2] for every 20 misqāl weight ; for silver bullion 2½ per cent. provided it exceeds the weight of a rupee, 1 tolā, 3 drachms, or 179 grains ; for minerals, if the value be upwards of 240 dirhams, each worth about 5*d.*, a fifth is to be given, and if the capital is invested in business, alms are to be given on the profits.[3]

The legal alms may be given to the following classes : pilgrims who are unable to defray the cost of their journey ; Faqīrs and beggars ; debtors unable to pay their debts ; champions in the cause of God ; travellers who are without food ; proselytes to Islām. It is only the very poorest of these classes who are entitled to the grant, religious mendicants never accepting any provision of this kind. Alms are not to be given to Sayyids, unless they particularly desire assistance, nor to the rich, to near relations, or to slaves. It is considered

[1] Yule-Burnell, *Hobson-Jobson*, 2nd ed. 317 f.

[2] Ibid. 568.

[3] Baillie, 554 ff. ; Hughes, 699 f. ; Sell, 218 ff. ; Sale, *Korān*, *Preliminary Discourse*, 79.

disgraceful for Sayyids, descendants of the Prophet, to beg, but there is a class of Sayyid beggars in Gujarāt.[1]

It is incumbent on Sunnīs, both men and women, to undertake the pilgrimage to Mecca and Mount 'Arafāt, Shī'as to Karbalā or Mashhadu-l-Husain and Mazār-i-sharīf in Afghān Turkistān, the burial place of 'Alī, at least once during their lives, provided they have means to pay their expenses and maintain their families in their absence. He who makes pilgrimage for God and does not talk loosely or act wickedly shall return free from faults as on the day when he was born. If he be of the Hanafī sect he may appoint a deputy in case he desires to make the pilgrimage but is prevented through sickness or by fear of an enemy. Or if a rich man or prince, without any excuse, sends another person to perform the pilgrimage on his behalf, he gains the merit of it. A woman going on pilgrimage must have a guardian (*mahram*)—her father, brother, husband, son, or some relation within the prohibited degrees. Though the poor are not obliged to perform the journey, many families go to the holy places in bounty (*faiz-i-billāh*) ships, on which charitable people supply them with food, drink, and a couple of pieces of cloth, each five cubits long, transport them thither and bring them back. In recent years the British Government has taken measures to ensure the comfort and safety of pilgrims by supervising the transport service, providing rest-houses and hospitals at Jeddah, and by appointing representatives to assist travellers.

On arriving near Mecca, or while still on board, the pilgrim (*hājī*, *hājjī*) assumes the pilgrim dress (*ihrām*), consisting of two new cotton cloths, each 6 feet long by 3½ broad, with narrow red stripes and fringes, one (*ridā'*) thrown over the back, exposing the arm and shoulder, knotted at the right side, the other (*izār*) wrapped round the loins from the waist to the knees or tucked in at the middle. When Sultān Khwāja was appointed by Akbar Mīr Hājī or pilgrim-leader, the Emperor, by way of joining the pilgrimage which he was never able to perform, stripped himself, put on the dress (*ihrām*) and walked some steps with the Khwāja.[2] In the time of the Prophet the circuit of the Ka'ba was made in

[1] Hughes, 700; *BG* part 2, 8. [2] Elliot-Dowson, v. 401.

a state of nudity, or in clothes borrowed from one of the religious communities of the holy city. Musalmāns explain the custom of using a special dress on the ground that they cannot perform the rite in clothes stained by sin, but the real reason is different. It was because the pilgrim's own clothes became taboo by contact with the holy place and function; he could not wear them again, but he was obliged to leave them at the gate of the sanctuary, hence the name *ihrām*, root *haram*, meaning 'sacred' or 'taboo'.[1] On the day the pilgrim assumes this new dress he bathes, recites a two-bow prayer, and puts on the two wrappers without seam, the head being left uncovered. He may wear wooden shoes (*kharāūn*). He must wear these two garments until he has sacrificed the victim at Minā, and has shaved and bathed.

The pilgrim must submit to certain taboos. He must avoid quarrels, immorality, bad language, light conversation; he must not kill game, cause a bird to fly, or even point it out for destruction; he may scratch himself only with his open palm lest vermin may be destroyed, or a hair be uprooted by the nails; he must spare trees and not pluck a blade of grass, abstain from the use of oils, perfumes, and unguents, from washing his head with mallow or lote leaves, from dyeing, shaving, cutting or plucking out a single pile or hair, from wearing clothes that are sewn, and, for the same reason, boots; shade may be enjoyed, but the head remains uncovered. The prohibition against killing animals does not apply to noxious creatures, such as a kite, crow, scorpion, mouse, or mad dog. For each violation of these rules a sheep must be sacrificed. Should a person after assuming the pilgrim habit indulge in sexual intercourse or even kiss his wife, the whole merit of the pilgrimage will be lost.[2] There are four stages (*mīqāt*) at which the habit must necessarily be assumed; on the Medīna road, Zū-l-halīfā; on the 'Irāq road, Zātu-'arq; on the Syrian road, Hujfa; on the Najd road, Qarn; on the Yemen road, Yalamlam.[3] Some put on

[1] R. Smith, *Religion of Semites*, 451; *ERE*. v. 65; Crawley, 88.

[2] On the rule of continence in holy places, see R. Smith, *op. cit.*, 45 ff., 481 ff.; cf. Herodotus, ii. 64.

[3] *Mishkāt*, i. 601; Hughes, 156.

the sacred habit, by which is properly meant the interdiction of all worldly enjoyments, a month or a fortnight before they reach Mecca, while others defer it to the last day or two, each one according to his powers of self-denial.

Immediately on their arrival at Mecca the pilgrims perform the minor ablution (*wuzū*ʻ) and proceed to the Masjidu-l-harām, or the Sacred Mosque, and kiss the Hajaru-l-aswad or Black Stone, which is said to be an aerolite. Then they make a circuit of the Ka‘ba, the ‘ Cube ’, seven times, presenting the left shoulder to the sacred building,[1] the first three circuits being with the pas gymnastique (*harwala*), or quick step, and four times by the limping pace (*tarammul*), moving the shoulders as if walking in deep sand.[2] The Ka‘ba is a square building, situated in the centre of the Baitu-l-lāh, or House of God. The rain water which falls on its terrace flows through the ‘ water-spout of pity ’ (*mizābu-r-rahma*) on to the grave of Ismāīl or Ishmael, where pilgrims stand struggling to catch it. In the corner of the Ka‘ba is the Alabaster Stone (*ruknu-l-yamanī*) where pilgrims extend their arms, press their bodies against the building, and beg pardon for their sins.[3] Then they go to the Station of Abraham (*qadam-i-Ibrāhīm*), a stone bearing the impression of the feet of the patriarch, repeat a two-bow prayer, and retiring kiss the Black Stone again. This stone is said to have been originally white, but by the constant touching and kissing of it by pilgrims it has become black. It is set in silver, fixed in the wall of the Ka‘ba ; it is said to float in water, and whoever kisses it obtains forgiveness of his manifold transgressions, yea they fall from him as the withered leaves fall off the trees in autumn. On the ninth day of the pilgrimage the pilgrims perform the rite of running between the hills Safā and Marwa seven times. On reaching the top of each hill they stand for a few minutes with open hands raised to Heaven, and suppli-

[1] Hindus perform the circumambulation of a sacred place (*pradakshina*) in the reverse way, moving in the direction of the hands of a clock. For an account of the Ka‘ba, see Margoliouth, *Mohammed*, 386 ; *ERE*. viii. 511 ff.

[2] Burton, *Pilgrimage*, ii. 167. This is an ancient religious rite, as the priests of Baal limped round the altar, 1 Kings xviii. 26, R.V. margin.

[3] Burton, *Pilgrimage*, ii. 303.

cate the Almighty for whatever their hearts desire, for their prayers at this time will undoubtedly be heard and answered.

The origin of this custom is as follows: When Hagar, Bībī Hājar, brought forth Ismāīl—on whom be the Peace!—in the wilderness of Mecca, there being no water or dwelling there, she in her distress left the babe, ran frantically from hill to hill in search of water and frequently returned lest the child should be devoured by jackals, dogs, or foxes. Meanwhile the child as he was crying chanced to strike his heel against the ground, when water gushed out of the sand. Hājar made a sort of well and purified herself and the child by bathing in it. This is now the holy well Zamzam, called in Arabic Bīr-i-Zamzam and in Persian Chāh-i-Zamzam, *zamzam* meaning 'a confused noise of waters'. Pilgrims on their return bring some of the water with them in gugglets, bottles, or in cotton steeped in it. On breaking the Ramazān fast they drink a little of this water, or squeeze the cotton into common water in order that their sins may be forgiven, and apply a little to their eyes to strengthen their sight. They also drink it at other times as a meritorious act, and when they cannot procure much of it they dilute it with common water and drink it. It is likewise administered to the dying, either pure or made into lemonade. It is said that if anybody finds difficulty in pronouncing Arabic he has only to sip a little of this water and it will immediately become easy. The well at Medīna, also called Zamzam, is known as the Bīr-al-Nabī, or 'the Apostle's well'. Another reason is also given for the running between Safā and Marwa. It is said that in the old time a man and a woman were turned into stone for committing fornication within the temple. The Quraish tribe placed one of them on Mount Safā, the other on Mount Marwa, and used to worship them. The Prophet—on whom be the Peace!—not approving of this practice, forbade it, but finding that his order was not observed he permitted the people to visit these hills in the hope that this example of God's vengeance would deter others from committing a similar crime.[1]

[1] The extreme hurry and noise must originally have possessed some magical meaning (*ERE*. x. 9).

On the 8th day of the month Zū-l-hijja or Zī-l-hijja,[1] the last month of the Musalmān year, the pilgrims assemble at Minā, where they recite prayers and spend the night. On the 9th day of this month, the festival of the Baqar 'Īd, before they go to Mount 'Arafāt to read the prayers with the Imām, they recite two two bow prayers in the name of each of their relations, except their father, because no one can be sure who was his father, and friends dead and living, supplicating the Almighty to vouchsafe a blessing on them. After the morning prayer they rush impetuously towards Jabalu-l-'Arafāt, 12 miles due east of Mecca, where having recited two bow prayers with the Imām and having heard the sermon or bidding prayer (*khutba*) they remain on the hill till sunset, and then run quickly to Al-Mazdalifa, 'the approacher', where they recite the evening prayer and stay all night.[2]

Next morning, the 10th, they start for Minā. On their arrival at the Mashar-al-harām, 'the place dedicated to religious rites', they stop and offer up supplications to God. Before sunrise they proceed quickly by the way of Satan, 'the Troubler', Batu-l-Muhassar, till they come to the place called Jamrat-al-Akaba, *jamra* meaning 'pelting', or Shaitān-al-kabīr, 'the Great Devil', the latter being the name of one of the pillars, the others being called Wasta, 'Central Place', and Al-Aula, 'First Place'. At each of these three pillars they pick up seven small stones or pebbles, and having recited a prayer and blown upon them, they fling them at the pillars. This rite is known as Ramyu-r-rijām or Ramyu-l-jimār, 'the throwing of the pebbles'. As they fling the pebbles they say, 'In the name of God, the Almighty, I do this, and in hatred to the Devil and his shame!'[3]

The origin of this rite is as follows: As His Highness the Prophet Abraham—upon whom be the Peace!—was taking

[1] 'The owner of pilgrimages', known also as Tarwiya, 'satisfying thirst'; Zū-l-qa'da, the eleventh month, meaning 'owner of truce', no warfare being allowed (*Encyclopaedia Islām*, i. 959).

[2] Burton, *Pilgrimage*, ii. 181, 186 ff.

[3] The throwing of the pebbles is a symbol of throwing away the sins of the pilgrimage, and a charm against punishment and misfortune (*ERE*. x. 10); and see Frazer, *GB*., The Scapegoat, 23.

his son Ismāīl to Mecca to sacrifice him,[1] Satan—curses be on him !—appeared to Ismāīl in human form and said, 'Boy, thy father is leading thee to sacrifice thee to idols, do not consent to go'. Ismāīl immediately informed his father who replied, 'O my child ! this is none other than the accursed Devil himself who comes to tempt and deceive thee ; do thou repeat the invocation "Lā haula wa lā quwwata illā bi' l-lāhi 'l-'alīya-l-'azīm", "There is no strength and power save in Allāh, the High, the Great !" and cast stones at him, when he will instantly depart'. After this fashion Satan appeared at three places, and each time Ismāīl repeated the 'Lā haula', and flung pebbles at him. Hence arose the custom that pilgrims at these places repeat 'Lā haula', and fling the stones.

After flinging the pebbles in these three places the pilgrims go to Minā to perform the sacrifice (*qurbānī*), which persons wealthy enough to be responsible for the payment of the legal alms (*zakāt*) are required to perform. They must offer a ram or a he-goat for each member, old or young, of their family, or for every seven persons a camel or a cow. The flesh of the victims is divided into three portions : one for the relatives of the giver of the sacrifice, one distributed among Faqīrs, the third reserved for the use of the giver.

The origin of this sacrifice is thus told : When Abraham—on whom be the Peace !—founded Mecca, the Lord desired him to prepare a feast for Him. When Abraham, Khalīlu-llāh, 'the Friend of God', asked what he desired, the Lord answered, 'Offer up thy son Ismāīl'. In accordance with this order Abraham took Ismāīl to the Ka'ba to sacrifice him, and having laid him down he made ineffectual attempts to slay him. Then Ismāīl said, 'Thine eyes being uncovered, it is through compassion for me that thou causest the knife to miss my throat. Blindfold thyself with the end of thy turban and then slay me'. Abraham wondering at the boy's fortitude and wisdom

[1] Though there is evidence in the Korān (xxxvii. 101) that Abraham intended to sacrifice Isaac, not Ishmael, both Sunnīs and Shī'as believe that Ishmael was the selected victim ; see Sale's note on the above passage in the Korān ; Hughes, 216 ; Hastings, *Dict. Bible*, iii. 437 ; *Encyclopaedia Biblica*, iii. 3200 f.

pronounced a blessing upon him and did as he said. Repeating the words 'Bi-'ismi 'llāhi 'l-akbar!' 'In the name of Allāh, the Great!' he drew the knife across his son's throat. In the meantime, however, the Archangel Gabriel, snatching Ismāīl from under the blade, substituted a broad-tailed sheep in his stead. Abraham on opening his eyes saw to his surprise the sheep slain, and his son standing beside him. Then he and his son joined in prayer, blessed God for His mercy and recited a two-bow prayer which every one going to Mecca is commanded to recite.

After the sacrifice the pilgrims get themselves shaved,[1] their nails pared, the cuttings of both being buried there. They bathe, take off the pilgrim habit, and consider the pilgrimage finished. The shaving and bathing at Minā are carried out with difficulty owing to the scarcity of water and barbers. Rich people out of charity get the poorer pilgrims shaved and bathed at their expense. A thorough shaving or hair-cutting is not necessary, a stroke or two of the razor, and a little hair clipped with a pair of scissors being sufficient. In bathing also it is enough if a cup of water be thrown over the head, or if water cannot be procured, purification (*tayammum*, 'intending to do a thing') with sand or dust is enough.

At the Minā market large quantities of goods are sold, and pilgrims say that the merchants are so absorbed in business that they have no leisure for devotion, and that with the view of protecting their goods they remain in their shops and omit to perform the rites. The day after the Aiyām-i-nahr, or day of sacrifice, pilgrims remain at Minā, and hence that day is called Aiyāmu-l-qarr, 'the Day of Rest'. Some halt there till the 11th, 12th, and 13th day of the month, and these are called 'Days of Communion' (*tashrīk*). On leaving they revisit the Ka'ba to take final leave of it, on their way throwing pebbles at the pillars as they pass them, and then

[1] When Burton made the pilgrimage he was shaved at Marwa. After being shaved the pilgrims throw the skirts of their garments over their heads, to show that the ihrām, or taboo robe, has now become *ihlāl*, or normal (*Pilgrimage*, ii. 246). The shaving implies union with the Deity, a sign that some sacrifice or other religious rite has been performed (R. Smith, *op. cit.*, 331). The hair is buried to prevent its use in Black Magic.

perform the final circuit as already described. After the circuit of the Ka'ba it is necessary to proceed to Medīna and visit the tomb of Muhammad Mustafā, 'The Chosen',—on whom be the Peace! The legend told by Christian writers, but unknown to Muslim tradition, that the tomb is suspended in the air by means of magnets, is a modern invention, probably due to the incorrect perspective of the popular engravings of it.[1] He that performs the circuit of the Ka'ba and does not visit Medīna defeats the object of his pilgrimage.

I learn, says the author, from my esteemed friends of the Maulavī, Mashāikh and Hāfiz classes, that some pilgrims from Hindostān go so far in their reverence for the holy tomb of the Prophet as to make prostration (*sijda*) before it, and do the respectful bows (*taslīm, kornish*) at it. The Arab attendants (*khādim*) resent this, and tell them that since the Prophet has not commanded that any should prostrate themselves before him, such worship being due to God alone, their worship is improper. Some foolish people, too, at the Muharram festival prostrate themselves before the cenotaphs and standards, as also before the tombs of Apostles or Saints. This only shows their ignorance and folly, because if it be improper to pay such homage to the Prophet, it is equally so in the case of his inferiors. It is the duty, however, of the Mashāikh or holy men to make the bow of salutation (*sijda tahīyat*) to the Prophet, of the Murshid or spiritual guide to his parents, of slaves to their masters, and of subjects to their king. This bow of salutation consists in stooping forward, as in the bow prayers while in the sitting posture with the knees touching the ground, the hands tightly closed on the ground, and in that position the extended thumb of the superior should be kissed.

Few Shī'as ever perform the pilgrimage, for two reasons, first, because on Mount 'Arafāt, after the sermon and adoration to God and praise of the Prophet, they praise the three Companions, Abū Bakr, the first Khalīfa, known as Siddīq-i-akbar, 'the veracious, the very great', 'Umar, the second Khalīfa, known as 'Ādil, 'the just', 'Usmān, the third Khalīfa, known as Ghanī, 'independent' or Zū-n-nūrain, because he married

[1] E. Gibbon, *Decline and Fall*, ed. W. Smith, vi. 262.

two of the Prophet's daughters, Ruqaiya and Ummu Kulsūm —may God reward them!—and lastly, 'Alī-um-murtazā, 'the chosen'—may God reward him! This is so displeasing to Shī'as that some refuse to go on the pilgrimage. They would have it that 'Alī should be praised first. Besides this Shī'as refuse to recognize six other Companions—Tulha, Sa'īd, Sa'd, Abū 'Ubaida, Zubair, and Abdu-r-rahmān bin 'Auf.[1] They cannot bear to utter the names of these six last Companions, and should they do so they would be obliged to recite the Fātiha at their tombs. These six with the preceding four formed the ten Companions who followed the example of the Prophet when, at the desire of the Archangel Gabriel, he turned his face in prayer from Jerusalem towards the west to Mecca, and of whom the Prophet declared that they had by this act secured Heaven for themselves. Secondly, because on entering the Ka'ba every one is asked to what sect (*jamā'at*) he belongs, the Sunnīs alone being admitted to the sanctuary. Some Shī'as, however, gain admission by concealing their sect and calling themselves Sunnīs. But they never venture near the illustrious Medīna, because there near the tomb of His Highness Muhammad Mustafā—on whom be the blessing!—are those of Abū Bakr as-Siddīq and 'Umar-i-farūqī, 'the Discriminator between truth and falsehood'—may God reward them!

Many Musalmāns live for years in the joyful anticipation of being able some day to perform the circuit of the Ka'ba; nay, very many never dismiss the idea from their minds. Much has been said on the many blessings attending the pilgrimage. Amongst other things it is said that for every step a man takes towards the Ka'ba he has a sin blotted out, and that hereafter he will be highly exalted. If a man happens to die on the way to Mecca he obtains the rank of a martyr (*shahīd*, literally 'present as a witness'), the reward of the pilgrimage being instantly recorded in the Book of Remembrance.

The souls of the martyrs (*shuhadā*) are stowed away in the

[1] The Companions, known as Ashāb or Sahāba, were partly leaders (*naqīb*) from Medīna, partly leaders of expeditions. See the list in *EB*. xvii. 410.

crops of green birds till Resurrection Day, eating of the fruits and drinking of the streams of Paradise.[1] There are many modes of death which raise the dead to the rank of martyrs: if a man dies in the act of reading the Korān, in the act of praying, in the act of fasting, on a pilgrimage to Mecca, on the Friday Sabbath, in defence of the Faith, as a result of religious meditation, if he be executed for speaking the truth, if he suffer death at the hands of a tyrant or oppressor with patience and submission, if he be killed in defending his own property, if a woman die in labour or in child-bed, if a man be slain by robbers, devoured by a tiger, killed by the kick of a horse, struck dead by lightning, burnt to death, buried under the ruins of a wall, drowned, killed by a fall from a precipice or down a dry well or pit, and if he meet death by apoplexy or sunstroke.

[1] *Korān*, ii. 149.

CHAPTER XI

PRAYER

If any of the greater ablutions (*ghusl*) be required, they must be performed before prayer.[1] Should this be not necessary, at each time of prayer the worshipper must perform the minor ablution (*wuzū'*), which frees the worshipper from impurity (*hadas, nāpākī*), for this is the command of God. The rule of lustration was perhaps prescribed at Mecca, but however that may be it was obviously borrowed from the Jews, with whose teaching the ordinances established by the Prophet respecting ceremonial impurity and ablutions closely correspond.[2]

In the minor ablution the Prophet used to wash both his hands as far as the wrist, each twice ; then he put water into his mouth, blew his nose, after throwing water into it, thrice ; then he washed his face thrice ; then both his arms from the tips of the fingers up to the elbows ; then drew both his hands, still wet, from the forehead to the rear of the head and then back again.[3] The present method follows the traditional rule. First, the teeth must be thoroughly cleansed with dentifrice (*manjan*) or with the tooth-stick (*miswāk*). Then having washed both hands as far up as the wrists three times and gargled thrice, water must be snuffed up each nostril thrice, and the cavities must be cleansed by introducing the little finger of the left hand. Hence the rule that the left hand, which is used in this and other modes of ablution, must not be employed in taking food. Then taking up water in both hands the face must be well washed three times, from the upper part of the forehead to the chin, including the beard,

[1] See 'Holiness, Uncleanness, and Taboo', R. Smith, *Religion of the Semītes*, 446 ff. ; *ERE*. x. 496 ff. ; Burton, *AN*. iv. 153.

[2] Hastings, *Dict. Bible*, iv. 825 ff. ; *Encyclopaedia Biblica*, i. 536 ff. On Musalmān prayer, *ERE*. x. 197 ff.

[3] *Korān*, v. 9 ; *Mishkāt*, i. 91 f. ; Lane, *ME*. i. 85 ff.

and from ear to ear. After this the arms are washed, from the ends of the fingers up to the elbows, first the right, then the left. Then a little water is poured into the palms of the hands, and made to flow along the forearms three times. It must be borne in mind that each operation is repeated thrice, whereas the wiping (*mash*) is done only once. The wiping is thus done. The right hand slightly wetted in water is drawn over a quarter, half, or the whole of the head. Then, if the worshipper has a long beard and whiskers, he takes a little water separately, wets and combs the hair with the fingers of his right hand, in the case of the beard moving them with the palm facing downwards from the lower and back to the upper and front of it. Then putting the tips of the forefingers into each ear he twists the fingers round when the thumbs are behind the ears, and rubs them along the back part of the ear cartilages from below upwards, bringing them round the top. With the back of the fingers of both hands touching the neck he draws them from behind forwards. After that the inside of the left hand and fingers is drawn along the outside of the right arm from the tips of the fingers to the elbows, and the same operation is gone through on the other arm with the hands reversed. The hands are clasped together, the palms necessarily touching each other. This concludes the wiping. After that the feet and ankles are washed, first the right, then the left. This concludes the minor ablution. Lastly, the water that remains in the vessels (*lotā*, *badhnā*) used, in which they usually take the amount of water required, is drunk with the face turned to the Qibla or Mecca, which is considered a meritorious act. These different ablutions are accompanied by a number of supplications detailed in the sacred *Mishkāt*,[1] but owing to their length they have been omitted.

The observance of this minor ablution is of great efficacy, for the Prophet has declared that the countenance, hands, and feet of him who purifies himself for prayer will at the Day of Judgement be recognized among the crowd by their shining in all the effulgence of the full moon. 'Verily my sect will be called towards Paradise on the Day of Resurrection

[1] i. 99 ff.; Lane, *ME*. i. 85 ff.

with bright faces, hands, and feet; then he amongst you who has power to increase the brightness of his face, let him do so.'[1] According to the Shafāī doctrine, ablutions are lawful only if performed in running water, and hence in the time of Shāhjahān a canal was dug at Siālkot to provide it.[2] It is not necessary to perform the greater ablution each time when one goes to prayer, but only when the body has been defiled in any one of the following ways: by obeying a call of nature, *crepitus ventris*, discharge of blood or matter in any part of the body, vomiting, sleeping, fainting, loud or immoderate laughter during prayer, and *coitus*.[3] Any of these is enough to defile a man, and then ablution is required before prayer.

If on account of illness a person cannot use water in either the greater or minor ablution, he may use earth for the purpose of purification (*tayammum*, 'betaking oneself' to dust). If water be at a great distance, in a well from which there is no means of drawing it, if in procuring it there is risk of life, if water be scarce and a neighbour be dying of thirst—under these circumstances any one who does the water ablution and does not give the water to him who needs it is in danger of the Divine wrath. All the circumstances mentioned above which necessitate the water ablution apply also to the earth purification, and the virtue of the latter ceases on the sight of water. The earth purification (*tayammum*) is done in this way: the person recites a vow in Arabic: 'I vow by this act of earth purification, which I substitute for the greater and minor ablution, as the case may be, that I purify myself for prayer by cleansing my body from all filth and corruption'. Repeating this he claps his open hand on sand or dust, shakes off the dust, draws his hands over his face, again claps his hand on the sand or dust, draws the left hand over the right, and in like manner the right over the left. The practice is authorized in the Korān: 'And if ye have become unclean, then purify yourselves. But if ye are sick or on a journey, or if one of you come from the place of retirement, or if ye have touched women, and ye find no

[1] *Mishkāt*, i. 72. [2] Rose, i. 498.
[3] Crawley, 200 f.

water, then take clean sand and rub your faces and your hands with it '.[1]

It was the command of the Prophet to proclaim the summons (*azān, bāng*) to prayer, at the five seasons, as a warning to the people of the will of God and as an exhortation to them to flee for salvation. The call must be listened to with the utmost reverence; if a person be walking at the time he should stand still, if lying down he should sit up, and he should reply to the call of the Muazzin or crier by some appropriate ejaculation, such as 'Labbaik da' watu-l-Haqq', 'Here I am awaiting God's invitation!'

'The summons to prayer was at first the simple cry, "To public prayer!" After the Qibla was changed [from Jerusalem to Mecca] Muhammad bethought himself of a more formal call. Some suggested the Jewish trumpet, others the Christian bell (*nāqūs*);[2] but neither was grateful to the Prophet's ear. The Azān or call to prayer was then established. Tradition claims for it a supernatural origin. While the matter was under discussion a citizen dreamed that he met a man clad in green raiment carrying a bell, and he sought to buy it, saying that it would do well for assembling the faithful to prayer. 'I will show thee', replied the stranger, 'a better way than that; let a crier call aloud, "Great is the Lord! Great is the Lord! I bear witness that there is no God but the Lord! I bear witness that the Prophet Muhammad is the Prophet of God! Come unto prayer! Come unto Salvation! God is Great! God is Great!"' Awaking from sleep he went straightway to Muhammad and told him the dream, when perceiving that it was a vision from the Lord, the Prophet forthwith commanded Bilāl, his negro servant, to carry out the divine behest.'[3] Ascending the roof of a lofty house near the mosque while it was quite dark, Bilāl watched for the break of day,

[1] *Korān*, v. 9.

[2] 'The Musulmāns of Hindostān consider the Nāqūs, a thin, oblong piece of wood, beaten with a flexible rod (*wabīl*) to be, and call it, the conch-shell, blown by Hindus at divine worship: they believe the Jews use this' (Author's note, but this is doubtful; see Hughes, 430).

[3] Muir, *Life*, 189; for the story of Bilāl, and for his last call to prayer, Ibid. 204, 235; Margoliouth, *Mohammed*, 222, 387.

and on the first glimmer of light, with his far-sounding voice aroused all around from their slumbers, adding to the divinely appointed call the words, 'Prayer is better than Sleep! Prayer is better than Sleep'. Musalmān tradition ascribes the dream to a youth named 'Abdu-llāh, the Kharijite, son of Zaid Ansārī, and states that at the same time the Commander of the Faithful, Amīru-l-mūminīn, 'Umar—May God reward him!—got up and said, 'O Prophet of God! I likewise saw that same thing in my dream, and I was about to inform your Holiness, when I found that 'Abdu-llāh bin Zaid had already done so'.

The manner of proclaiming the call is as follows. At the proper time for prayer that member of the congregation who comes first to the mosque (*masjid*), or a man known as the Muazzin or crier, in western India Bāngī (*bāng*, 'the call to prayer'), standing on an elevated platform (*chabūtrā*) in front of the mosque, on a pulpit (*mimbar*, *minbar*) or on a minaret (*manāra*), turning his face in the direction of the Qibla or Mecca, thrusting the points of his forefingers into his ears, and pressing his hands over them, calls out four times successively, 'God is Great!' 'Allāhu akbar!', twice; 'I certify that there is no God but the Lord!' 'Ashhadu an lā ilāha illa-llāh!' twice; 'I certify that Muhammad is the Prophet of the Lord!' Then turning to the right hand he repeats twice, 'Come to prayer', 'Hayya 'ala-s-salāti!' Then to the left twice, 'Come to salvation!' 'Hayya 'ala-l-falāh!' Then he finishes by repeating twice, 'God is Great!', 'Allāhu akbar!' Lastly, he says once, 'There is no God but the Lord!', 'Lā ilāha illa-llāh!' In the call at the early morning after the words 'Come to salvation!' is added twice, 'Prayer is better than sleep!', 'As-salātu khairun mina-n-naumi!' Shī'as make one slight alteration by adding twice the words, 'Come to the best of works!', 'Hayya 'ala khairi-l-'amali', and by repeating the last sentence of the call, 'There is no God but the Lord!' twice instead of once as in the Sunnī call. The crier having recited a supplication, ends by drawing his hands over his face. There are four classes of people for whom it is unlawful to sound the call: an unclean person, a drunkard, a woman, a madman. In some places a blind man is preferred as a crier, because he is unable to overlook the neighbouring quarters of the women from the summit of the minaret.

Prayer (*salāt, namāz*) is the second of the foundations of Islām. ' There are five prayers ordered by God, and whoever performs ablution (*wuzū*') for them properly and says them at the stated time, and exactly observes the rules and precepts regarding them, God has promised to forgive him on the Day of Resurrection '.[1]

The form of prayer is known as the bow (*rukū*', *rak'at*), the inclination of the head with the palms of the hands resting on the knees. The periods with the necessary prostrations are as follows : i. From dawn to sunrise, Salātu-l-fajr, Namāz-i-subh, Fajr kī namāz, four prostrations, two of which are ' traditional ' (*sunnat*) and two obligatory (*farz*). ii. When the sun has passed the meridian, Salātu-z-zahr, Namāz-i-peshīn, Zuhr kī Namāz, twelve prostrations, of which four are ' traditional ', four ' obligatory ', two ' voluntary ' (*nafl*). iii. Afternoon prayer, Salātu-l-'asr, Namāz-i-dīgar, 'Asr kī Namāz, eight prostrations, four recited by few (*sunnat ghair mu'aqqada*), most people reciting only the four ' obligatory '. iv. After sunset, Salātu-l-maghrib, Namāz-i-shām, Maghrib kī Namāz, seven prostrations, three ' obligatory ', two ' traditional ', and two ' voluntary '. v. When night has closed in, Salātu-l-'ishā, Namāz-i-khuftan, 'Ishā kī Namāz, seventeen prostrations, four of which are omitted by most people, the generality reciting four ' obligatory ', two ' traditional ', two ' voluntary ', three ' special ' (*wājibu-l-watar*), and two ' consolatory ' (*tashaffiu-l-watar*).

The ritual of prayer is as follows : The worshipper spreads a prayer-carpet (*musallā, jā-i-namāz, jānamāz, sajjāda*), stands on it with his face towards the Qibla or Mecca,[2] repeats the prayer of deprecation or asking for forgiveness (*istighfār*), and two ' obligatory ' prayers, proclaims his ' purpose ' (*nīyat*) : ' I have purposed to offer up to God only with a sincere heart this morning [or as the case may be] with my face turned to the Qibla two [or as the case may be] bow prayers, " obliga-

[1] *Mishkāt*, i. 129.

[2] The original Qibla was Jerusalem ; for the change of it to Mecca, see Muir, *Life*, 184.

tory ", " traditional ", or " voluntary ".' Having repeated the words ' Allāhu akbar ! ', ' God is Great ! ' he places his right hand upon the left below the navel. This done, he is not to look about, but directing his eyes to the spot which he is to touch with his hand, in the posture of prostration (*sijda*) he must stand with the most profound reverence and self-abasement, as if in the presence of a mighty monarch. Then he repeats the ejaculation (*ta'awwuz*), ' I seek refuge from God from Satan, the accursed ! '; the ' naming of God ' (*tasmiya*) : ' In the name of God, the Compassionate, the Merciful ! ' Then follows the recital of the Sūratu-l-fātiha, Sūratu-l-hamd, the first chapter of the Korān, followed by any other, without repeating the ' blessing ', ' Bi'smillāh ', ' In the name of God ! ' He then comes to the bow position, repeats three or five times the ' ejaculation ' (*Ruku' kī tasbīh*) : ' Subhān illāh, subhāna Rabbu-l-'azīm ', ' I extol the holiness of God ! ' Reassuming the erect position he recites : ' Thou, Almighty God ! Art the hearer of my praises ! Thou art my support ! ' Then he takes the posture of prostration (*sijda*), and repeats three or four times : ' O thou holy and blessed Preserver ! ', sits up and resting for a few seconds again performs the prostration and repeats the ' ejaculation ' (*tasbīh*) as before. This constitutes the first bow prayer. It must be remembered that the assumption of each new posture must commence with the words ' God is Great ! ' ' Allāhu akbar ! ' From the prostrate position he assumes the standing attitude (*qiyām*), recites the first chapter of the Korān with the blessing, and then another without it, makes the bow, then sitting he repeats the ' greetings ' (*at-tahīyāt*), or concluding portion of the prayers, finishing it with its accompanying part, the ' blessing ' (*durūd*). Then turning first to the right and then to the left he says the ' salutation ' (*salām*) : ' The peace and mercy of God be with you all ! ' ' As-salāmu 'alaikum, rahmat ilāhi '. Musalmāns do not after the conclusion of prayers repeat ' Amen ', ' Āmīn ', but they invariably do so after reciting the Fātiha or first chapter of the Korān, and after ' supplication ' (*munājāt*) the congregation say ' Āmīn '. Then joining his two hands from the wrists, both spread out and held up in line with the shoulders, he makes the ' supplication' (*munājāt*). The manner of reciting it is as follows: Having raised the extended arms meeting at the wrist to a level with the shoulder, or rather the middle of the arm, with eyes half open, he should confess his sins, and ask pardon and mercy. He repeats that he dreads the miseries of Hell, and prays for protection from the crafts and subtleties of the Devil; and by making use of an appropriate sentence or verse of the Word of God, or by some established prayer suitable to his case, or in his own words, in any language he pleases, he makes known his requests. Then drawing his hands over his face he ends the second prayer.

Should the performance of four prayers have been vowed, it is observed with the following trifling variation. The two first are gone through as just described, with this difference, that only half of the 'greetings' (*at-tahīyāt*) is recited in the second prayer, and after pausing a while, instead of repeating after it the blessing and salutation, the worshipper begins the third prayer by rehearsing the first but beginning with the *tasmiya*, omitting the *sunna* and *ta'awwuz*, which is done in every prayer except the first. The third and fourth are repeated like the two first, but the whole 'greeting' is this time recited. The above four *rak'at* comprehend what are called *sunnat rak'at.*

In the three *farz rak'at* the two first are performed like those preceding, except that the chapter after the Alhamd is omitted, and the whole of the *at-tahīyāt* recited in the third *rak'at,* and they conclude with the Salām.

In the four *farz rak'at* there is this difference, that in the first and second *rak'at* after the first chapter of the Korān another must be recited, as in the preceding forms, but not so in the third and fourth, where the latter chapter is omitted. And, again, previous to the vow at the commencement, the Takbīr or Creed, which differs little from the Azān or call to prayer, must be repeated four times in succession.

In the 'Ishā, or night prayers, in the third bow of the 'special' or 'voluntary' prayers, after reciting the first chapter of the Korān and another chapter, on assuming the bow position the worshipper, touching the lobes of his ears with his thumbs, calls out, 'God is Great!' Then placing his hands on his navel he repeats the 'prayer of adoration' (*du'ā-l-qunūt*). Then resuming the bow position and proceeding with the prostrations and blessings, he finishes as before.[1]

It is the Divine command that when persons, male and female, have reached maturity and the age of discretion they should observe the five appointed seasons of prayer, and at the moment of prayer spread the prayer-carpet on a clean spot to the west of the worshipper and engage in devotion. Should a street happen to be in front of him, or a large concourse of people coming and going present an obstacle, he should place a 'mark of defence' (*satr*), such as a stick two feet long, a sword, or anything else stuck in the ground, or placed in front of the carpet, in order to concentrate his attention. Prayer should never be neglected. If a sick person cannot stand up to say his prayers he must repeat them lying down, and if he be so unwell as not to be able to say them aloud he must pray mentally. However, it is only the pious and devout that observe these rules. Where do we find every one able to comply with them? If a person be pressed by lack of time, as when he is required to obey the orders of a superior officer, the prayer may be deferred to a more convenient season, but never wholly omitted. A traveller also may curtail the four obligatory, but not the four traditional, by reciting only two, but a two or three bow prayer must not be diminished; and he alone is deemed to be a traveller who has been on his journey for three days and three nights.

After the supplication (*munājāt*) some recite the praises (*tasbīh*) of God: 'The Great God hears whatever praises I offer to Him. O, my Protector, I thank Thee!' This is desirable (*mustahabb*), that is, the observance of it is beneficial, but the neglect of it is not sinful. To recite prayers with the aid of the rosary (*tasbīh*) is meritorious, but it is an innovation, since it was not enjoined by the Prophet—on whom be the Blessing!—or his Companions, but by certain divines (*mashāikh*). They use it in reciting the Kalima or Confession of Faith or the Blessing (*durūd*) once, twice, or even hundreds of times.

[1] It is difficult to follow this complicated ritual without much greater detail than that supplied by the author, and in the absence of illustrations of the successive postures, which are supplied by Lane, *ME.* i. 95; Hughes, 465 ff.

CHAPTER XII

VOWS AND OBLATIONS ; SOME INDO-MUSALMĀN SAINTS

THERE are various kinds of vows, oblations, and dedications (*nazr o niyāz*). Men and women, both Shī'as and Sunnīs, so far as they believe in such things, vow that when what they desire comes to pass they will present offerings and oblations in the name of God, the Prophet, his Companions, or some Walī or Saint. For instance, if a man recovers from sickness, finds a lost sheep, obtains employment, is blessed with offspring, if his enemy be ruined or killed, if his master be pleased with him, or if he gains promotion—in such cases special forms are observed and special food is cooked. The following are a few examples.

Nazru-llāh, an offering to God. This consists in preparing stews with bread, distributing it among friends and the poor, giving grain, a sacrificed sheep, and money in alms. Some women make sweetmeats and cakes, offer the Fātiha over them, and distribute them to all comers. It is not necessary that the Fātiha should be said in the name of God ; it is sufficient at the time of making the vow to say that the oblation is in the name of God. It is only ignorant people who never dispense with this custom, or eat the food without saying the Fātiha over it. Such sweetmeats are called 'offerings to God, the Merciful' (*Allāh rahīm kī pindiān*) or merely 'Mercy' (*rahm*). Some do this in what is called the easy (*āsān*) way by cooking cakes with sugar and fruit and saying the Fātiha over them. Many prepare this 'Mercy' offering and keep a night vigil with dancing and singing.

Some women at weddings prepare food in the name of the Saint Pīr Shitāb. A married woman or a widow is bathed, dressed in her best, and supplied with a twisted thread on which nine, eleven, or nineteen knots are made. She is then sent to beg from all relatives and friends of the family. When she comes to a house she calls out, 'I am going to untie the knots of Pīr Shitāb '. Then the house people throw in her lap some raw rice, and then she unties one of the knots. When all the knots have been thus untied she brings the rice back and the mistress cooks it in balls, one of which is sent to every house which contributed. Others in the name of Pīr Milāo make cakes of wheat and pulse (*mothī, phaseolus aconitifolius*), recite the Fātiha over them, and distribute them in the house, not out of doors. Some dig a fire-pit (*alāwā*) in the corner of a room and wash their hands, not as Europeans do, but by pouring water over them from an ewer, the water falling into a basin. Then they bury the food with the remnants of the meal and fill the hole with earth. Or they fill a pot with curds and boiled rice in the name of the Saint Pīr Dīdār. Others in the name of Kath Bāwā Sāhib make a curry of a fowl and bake bread which is dedicated after the Fātiha has been said over it, and distribute it.[1]

Some women keep one to five locks (*chontī*) of hair uncut on the heads of their children and consecrate them in the name of some celebrated Walī or Saint with the words, ' I dedicate this to so and so, and when the child has reached such and such an age I vow to prepare food, offer the Fātiha, and then have the hair cut by a barber '.

Others in the Deccan after their wishes have been fulfilled set afloat little boats (*jahāz*), as in the rite of Khwāja Khizr described later on. Or they take one, two, or three lamps made of paste or clay, light them with cotton wicks soaked in butter, put them on an earthen or brass tray with some cowry shells and money, as far as they can afford, take them to the sea beach or a river bank, or well, recite the Fātiha over them and leave them there. As they are conveying them, shopkeepers and passers-by put cowries into the trays. After the Fātiha has been said, children scramble for the money, but the women bring the brass trays home. In Gujarāt the officiant in such rites is the Bihishtī or water-carrier.[2]

In Gujarāt women make the Bahlīm vow, which should be

[1] The above are probably local South Indian saints, regarding whom no information is available.

[2] *BG.* ix part 2, 152.

performed at the beginning of the rites of marriage, pregnancy, and initiation of children. It consists in engaging to crush some five pounds of live coals. This is done under the superintendence of a Phadālī, or spirit medium. The woman in a state of ecstasy crushes the burning cinders with her hands and steps into the fire-pit where she stamps out the fire with her feet. If any injury occurs it is attributed to disregard of the rules of purity and cleanliness in cooking the food for the rite, or in plastering the floor of the place where the rite is performed.[1]

Some people on every Thursday in the year put a few flowers and some sugar in a leaf plate (*daunā*) and launch it in the water in the name of Khwāja Khizr, and they also throw some cowry shells into the stream. The festival of the raft (*berā*) should be observed on the last Thursday of the Musalmān year, but in eastern Bengal it is held on the last Thursday of the Hindu month Bhādon (August–September), the middle of the rainy season. The raft, usually made of paper and ornamented with tinsel, has a prow resembling a woman's face with the crest and breast of a peacock, in imitation of the figure-head on the bow of the Morpankhī boat, or 'peacock-winged', a barge used in festivals on the Ganges. This effigy placed on a raft of plantain leaves is set afloat at sunset. The festival is specially popular on the river Bhagīrathī at Murshidābād. The person launching the craft deposits on the bank a few slices of ginger, a little rice, and two or three plantains which are usually snatched up by some beggar.[2] In other places poor people lay on an earthen plate two bundles each of a hundred betel leaves with five areca nuts in each, a little sugar folded up in plantain leaves, two lamps fed with butter, with five, nine, or twenty-one cowries in an empty water-pot, and go to the river bank. There they light the lamps, have the Fātiha said in the name of Khwāja

[1] *BG.* ix, part 2, 151. Bahlīm is a name applied in the United Provinces to sections of castes, like the Banjārā, Bihishtī, Nāī, Shaikh, and Telī; but it is not known how the name came to be applied to this vow in Gujarāt.

[2] Wise, *Notes*, 12 f. Frazer regards these customs as means of periodically expelling evils (*GB.*, The Scapegoat, 198 ff.).

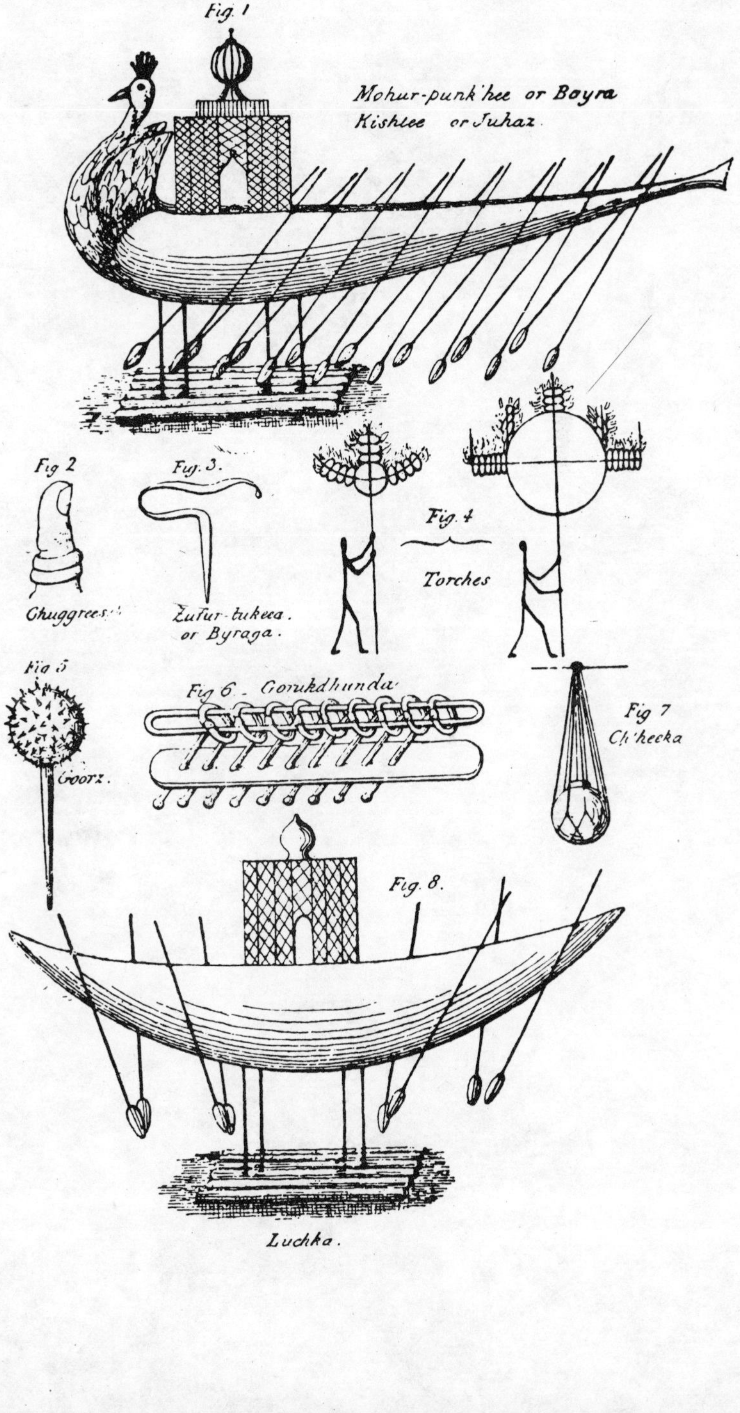

Fig. 1
Mohur-punk'hee or Bayra
Kishtee or Juhaz
Fig 2
Chuggree
Fig. 3.
Zufur-tukeea
or Byraga.
Fig. 4
Torches
Fig 5
Goorz.
Fig 6. Gorukdhunda
Fig 7
Ch'heeka
Fig. 8.
Luchka.

Khizr by the Mullā, who gets the cowries as his fee, and as they float the plates in the water, children scramble for the contents. In the end the person who has made the vow fills the water-pot from the river, brings it home and breaks his fast with a mouthful of the water. In the same way they put on their children various articles of jewellery in the names of Saints and other holy men.

It is a general custom when a person is about to travel, or when evil befalls him, to tie a copper coin and a metal ring in a bit of cloth dyed with turmeric in the name of the personal guardian, the Saint Imām Zāmin,[1] and to wear this tied on the left upper arm. When the traveller reaches his destination in safety, or gets rid of his trouble, he takes off the coin, and sometimes adding something to it, buys sweets, or makes cakes or stew, and offers the Fātiha in the name of the Saint. Learned people beside the offering to the Almighty (*nazru-llāh*), or that in the name of the Prophet (*niyāz-i-rasūl*), or the Fātiha in the name of Hazrat Shāh or 'Alī, or the Saint Pīr Dastagīr, give other oblations, such as the viaticum or provision for a journey (*tosha*) in the name of the Saint Ahmad 'Abdu-l-haqq of Radhaulī. They make sweets, and those who are specially devout prepare and eat them themselves, never giving any to smokers of tobacco or to women. In the same way they make and distribute food in the names of the Saints Shāh Sharaf Bū 'Alī Qalandar, Shāh Sharafu-d-dīn Yahyā Munārī, Ahmad Khān and Mubāriz Khān.

They also prepare an offering (*tosha*) in the names of the Ashābu-l-kahf, 'the Companions of the Cave', the Seven Sleepers.[2] It is said that seven brothers, Alīkha, Maksalimta,

[1] Zāmin means 'one who is responsible for another, or enters into bail for him'. *Imām Zāmin kā rupayā* means 'a rupee worn as a protective against disaster or death'; see Mrs. Meer Hassan Ali, 136; Rose, i. 874.

[2] For the famous tale of the Seven Sleepers, see *Korān*, xviii, with Sale's notes. The Prophet did not know the exact number of them: 'Some say, "They were three; their dog the fourth"; others say, "Five; their dog the sixth", guessing at the secret; others say, "Seven; and their dog the eighth". Say, my Lord best knoweth the number; none, save a few, shall know them' (*Korān*, xviii. 22, 23). For this legend see Gibbon, *Decline and Fall*, ed. W. Smith, iv. 188; Rydberg, *Teutonic Mythology*, 479 ff.; *EB.* xxiv. 709 f.; *ERE.* iii. 458.

Tabyanas, Kashfūtat, Adargat, Yūnas, Yuānus, were devoted to each other, and the most virtuous of the children of Israel, and they had an affectionate dog, Qitmīr. In the name of these seven they take out seven plates of food, recite the Fātiha over them, eat some and distribute the remainder. A special plate is reserved for the dog, which is not placed with the rest but given to a dog to eat.

Shī'as prepare breakfast (*hāzirī*) in the name of His Holiness 'Abbās 'Alī, 'Alambardār, or standard-bearer, step-brother of Husain, by cooking and distributing food, but to none save Shī'as. In fact, after the Fātiha they revile the Companions of the Prophet before they eat the food. Most women vow food in the name of Imām Ja'faru-s-sādiq, the Veracious, the sixth Imām—May God be pleased with him!—by distributing cakes. Some women make the Kandūrī[1] or offering to Bībī Fātima by making various kinds of food in secret, because this being the lady's food, it is improper that any men should see it, and only respectable, virtuous matrons partake of it. The Fātiha must be said over it behind a curtain. Sometimes also they do the rite of Bībī kī sahnak or Bībī ka bāsan, 'the lady's dish or vessel', as described in connexion with marriage. Some women make and distribute food in the name of the Saint Shāh Dāwal.[2] Some of this is made at the expense of the person who offers it, part is procured by begging. The man or woman sent to beg calls out 'Shāh Dāwal' at the house door and receives some grain. Some sacrifice a sheep in his honour, eat some of the meat and distribute the rest.

Some people when any trouble befalls them go out begging with their wives and children, all dressed in blue, and live on

The tale is localized in many places, as in Babylonia, A. H. Layard, *Discoveries in the Ruins of Nineveh and Babylon*, 206.

[1] Kandūrī primarily means a leather or linen tablecloth.

[2] Shāh Dāwal was the title of 'Abdu-l-latīf, son of one of the nobles of Mahmūd Bīgarhā of Gujarāt (A. D. 1459–1511). His title Dāwaru-l-mulk, 'lord of the kingdom', was changed into Dāwal Shāh. He became a disciple of Shāh 'Alam Bukhārī, and was slain in A. D. 1474. He was engaged in religious war (*Jihād*), and is highly venerated by both Musalmāns and Hindus in Gujarāt and the Deccan, where his followers observe many Hindu customs (*BG.* v. 89).

what they receive as alms. When their troubles are removed they go home and make a vow as far as their means allow.

Some impious women fix a day, dress themselves in men's clothes and have a night session (*baithak*). They collect flowers, betel, perfumes, and sweets, and get women of the Dom caste to play before them on the timbrel (*pakhāwaj*) or the small drum (*dholak*). Then a woman becomes possessed by Shaikh Saddū,[1] and as she whirls her head about foolish women who want something ask her how to attain it. For instance, a woman says 'Master ! (*miyān*) I offer myself (*sadqī*) to thee that I may have a child '. Then if she pleases, the possessed woman gives her a packet of betel leaves, some of the betel which she has chewed herself (*ugāl*) or some sweets, all of which she eats in perfect faith. However, God is Lord of all, and it depends on His will and pleasure whether she comes to be in child or not. If, perchance, she gives birth to a child, the belief of these unfortunate people in this form of magic is strengthened, and they become real infidels. Should she fail to become in child she concludes that the Master is angry with her, and she repeats the rite with increased credulity. Sensible people have no faith in Shaikh Saddū, and hold that he is a devil. His tomb, or rather the place where he disappeared, is at Amrohā in the Morādābād District, where much noise and disturbance always goes on.

Besides these there are other objects of superstition. Musalmāns in south India, being to a large extent converts from Hinduism, believe in malignant spirits, fairies, Narasinha, the lion incarnation of Vishnu, Mātā, the Mother goddess. May God blacken the faces of such people ! Some, again, in order to obtain their wishes, pray to His Majesty Sikandar or Iskandar, Alexander the Great, known as Zū-l-qarnain, 'he of the two horns ', vowing that if their desires are accomplished they will offer horses in his name.[2] Accordingly, when they

[1] Shaikh Saddū, whose real name was Muhīu-d-dīn, was an impious personage, who was finally torn in pieces by the Jīnn. He is a favourite saint of woman (Mrs. Meer Hassan Ali, 375 f. ; Crooke, *Popular Religion*, i. 217 ; *Dabistān*, iii. 234, 325 ; *Indian Antiquary*, xxxiv. 125 ff. ; Rose, i. 638).

[2] Zū-l-qarnain, 'he of the two horns ', is Alexander the Great, an important personage in Oriental folklore, but he has become the centre

gain their wishes, they have little horses with their riders made in pottery, recite the Fātiha over them in his name, take them with great pomp to his shrine (*āstāna*) and dedicate them there. At such places hundreds of such horses lie in heaps, and some fix these horse images in front of their houses or over their doors.[1] Hindus as well as Musalmāns have great veneration for this personage, and it is often difficult to ascertain whether such places are Musalmān shrines or Hindu temples.

Besides these personages already mentioned, there are innumerable other Saints at whose shrines, especially at the annual celebrations of their deaths (*'urs*), offerings are made, and at many of them by Hindus as well as by Musalmāns. The following are a few of those most generally known.

Bābā Budan was a Faqīr who introduced coffee into Mysore in the fourteenth century. He is also known as Hayāt Qalandar and Hayātu-l-bahr, and the Bābā Budan hills, in which his shrine is situated, take their name from him.[2]

Bābā Ghor was an Abyssinian saint who is venerated by the Abyssinian Sidīs in Gujarāt. He gives his name to the Bābāghorī or white agates of Cambay.[3]

Bābā Lāl. There were several saints of this name, but the best known is a Hindu who became the preceptor of the unfortunate Dāra Shukoh, brother of the Emperor Aurangzeb.[4]

Bahāu-d-dīn Zikaria is one of the most renowned Saints

of a mass of tradition at variance with true history. His legend is given in the *Korān* (xviii. 82–96, see Sale's note *ad loc.*). The title is explained in various ways—from two protuberances on his head or helm, from his two long locks, from the ram horns of Jupiter Ammon, or from the story of Moses (Exod. xxxiv. 29, R.V. margin; see *Encyclopaedia Biblica*, ii. 2111; Burton, *AN.* iv. 203).

[1] The dedication of horse images, to serve as coursers for the gods, is common. In south India the practice is connected with the cult of Ayenār, who rides over the country at night, driving off the demons (Monier-Williams, *Brahmanism and Hinduism*, 4th ed., 218 f.; G. Oppert, *Original Inhabitants of Bhāratavarsa*, 504 ff.). Bhīls use horse images in their magical rites (*Census Report*, Central India, 1901, i. 53; *BG.* ix, part 1, 304).

[2] B. L. Rice, *Mysore*, ii. 374; Balfour, *Cyclopaedia*, i. 214; ii. 132.

[3] *BG.* ix, part 2, 12; Yule-Burnell, *Hobson-Jobson*, 43.

[4] Wilson, *Sketch of the Religious Sects of the Hindus*, i. 347 ff.; *Census Report*, Panjāb, 1891, i. 126 f.; Rose, i. 394; *ERE.* ii. 308 f.

in northern India. He was born at Kotkaror in Multān, A.D. 1170, went to Baghdād and became disciple of Shaikh Shihābu-d-dīn Saharwardī, and died at Multān in 1266, where his tomb stands in the citadel. He was a close friend of the other great Saint, Shaikh Farīdu-d-dīn Shakarganj.

Dūlā or Daulā Shāh was born about A.D. 1567, and the tale that he met the Emperor Humāyūn, who died in 1556, is an anachronism. His shrine is at Gujarāt in the Panjāb, and it is chiefly remarkable for the collection of deformed, idiotic children, known as the Chūhā or 'rats' of the Saint, who congregate there.[1]

Farīdu-d-din Shakarganj, 'sugar treasury', so called because he is said to have been able to transmute dust or salt into sugar, was a disciple of Khwāja Qutbu-d-dīn Bakhtyār Kākī, born A.D. 1173, died 1265. His shrine at Ajodhan or Pākpattan in the Montgomery district, Panjāb, attracts vast crowds of worshippers at his festival during the Muharram, from Afghānistān and Central Asia. The Qutb Minār, the great minaret in Old Delhi, takes its name from him.[2]

Gesū Darāz, 'he of the long locks', is the title of the saint Sayyid Muhammad Sudaru-d-dīn Muhammad Husainī. He was born at Delhi in A.D. 1321, lived in the Deccan under the Bahmanī dynasty, and died at Kulbarga or Gulbarga, where his tomb is visited by large numbers of votaries.[3]

Ghāzī Miyān is the title of Sālār Mas'ūd, nephew of Sultān Mahmūd of Ghaznī. He invaded Oudh and was killed in battle at Bahrāich in 1033 at the age of nineteen. He is venerated as a martyr by Musalmāns, and is regarded by Hindus as one of the youthful heroes who are widely venerated.[4]

Jalāl Jahāniān Jahāngasht, 'he that wandered over the world', is venerated at Uchh in the Bahāwalpur State. He brought from Mecca a foot-print of the Prophet and became

[1] Rose, i. 630 ff.; Manucci, i. 117, 119.

[2] Sleeman, *Rambles*, 494, 500; *Aīn*, iii. 363 f.; Ferishta, i. 271.

[3] Bilgrami-Willmott, *Sketch of the Nizām's Dominions*, ii. 669 f.; *Āīn*, iii. 372; Ferishta, ii. 388, 398; Jadunath Sarkar, *Life of Aurangzīb*, i. 276.

[4] Elliot-Dowson, ii. 513 ff.; *NINQ*. ii. 109; Crooke, *Popular Religion*, i. 207 f.

the preceptor of Sultān Fīroz Tughlaq (A. D. 1351–90). He was the founder of the Orders of the Malang and Jalāliya Faqīrs.[1]

Lāl Shāhbāz, 'the royal hawk', the great saint of Sind, was a Qalandar and rigid celibate who died at Sehwān in A. D. 1274. His tomb is highly venerated and every year a girl of the Khonbatī caste is married to it, and she is never allowed to contract a real marriage.[2]

Makhdūm Faqīh, the great Saint of Bombay, was of Arab origin, born in the fourteenth century, and became law-officer of the Musalmāns at Mahim in Thānā District. His tomb, built close to the sea-shore, is the scene of a large gathering on the anniversary of his death. One of the chief rites is the drinking of water which has been waved over the tomb, and eating the ashes of incense burnt there. The Saint enjoys a high reputation for the cure of hysterical and other spirit-possessed patients.[3]

Mīr or Miyān Mīr, Shaikh Muhammad, flourished at Lahore between A. D. 1550 and 1635. His disciple Mullā Mīr was a spiritual guide of Dāra Shukoh, brother of Aurangzeb. The saint has given his name to the well-known military cantonment, Miyānmīr, near Lahore.[4]

Mīrān Sāhib lived about four centuries ago, performed many miracles, and is buried at Nāgor, a suburb of the town of Negapatam in Tanjore District, Madras. Crowds of pilgrims from long distances visit his tomb, and Hindus, even Brāhmans, make vows there. On the ninth evening of his festival a Faqīr sits motionless in his Dargāh, and must remain so for thirty-six hours.[5]

Mu'īnu-d-dīn Hasan Chishtī, known as the Khwāja, was born at Sīstān, A. D. 1142, and died at Ajmer 1236. His Dargāh or tomb is one of the great places of pilgrimage in northern India, and Akbar used to make pilgrimages there on foot.[6]

[1] Temple, *Legends of the Panjāb*, iii. 184; *NINQ*. i. 5; iv. 53.
[2] Burton, *Sindh*, 211 f.; *IGI*. xxii. 163.
[3] Edwardes, *Gazetteer Bombay City*, iii. 301 ff.
[4] Temple, *Legends of the Panjāb*, ii. 508; iii. 188; Rose, i. 615 f.
[5] F. B. Hemingway, *Gazetteer Tanjore District*, i. 243.
[6] *Āīn*, iii. 361 f.; C. C. Watson, *Gazetteer Ajmer–Merwāra*, 17, 40; Smith, *Akbar*, 57, 96, 102.

Nizāmu-d-dīn Auliyā, known as Sultānu-l-mashāikh, 'chief of holy men', was one of the noblest disciples of Shaikh Farīdu-d-dīn, born at Budāun A. D. 1236, died at Delhi 1325, where a lovely shrine was erected to his memory.[1]

Panj Pīr, the group of five Saints who give their name to the Pachpiriyā sect, a strange mixture of Musalmān and Hindu hagiology.[2]

Qutbu-d-dīn Bakhtyār Kākī came from Ūsh in Persia and died at Delhi, A. D. 1235. He is the favourite Afghān Saint, and pilgrims visit his shrine at Mahraulī near Delhi.[3]

Shamsu-d-dīn Muhammad Tabrīzī, a famous Sūfī martyr, who, when he was flayed, is said to have walked about carrying his own skin. When no one would help him he prayed to the sun to broil his meat, and when it descended for this purpose, the world being on the point of being consumed, the Saint ordered the sun to return to heaven. His followers, known as Shamsī, 'sun-worshippers', combine Hindu beliefs with those of Islām, and at his shrine at Shamspur in the Shāhpur District, Panjāb, people come to be bled and the place reeks with blood.[4]

Sultān Sakhī Sarwar settled at Siālkot in A. D. 1220. His shrine is at a place of the same name in the Derā Ghāzī Khān District, which is a resort of Hindu and Musalmān mendicants. His devotees are known as Sultānī, Phirāī, or Pirāhin, and his attendants (*mujāvir*) sleep on the ground.[5]

[1] Fanshawe, *Delhi Past and Present*, 235 ff.; *Āīn*, iii. 365; Sleeman, *Rambles*, 490 ff.; Rose, i. 491; Ferishta, i. 377; ii. 285.

[2] *ERE.* ix. 600 f.; Crooke, *Popular Religion*, i. 205 ff.; Rose, on Lālbeg, iii. 20 ff.

[3] Fanshawe, *Delhi Past and Present*, 280; Rose, i. 491; ii. 3; *Āīn*, iii. 363; *PNQ.* i. 143.

[4] *Census Report*, Panjāb, 1891, i. 138; Rose, iii. 402 f.; J. W. Redhouse, *Mesnevi of Jelālu-dīn*, 99 ff.

[5] Rose, i. 566 ff.; iii. 435, 566; *PNQ.* i. 133; *ERE.* vii. 490.

CHAPTER XIII

RELIGIOUS BUILDINGS AND OTHER APPLIANCES FOR WORSHIP

THE religious buildings of Islām in India constitute an architectural group of great interest and beauty. Here no attempt will be made to consider them from the architectural aspect, but merely for their religious purposes.[1]

The Dargāh (Persian *dar*, 'door', *gāh*, 'place') is usually the shrine or tomb of some reputed Saint at which pilgrims assemble at the festival (*'urs*) which commemorates his death. In southern India there are two noted buildings of this class near Mangalore in the South Kanara District, Madras. The first is that known as Shaikh Farīd kī Dargāh. It consists of a cavern in a precipitous laterite rock, which is said to reach as far as Hyderābād, 45 miles distant. The cavern is very dark and, as no one ventures to enter it, its extent is unknown. The square opening is just large enough to allow a visitor to creep in, and it is reached by a flight of stone steps. Tradition runs that nearly two hundred years ago a Pīr or Saint, Shaikh Farīd, did the Chilla or forty days' penance at a time, neither speaking, eating, nor drinking during that period. At Kadiri in the Cuddapah District, Madras, he used to do similar penance, eating only the leaves of the plant known as Farīd būtī (*coculus villosus*, or more properly *pedalium murer*).[2] At the end of twelve years he disappeared, and is said to have travelled underground to Mecca. Musalmāns in numbers visit his shrine and on the Friday Sabbath cook food, say the Fātiha prayer over it and then distribute it to Faqīrs.

[1] On Musalmān architecture, see G. T. Rivoira, *Moslem Architecture, its Origins and Development*, Oxford, 1919; J. Fergusson, *History of Indian and Eastern Architecture*, London, 1910; Smith, *History of Fine Art in India and Ceylon*, Oxford, 1911; *IGI*. ii. 181 f.; *ERE*. i. 755 ff., 874 ff.

[2] Watt, *Econ. Dict.* vi, part 1, 123 f.

Fig 1

Tukht-e-rowan

Fig 2

Eed-gah or Numaz gah

Fig 3

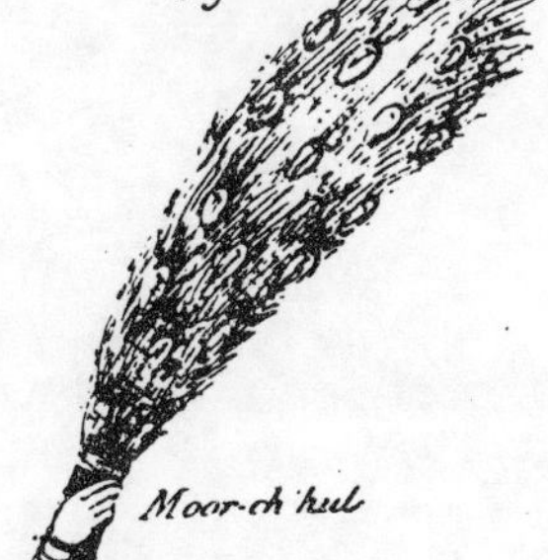

Moor-ch'hul

Fig. 4

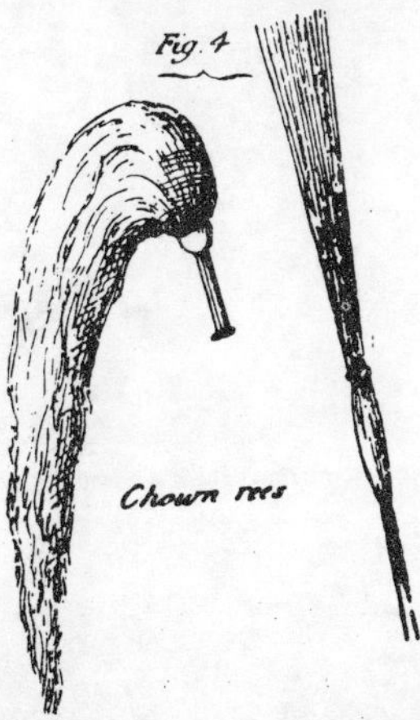

Chown rees

If materials for cooking are not procurable, sweetmeats are distributed. The guardian of the Dargāli is appointed from among those best qualified by piety and zeal, by a committee of the Makānwālā (*makān*, 'a place, station') or resident Faqīrs and their Murīds or disciples. In the days of Tipū Sultān (A.D. 1782–99) the superintendent used to receive a rupee for every mast of a ship entering the harbour of Mangalore, a right which has been abolished since the British occupation. The second Dargāh at Mangalore is that of Loh Langar Shāh, 'he of the iron anchor', visited both by Musalmāns and Hindus, by those who wish to be freed from disease or misfortune. Lamps are lighted there every night, food is distributed, and dancing-girls entertain the visitors. The shrine is a large long tomb with minarets at each end. Rich people visit it on any night in the year, the poor every Monday and Thursday, or once a week or month. There are many famous Dargāhs and tombs in the Deccan and northern India, of which the following are some examples. In the United Provinces at Ajodhyā are the reputed tombs of Noah, Seth, and Job, that of Shāh Qāsim Sulaimānī at Chunār, of Shaikh Salīm Chishtī at Fathpur Sīkrī, of Kabīr at Maghar. In Rajputāna, at Ajmer, is that of Muīnu-d-dīn Chishtī. In the Panjāb are those of Shaikh Nizāmu-d-dīn Auliya in Old Delhi, Bābāwālī Kandhārī at Hasan Abdāl, Bū 'Alī Qalandar at Karnāl, and several of great repute at Uchh in the Bahāwalpur State. In the Central Provinces is that of Khwāja Shaikh Farīd at Girar, and in southern India that of Bābā Budan at Attīgundī in Mysore.

An 'Īdgah is the place where the rites at the 'Īd festivals are performed, known also as Namāzgāh or 'place of prayer'. It is usually a building erected outside a town, which is used only by Sunnīs, and consists of a court or stone pavement raised some three or four feet above the level of the ground, along the west side of which is a wall which generally has small minarets at each end. In the middle of the wall three or four slabs rise from the pavement and form a pulpit (*mimbar*, *minbar*), from which at the Ramazān and Baqar 'Īd festivals the sermon or bidding-prayer (*khutba*) is delivered. Near it is a niche (*mihrāb*) facing the worshipper, which points to the direction of Mecca. The prayer-niche and the minaret are by some supposed to be derived from Hinduism, while the mosque dome follows the precedent of Assyrian temples.[1] It is said that the Prophet while addressing the congregation used to stand on the uppermost step of the pulpit, Abū Bakr, his successor, on the second, ʻUmar on the third or lowest, but ʻUsmān fixed upon the middle stage as that from which the sermon should be delivered, and since then this rule has been followed. ʻ In the beginning the Prophet leaned when fatigued against a post while preaching the khutba or Friday sermon. The Mimbar or pulpit was an invention of a Medīna man of the Banū Najjār. It was a wooden frame two cubits long by one broad, with three steps, each one span high ; on the topmost of these the Prophet sat when he required rest. The pulpit assumed its present form about A.H. 90, A.D. 708, during the artistic reign of El Walīd ʼ (A.D. 705–14).[2] No special sanctity attaches to the ʻĪdgāh.

The Imāmbārā, ʻ enclosure of the leader or guide ʼ, belongs particularly to the Shīʻas, being the mourning chapel in which the elegies for the martyrs Hasan and Husain are recited, and in which their cenotaphs (*taʻziya, tābūt*) are stored. One of the most famous buildings of this class is that at Lucknow, 162 feet long by 54 wide, with a wonderful concrete vault, built by the Nawwāb Asafu-d-daula (A.D. 1775–97).[3]

The mosque (*masjid*, ʻ place of prostration ʼ) is, of course, a sacred building, and attempts to pollute it have often given rise to serious riots. But it marks Akbar's feeling towards orthodox Islām that when he introduced the Dīn Ilāhī, or Divine Faith, he changed the mosques and prayer-rooms into store-rooms, or put them in charge of Hindu watchmen.[4] Except in the poorest villages, where it is built of clay like

[1] Burton, *Pilgrimage*, i. 361 ; *Dabistan*, i. 49 ; M. Jastrow, *Civilization of Babylonia and Assyria*, 379. See the account of the Mihrāb in the Jāmiʻ Masjid at Bījāpur (Cousens, *Bījāpur*, 59, with a fine coloured drawing as a frontispiece) ; that at Fathpur-Sīkrī is figured by Smith, *HFA.*, plate c.

[2] Burton, *Pilgrimage*, i. 362. In ancient Arabia the pulpit was the judge's chair (*ERE*. i. 875).

[3] Fergusson, *Hist. Indian and Eastern Architecture*, ed. 1899, p. 605.

[4] *Āīn*, i. 200 ; Smith, *Akbar*, 253.

the houses of the peasantry, the mosque is of stone or brick in the form of a square. To the west is the service portion of the building (*al-īwān, al-aiwān, līmān*). In the centre of the open court (*sahn*) is a tank (*hauz*) used for the minor ablution (*wuzū'*), while the greater (*ghusl*) is done in a special lavatory. The court is often surrounded by cloisters (*riwāq, rawāq*). In the covered part of the building on the east, or Mecca-pointing wall, is the arch (*mihrāb*) and near it the pulpit (*mimbar, minbar*), beside which stands the stick (*'asa*), on which, according to ancient custom, the preacher leans, or holds it in his hand. The mosque in its simplest form is based on the model of the ancient Semitic temple, but on the frontier, as in Balūchistān, we find mosques consisting only of a ring of stones, with an opening to the east and a small arch to the west, which is probably a survival from the pre-Islāmic period.[1] The roof is generally formed of a series of domes (*gumbad, gumbaz*), and the walls are all white, the only decoration allowed being the Names of Allāh inscribed in Arabic characters.

Lamps hang from the roof and curiosities like ostrich eggs are suspended in the same way. The use of pictures is prohibited, except in a few instances beyond India, as in Persia where the Shī'a kings paid little regard to the Mosaic and Koranic prohibition, and thus a school of art was formed which became extended to India under the patronage of Akbar.[2] Muhammad cursed the painter of men and animals, and hence the prohibition which Akbar and other Mughal emperors followed. In the Gol Gambaz, the tomb of Sultān Mahmūd (A.D. 1626–56), at Bījāpur, it is said that an aerolite which fell in his reign was suspended from the archway, but when it was taken down in 1879 it was found to be a water-worn pebble of green quartzite.[3] The most authenticated relics of the Prophet were two rosaries, his cloak, the vessel in which he kept his eye collyrium, and a woollen sheet. But other relics are shown in India, such as a hair at Bījāpur, a hair and a slipper in the Jāmi' Masjid at Delhi.[4] A remark-

[1] *Census Report*, 1911, p. 61. On mosque architecture see *EB*. ii. 424 f.

[2] Smith, *HFA*. 422, 455.

[3] *BG*. xxiii. 606.

[4] Ferishta, iii. 187; *BG*. xxiii. 621 ff.; Fanshawe, *Delhi Past and Present*, 42. On relics of the Prophet see Lane, *ME*. i. 314 f.; *ERE*. x. 662.

able form of mosque is found among the Māppillās of Malabar, where it follows the model of the turret-like Saiva temples.[1]

The Prophet did not forbid women to pray in the mosque, but it is considered better that they should pray in private.[2] In Cairo neither women nor young boys are permitted to join in or to be present at mosque prayers ; formerly women were admitted, but they were obliged to place themselves apart from men.[3] There are ladies' galleries in some of the Indian mosques, as in the Motī Masjid or 'Pearl' mosque at Agra, where they had one of their own called Nagīna or 'Precious Stone', and at Ahmadnagar. Such galleries are screened from view by a lattice (*jālī*) of carved marble, one of the most beautiful productions of Indo-Musalmān art.[4]

Connected with the mosque are one or more minarets (*mīnār*, *manār*), sometimes rising from the roof, sometimes detached from the main building, the finest example of the latter type being the Qutb Minār in Old Delhi. A hostelry (*musāfirkhāna*), in which strangers enjoy the right of entertainment for three days, and a school, in which boys are taught to repeat the Korān and other religious books, are often attached to the mosque, with shops the rental of which is devoted to mosque expenses. The Korān is usually kept in a folding stand (*rahīl*, 'that which is fit for travelling'). The tomb of the founder is sometimes covered with a pall of green velvet or satin, lights are lit and prelections of the Korān held near it. Worshippers naturally remove their shoes before entering the mosque. The floor of the court is sometimes covered with matting, arranged in strips to mark out the lines of worshippers, or in the greater mosques the slabs of the stone pavement answer the same purpose. The worshipper steps barefoot into the square (*musallā*) allotted to him, putting his right foot first in the space. On leaving the mosque he puts on his left shoe first as he crosses the threshold, and then the right shoe. Some of the older mosques, like

[1] Thurston, *Castes*, iv. 470.

[2] *Mishkāt*, i. 223. According to Lane (*ME*. i. 102) very few women in Egypt pray, even at home ; but Leeder (p. 358) denies this.

[3] Lane, *ME*. i. 102.

[4] Burton, *Pilgrimage*, i. 434 ; Syad Muhammad Latif, *Agra*, 91, 94 ; *BG*. v. 431 ; Smith, *HFA*. 432 ff.

the Quwwatu-l-Islām, 'might of Islām', near the Qutb Minār in Old Delhi, and the Arhāī Din kā Jhonprā, or 'the shed built in two days and a half', at Ajmer, were built from the materials of Jain or Hindu temples.[1]

To meet the expense of maintenance there is sometimes a small endowment (*waqf*) derived from the rent of lands dedicated to the mosque. The religious local officials, more or less closely connected with the mosque, are the Qāzī, formerly the ecclesiastical judge whose judicial functions have now ceased; the Khatīb, who sometimes makes the call to prayer, officiates at funerals, or as Imām, or Peshnamāz, the prayer leader, or as a beadle, a duty often assigned to the Mujāvir or Farrāsh who sweeps the building; the Ghassāl who washes the dead; the Daurāhābardār or Piyāda who acts as messenger and attendant. In the smaller mosques one man often discharges most of these duties.[2] The affairs of the mosque are regulated by a committee with a Mutawalī or superintendent.

The rosary [3] (*tasbīh, subha*) used by Musalmāns consists of one hundred beads, and it is employed only in reciting the ninety-nine names of God with that of Allāh. It is said that in early times pebbles were used for this purpose, or the names were counted on the fingers, and some Wahhābīs contend that the Prophet did not use a rosary. The use of the rosary is said to have been borrowed from the Buddhists by Musalmāns and from the latter by Christians, but the Christian use of it dates from a period much earlier than the Crusades. Some

[1] Fanshawe, *Delhi Past and Present*, 258 ff.; *IGI*. v. 170; *BG*. xi. 385; xxiii. 635. 'In spite of the widely differing character of their places of worship, the dark Hindu shrine where only one or two can enter, the well-lit hall where the whole congregation of the faithful may meet, a pillared Gujarāt temple, with its courtyard, porches, and colonnades, can, with ease, be turned into a mosque. The chief cell and its porch taken from the middle of the court, and the entrances of the surrounding cells built up, there remains the typical mosque, a courtyard girt with a double colonnade. For the remaining feature, the important Mecca wall, all that is wanted is to raise these two tall porch pillars and dome, with, if they are to be had, a smaller dome on either side' (*BG*. iv. 264; Fergusson, *Hist. Indian Architecture*, 500 ff.).

[2] On the varied functions of the Mullā, see *ERE*. viii. 909 f.

[3] For a full account of the rosary, see ibid. x. 847 ff.; Hughes, 546.

of the materials from which the beads are made are ebony (*abnūs*), seeds of the Indian shot plant (*aqalbār*, *canna indica*), cornelian (*'aqīq*), Mocha stone (*'aqīqu-l-bahr*), seeds of the umbrella-bearing palm (*bajrbattū*, *corypha umbraculifera*), coral (*gulī*), the country gooseberry or Brazil cherry (*harfaleuri*, *chilmilī*, *charmelā*, *phyllanthus emblica*), the curative dust from the field of Karbalā (*khāk-i-shafā*) used by Shī'as, amber (*kahrubā*, 'straw attracting'), wood (*kāth*) of various kinds, date stones (*khajūr kā bīj*), a red wood spotted with black (*lail o nahār*, 'night and day'), pearl (*motī*), agate (*pīr patārī*), wood of the basilic basil (*rehān*, *raihān*, *ocymum basilicum*), mother of pearl (*sadaf*), sandalwood (*sandal*), onyx (*sulaimānī*), yellowish stone beads used by Faqīrs and learned men (*sang-i-maqsūd*), olive stones (*zaitūn*).[1]

The prayer-carpet (*jānamāz*, *jāēnamāz*) should have the background green, the Prophet's colour, and on it is woven a representation of a mosque with its domes and minarets in some contrasting colour, such as red, the whole being a picture of the Ka'ba at Mecca.

[1] Full details are given by Watt (*Econ. Dict.* i. 426 ff.).

CHAPTER XIV

THE MUHARRAM FESTIVAL

THE name Muharram means that which is 'forbidden' or 'taboo', and hence 'sacred', the first month of the Musalmān year.[1] According to the Author, the festival in this month, and called by the same name, was in existence in the time of the Prophet, the Chosen—May God bless him!—it having been observed as such by prophets before his time. But the Prophet, the Messenger of God, ordered that his followers should observe certain additional customs on the 'Āshūrā or tenth day, bathing, the wearing of apparel finer than ordinary, the applying of antimony (*surmā*) to the eyes, fasting, prayer, cooking of more food than ordinary, making friends with enemies and establishing friendship among others, associating with pious and learned divines, taking compassion on orphans and giving alms to them, and bestowing alms in charity. The month derives its special importance from the festival in honour of the martyrs.

In certain historical and traditional works it is stated that on the tenth day of Muharram the following events occurred: the first fall of rain, the appearance of Adam and Eve upon earth and the propagation of the human race, the creation of the ninth Heaven ('*arsh*, a term applied in the Korān[2] to the throne of God), the divine mission granted to the spirits of ten thousand prophets, the creation of the eighth or, as some say, the ninth crystalline sphere, the seat of judgement (*kursī*) of God, of Paradise (*bihisht*), or the seven Heavens, of Hell (*dūzakh*), of the 'guarded tablets' (*al-haula-l-mahfūz*),

[1] The Prophet is said to have fixed the 10th, or 'Āshūrā of Muharram as a time of fast, which was subsequently transferred to Ramazān. The Muharram seems to have been originally a harvest feast (*ERE.* iii. 126; v. 882). The question of the ancient sanctity of the month is discussed by Sale (*Korān*, *Preliminary Discourse*, 81).

[2] ix. 121.

on which the decrees of God are written, of the pen (*qalam*) with which these decrees are inscribed, of fate or destiny (*taqdīr*), of life (*hayāt*), and of death (*maut*): these things did the Almighty create in His infinite wisdom.

Musalmāns count seven Heavens,[1] which are evidently based upon the Ptolemaic astronomy: i. Dāru-l-jalāl, 'house of glory', made of pearls; ii. Dāru-l-salām, 'house of peace', of rubies and jacynths; iii. Jannātu-l-m'awā, 'garden of mansions', of green chrysolite; iv. Jannātu-l-khuld, 'garden of eternity', of yellow coral; v. Jannātu-l-na'īm, 'garden of delights', not a sensual Paradise,[2] of white silver; vi. Jannātu-l-firdaus, Paradise, of red gold; vii. Jannātu-l-'Adn, Eden, or Al-Qarār, 'everlasting abode', which some number viii, of red pearls or pure musk; viii. Jannātu-l-Illyūn, 'the sublime'.

There are also seven Hells according to Musalmān belief: i. Jahannum, the purgatorial Hell, the Hebrew Gehenna, 'the valley of Hinnom', borrowed probably from the Jews and Magians;[3] ii. Lazā, 'a blazing fire', reserved for Christians; iii. Hutama, for Jews; iv. Sa'īr, 'a flaming fire', for the Sabians and those who unjustly devour the property of orphans; v. Saqar, 'a scorching heat', for the Magians and Ghabr or fire-worshippers; vi. Jahīma, 'a great hot fire', for Pagans and idolators; vii. Hāwiya, 'a dark bottomless pit', for hypocrites.

Musalmāns also believe that the earth and heaven are each divided into seven parts. Those of the earth: i. of ashes; ii. of crystal; iii. of gold; iv. of pewter; v. of emerald; vi. of iron; vii. of pearl. Of these No. i. is occupied by men, Jinn, and animals; ii. by the suffocating wind which destroyed the infidel tribe of 'Ād;[4] iii. by the stones of Hell; iv. by the sulphur of Hell; v. by the serpents of Hell; vi. by the scorpions of Hell; vii. by the Devil and his angels. The

[1] *Korān*, lxv. 12; *ERE*. iv. 174; Redhouse, *The Mesnevi* of Jelālud-dīn, 253 note.

[2] Burton, *AN*. vii. 381; but see Hughes, 449 f.

[3] Hastings, *Dict. Bible*, ii. 119, 345; Sale, *Korān*, *Preliminary Discourse*, 67.

[4] They lived in South Arabia, and to them the Prophet Hūd was sent (*Korān*, vii. 63 ff.; xi. 52 ff.; xxvi. 123 ff.; Hughes, 181 f.).

seven heavens are: i. the firmament, the abode of Adam, made of pure virgin silver; ii. the abode of Enoch and John the Baptist, of gold; iii. of Joseph, of pearls; iv. of Jesus, of pure white gold; v. of Aaron, of pure silver; vi. of Moses, of ruby and garnet; vii. of Abraham, of crystal.

There are various accounts of the history of the martyrdom of Their Highnesses Imām Hasan and Husain—May God reward them!—but all agree in the fact that it was caused at the instigation of Yazīd who, wretched from all eternity, was the ringleader, and it was preordained that he should be the author of their martyrdom. How is it possible for one to be deprived of life by the mere enmity, tyranny, or command of another? But thus it is that whatever the Munshī or Eternal Registrar has recorded as man's destiny must necessarily come to pass. As a proverb justly says: 'Diversified are the modes of dying, and equally so are the means of living'. That is, though the hand of the Almighty does not appear visibly in either, yet He is the Author of both.

In A.D. 639 the Khalīfa 'Umar conferred the government of Syria on Mu'āwia, son of Abū Sufiān, and on his son as his successor.[1] The house of Ummaya was founded in 644. In 676 his son Yazīd was declared heir-apparent, and Mu'āwia set out for Mecca with the object of securing the assent of the leading dissentients at Medīna, led by His Highness Imām Husain, second son of 'Alī who was elected Khalīfa in 655 on the death of 'Usmān, the third Khalīfa, and was murdered at Kūfa in 661. Mu'āwia died in 680 and Yazīd succeeded him. The subjects of Yazīd excited enmity between Husain and Hasan, the second and eldest sons of 'Alī, representing the latter to be a mere boy, the son of a Faqīr, a poor miserable wretch, possessing no army, while he, a mighty monarch, had an inexhaustible treasury at his disposal. It was surprising that he should submit to be ruled by a man of Medīna. Yazīd, known to Shī'as as Palīd, 'the polluted', or Mal'ūn, 'accursed', thus influenced and elated by pride, demanded homage

[1] For a full account of these events see Muir, *Annals of the Early Caliphate*, chaps. 40, 41, 42. The narrative in the text follows the original version by the author, as it embodies some curious legends; but much which is of little value has been omitted.

from Hasan. He wrote to him in these terms: 'Come and be subject to my sway, and I will of my own accord not only make you King of Medīna and Mecca, but I will bestow on you great wealth'. Hasan replied, 'This is passing strange! Pray, whose duty is it to pay homage? Whence did this state of subjection and sovereignty originate? Consider the matter calmly. Do not presume on worldly wealth, to-morrow you may have to answer for this to God'. This answer further increased the jealousy of Yazīd.

After this another affair occurred. Yazīd learned that 'Abdu-llāh ibn Zubair,[1] an inhabitant of Mecca in his service, had a beautiful wife, and being a debauched character he endeavoured by some means to gain possession of her. On one occasion he said to 'Abdu-llāh, 'You are a man of Medīna and I have a virgin sister, quick, sensible, virtuous. If you choose I will give her to you in marriage'. He, being unaware of the plot, replied, 'O King of the whole earth! I agree with all my heart and soul'. Yazīd then took 'Abdu-llāh to his palace and desired him to be seated. In an hour or so he came out and said, 'The girl knows that you are a married man, and unless you divorce your present wife she refuses to marry you'. The moment he heard this he gave his wife the 'unconditional' divorce (*talāq-i-mutlaqa*). Yazīd left him, and returning after some time said, 'The girl agrees to marry you, but she wishes that the marriage settlement should be first paid, and until this is done she will not consent to the union'. 'Abdu-llāh answered, 'I am a poor man and the portion will probably be large. Where can I procure it?' Yazīd satisfied him by granting him the governorship of a distant province to which he sent him. In the meantime he wrote to the holder of that office and directed him to put 'Abdu-llāh to death by some means.[2] This was accordingly done.

Then Yazīd dispatched Mūsa Asha'rī as his envoy to 'Abdu-llāh's wife with this message, 'Behold! Your husband

[1] This man, a rival claimant of the dignity of Khalīfa, was besieged at Mecca by Hajjāj, general of 'Abdu-l-malik, and was killed in battle in 692. (Muir, *op. cit.*, chap. 50.)

[2] One of the 'letters of death', so common in folklore. The Arabs called them 'letters of Mutalammis' (Burton, *A.N.* xii. 68).

without any cause and through covetousness has divorced you. Now if you consent to be mine you may be the wife of a King'. On the arrival of the envoy at Mecca His Highness Hasan asked whence he came and where he was going. He replied, 'I am sent by the King of Syria to 'Abdu-llāh's wife, whose husband is dead, offering marriage'. Hearing this Hasan said, 'O Mūsa Asha'rī! In case she does not consent to Yazīd's proposals, deliver the same message in my name'. When the envoy gave his message to the lady and praised the grandeur of Yazīd, she asked, 'Well, what next?' He said, 'Imām Hasan, Khalīfa of this city, the son of 'Alī and of the daughter of the Prophet—on whom be the Blessing!—has also made proposals to you'. She asked, 'Anything else?' 'Why', said he, 'if you desire manliness and beauty I am here.' Then peeping at him from behind a screen and seeing him to be an old man, she said, 'O Asha'rī! You are old enough to be my father, and as for your beauty it cannot exceed mine. As for Yazīd, who can depend on his wealth which is only of a day or two? And like the noonday sun it may incline one way or the other. It is better for me to accept Hasan whose wealth will last till the Day of Judgement, and whose dignity and grandeur are in the very presence of the Deity'

The envoy informed Hasan that she had decided in his favour, and told him that according to Musalmān custom he might be married at the bride's house and bring her home. So Asha'rī took Hasan to her house, performed the ceremony, and Hasan brought her home. Asha'rī told Yazīd all that had happened, and he finding that his schemes had miscarried, became from that time indignant with Asha'rī and the mortal enemy of Hasan. Yazīd used to send order after order, urging them to slay Hasan and promising the post of Wazīr to his murderer. The Kūfa people also complained to Hasan of Yazīd's treatment of them and invited him to join them. Hasan trusted their promises and started for Kūfa. Yazīd sent his Munshī Marwān to Medīna, and on his way a man at whose house he stayed tried twice to poison Hasan. Yazīd urged him to make another attempt and promised him the post of Wazīr if he succeeded. Learning of this Hasan left the place, and on the way a man pretending to be blind thrust a poisoned lance into his thigh, and he long suffered from the injury. Hasan returned to Medīna, and there Marwān induced a woman named Ja'da to put poison in his water-bottle, from the effects of which he died. He was buried in the cemetery at Medīna known as Jannātu-l-baqi' or Baqi'u-l-gharkad, 'the garden of roots'.[1]

Husain thus left alone in his distress was invited by the men of Kūfa, and he sent his cousin, nephew of 'Alī, Muslim ibn 'Uqail, who urged him to come and win his revenge on Yazīd. So Husain went to Kūfa in A.D. 680. Muslim, in fear of attack, concealed himself in the house of a man named Hānī. When 'Abdu-llāh, the new governor, came, he ordered Hānī to surrender Muslim, and on his refusal had him scourged to death. Muslim, too, was slain, and his two sons suffered martyrdom at the hands of a man named Hāris with whom they sought refuge. When Husain heard of these events, he fell into despair, and an order came from Yazīd that Husain was to be slain. Yazīd's army encamped on the banks of the Furāt or Euphrates,[2] and that of Husain at a place called Māriya or Dashtbalā Karbalā.[3] In the end Husain with his family gained martyrdom. It is said that at the last Ja'far, king of the Parī or fairies, offered to help Husain, but he declined their aid.

The funeral service (*namāz-i-janāza*) was said over the bodies, and the family of Husain were sent with the heads of the martyrs to Syria. Among the mourners was Bībī Shahrbānū, daughter of the unfortunate Yazdigard III, the last of the Sassanian dynasty, thus uniting the house of Sāsān with that of the Prophet. 'To this union is perhaps to be attributed in some degree the enthusiasm with which the Persians, bereft of their old religion, espoused the cause of 'Alī and his successors, in other words the Shī'ite faction of the Muham-

[1] Hasan died by poison March 17, 669–70. The story that his wife was bribed to poison him is improbable, and his death was probably due to jealousy in his harem (Muir, *Annals*, 422).

[2] The Euphrates was called in Sumerian Pura-nun, 'the great water', or Pura, whence the Semites derived their Purat or Purattu, old Persian Ufrātu, and thence the name Euphrates and modern Persian Furāt.

[3] Mrs. Meer Hassan Ali, 11.

Fig. 1

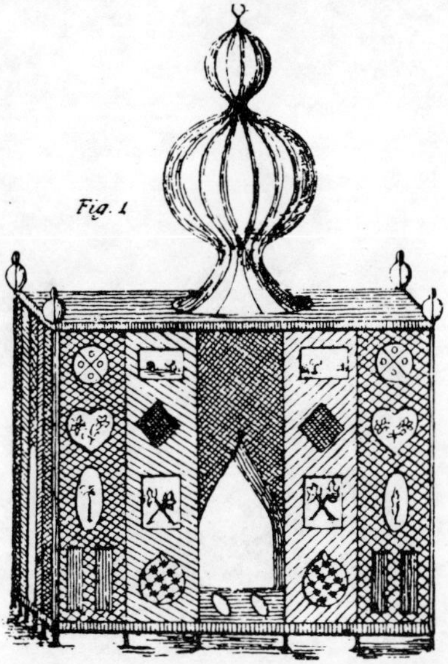

Taboot, or Tazea

Fig. 2.

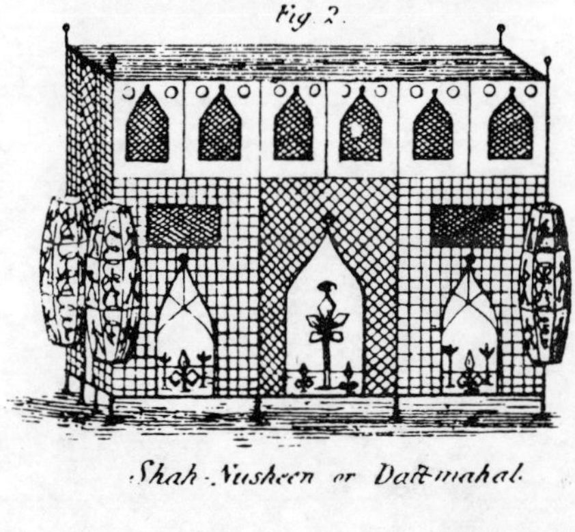

Shah-Nusheen or Daftmahal

Fig. 3

Churkhee-fanoos
or Fanoos-e-kheal

Fig. 4

Bootaq

madans, against the usurpation of those whom the Sunnīs dignify with the title of Khalīfa, or vice-regent of the Prophet '.[1]

Various miracles occurred as the heads of the martyrs were taken to Syria, under orders of Yazīd, in spite of the protests of Zainu-l-ābidīn, son of Husain, in whose charge the heads were sent to Medīna, whence, it is said, they were taken back to Karbalā. According to others, the head of Husain was buried at Cairo.[2] The Persians observe the 20th day of the month Safar in commemoration of the burial of Husain's head at Karbalā. They say that it had been removed by Mu'āwia to Damascus and thence to Karbalā, where it was buried forty days after his death. But Mu'āwia died in April 680, and Husain was killed on the 10th October following.[3]

The Muharram festival begins on the evening when the new moon becomes visible, but by the Musalmān calculation from the morning following. During the ten days of mourning it is believed in Egypt that the Jinn visit people at night.[4] The Muharram, including the tomb visitation (*ziyārat*), may be said to last till the 12th day of the month, but the festival really lasts ten days, known as the 'Āshūrā or tenth. Special buildings are provided in which they set up the standards (*'alam*), the cenotaphs of the martyrs (*ta'ziya, tābūt*), the royal seats (*shāhnishīn, dādmahall*), the representations of Burāq, the mule on which the Prophet made his journey (*mi'rāj, isrā*) to Jerusalem and to Heaven. Sometimes these buildings are decorated with screens (*tattī*) made of mica and other glittering substances. They are known as the 'Ten Day houses' (*'āshūrkhāna*), 'the house of the cenotaphs' (*ta'ziyakhāna*), or 'the Faqīrs' lodging' (*āstāna*). Strangers are not allowed to approach these buildings, as they must be kept pure for prayers.

The moment they see the new moon they do the 'mattock-

[1] Browne, *A Year amongst the Persians*, 88. For details of the tragedy see Muir, *The Caliphate*, 317 ff.; *Annals of the Caliphate*, 433 ff.; Sir Lewis Perry, *The Miracle Play of Hasan and Husain*, Preface.

[2] Burton, *Pilgrimage*, ii. 40; S. Ockley, *Hist. of Saracens*, 412, 415 note.

[3] Malcolm, *Hist. of Persia*, i. 264.

[4] Lane, *ME.* ii. 146 ff.

wielding' rite (*kudālī mārnā*). They recite the Fātiha over sugar in the names of the martyrs, and go to the spot selected for the fire-pit (*alāwā*). A sod of earth is turned and a day or two after the pit is dug. It is 1½ to 8 cubits in diameter, with a low wall built round it, and every year it is dug in the same place. After the pit is dug they light fires in it every evening during the festival, and ignorant people, young and old, fence across it with sticks or swords. Or they run round it calling out 'Yā 'Alī! Yā 'Alī! Shāh Hasan! Shāh Husain! Dulhā! Dulhā! Hāē Dost! Rahiyo! Rahiyo!' 'O 'Alī! King Hasan, Husain! Bridegroom! Alas! Friend! Stay! Stay!' In performance of vows some leap into the burning embers and out again, while others leap through the flames or throw handfuls of fire about. Women, too, make a fire-pit, sing the funeral elegies (*marsiya*) and beat their breasts. In Gujarāt 'a hole is dug about a foot broad and a foot deep. In this hole a fire is kindled and the person who has vowed to become a Dūlā, Dulhā, or "bridegroom", goes round the fire seven or eleven times. If any of his friends notices the bridegroom spirit moving the devotee, they wave a rod with feathers on it up and down before his face, fanning him gently, while incense is freely burnt. The people round keep up a chorus of "Dūlā! Dūlā! Dūlā!" to the measure of which the person wishing to be possessed sways at first in gentle, and by degrees in more violent, oscillations. When the full power of the "breath" (*hāl*) fills the devotee, that is, when his eyeballs turn up and become fixed in a steady stare, and his body grows cold, he is made to keep his face bowed among the peacock feathers. After his face has been for some time pressed in the feathers, the spirit seizes him and he rushes out heedless of water or of fire. As he starts, one of his friends holds him from behind, supporting and steadying him. He guides the Dūlā's aimless impulses to the Akhārā or place of other Dūlās or of the Ta'ziya cenotaphs, where fresh incense is burnt before his face. On the way from place to place the Dūlā is stopped by wives praying for the blessing of children, or the removal of a rival, or the casting out of a Jinn or other evil spirit. To secure a son the Dūlā generally directs a flower or two to be plucked from the jasmine garlands that deck his rod, a bar of silver or iron ending in a crescent or horseshoe, and covered with peacock feathers. On returning to his own Akhārā or place the Dūlā falls senseless and after remaining so for an hour or two regains consciousness. Only those can become possessed who have vowed to become Dūlās. Even to these the afflatus is sometimes denied. No woman can be possessed by the Dūlā spirits.'[1] In Sūrat, where the Muharram rites are more fully performed than in other parts of Gujarāt, on the evening of the eighth day of the feast children are dressed in green, and clothes are sent to families connected by betrothal. Besides dressing as tigers, men and boys often join hands and go about singing the Muharram dirges, dressed like Hindu Gosāīn ascetics or half-Hindu, half-Musalmān Husainī Brāhman beggars.[2]

Women doing the breast-beating (*sīnazanī*), a Shī'a practice prohibited to Sunnīs, call out with screams, 'Hāē! Hāē! Shāh Javān! Tīnon! Tīnon! Lohū mēn! Dūbē! Dūbē! Girē! Girē! Marē! Marē! Yā 'Alī!' 'Alas! Noble youths! All three! Drowned in their blood! Fallen! Fallen! O 'Alī!' If they remember any of the dirges they scream them out and beat their breasts. Some women in place of the fire-pit put a lamp on a wooden mortar or on an inverted earthen pot, and make their lamentations over it.

The 'Āshūrkhāna of southern India is replaced in the north by the Imāmbārā, 'the place of the prayer-leader'. On the first, third, or fourth day after the new moon the building is decorated, and the standards (*'alam, shaddā, panja, imāmzāda, pīrān, Sāhibān, Imāmain*) are placed there. Those that are paraded before the tenth day are called the 'mounted' (*sawārī*), and they are distinguished by having

[1] *BG.* ix, part 2, 138. The meaning of the fire-walk is obscure. It has been interpreted as a form of fertility or purification magic (Frazer, *GB.*, Balder the Beautiful, ii. 1 ff.; *ERE.* iv. 852; vi. 30 f.; ix. 510, 512 f., 518). It has been alleged that the walking through the fire is an optical delusion, the trench being so arranged that the performer can tread on its sides without touching the fire (Risley, *Tribes and Castes of Bengal*, i. 253; cf. *Man*, iv. 57). Also see Hartland, *Primitive Paternity*, i. 99. Rival theologians in India have challenged each other to walk through fire (Ferishta, i. 299; Smith, *Akbar*, 176).

[2] *BG.* ix, part 2, 138 f. For the Husainī Brāhmans see J. Wilson, *Indian Caste*, ii. 29, 134; Rose, ii. 141 f.

lemons suspended from them.[1] In all Shī'a houses the fish standard (*māhī*) is conspicuous, being the head of a fish made of gold or silver suspended from a pole decorated with brocade.[2] The 'dignities' (*marātib*) is also a standard fixed on a bamboo, decorated with rich cloth. These are carried on elephants, like colours. Some are known as those of Haidar, 'the lion', a title of 'Alī, 'the hand' (*panja*[3]) of 'Alī, those of Fātima, 'Abbās, the standard-bearer ('*alamdār*), that of Qāsim, of the twelve Imāms, of the 'protecting Imām' (*Imām zāmin*), the 'noble shield' (*dhāl sāhib*), the double sword presented by the Prophet to 'Ali (*barzakhī*, *qudratī*, *zū-l-faqār*), the horse-shoe (*na'l sāhib*), that of the charger ridden by Husain at the battle of Karbalā, which is said to have been found by a pilgrim and brought to Bījāpur, whence on the downfall of that kingdom it was removed to Hyderābād. These standards are generally made of copper, brass, or steel, inlaid with precious stones, or of paper or wood. Those of metal, whether new or old, are brought in state with music, after being polished, to the 'Āshūrkhānas, in each of which four, five, six, or seven are set up. They are fixed on staves of silver or wood, decked with coloured cloths. On the first, fourth, or fifth evening after the new moon they are fixed in holes in the ground or fastened to stools, and in front of them are placed lights, fly-whisks (*morchhal*), censers for burning aloes wood ('*ūdsoz*), toys, and other decorations. Sometimes on one side is placed a footmark of the Prophet (*qadam-i-rasūl*). Incense is burnt, and food and sherbet over which the Fātiha is said in the name of the martyrs are distributed.[4] Every evening the Fātiha is recited, and there is a lection of the Korān (*khatm-i-qurān*). In the morning they read only the Korān and at night the Rauzatu-sh-shuhadā, 'The Garden of the Martyrs', sing dirges (*nahhā*, *marsiya*), make lamentation

[1] A lemon speared on a knife is a powerful charm against evil spirits (Russell, ii. 179; iii. 181, 557; *BG*. ix, part 1, 420; xi. 61; xviii, part 1, 304, 345; L. Rice, *Mysore from the Inscriptions*, 185).

[2] See Sleeman, *Rambles*, 135, 137; Mrs. Meer Hassan Ali, 43.

[3] *Panja*, 'five', the hand with the fingers extended, a favourite protective amulet (Crooke, *Popular Religion*, ii. 39; *ERE*. iii. 459; F. T. Elworthy, *The Evil Eye*, 241 ff.).

[4] On the mourning see *BG*. ix, part 2, 137.

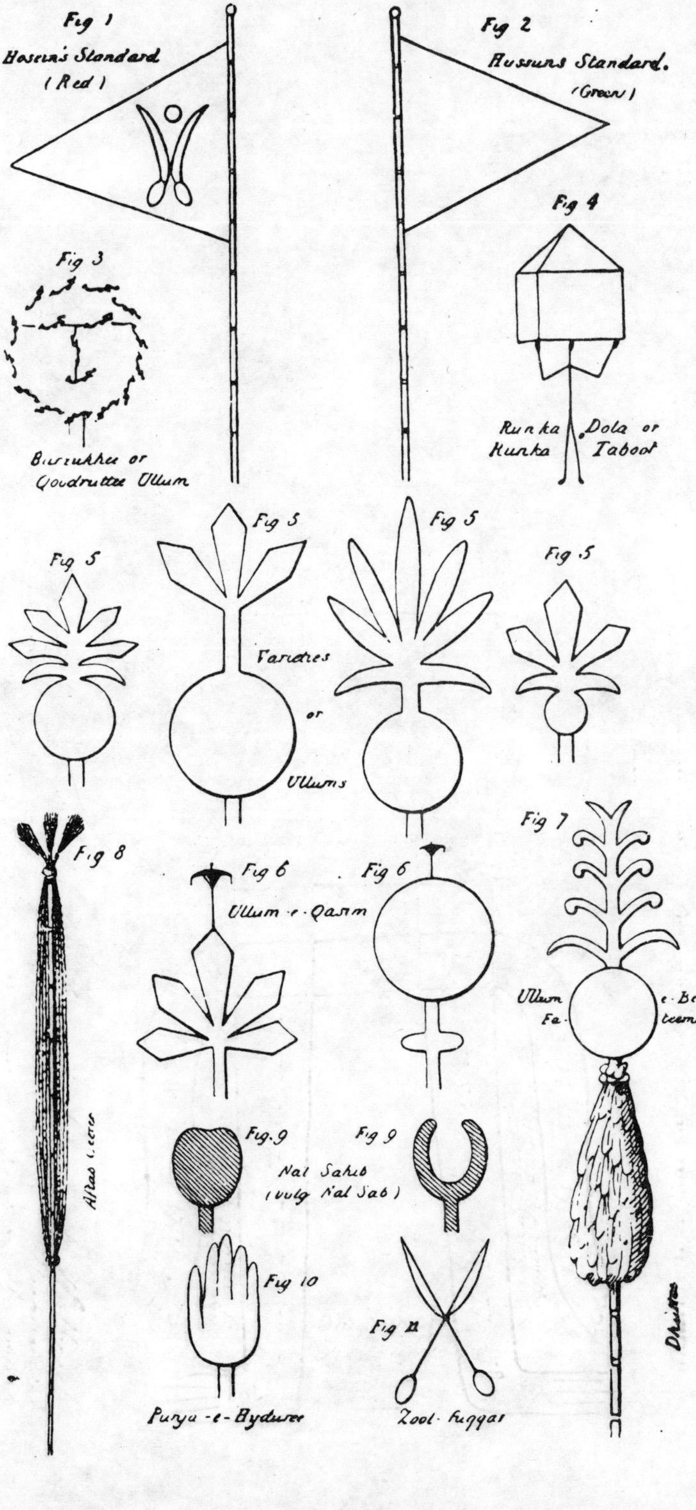
Fig 1
Hoseins Standard
(Red)
Fig 2
Hussuns Standard.
(Green)
Fig 3
Burzukhee or
Qoodruttee Ullum
Fig 4
Runka
Hunka
Dola or
Taboot
Fig 5
Fig 5
Fig 5
Fig 5
Varieties
or
Ullums
Fig 8
Fig 6
Ullum-e-Qasim
Fig 6
Fig 7
Ullum
Fa-
e-Beebee
teema
Fig. 9
Fig 9
Nal Sahib
(vulg Nal Sab)
Fig 10
Fig 11
Purya-e-Hyduree
Zool-fuqqar

and beat their breasts. Food over which the Fātiha is said is given to the poor.

Every night the funeral elegies are sung by boys trained for the duty, and Faqīrs and friends keep vigil (*shab-bedārī*). In south Gujarāt after the fourth day the mourning changes to merriment and masquerade, and the only observance till the tenth day is the offering of sherbet at the side of the roads to children and travellers. This seems to be, in part, a reaction after the intensity of the mourning, partly, an imitation of the revelry at Hindu festivals like the Holī or fire feast. In Hyderābād, from the first to the seventh day, except the recital of the Fātiha and of the benediction (*durūd*), reading of the Korān and the dirges [1] with preparation of food and sherbet, nothing else is done. On the seventh day of the moon, by the ignorant on the seventh day of the month, the standard of the martyr Qāsim, distinguished by a little silver or gold umbrella fixed on it, is paraded. He is one of the sacred bridegrooms, for at the age of ten he was betrothed to Fātima, daughter of Husain, and was slain in the battle.[2] In Lucknow this is known as the marriage procession (*menhdī*) of the little bridegroom. His standard is carried by a man on horseback, and the dancing-girls who follow sing elegies and beat their breasts. Sometimes it is carried by a man on foot who reels like a madman calling out 'Dulhā! Dulhā!' 'Bridegroom!' As he passes any 'Āshūrkhāna on the road he salutes the standards and recites the Fātiha over the smoke of burning aloes wood. Then he is escorted back to his own 'Āshūrkhāna, where he is laid on a stool as he is believed to impersonate the dead martyr, shrouded and treated as a corpse, while lamentations are made. Here sherbet, known as that of the battle (*ran kā sharbat*), is distributed.

On the seventh day the spear (*neza*), covered with cloth and having a lemon fixed on the top, emblematical of the spear on which the head of Husain was taken away, is paraded. As they pass, the people throw pots of water on the spear-bearer's feet and give him money or grain. The superintendent

[1] For translations of several dirges see Sir L. Pelly, *Miracle Play, passim*.

[2] Muir, *Annals*, 439; *The Caliphate*, 322.

of each 'Āshūrkhāna, as he passes, gives him a little ashes of the burnt aloes wood, which he takes with devotion, rubs it on his own eyes and those of his children, eats a little and makes his children do the same. On that evening they parade the standard of Bībī Fātima, that of Husain, the holy horseshoe (*n'al sāhib*) and the sword of 'Alī (*zū-l-fiqār*). Elegies are sung and lamentation is made.

The holy horseshoe is made of gold, or other metal, or of wood, or paper smeared with sandalwood paste. It is rather larger than a common horse-shoe. The bearers rush through the crowd upsetting infirm men, women, and children to the diversion of the lookers-on.

Some, in ignorance of the Law, make a thing like a human figure, and put the horseshoe on it as a head. Others carry a parasol (*āftābgīr*), a fan in the shape of a leaf of the sacred Pīpal tree (*ficus religiosa*), made of decorated coloured paper, and this is carried by a man who rests the pole on his waist-cloth while others hold it up with ropes. Whenever the bearer halts they lower the parasol and shake it over his head, but in their excitement they often knock one parasol against another and break them. Many do this in fulfilment of a vow. A woman makes a vow to the horseshoe, 'If through thy favour I am blessed with a son I promise to make him run with thy procession'. Should a son be born to her she puts a parasol in his hand and makes him run with it. Rich people let their sons go only a short way, and after that servants run for them. In the same way on the eighth evening they take out the Barzakhī or Qudratī standard, and in Lucknow on the following night those of 'Abbās and Husain. If two processions happen to meet on the road they make the standards embrace each other, and then pass on after saying the Fātiha and burning incense. In Ajmer an exciting spectacle is provided by the people of the Indarkotī Muhalla or quarter, in which a crowd of men armed with sharp swords dance and throw their weapons about in wild confusion.[1] Something of the bridegroom's spirit is supposed to dwell in the horseshoe, which works miraculous cures. To gain this inspiration a silver or iron rod ending in a crescent or horse-

[1] C. C. Watson, *Gazetteer Ajmer-Marwara*, 1 A, 40.

shoe, and covered on all sides with peacocks' feathers, is set up with the burning of incense. In the Deccan, particularly in Hyderābād, after each Muharram many such rods with horseshoes mounted on the tops are thrown into a well, and before the next Muharram all those who have thrown their rods into the well go there and await the pleasure of the martyr who makes the rod of the person he has chosen to represent him to rise to the surface. In Gujarāt this miracle is not vouchsafed.[1] On the tenth day in Hyderābād all the standards and the cenotaphs, except those of Qāsim, are carried on men's shoulders, attended by Faqīrs, and they perform the night procession (*shabgasht*) with great pomp, the lower orders doing this in the evening, the higher at midnight. On that night the streets are illuminated and every kind of revelry goes on. One form of this is an exhibition of a kind of magic lantern, in which the shadows of the figures representing battle scenes are thrown on a white cloth and attract crowds. The whole town keeps awake that night and there is universal noise and confusion.

The simplest form of the cenotaph or shrine is that made by Brāhūī and Baloch women, effigies made of cloth representing Husain, before which they gather and beat their breasts.[2] In Persia 'a litter in the shape of a sarcophagus which was called Qabr-i-Paighambar, or the tomb of the Prophet, was borne on the shoulders of eight men. On its front was a large oval ornament entirely covered with precious stones and just above it a large diamond star. On a small projection were two tapers placed on candlesticks enriched with jewels. The top and sides were covered over with Cachmerian shawls, and on the summit rested a turban, intended to represent the head-dress of the Prophet. On each side walked two men bearing poles from which a variety of beautiful shawls was suspended, at the top of which were representations of Mahomed's hand studded with jewellery.'[3] This is, perhaps, not connected with the Muharram, but it

[1] *BG.* ix, part 2, 138. For a photograph see Russell, i. 252.

[2] *Census Report*, Balūchistān, 1901, i. 43.

[3] Morier, *Second Journey*, 181, with an illustration; see Hughes, 408 ff. The Persian cenotaphs are described by Wills, 279 ff

is analogous to the shrine paraded by the Indo-Musalmāns. In India the cenotaph (*ta'ziya, tābūt*) consists of a framework of bamboo in the shape of a mausoleum, intended to represent that erected in the plain of Karbalā over the remains of Husain. It is usually covered with a network of paper neatly cut, and it is sometimes decorated on the back with plates of mica (*talq*). It is also ornamented with coloured paper formed into various devices and has tinsel fringes, the whole structure being surmounted by a dome which is often contrived so as to move round at the slightest breath of air. Its beauty appears when it is lighted up within and without. In shape it is square, its sides varying in height. Within are set up standards or a couple of small tombs intended to be those of the martyrs. Some instead of covering it with a paper network make strings of glass bangles (*bangrī*), with white paper flowers, and behind they tie saffron-coloured cloth or paste red paper. This is known in the Deccan as the 'bracelet bier' (*bangriān kī tābūt*). Others, again, replace the paper network with wax flowers and leaves of various colours, such as roses and tuberoses, and when they carry it about at night they squirt water on it to prevent the wax from melting in the heat of the torches and blue lights. This looks like a flower garden (*chaman*) and is known as the 'waxen bier' (*mom kī tābūt*). Others make the bier to represent the tomb of the Prophet at Medīna. This is decorated with gold and enamel and attracts crowds of admirers. Again, instead of the network, some people substitute cloth on which they sow the seed of mustard (*sarson*), so that at night the young plants make it look as if made of emeralds. Some make a representation of a camel, the spread hand (*panja*) or standards with mustard or jasmine growing on a shed (*manduā kī chamelī*), and as they carry this about on the Shuhadā or martyrs' day, the tenth, people throw bracelets made of coloured threads on it. The making of these biers or cenotaphs is said to date from the time of Amīr Tīmūr, who invaded India in A.D. 1398. On his return from a pilgrimage to Karbalā he made a miniature tomb of Husain which he added to the mourning rites of the Muharram.[1]

[1] *BG.* ix, part 2, 139.

In Hyderābād some people, instead of the cenotaphs, erect a 'royal seat' (*shāhnishīn*) or a 'palace of justice' (*dādmahall*), which, like the cenotaphs, are made of bamboo, paper, and tinsel. This is placed against the wall of the 'Āshūrkhāna, and standards are set up within it. It has sometimes a transparency in the form of a lamp-shade which moves with the slightest breeze, and is called the 'revolving shade' (*charkhī fānūs*) or the 'fancy shade' (*fānūs-i-khayāl*), the latter being a lantern which revolves through the heat of the candle placed inside, and has outside figures of camels and other animals. These shades are sometimes made independently, and are placed in front of the 'royal seat'. Some set up what are called 'screens' (*tattī*), made of square pieces of mica and mercury, like looking-glasses, which shine brightly in the glare. Large sums of money are spent in making these 'screens', which are specially in vogue in the city of Hyderābād. Some set up in the 'Āshūrkhāna artificial trees—mangoes, pine-apples, or custard apples—which look like real trees laden with fruit and flowers, with pictures of birds and squirrels eating the fruit. Sometimes human figures of various shapes and colours are constructed, representing people praying, sitting, standing, making prostrations, or of a sepoy standing as a sentry with his musket on his shoulder. This is contrary to the practice of the Prophet, who cursed the painter or artist of men or animals, and hence the portraits of rulers are absent from the Musalmān coinage.[1] Near these they place figures of birds and animals, and an artificial dove is made to fly out of its cage and coo.[2]

At some 'Āshūrkhānas or fire-pits (*alāwā*) they set up on a platform a representation of a woman grinding corn in a hand-mill. Sometimes they attach a heavy stone to a cucumber, melon, or plantain, and, strange to say, if a knife is stuck into it, it does not cut it.

[1] Hughes, 458.

[2] The dove, perhaps a survival of some older cult, is associated with the martyrdom. Lady Burton (*Life of Sir R. Burton*, ii. 77) describes the miracle play: 'Then comes the bier with Hossein's corpse, and his son sitting upon it and embracing him, and a beautiful white dove in the corner, whose wings are dabbled with blood.' On the Minoan dove cult, see L. R. Farnell, *Greece and Babylon*, 72 f.

On the seventh night of the festival a figure of Burāq, 'the bright one', the gryphon-shaped animal on which the Prophet rode in his night journey (*mi'rāj*),[1] is made of wood, painted and decorated with the usual Musalmān jewels on its nose, arms, neck, and ears. It is brought in procession from the painter's workshop, accompanied by reciters of elegies and torch-bearers, to the 'Āshūrkhāna where it is placed facing the front before the standards. The Burāq was sent from Heaven by the Angel Gabriel to convey His Highness Muhammad Mustafā, 'The Chosen'—on whom be the Peace !—It has the head and face of a man, long ears, broad forehead, shining like the moon, eyes black like those of a deer, and brilliant as the stars. Its neck and breast are those of a swan, its loins those of a lion, tail and wings like a peacock, in stature like the Hindu cow of plenty[2] or a mule, swift as the lightning (*barq*), whence the name Burāq.

Many Hindus have so much faith in these cenotaphs, standards, and the Burāq, that they erect them themselves and become Faqīrs during the Muharram. In Gujarāt, as the cenotaphs pass in procession, poor Hindu and Musalmān men and women, in fulfilment of vows, often throw themselves in the roadway and roll in front of the cenotaphs.[3] Others hang red cotton threads round their necks, mark their brows with white powder, and live for the time on alms given by friends. In Gujarāt on the ninth day of the festival some Hindu women wear wet clothes, a symbol of the ceremonious bathing after a death in the family, and drop pieces of hot charcoal on their bodies. They fast all day, and in the evening lick one of their fingers dipped in wet lime as a chastity test, and eat rice and sugar. Next day when the shrines are being taken to the river some low-caste Hindus, in the hope of securing the well-being of their children or the cure of some disease, offer to the shrines various kinds of food, coco-nuts, red threads, cloth, and even camels and elephants or the

[1] *Korān*, xvii. 1.

[2] The Hindu Surabhī, Kāmadhenū, or Nandinī, produced at the churning of the ocean, which grants all desires, and is reverenced as the fountain of milk and curds.

[3] *BG* ix, part 2, 139.

flesh of cock, goat, or buffalo, and with a coco-nut in their hands roll in front of the cenotaph.[1]

On the other hand, whenever the Muharram, according to the lunisolar calendar, chances to coincide with Hindu festivals, such as the Rāmanavamī or Rāmnaumī, the birth of Rāma, the Charakhpūjā, or swing festival, or the Dasahrā, serious riots have occurred as the processions meet in front of a mosque or Hindu temple, or when an attempt is made to cut the branches of some sacred fig-tree which impedes the passage of the cenotaphs. Such riots, for instance, occurred at Cuddapa in Madras in 1821, at Bhiwandī in the Thāna District, Bombay, in 1837.[2] In the case of some disturbances at Hyderābād it is said that Hindus who act as Muharram Faqīrs sometimes take the part of the Musalmāns against their co-religionists, and during this time do not eat any meat save that of animals which have been slaughtered by the Musalmān ritual (*zabh*).

During the thirteen days of the festival Musalmāns are required to keep their houses and clothes clean, and their bodies pure and undefiled. They refrain from congress with women; some from the first, others from the fourth, fifth, sixth, or seventh day do not eat meat, fish, or betel-leaf, and will not sleep on a cot, or if they do so it is turned upside down, as it would be disrespectful to sleep on anything raised while their Imām or leaders stand on the ground. On the tenth day some partake of these luxuries, while others abstain from the tenth till the thirteenth day. Married women are not allowed to show their faces to their husbands during the ten days of the first Muharram after marriage, and live apart from them. They observe the same taboo during the first thirteen days of the month Safar, the second month, known as the Terah Tezī, of the sickness of the Prophet, during the Bārah Wafāt, from

[1] The coco-nut is believed by Hindus to represent the head of a victim (Crooke, *Popular Religion*, i. 46, 148, 227, 238; ii. 106). In parts of the Bombay Presidency it represents the sacred dead of the family (*BG.* xv, part 1, 205). Hence, as representing a human victim, it is thrown into rivers to check floods (ibid. ix, part 1, 350). See also Burton, *AN.* vi. 217; Forbes, *Rās Mālā*, 323.

[2] *BG.* xiii, part 2, 524; Edwardes, *Gazetteer Bombay City*, ii. 195 f. In the latter case the riots were between the Sunnī and Shī'a sects.

the first to the celebration of the Saint's death (*'urs*), in the month of Rabī'u-l-sānī, the fourth month, because these are times of mourning, held unlucky, and no enjoyment should take place at these seasons.

On the fifth day at every 'Āshūrkhāna, rich people at their reception halls (*dīwānkhāna*), merchants at their house gates, shopkeepers before their shops, set up a place (*ābdārkhāna*, 'waterman's house', *sabīl*, 'a way, road') which is covered with a cloth and otherwise decorated, at which milk, sherbet, cooled and scented water are distributed to all comers, and these places are illuminated at night. On this day at Hyderābād almost every body, men, women, old and young, especially those who are unmarried, seldom the married, wear a Faqīr's necklace (*selī*), made of cotton thread, silk, or hair, and bracelets (*gajrā*), made of coloured silk or flowers. Intelligent people think it unlawful to wear these ornaments as it is contrary to the Law. But in India people obey more than the obligatory (*farz*) rites, the rubbing of perfumed powder (*abīr*) on the faces of their children, dressing them in green clothes, and wearing such garments themselves. The higher and the more respectable of the middle classes content themselves with merely tying a necklace on their necks and a bracelet on their wrists.

During the festival many persons adopt the garb and mode of life of Faqīrs, some wearing this dress on the fifth, a few on the second, and still fewer on the sixth or seventh.

The following are some of these classes in southern India:

The Sēlīwālā, vulgarly called Suhelīwālā (*suhelā* 'easy, feasible'), wear a Faqīr's necklace (*selī*, *ānti*), made of coloured thread. This is emblematical of the two classes of Faqīrs, known as Āzād, 'free, unrestrained', and Benawā, 'those who possess no worldly goods', who become Faqīrs through grief for the fate of the martyrs. They usually wear a hair necklace, but during the Muharram it is made of green or red thread, the former colour being said to represent that to which the corpse of Hasan was reduced soon after his death from the effects of poison, the latter the blood which fell from the body of Husain on the battlefield. These necklaces are made by the 'Attār or perfumers, or by the Patwā, makers of fringe and tape, who also weave bracelets of coloured thread ornamented with gold or silver known as 'remembrance' (*sumaran*) or 'carrot-shaped' (*gajrā*). Before these are worn they put them on a tray with sweetmeats, fruits, rice cooked and dried in the sun (*churwā*), and a present in cash known as 'lamp-money' (*chirāghī, charāghī*), for lighting lamps at the tomb of a Saint. After offering the Fātiha over these things they first put a small bracelet or necklace round one of the banners (*shaddā*) and then on their own wrists or necks. If the bracelet is worn only on one arm it is always the right, and the 'remembrance' is worn on the right wrist. They wear the usual costume of Faqīrs. After the Fātiha is recited, the Mujāwir or tomb superintendent takes the lighting fee, some of the fruit, and returns the rest. In addition to these ornaments some tie pieces of green cloth on both the upper arms, while some Faqīrs rub their faces with perfumed powder, hold in their hands an aloes wood pastile (*'ūd-battī*), and go about begging.

The Benawā or 'indigent' are also called Āzād, 'unrestrained', or Alif shāhī, because they make a black line like the Arabic letter Alif or A down the forehead and nose. They wear on the head a tall Persian woollen cap (*tāj, topī*), a shawl or turban with a gold band round it (*mandīl*), and on the neck a piece of cloth with a slit in the centre of its breadth through which the head is passed, and to which a collar is sewn on. One-third of the cloth hangs behind as low as the calf, and two-thirds is tucked in front into the waist-band (*kamarband*), so as to form a sort of bag to receive the contributions of the faithful. This dress is known as 'the shroud' (*kafan*) or Alfa, because the Arabic letter Alif is marked on it. They also wear a thread necklace (*selī*), a rosary (*tasbīh*), bangles on the wrist, a loin-cloth (*lūng, langotī, dhotī*), and round the right ankle an ornament (*dāl*), flat, of the size of a crown piece, made of stone, bone, or mother of pearl, with a couple of holes through which it is fastened by threads below the outer ankle joint. This is sometimes replaced by a silver bell anklet (*torā*), but some wear no ornament on the feet, apply coloured powder (*abīr*) to the face, and carry in their hands a fan, a switch (*chharī*), a sword, or an iron javelin (*sāng*).

Faqīrs of this class form a band (*guroh*) with various ranks and titles, under a director (*murshid*) or a leader of the troop (*sarguroh*), whom all agree to obey. Under him there is, first, the Khalīfa, who is second in command, like a Wazīr to a King; secondly, the Bhandārī Shāh, house steward or chief of the commissariat; thirdly, the Iznī Shāh, the 'caller' or adjutant who assembles the troop and conveys orders; fourthly, the 'Adālat Shāh, the 'lawgiver', who is the director of movements or quarter-master; fifthly, the Kotwāl, or chief police officer who maintains order and discipline; sixthly, the Dost or 'friend'; seventhly, the Al-hukm-i-lillāh, or commander; eighthly, the Amr-i-lillāh, or God's officer; ninthly, the Naqību-l-fuqarā, 'the Faqīrs' leader', who marches in front of the troop and proclaims the praises and attributes of God, as an example to the other Faqīrs.

When they arrive at an 'Āshūrkhāna they draw up in two or three lines before it, and the Dost or 'friend' calls out his title. The Kotwāl replies 'Whatever pleases Him, the Almighty!' Then the Al-hukm-i-lillāh calls out his own name twice from the right, and his colleague, the Al Amr-i-lillāh re-echoes his name twice. After this the 'Adālat Shāh repeats the introduction (*darja*) of the Fātiha by himself in a loud voice, and at the end calls out 'Fātiha', on which all the Faqīrs repeat the first chapter of the Korān, the Sūratu-l-hamd or Fātiha, once, and the Declaration of the Unity of God, Qul huw'Allāh, Suratu-l-ikhlās, three times, recite the Benediction (*durūd*), and finish by drawing their hands over their faces. Then the 'Adālat Shāh repeats sentences or couplets describing the excellence of his own profession, the Law, to which the others respond 'Ek nārā-i-Haidarī!' an appeal to 'Alī, to which the others respond 'Yāhu!' 'O He! (God)'. Again he shouts a call to the Sacred Five—Muhammad, 'Alī, Fātima, Hasan, Husain: 'Ek nārā Panjtan, Panjpāk!' and they answer 'Yāhu!' 'O He!' an appeal to the Four, Abū Bakr, 'Umar, 'Usmān, 'Alī; 'Ek nārā-i-chār yār bāsafā!' to which they answer as before; an appeal to the martyrs on the plain of Karbalā: 'Ek nārā-i-shahidān dasht-i-Karbalā!' with the same answer.

Then he shouts, 'O God! Thou art the only true God, and there is none else!' to which they answer, 'He is One and there is no other with Him!' 'I give witness that the man Muhammad is His Apostle!' Then he cries out 'Grant me the dust that lies beneath that foot ! ' to which they answer, ' As collyrium for my eyes ! ' As they march the Naqību-l-fuqarā calls out, ' Guard your breath ! ' that is ' Have God's name always on your lips ! ' ' Keep your eyes on your feet as you walk ! ' that is, ' Constantly repeat the Kalima or Creed ! ' ' Travel in your homeland ! ' that is, ' Contemplate God and His works ! ' ' In assemblies have private conference ! ' ' Even in a crowd have communion with God ! ' ' By the grace of the Holy Five ! O 'Alī help me ! '

If the band halts at any 'Āshūrkhāna the superintendent gives them pipes and tobacco, sherbet, cloves, and cardamoms, and if he can afford it, a meal of rice boiled with pulse. These men are called Dasmāsī or ' Ten Month Faqīrs ', that is, for the ten days of the festival, as contrasted with the Bārahmāsī, ' Twelve Months Faqīrs', those who are permanent Faqīrs all through the year. Amongst themselves they use as forms of address, ' Yā Hādī Allāh ! ' ' O Allāh, the Guide ! ' ' Yā Murshid Allāh ! ' ' O Allāh, the Teacher ! ' ' O Husain ! O Imām ! ' or Leader. If they call one they address him as Bāwā, ' Father ', Dātā, ' Giver ', Dunyādār, ' He that possesses everything '. Rupees they call ' a trifle ' ; ' What will you not give a trifle ? ' (*haurā-kaurī*) to buy arsenic (*sanbul*), which they eat. If any one refuses to give alms they repeat the verse :

' The generous are dead and only misers are left, There is no giving or taking, nay, they are ready to fight us ! '

When they are ready to start the Naqīb says :

' Were the world filled with wind it could not blow out the light of the Elect ! '

' Sugar to the thankful, a thump to the denier ! ', to which they reply, ' We are on the road to Heaven, and our belief is that of the Prophet ! '

The word Majnūn means ' possessed by the Jinn, demented '. They dress with a kind of fool's cap or long sugar-loaf cap of paper with a queue of paper hanging behind and trailing on the ground, ornamented with gold leaf. Sometimes this cap is made with panes of glass all round in the form of a lantern, with strips of tinfoil (*begar*) or tinsel, or white and red net-work paper hanging from the outside. Inside this they put a candle when they walk about at night. Instead of the cap they sometimes wear a shawl, a red sheet or a piece of cloth, while others have a string of ripe lemons dangling round their heads. Round the neck a red, yellow, or white scarf is twisted and worn in the shape of a necklace (*baddhī, hamel*), or a shawl or handkerchief is passed through rings. They smear their bodies with powdered sandalwood and pipe-clay (*kharī*). On each arm two or three handkerchiefs are tied and sometimes an armlet (*bāzūband*) over them. At the waist they wear breeches (*gurjī*) or a loin-cloth, in which they carry a whip (*korlā, korā*), a dagger (*katār*), a sword, a 'scorpion' dagger (*bichhuā*), a weapon (*mārū*) made of two antelope horns joined at the base, an iron javelin (*sāng*), a scourge (*qamchī*), and a switch (*chharī*). Their ankles are bound with strips (*ghantī*) of coloured cloth, or they wear bell anklets (*ghungrū*). Some get a couple of 'scorpion' (*bichhuā*) toe-rings, fix lemons on the points of them, and fasten one on each arm. Thus equipped they go to the 'Āshūrkhāna and dance a circular whirling dance (*ghūmnā*) to the sound of the tambourine (*daf*). There are four figures in the dance to which they keep time by chanting, ''Alī! 'Alī! 'Alī Bhum!' 'round we go!'

The Lailā take their name from the famous Bedouin love story of Lailā and Majnūn, told by Persian poets, especially Nizāmī. The man who represents Lailā has the whole of his body, from head to foot, glued over with cotton wool, covering even his waistcloth, the only dress he wears. In his hands he holds a cup, sometimes full of pounded sandalwood or sherbet, or a human skull cap, a coco-nut shell, or the calabash (*chippī*) of a turtle, and a fan or paper nosegay. On his head he wears a three-cornered paper cap.

The Bharang or Bharbhariyā, 'foolish chatterer', has his whole body besmeared with red ochre (*lāl gerū*) mixed with water. His head is covered with a shawl, handkerchief, or coloured cloth with a small flag fixed in the top of it, and like the Majnūn he wears shoulder-belts (*hamel*) made of cloth. On his legs he carries tinkling bells (*ghungrū, ghantī, zang*), and he wears breeches (*gurjī*). His loins are tightly girt, and as he dances he kicks his posteriors with his heels, calling out, ''Alī! 'Alī! 'Alī! Zang!'

The Malang are said to be disciples of Jamanjatī, a disciple of

Zinda Shāh Madār.[1] The term is usually applied to any 'unattached' religious beggar who smokes drugs to excess, dresses in nothing but a loin-cloth, keeps fire always near him, and wears his hair very long tied into a knot behind. They are by religion half Hindus and half Musalmāns. In Hyderābād those who personate them at the Muharram wear on the head a knob or knot of hair or of cloth passed through an iron ring (*chakar*) round which they twist red thread, gold or silver lace-edging (*kinārī*), and narrow lace (*gotā*). On each wrist they wear two or three metal bracelets (*karā*). The edge of a handkerchief (*gulūband*) is passed under one arm and the two upper ends fastened over the opposite shoulder, while on the neck are strings of beads or rosaries (*kanthā*, *mālā*, *tasbīh*). A sash (*kamarband*) encircles the waist, a cloth covers the loins, while on the right ankle is an ornament (*dāl*) or an anklet with bells. These men wander about, visit 'Āshūrkhānas, and as they walk rattle their anklets and call out, 'Hail Shāh Madār, Hail to Him!' Then one repeats the verse: 'Whatever you have, spend it in the road to Him (God). They will never gain good until they bestow it.'

Angīthī Shāh, 'King Chafing-dish', has his head bare, or he wears only a red or green thread tied round it, a waist-cloth on his loins and an iron chain as a waistbelt. His body is rubbed with pipe-clay or cowdung ashes (*bhabhūt*), and he carries in one hand a pair of tongs (*dastpanāh*). He walks about carrying a chafing-dish (*angīthī*), a fragment of an earthen pot held on the palm of his hand, containing live coals in which he heats one end of an iron chain while the other end fixed to a rope hangs by his side. When he visits an 'Āshūrkhāna he holds up the chain by the rope, dips it in oil which suddenly blazes up on the hot part, to the surprise of the onlookers, who wonder that he is not burnt by carrying the fire. This he manages to do without danger by filling the bottom of the potsherd with a mixture of the pulp of aloes and cowdung covered with ashes, which remains cool and prevents the dish from burning his hand.

The Sidī or Sayyidī, 'Master', is an African negro, ten or twelve of whom blacken their bodies with lampblack and oil.

[1] Rose, i. 579; iii. 57.

On their heads they wear a rough hat made of the skin of a sheep or goat, with the wool or hair on, or of a blanket or mat. Round the waist they have a small loin-cloth, skins with the hair on, blankets, sackcloth, or mats. In the left hand they carry a bamboo bow and in the right a coco-nut fastened to a short stick, the former containing some gravel which rattles, or sometimes it is covered with a cloth to which bells are attached. They dance to the rattling of the coco-nut, which they strike with the stick. Or they sometimes carry a rice-pounder (*mūsal*) in the left hand, which they strike with the stick held in the right. They twist their limbs about and mimic the jargon of negroes, or one of the party dresses like a negress, her face painted black like that of the men and dressed in the same way, her sex marked by a pair of hanging breasts. She beats the ground with a rice-pounder while the men dance round her and make jokes.

The Baglā or Bagulā represent paddy birds (*ardea torra*). Ten or twelve men, all of the same height, smear their bodies all over with cowdung ashes, wear white paper caps on their heads, and loin-cloths. They go about holding each other by the waist and imitate the call of the paddy-bird. One of them calls himself Bhīrī or Bahrī Shāh, 'King hawk', and dashes at the paddy-birds, who escape and hide in the crowd, while sometimes they catch one and run round to prevent him from escaping.

The Kawwā Shāh, or 'King crow', smears his body with pipe-clay, wears a blanket coat with strings on his head and round his neck. They walk about making jokes, each of them holding a cage containing a crow, or a frog, or a branch of a tree with a crow fastened to it by its legs.

The Hāth-katorē-wālā, 'he that carries a jug in his hands', wears a shawl, strings, or a piece of cloth on his head, a red, green, or yellow handkerchief round his neck, his face covered with sandalwood paste. Jug in hand he goes about singing the Muharram elegies, tales of battles, eulogia on great men, and collects alms in the jug. His song runs:

'Paisā denā rē Bābū! Paisā denā rē Māī!
Paisā denā rē Allāh! Hāth katorā dūdh kā!'

'Give us pice, Master! Give us pice, Lady! To him that carries the milk jug!'

The Jalālī or Khākī are one of the regular Musalmān Orders, founded by Sayyid Jalālu-d-dīn, a disciple of Bahāwal Haqq, the Suhrwardī Saint of Multān, whose shrine is at Uchh in the Bahāwalpur State. Khākī means 'dust-covered'. They have no special dress, but wear fancy caps of various shapes and immense turbans made of straw, leather, or mat on their heads, rosaries and necklaces made of fruits. Some have their faces half blackened, their bodies covered with pipe-clay, garlands round their necks, and dried pumpkins hanging from their bodies. One of the band carries a hideous female doll which he says is the grandmother of one of the spectators, while others have a mock club made of leather with which they strike any poor man or woman who comes in their way.

The Naqshbandī are followers of Khwāja Pīr Muhammad Naqshband, the term meaning a cotton printer. They are specially revered by Afghāns.[1] They worship sitting silent and motionless, with bowed heads and eyes fixed on the ground. Their dress is like that of the Benawā already described, but they wear in addition a shirt (*kurtā*, *alfā*). Their chief characteristic is that they carry a lighted lamp in the hand and appear only at night. The lamp has two compartments, one holding the oil, the other empty to receive alms. They walk through the bazars singing the praises of God and the virtues of light.

'Lākhān kror kharch kā bāndhē agar mahall,
Khālī parā rahgayā, damrī kā nahīn chirāgh.'

'If you spend millions on a palace it will be void if you have not a farthing's worth of light!'

Men, women, and children follow them, and when any one brings a child to them they rub a little of the burnt wick of the lamp on his face to prevent him from crying and becoming ill-tempered.

The Hājī Ahmak or Hājī Bewuqūf, 'Pilgrim Fool, Pilgrim Idiot', wears a long cap, a shirt and coat with a necklace. Each has an enormous rosary, a wooden platter, and a long walking-stick. They have moustaches and beards reaching

[1] Rose, ii. 350; *ERE*. viii. 887.

to the waist, wigs made of flax, and immense artificial paunches. They carry on coarse buffoonery before the 'Āshūrkhānas.

The Buddhī, Buddhā, 'Old Woman and Old Man', are represented by two men on a platform, the man in a male mask, the woman in that of a female with an immense nose-ring. They carry on coarse buffoonery.

Bāgh, 'The Tiger', imitates a tiger, running about with a bit of meat in his mouth, and springs at children.

Matkī Shāh, 'King Pot', is represented by some Jalālī Faqīrs, who carry about a pot containing dried gram which they rattle. They offer some of the gram to people and then stuff it into their own mouths, singing ludicrous verses.

Chatnī Shāh, 'King Pickles', dresses like a Jalālī and pounds up spices in a mortar, saying, 'I am making pickles for the Qāzī, the Kotwāl, or head police officer, the Sūbahdār, or captain'. Sometimes he adds intoxicants to the pickles and tries to induce people to eat them.

Hakīm, 'The Physician', dresses like a Benawā, and, mounted on a pony, he goes about with bags of herbs and makes ludicrous speeches. If any one asks him to feel his pulse he manages to touch it with cowhage or cow-itch (*kiwānch*, *macuna pruriens*), which causes intolerable itching.

Musāfir Shāh, 'King Traveller', dresses like the Benawā, pretends to be a traveller, cooks for himself, and distributes the food he makes.

Mughal, 'The Mogul', carries a rosary and a stick, and his attendants have each the title of Beg, or 'Carrot' (*gājar*), 'Turnip' (*shalgham*), 'Pepper' (*mirch*), 'Egg-plant' (*baingan*), with whom he makes jokes.

Byājkhor, 'The Eater of interest, the Usurer', makes jokes, pretends to offer his accounts, and demands payment.

Murda-firosh, 'The Corpse-seller, Carrier of the dead', carries about a representation of a corpse, and people pay him to take it away. If a bribe is refused he burns chillies, hair, and other offensive substances on a plate, and says, 'This is the scent which your souls will smell when you are dead!'

Jhār Shāh, 'King Tree', dresses like a Jalālī, takes a small tree, hangs all kinds of fruit on its branches and ties to it a crow by the legs, calling out, 'Take care! Crouch! A black owl has devoured the Prince of Fruits! Off with you!'

The Jogī is one of the Hindu Orders of ascetics. Men dressed like them come to the 'Āshūrkhānas playing on the guitar (*sitār*), tambourine (*daf*), the small drum (*dholkī*), and small tambourines (*khanjarī*), sing songs and funeral dirges with much skill.

The Baqqāl is the Hindu Banyā or shopkeeper, in Arabic and Persian a greengrocer. He is dressed like one of that caste, wearing a turban, streaks of ashes on his forehead with a spot in the centre made with a mixture of turmeric and quicklime, or sandalwood and turmeric. He has on his ears large Hindu earrings (*pogal, kundal*), bangles on his wrists, gold and silver finger-rings, round his waist a chain for holding his keys (*kardhanī, kardorā, kordalā*), and a white cloth round his loins. He carries in his hand an iron stile and a bundle of palmyra leaves on which he writes his accounts. A sepoy goes with him who threatens him, 'You rascal! You have overcharged me!' Pretending not to understand him, he abuses him in return.

Shāhbālā, the 'best man' at a wedding, the boy who attends the bridegroom to represent him and relieve him from spirit danger and the Evil Eye, comes dressed as a girl in fine clothes and jewels and is seated on a platform. People from below chaff him and try to make him smile. If he shows a sign of a smile the curtain is dropped and raised when he regains serenity.

The Sar bē tan and the Tan bē sar, 'the head without a body, the body without a head', is a trick played by a man concealing his head in a hole or under a bed and showing only his body while another buries himself, leaving only his head overground. A blood-stained sword is laid near them and the ground is stained to imitate blood. Or two men personate robbers, while one dressed as a woman cries out, 'They have murdered my husband (or brother). Give me something that I may go and bury him'. The headless body is a common show at fairs in northern India.

Naqlī Shāh, 'King Story-teller', dresses like a Jalālī, brings with him a dog, cat, rat, crow, and ass, and tells funny tales.

Kammal Shāh, 'King Blanket'. Two or three people cut a hole in a blanket and peeping through repeat verses, such as, 'One cock was killed at my wedding and a pound of rice distributed to thousands. One pice paid for all, but when the accounts were made up three-quarters remained!' Or, 'My doting mother tenderly reared me. She decked me in a blanket and turned me out!'

Khogīr Shāh, 'King Saddle'. A man dressed like a Jalālī wears a Musalmān saddle on his neck and red and white strings tied round his head, while he pretends to give chase to boys. Or he sings: 'In every lane I saw heaps of sweets and a lady with a nose-ring cast longing eyes on them.'

Sharābī, 'The Drunkard', is dressed like a Jalālī and has a mark like the Arabic letter A painted on his forehead, while he carries a bottle full of sherbet and water, repeating mock verses from the Korān in praise of wine and drinking freely. Much debate goes on between him and the other Muharram Faqīrs about the use of wine or pork. Sometimes he wears a leather Brahmanical cord (*janeo, zunnār*) round his neck.

Qāzī-i-la'īn, Qāzī-bē-dīn, 'The cursed and irreligious Law Officer'. He wears a sleeveless shirt, his beard and moustaches are made of flax, and he counts a rosary while he preaches various absurdities contrary to the Law of Islām.

Nawwāb, 'The Prince, Nabob', has his whole body wound round with straw, an enormous cap or turban of the same and beard and moustaches made of flax. He goes on horseback with attendants who carry an absurd tobacco pipe. He gives orders to his servants, and when he mounts he very often falls off on the other side.

Mekh Shāh, 'King Tent-peg', is dressed like a Jalālī, and drags bundles of tent-pegs tied by a rope to his waist. He threatens to drive a peg with his mallet into any one who dares to look at him or speak to him.

Khodūn-gārūn, 'Digging and burying'. He wears on his head a straw cap or turban encircled with ropes, his body is covered with a mat through a hole in which his head is thrust, his waist is encircled with ropes, on his shoulder he carries a spade and on his back a screen. He goes about singing, 'I throw down and bury whom I please; for a small grave

I charge a hundred rupees, five for a big one'. Then he seizes a rustic and pretends to bury him.

Hunar Husain's Faqīrs are two men dressed like the Benawā, save that their shirts are dyed with red ochre ; they have over their ears ringlets of natural or artificial hair, carry a small tray or winnowing basket (*suplī*) with a couple of cakes of cowdung in it covered with fine handkerchiefs, adorned with flowers, and holding a fly-flapper they go about saying, 'The remains of a great man who did wondrous miracles are hidden here. Whoever makes the circuit (*tawāf*) of his grave will never feel the torments of Hell fire. So make your wishes known to him!' Whenever any one asks to see him he shows him the contents of the tray, on which the inquirer retires abashed.

The Nānakshāhī or Nānakpanthī are followers of the Sikh Saint Nānak (A. D. 1469–1539).[1] Four or five men assume this dress with coloured strings (*seli*) round their necks, a spot of lampblack in the centre of their foreheads, their faces smeared with sandalwood paste, on their necks a handkerchief in which a small copy of the Korān (*hamāil*) is fixed as an amulet,[2] a necklace of conch-shell such as that worn by Rājputs, and two coloured sheets round their waists. They carry a couple of clubs, visit 'Āshūrkhānas, and, striking the clubs together, sing verses in honour of Husain.

The Ghagrīwālā are so called because they wear on their thumbs brass rings (*ghagrī*), inside which are little tinkling brass balls. Their dress is either white or red, their faces and bodies are rubbed over with cowdung ashes, they wear on their heads a sheet with coloured threads or fringes hanging to it, on their ears a feathered plume (*turra*), round each arm handkerchiefs tied like those of the Majnūn, armlets (*bāzūband*, *bhujband*), a waist-cloth and a tinkling ornament (*torā*) on the right ankle. One of them, lamp in hand, goes in front, and two standard-bearers carry white, green, or red colours. All of them with the exception of the 'Adālat Shāh wear rings on the right thumb, and these they rattle as they sing ballads of the martyrdom and the praises of Husain. In front of them a couple of Ramanīyā, or dancing-boys, walk, each having a painted earthen pot with gravel inside or a yak-tail fly-flapper (*chāmar*),

[1] Rose, iii. 152 ff. [2] Burton, *Pilgrimage*, i. 142, 239.

and so they dance and sway their legs, stooping or sitting down at the end of each verse. The leaders walk on each flank of the procession, and two men carry spears or long bamboos covered with coloured paper in front. While the troop halts they tie the spears crossways and stand with them so as to keep off other troops while they recite verses in honour of their spears.

The Gāruṛī Shāh are snake-charmers or buffoons.[1] They dress like the Jalālī, each wearing a feather ornament (*turra*) on his turban and carrying the pipe (*pūngī*) played by jugglers, Jogīs, and snake-charmers. When they halt they do juggling tricks.

Chindī Shāh, 'the Ragman', ties rags round his body from neck to feet and walks through the bazars without saying a word.

Khandar Shāh, 'the Tatterdemalion', or 'King Clout', wears rags, a tattered quilt (*khandarī*) and short breeches (*cholnā*) reaching to the knees. They beat each other with ragged handkerchiefs and at the 'Āshūrkhānas fall down and roll on the ground.

Ghalīz Shāh, 'King Filth', has his forehead marked with a black spot, with a leather handkerchief round his neck, and wearing a loin-cloth. He has his whole body covered with honey to attract flies, and goes about reciting ludicrous and satirical verses.

Rīchh Shāh, 'King Bear', is dressed in a black goat's skin with the hair outside, while two or three fellows in blankets imitate the growling of bears and frighten women and children.

Burburgā Shāh, 'King Doubledrum', is apparently identical with the Budbudgē of the southern Deccan, Marāthā fortune-tellers and beggars.[2] In Hyderābād they wear big turbans of different colours and carry a double drum. When they see a man coming they say, 'I saw a good omen to-day. You will become a rich man and get a palanquin, elephant and horse'. They twang their drum and bless those they meet.

The Mārwārī dress like the people of Mārwār or Jodhpur, the well-known moneylenders of western India and the Deccan.

[1] The Gārudī are a caste of snake-charmers found in the Bombay Presidency (*BG*. xiii 197; xix. 142; xxi. 224; xxiv. 116).

[2] *BG*. xxii. 200 f.

With pen in ear, they carry account books, bags filled with potsherds to imitate coins, and strut about saying, 'Let us settle our accounts as we are going home'. They make coarse jokes to annoy any real Mārwārīs they meet.

Ūnt Shāh, 'King Camel'. They make a camel of bamboos covered with paper, and a man standing in a hole within it walks along and personates the driver.

Men and women often make a vow that if a child is born to them they will 'take out the anchor' (*langar nikālnā*) yearly for three or twelve years, or so long as the child lives. This is done on the fourth or sixth day of the feast. They tie round the child's neck a string of flowers or leaves of the basil (*sabza, ocymum basilicum*), to which is sometimes added an iron chain trailing on the ground to represent an anchor. The child also carries a pastille of aloes wood shaped like a tree (*'ūd battī kā jhār*) and a standard, while boys with coco-nut leaves or little flags make a canopy over him. Coolies carry jars full of sherbet in the procession, which at night is accompanied by torches, and fireworks are discharged, and as they walk they shout 'Shāh Husain! Yā Imām! Yā 'Alī!' When they come to an 'Āshūrkhāna they walk thrice round the fire-pit and throw wood on it, the superintendent recites the Fātiha over food, some sherbet is poured into the pit and the attendants are fed. Other people, Hindus as well as Musalmāns, vow to give flags, sherbet, food, money to light lamps, perfumes and flowers if they are blessed with a child. When rich people 'take out the anchor' they do so in state mounted on elephants with matchlockmen, drummers, and dancing-girls singing the elegies. The offerings are sometimes carried under a canopy (*shāmiyāna*), the person giving them riding in a litter (*'amārī, ambārī*), or on an elephant.

Women often make vows to be performed at the Muharram. Thus a woman vows that if her wish is granted she will sweep the ground about the 'Āshūrkhāna with her wet hair or bathe her head in fire. In the latter case she covers her head with a sheet, and the superintendent with a pot-skimmer (*kafgīr*) throws some fire three times on her head and then brushes it off with a whisk. Or she vows that she will break her fast with no food save that which she has gained by begging, or that she will light a lamp with butter and have the Fātiha said over food, or that she will hang a flower (*gend-gahvārā*) on one of the standards. When their wishes are granted they perform the vow. Some beg at a few houses, add some money of their own and have a gold ring (*dur*, *bāolī*) made which they get a goldsmith to fix in the ear of their son on the tenth day of Muharram. In the case of a girl they fix a ring (*bulāq*) in the cartilage of her nose. Shī'as in Persia, when a girl is dangerously ill, vow that if she recovers they will marry her to a Sayyid, and a similar vow is made if they have been disappointed of children.[1] In the Panjāb barren women vow to offer a cloth, light a lamp and have the child's first tonsure done at a shrine, to put a necklet on the child, adding a coin to it yearly, and to give all to the poor when the child reaches the age of ten or twelve, to shave only half the child's head at a time, every week, or to leave a lock on his head to be shaved at a Saint's tomb.[2] In Baroda there are three kinds of vows: to Saints, to the Muharram cenotaphs, and to spirits.[3] In the Central Provinces Hindu Dhīmar fishermen beg food for an offering, take it to a Faqīr who dedicates it to the cenotaphs, and gives it to the people who dedicated it, this being the only occasion on which they will eat food touched by a Musalmān.[4]

On the tenth day, known as Shahādat kā Roz, 'the day of martyrdom', between 9 a.m. and 3 p.m. all the standards are taken to an open place near the sea, a tank or river, known as Karbalā ka Maidān, 'the plain of Karbalā'. Fire is lighted in the fire-pits round which they walk thrice and recite the Fātiha facing Mecca. Then they put a small coin with some milk and sherbet into an earthen pot, cover it, and lay it in the fire-pit which they fill up with earth, and fix a pomegranate branch on the mound. Next year the pot is dug up and some women for a consideration get the coins from the superintendent, bore holes in them, and hang them from the necks of their children to protect them from evil spirits. Some people after the fire-pit is closed pour sherbet over it and burn a lamp there for three or four days, as they do in the case of a real

[1] Sykes, *The Glory of the Shia World*, 67.
[2] Rose, i. 780; *JRAI*. xxxvii. 256.
[3] *Census Report*, 1911, i. 100 f.
[4] Russell, ii. 513.

grave. As the standards pass their shops, the owners, in fulfilment of a vow, throw handfuls of sweetmeats or cowries on them, and people pick up the cowries as amulets for their children. Some people vow that if they recover from a disease they will roll on the ground in front of the standards as far as the Karbalā plain. Men do this wearing only a loin-cloth, while women pour water over them to cool them, and their friends go in front removing stones and other obstacles from the road.

In the Karbalā plain a great crowd assembles, where sweetmeats and food are sold, tumblers, bear and monkey leaders perform, and swings are set going. Water and sherbet are dispensed to the thirsty, either gratis (*sabīl*) or for a small sum. When the standards and cenotaphs are brought to the water edge, the Fātiha is recited in the names of the martyrs over food and sweetmeats, some of which are distributed, and some regarded as sacred and brought home. The tinsel is removed from the cenotaphs, and the standards which they contain are removed. Then the structures are dipped in the water.[1] Some are thrown away, others reserved for future use. Men and boys, Hindus as well as Musalmāns, try to catch the drops of water which fall from them and rub it on their eyes to strengthen the sight. Then the standards are packed up and the food is distributed. The Burāq and Na'l Sāhib are not dipped but taken back, the former to be painted afresh and the latter annually smeared with sandalwood paste. They wave flags over them, burn incense, repeat elegies, and bring them back to the 'Āshūrkhānas, where they make lamentations over them and distribute food. Those who have acted as Faqīrs during the festival now lay aside the garb of mendicants and wash themselves and their ornaments. The members of every band, before removing their Faqīr dress, offer the Fātiha over sweetmeats, give some to their leaders, and eat the rest themselves. Some do not change their dress for three days. On this, the Day of Martyrdom, food is cooked in every house, the Fātiha is said over it in the name of Maulā, 'Lord', 'Alī, and the martyrs, and it is distributed to friends or given in charity.

[1] This was, perhaps, originally a rain charm (Frazer, *GB.*, The Magic Art, i. 247 ff.).

From the eleventh day, or sometimes from the twelfth or thirteenth, the people resume the eating of meat.

On the Day of Martyrdom some people take out in the afternoon the 'war bier' (*ran kā dolā, ran kī tābūt*), intended to represent the boxes or coffins in which the heads of the seventy-two martyrs were carried. Sometimes, as in Bengal, boxes of that number are used. They are made of strips of bamboo covered with white cloth. Like the cenotaphs they are taken in procession to the Karbalā plain, and as they return people run beside them calling out, 'The Faith! The Faith!' (*dīn! dīn!*), every now and then halting, reciting the elegies and beating their breasts. When the boxes are brought back they are set up as before till the third day, when they are broken up and the pieces reserved for future use.

On the third day comes the visitation of the standards, the terms used, 'third day' (*tījā*) and 'visitation' (*ziyārat*) being those used in the death rites. On the twelfth day, again, they sit up all night reciting elegies, reading the Korān and the praises (*madh*) of Husain. Early next morning, the thirteenth, they cook, eat, and distribute food in the name of the martyrs. That night they lay fruit, flowers, and other things near the standards, and after the Fātiha distribute the food of the dead. They then take down the sheds erected in front of the 'Āshūr-khānas and store away the standards. Cloths borrowed for the festival are returned, but those which are ornamented are put away for future use. If any one wants any of them he may have them on payment (*nazr*). Some people in pursuance of vows take some of the cloth and hang it round the necks of their children to prevent the shadow of the Jinn and the Parīs or fairies from falling upon them. Some in the same way observe the tenth, twelfth, and fortieth days of mourning by the distribution of food. On the tenth of the following month, Safar, dirges are sung and prayers offered for the souls of the martyrs, and on the fourteenth day, which corresponds to the twentieth of Safar, they observe the commemoration of the union of their heads and bodies (*sar o tan*) in the grave at Karbalā. The fortieth day is known as 'the tumultuous assembly', and the host provides coffee, betel, and sweetmeats for the reciters of the elegies.

This ends the Muharram mourning for that year. During the ten days of the festival Musalmāns should not work, have congress with women, drink any intoxicating liquor, or marry. If a death happens to occur during this period they must perform the funeral rites, but this is the only work allowed. This, of course, does not apply to duty as public servants or to other work of necessity. The rites observed in southern India, of which the above is mainly an account, differ greatly from the distinctive mourning observances in the north, where no buffoonery such as that of the Muharram Faqīrs takes place. Mummery of this kind is also practised by the Sunnī Musalmāns in Bombay, while the Shī'as regard it as a real time of mourning. This is said to be largely based upon spirit beliefs and ghost-scaring borrowed from the Hindus.[1] Such customs naturally are more prevalent in those parts of the country where the Musalmāns are largely converts from Hinduism.

[1] Edwardes, *Gazetteer Bombay City*, i. 184 ff.

CHAPTER XV

THE TERAH TEZĪ AND ĀKHIRĪ CHAHĀRSHAMBA FESTIVALS

THE Prophet, who died on the twelfth day of the month Rabī'u-l-awwal, in the eleventh year of the Hijra, June 8, A.D. 632, had been attacked by illness for thirteen days before his death. Hence the first thirteen days of the month Safar, which is called 'victorious, auspicious' (*muzaffar*), are known as the 'Thirteen of heat or fever', Terah Tezī, and they are held to be unlucky because the Prophet—on whom be the Blessing!—was seriously ill, and his condition is said to have shown signs of improvement on the thirteenth day. Should a marriage take place about this time, bride and bridegroom are not allowed to meet, nor should any good work be undertaken. On the thirteenth, or rather on the twelfth, calculated from the evening on which the moon becomes visible, all bathe. They take some pulse (*māsh*, *phaseolus radiatus*), wheat and sesamum, mix them, put a small cup of oil on the tray in which the grain is laid, look three times on their faces reflected in the oil, and each time drop a few grains of the corn into it. They also put some eggs and small coppers in the tray, and the whole contents are given away to Faqīrs and the Halālkhor outcasts, 'those to whom all things are lawful food'. They themselves on that day eat rice and pulse, sheep's head and its offal, and send some to relations and friends. Others mix gram and wheat with sugar, coco-nut kernels, and poppy seed, and reciting the Fātiha, in the name of the Prophet—on whom be the Blessing!—throw some on the roof of the house, eat and distribute the rest. There is no reason for ceremonial bathing on this day, a new custom introduced by women.

The Ākhirī Chahār or Chār-shamba, meaning 'the last Wednesday', is the last Wednesday of the month Safar, the second month of the Musalmān calendar. On this day the Prophet showed some relief from the disease which ended his life on the twelfth of the following month. On this day, therefore, every Musalmān, early in the morning, writes or causes to be written the seven Salāms or 'greetings' with saffron water, ink, or rose-water on the leaf of a mango tree or a sacred fig-tree (*pīpal*), or that of a plantain. The Salāms with the Koranic references are as follows : 'Peace ! shall be the word on the part of the Merciful Lord !' (xxxvi. 58) ; 'Peace be to Noah throughout the worlds !' (xxxvii. 77) ; 'Peace be to Abraham !' (xxxvii. 109) ; 'Peace be on Moses and Aaron ! (xxxvii. 120) ; 'Peace be on Elias !' (xxxvii. 130) ; 'All hail ! Virtuous you have been ; enter then [into Paradise], to abide there for ever !' (xxxix. 73) ; 'And all is peace till the breaking of the morn !' (xcvii. 5). They then wash off the writing in water and drink it in the hope that they may be preserved from affliction and enjoy peace and happiness.[1] This is a Sunnī observance, but Shī'as consider the day unlucky and call it Chārshamba-i-Sūrī, 'The Wednesday of the Trumpet', that is, of the Day of Judgement, an opinion now held in Hyderābād, and hence baths are usually taken the day before.[2] These writings are done gratuitously by Maulavīs and teachers. It is proper to bathe on this day, to wear new clothes, to use rose-water ('*itr*), to make sweet cakes (*gulgulā*) fried in butter. Over these the Fātiha is said ; they eat some and distribute the rest, walk in the gardens and say prayers. Some of the lower orders employ dancing-girls to sing and dance in the garden or at home, and regale themselves with toddy (*sendhī*) and other liquors. On this day schoolmasters give their pupils the gifts of the festival ('*īdī*), verses written on coloured paper with the boy's name inscribed below, and the boys are told to take them to their parents and read them, in return for which a present of a rupee or two is sent to the teacher.

[1] For charms written, washed off in water and drunk, see Frazer, *Folklore in O.T.*, iii. 412 ff. ; Crawley, 116 ; Thurston, *Castes*, iv. 489 ; *Ethnographic Notes*, 357 ; Lane, *ME.* i. 320. For the remarkable vessels engraved with charms, out of which potions were drunk in Babylonia, see A. H. Layard, *Nineveh and Babylon*, 509 ff.

[2] Bilgrami–Willmott, *Sketch of Nizam's Dominions*, i. 364.

CHAPTER XVI

THE BĀRAH WAFĀT; NEW YEAR AND SPRING FESTIVALS

THE third month of the Musalmān year, Rabī'ul-awwal, is commonly called that of the twelve days of sickness ending in death, Bārah Wafāt, because on the twelfth day His Excellency the Prophet, Muhammad Mustafā, the Chosen—on whom be the Peace!—departed this life. On this day accordingly the following Fātiha should be observed by all Musalmāns, both Arabs and foreigners. All must perform it because its virtues surpass those of the Muharram and every other Fātiha. It is one of the three days on which Sunnīs mourn, the others being the Muharram and the Shab-i-Qadr, or Night of Power. Men employed in the public service should obtain leave of absence for a couple of days to enable them to celebrate the Sandal on the eleventh and the 'Urs, or death day rite, on the twelfth. Learned men at mosques or at home rehearse during the first twelve days the praises and excellency of Muhammad Mustafā—on whom be the Peace!—as contained in the Hadīs or Traditions, and explain them to the lower classes in their own language. Some assemble daily, morning and evening, at their houses or in the mosques, read the Korān and cook stew, rice, and pulse, unleavened bread, meat stew (*qaliya*) or rice boiled in milk (*shīrbirinj*). Each man's portion is arranged separately on the table-cloth (*dastarkhwān*), aloe wood is burnt, the Fātiha is said both before and after eating in the name of the Prophet—the Peace be on him!—so that the benefits of the Korān may influence their souls.

Musalmāns believe that men have three souls or spirits: the lower or animal spirit (*rūhu-s-suflī*); the travelling spirit (*rūhu-l-jārī*) which leaves the body in sleep and causes dreams; the lofty spirit (*rūhu-l-ulwī*) which never leaves the body, even after death.[1]

Some people keep in their houses the Qadam-i-rasūl, or

[1] Others add to these: *rūhu-n-nabātī*, the vegetable spirit; *rūhu-t-tabī'ī*, the animal spirit; *rūhu-l-Ilāhī*, the divine spirit; *rūhu-l-muhkam*, the resident spirit; *rūhu-l-ilqā'*, the spirit of casting into, used for Gabriel and the spirit of prophecy (Hughes, 547).

footprints of the Prophet in stone,[1] preserved in a box covered with rich clothes. On this day the plate on which the stone is kept is decorated, the chest is covered with brocade and the Qadam-i-mubārak, or ‘ blessed foot ’, is placed in it, or in a cenotaph surrounded with fly-whisks. As is the case at the Muharram the house is illuminated, music is played, frankincense is burnt, and the fly-whisks are waved over it. Five or six persons in the form of an elegy (*marsiya*) repeat the birth service and the benediction (*maulūd, durūd*), the miracles (*mu'jizat*) and the account of the death (*wafātnāma*) of the Prophet, the last in Hindostānī, so that people may understand and feel sympathy and sorrow for him. On the eleventh and twelfth days, processions, as on the night of the Muharram, take place.

On the eleventh day in the evening or a little before sunset some people perform the Sandal of the Prophet—on whom be the Peace !—that is to say, they put one or more cups full of perfumed powder (*argajā*) or sandalwood paste on one or more models of Burāq, in a tray, or in a cenotaph which is called ‘ the Henna ’ or ‘ the Mosque ’ (*menhdī, masjid*), and cover it with a flower sheet. Along with these are carried trays of cakes with music and fireworks, while the benediction and birth service are recited. Thus they proceed to the place where the footprint of the Prophet is kept. On arriving there, after saying the Fātiha, each person dips his hand in the sandal paste or perfumed powder and rubs a little on the foot-print. The flower sheet is spread over it and the cakes are given to those present. The reason why the sandalwood is carried on an image of Burāq is that this was the steed of the Prophet. The Burāq really should not be brought out at the Muharram, but only at this rite, so that the people may know that it was on this animal that Muhammad Mustafā—Peace be on him !—ascended into Heaven.[2] But according to the Shar', or Law,

[1] Compare the veneration of the footprints of Buddha, the Buddhapada, which preceded the use of images, and the Vishnupada, or footprints of Buddha (A. Grünwedel, *Buddhist Art in India*, 71 f. ; Monier-Williams, *Brāhmanism and Hindūism*, 309 ; Crooke, *Things Indian*, 231 f.)

[2] ‘ After this an animal was brought for me to ride, its sex between a mule and an ass ; it stretched as far as the eye could reach ’ (*Mishkāt*, ii. 691).

the keeping of such models, as well as pictures, in the house is unlawful. The Burāq is left near the foot-prints till the thirteenth day. As a rule, the person in charge of the foot-print makes a Burāq and carries out the sandalwood on it, and people in performance of vows make offerings to the foot-print.

On the twelfth or 'Urs, the day of the union of a Saint with the Supreme Spirit, they sit up all night reading the Korān and other sacred books, and cook stew and distribute it. The women bring food, aloes wood and money for lighting the lamps to the foot-print, burn frankincense, recite the Fātiha, give some sweets to the man in charge, pour butter into the lamps, and bring the rest home. More butter than what is wanted for the lamps is usually offered, and the man in charge keeps the surplus for his own use. Aloes wood pastilles are burnt near the foot-print for the first twelve days of the month. This food for the Prophet usually consists of rice boiled in milk, because he was particularly fond of that, and used to call it the 'Sayyid among foods' (*sayyidu-t-ta'ām*). When rice-milk and cakes are offered the rite is called 'full' (*pūrā*). Some people keep a sacred relic (*asar-i-sharīf*, *asar-i-mubārak*), that is to say, a hair of the beard or moustache of the Prophet. This is preserved in a silver tube surrounded with coloured powder (*abīr*), and this is held in higher honour even than the foot-print. Food is offered before it, the benediction is said, and there are illuminations and music. But most of these hairs are counterfeit. Hairs of the Prophet are exhibited at many places, as at the Jāmi Masjid at Delhi. The 'blessed hair' (*mū-i-mubārak*) from the beard of the Prophet was placed in the Jāmi'Masjid or cathedral mosque at Rohrī in Sind by the famous mystic, 'Abdu-l-Qādir al Jīlānī.[1]

The Nauroz or New Year's Day festival was transferred by the Persians from the winter to the summer solstice, the former being known as the Mihrjān festival.[2] It is a distinctly Shī'a observance, hence it was abolished by Aurangzeb, a devoted Sunnī, who transferred it to the coronation festival in the month Ramazān.[3] 'It commences on the day when the Sun in splendour

[1] Burton, *Sind Revisited*, ii. 220.
[2] Albiruni, *Chronology of the Ancient Nations*, 199 ff.; *BG*. ix, part 2, 216.
[3] Jadunath Sarkar, *Life of Aurangzīb*, ii. 299; iii. 93.

moves to Aries [March 21], and lasts till the nineteenth day of the month Farwardīn, the first month of the Persian year. Two days of this period are considered great festivals, when much money and numerous things are given away in presents '.[1] In Persia it still retains ancient observances, modified by Islām. It lasts three days from the entrance of the Sun into the sign Aries, and it differs from the old Persian festival in the diminution of its duration and in the absence of all religious observances. There are no processions, still less any offerings of food to the dead, but all people as they meet say, 'Blessed be the feast!' (*'īd mubārak*), and send gifts to the poor. All are dressed in their best and share in amusements.[2] In the time of Aurangzeb 'the palaces were decked inside and out with high and costly hangings, made by order of Ṣhāhjahān along with the throne like a peacock . . . persons of the blood royal are weighed, according to ancient custom, in different ways—that is to say, first against seven kinds of metals, such as gold, silver, copper, iron, et cetera; the second, against seven kinds of cloth, cloth of gold, cloth of silver, velvet, et cetera. All the things weighed out are given to the poor, and what everyone has weighed is recorded in a book in memory of the occasion '.[3] Aurangzeb for himself abolished the custom, but he allowed it in the case of his sons, on their recovery from illness, on condition that the money should be distributed in charity.[4] In modern times it is observed by giving presents. If it occurs during the day, ladies throw a fresh-plucked rose, blossom downwards, into a basin of water, and this is supposed to turn of itself when the Sun passes into the sign Aries.[5] The Basant-panchamī, the Hindu feast held at the vernal equinox, March 31, was the form observed by the Kings of Oudh.[6]

[1] *Āīn*, i. 183, 276.

[2] Morier, *Journey*, 206; Malcolm, *Hist. of Persia*, i. 404 ff.; Browne, *A Year amongst the Persians*, 216; Benjamin, *Persia and the Persians*, 198 ff.; Wills, *Land of the Lion and the Sun*, 48.

[3] Manucci, ii. 348: On the weighing of Akbar, *Āīn*, i. 266 ff.; of Prince Khurram, Elliot-Dowson, vi. 341.

[4] Jadunath Sarkar, iii. 97.

[5] Mrs. Meer Hassan Ali, 152 ff.

[6] Ibid. 154.

CHAPTER XVII

THE FESTIVAL OF PĪR-I-DASTAGĪR

THE festival of the Saint Pīr-i-dastagīr or Pīr-i-dastgīr is held on the Gyārahvīn, or eleventh day of the fourth month, Rabī'u-l-sānī. His Excellency—May God sanctify his beloved sepulchre !—has no less than ninety-nine names. But the chief and best known are : Pīrān-i-Pīr, 'chief of Saints', Ghausu-l-a'zam, 'the great Saint', Ghausu-s-samdānī, 'the eternal Saint', Mahbūb-i-subhānī, 'the beloved, divine', Mīrān Muhiyu-d-dīn, 'the reviver of religion', Sayyid or Shaikh 'Abdu-l-qādir Jīlānī, Hasaniu-l-Husainī, the founder of the Qādiriya Order of mendicants, taking his name, Jīlānī, from his birthplace, Gīlān or Jīlān, properly Kil o Kilān, in western Persia. He was born in A.D. 1078 and died at Baghdād February 22, 1166, where his tomb is still held in great veneration. He is esteemed the chief Walī or Saint, a worker of miracles, who appears at times to his disciples and gives them instruction. In the Panjāb he is venerated by the Hijras or eunuchs.[1] The Author, Ja'far Sharīf, speaks from experience, because when oppressed in mind concerning things which he desired he used to repeat his ninety-nine names, and make a vow before God Almighty imploring His aid by the spirit of Pīr-i-dastagīr, and, by the mercy of God, His Excellency Ghausu-l-a'zam presented himself to him in his sleep, relieved him from his perplexities, and accomplished his desires. Let men of my faith disbelieve this assertion if they please, or think that I make it in order to enhance the dignity of my Pīr or to aggrandize myself. If it proves true, may God's curses descend on those who disbelieve it, and may their religion and livelihood be annihilated ! Sunnīs consider Pīr-i-dastagīr a great personage and have a fervent belief in him, but some Shī'as in their ignorance slander him by asserting that this Pīr, Mahbūb-i-subhānī—May God have mercy on him !—occasioned the

[1] Rose, ii. 331.

death of His Excellency Imām Ja'far—May God bless him!—by causing him to swallow molten lead. This charge is based on malice, for no less than 250 years elapsed from the days of His Excellency Imām Ja'far Sādiq, 'the Just', the sixth Imām (A.D. 702–63) and those of His Excellency Mahbūb (A.D. 1078–1166).[1]

On the tenth of the month Rabī'u-s-sānī they perform his Sandal, and on the eleventh his Charāghan, or Chirāghan, or lamp festival. On the evening of the tenth they carry out a large green flag with impressions of the spread hand (*panja*) made on it with sandalwood paste, and bringing with it sandalwood, cakes (*malīda*), sugar, flowers, and aloes, with torches and music, they perambulate the town in state, go to the place appointed and set up the standard. Then offering the Fātiha in the name of the Pīr, they put flowers and sandalwood on the flag and distribute the cakes to the people. On the eleventh day they cook food, recite the birth service and the benediction (*maulūd, durūd*), give a recital of the whole Korān which takes two days, and repeat the ninety-nine names of the Saint. In Gujarāt the poor light eleven or twenty-two lamps, and in the houses of the rich small leafless trees or green embroidered frames (*mahdī*) are decorated with eleven lamps and covered with gifts of food and sweets for the children. At night powdered sugar bread (*malīda*) is eaten.[2]

When cholera or any other plague is raging they take out the flag (*jhandā*) of the Saint, perambulate the town, halting every now and then as the call to prayer (*azān*) is raised. Both Hindus and Musalmāns make gifts and put them in the pot ('*ūddān*, '*ūdsoz*) in which the aloes are burnt. Sometimes they offer the Fātiha over sweetmeats or sugar, bring the flag back and set it up in its place. This is done on one, three, five successive Thursdays in the month. Many people make little flags in the name of the Saint and set them up at their houses over the doors to secure themselves from misfortune. Usually by these means the plague is averted.

Some people vow that if, by the mercy of the Saint, they are

[1] Ja'far Sādiq, 'the veracious', so called on account of the uprightness of his character, the sixth Shī'a Imām.

[2] *BG.* ix, part 2, 140. Compare the Christmas tree of Europe.

blessed with a son or daughter, they will make him, or her, his slave. Should their wishes be accomplished, on the tenth or eleventh of this month they fix on the child a large silver anklet ring (*halqa*, *berī*), on which year by year they pass a smaller ring. They cook cakes, place on them eleven small lamps made of flour paste, and light them with red cotton wicks soaked in butter. They burn aloes and put the ring on the child, if it be an anklet on the right ankle, if it be a collarette (*tauq*) round the child's neck. Instead of these some people have a silver or leathern belt (*baddhī*) bound round the waist of the child. Most people say the Fātiha over a little stew, others invite friends and Faqīrs. This Fātiha is called the Gyārahvīn, or 'eleventh', the day of the Saint's death, but, as a matter of fact, he died on the 17th Rabī'u-s-sānī, February 22, 1166. But as for eleven days in every month he was in the habit of reciting the Fātiha in the name of the Prophet—on whom be the Peace!—the former date is kept for reciting the Fātiha in his name, but some perform this rite on any day in the month. Some have a cenotaph (*menhdī*) made of green paper or of wood painted green, ornamented with silver, and on his death day (*'urs*) they hang on it flowers, a bridegroom's veil (*siharā*) and fruits, fresh or dry, light lamps and set it up. Many people make a formal procession round the town and collect money or grain in a metal or earthen pot (*tambālū*, *matkī*) covered with cloth, in which a rent is made. Through this they put in a coin daily, either money or cowries. On the death day they take out the contents of the pot and with the money perform the rite.

The sister's son of the Saint was Sayyid Ahmad Kabīr Rafā'ī, from whom the Order of Faqīrs known as Rafā'ī, Gurzmār, Munhphorā, Munhchīrā, so called because they are in the habit of gashing their faces and bodies with a sort of spiked mace (*gurz*) hanging to a chain, is derived. By another account, however, this Order was founded at Baghdād in 876 of the Hijra era, A.D. 1471, by Ahmad-ar-Rifā'a.[1]

[1] Macdonald, 267; Rose, ii. 321 f.

CHAPTER XVIII

THE FESTIVAL OF THE SAINT ZINDA SHĀH MADĀR

By one account His Excellency Shāh Badiu-d-dīn or Zinda Shāh Madār, Ghāzī Miyān, was a converted Jew, born at Aleppo, A.D. 1050, who is said to have died at Makanpur, 40 miles from Cawnpore in that District of the United Provinces of Agra and Oudh. He is called Zinda, 'the living one', because he is supposed to be still alive, the Prophet having given him the power of living without breath. He used to wear black clothes, and neither married nor had congress with women. His shrine is visited by crowds of pilgrims, both Hindus and Musalmāns. Women are excluded from his shrine because it is believed that any woman entering is immediately seized with violent internal pains, as if her whole body were immersed in flames of fire. As in the case of Pīr-i-dastagīr, people make vows to him and in his name put belts (*baddhī*) of gold and silver round the necks of their children. He is supposed to have died on the seventeenth day of the fifth month, Jamādiu-l-awwal, and some people on that day, others on its eve, make dishes of wheaten flour, meat cakes (*satrī*), and other food, put seventeen lamps on it and then put the belt on the child.[1]

Some perform the rite of fire-walking in the name of the Saint. This is known as Dhammāl kūdnā, *dhammāl* meaning 'the place of virtuous conduct' (*dharma*), and *kūdnā*, 'to leap'. They kindle a large fire, send for the Tabaqātī, or Faqīrs of this Order, and give them a present. The Faqīrs recite the Fātiha, sprinkle sandalwood in the fire, and then the chief of the band leads the way by jumping into it, calling out, 'Dam Madār! Dam Madār!' 'the breath of Madār', this, as among the Persians,[2] being supposed to be a protective

[1] See Mrs. Meer Hassan Ali, 374; *Dabistān*, ii. 224; Rose, ii. 160 ff.; *Census Report*, Panjāb, 1891, i. 196 f.; Wise, *Notes*, 13 f.

[2] Morier, *Journey*, 101.

against the flames, the bite of a snake, or the sting of a scorpion. Then the rest follow him also shouting 'Dam Madār!', and tread out the fire. Their feet are washed with milk and water and they are found to have received no injury.

The rite of 'plundering the cow' (*gāī lutānā*) is done by vowing a black cow, usually on the supposed birthday of the Saint, 17 Jamādiu-l-awwal, either at one of their houses or at a lodge (*āstāna*) of the Order. It is slaughtered in the Musalmān ritual fashion (*zabh*), in the name of the Saint, and the meat is distributed among the Faqīrs. In some places a standard (*'alam*) is set up at one of the lodges with a black flag fastened to it, and on the seventeenth day they perform the death rite (*'urs*) of the Saint, or on the proceeding day they do the Sandal rite, as in the case of Pīr-i-dastagīr. On both nights they sit up singing the praises of the Saint. On the anniversary of his death they have illuminations and vigils. This standard is kept all the year round in its appointed place, and it is never removed, as is done with the Muharram standards.

CHAPTER XIX

THE FESTIVAL OF THE SAINT QĀDIRWALĪ SĀHIB

THE shrine of the Saint Qādirwalī Sāhib is situated in the town of Nāgor, a suburb of the town of Negapatam (Nāgapattanam, 'the town of the Nāga or serpent race') in the Tanjore District, Madras, a stronghold of the Marakāyyan traders, a mixed class of Musalmāns, who, with the Labbaīs and Māppillās, members of the Shāfī'ya sect, are his chief votaries.[1] The Saint has been by some authorities identified with Muīnu-d-din Chishtī, the famous Saint of Ajmer,[2] but he appears to be a local worthy. His Sandal celebration is held on the ninth of the month Jamādiu-l-ākhir or -sāni, the sixth month, and on the tenth his death anniversary ('*urs*) is observed in the usual way by preparing food, reading the birth service (*maulūd*) of the Prophet, by keeping a night vigil, and by illuminations. About Rs. 10,000 are spent on this occasion. On the eleventh day they 'break the rice and milk pot' (*khīr kī hāndī*), that is to say, when they observe the new moon, or on the second or fourth day after it, a leader (*sarguroh*) of one of the groups (*silsila*) of his devotees, or a Faqīr of the Malang Order, sits on a mattress or quilt spread on the ground in a closet, and spends the whole time there without drinking or obeying the calls of nature, engaged in the worship of the Deity. He does not leave this place or speak to any one till the eleventh, when the attendants (*mujāvir*) cook rice milk in a large pot, which is carried on the head of one of them to this Faqīr. He recites the Fātiha over it and tastes a little. Then leaving the closet, he joins the band of Faqīrs to which he belongs, while the attendants take the pot in procession to

[1] *IGI*. xix. 2 ff.; Thurston, *Castes*, v. 1 ff.; iv. 198 ff., 455 ff.

[2] Garcin de Tassy, *Mémoire sur des particularities de la religion Musalmane dans l'Inde*, 63.

the sea beach and there dash it in pieces. All the people present scramble for some of the rice milk, and take up so much of the sand that they leave a large hole. But strange to say, it is said that no one is ever hurt in the struggle. A few days after the death celebration many bodies of Faqīrs, from far and near, assemble (*chauk baithē hain*) in this place, but the different bands, each under their own leaders, sit apart. If any Faqīr has been guilty of a breach of discipline he is punished by the leader at this meeting, the penalty being that he is compelled to carry the bedding of all the assembled Faqīrs, or in some other way he must express his contrition, beg for mercy, and give a written engagement to behave better in future. He is then restored to membership, but if a serious charge is proved in the presence of the assembly (*jamā'u-llāh*), his leather loin strap is cut in two and he is excommunicated. In this case he can never rejoin the Order. The same procedure is followed at the annual death rites of other Saints, such as Tabar-i-'alam, Bābā Budan or Hayāt Qalandar, Bābā Faqru-d-dīn, and others. When a Faqīr, or one of their Pīrs or leaders, has never attended one of the Saint's death rites he is considered an unfit member of the Order. At some of these celebrations Faqīrs accept money from the attendant (*mujāvir*), distribute it among themselves and depart. Musalmān ship captains and sailors make vows and oblations in the name of His Excellency Qādirwalī Sāhib. For instance, when they meet with disaster at sea, they vow that if they and their cargo reach land in safety they will spend a certain sum of money in offering the Fātiha in his name. When they first see the new moon of the month in which he died they set up a flag, known as 'the centipede' (*gom*), five or six cubits long and shaped like a centipede. In other places, too, devotees of the Saint fly a 'centipede' flag in his honour and offer the Fātiha yearly in his name, but some merely say the Fātiha over some cakes in his honour. The cult of this Saint is a remarkable instance of the devotion of Hindus to Musalmān worthies; in fact, both creeds claim him as a member, the explanation being that he used to preach to both classes. A Hindu Rājā once made a vow that if he was blessed with a son he would enlarge and beautify the mosque near the

Saint's tomb, and there was a close connexion between the Hindu royal family of Tanjore and this Saint.[1]

Innumerable miracles of the Saint are described, of which the following are the best known. A ship sprang a leak at sea and the Nākhudā, or captain, vowed that if Qādirwalī stopped the leak he would on reaching land dedicate to him the profits of the cargo and offer a couple of gold and silver models of the ship.[2] The Saint at the time was being shaved, and learning the danger of the ship he threw away the barber's looking-glass, which, by the dispensation of Providence, flew through the air to the vessel, stuck to its side, and stopped the leak. When the ship came safe to land the captain, in obedience to his vow, brought his offering in gold and a gold and silver model of his vessel. The Saint ordered him to restore the looking-glass to the barber, and when the skipper in amazement asked what looking-glass he meant, the Saint replied that it was that which stuck in the leak. The skipper found it there and returned it.

On another occasion the Saint, who is said to have passed his life in the desert and never to have seen a woman, was bathing at a tank and noticed a woman with unusually large breasts, it being the custom of women in this part of India not to cover the upper parts of their bodies. He imagined that she was suffering from abscesses, and in compassion for her he prayed, 'Grant, O God, that these abscesses may be removed!' On this her breasts withered away. In her grief she told her friends that a Faqīr had seen her, and by mumbling some words had caused her breasts to disappear. They went to the Saint who told them that he supposed that she was suffering from disease, but as he now learned that they were natural he hoped the Almighty would restore them to their original state. When he said this her breasts reappeared. Near the tomb of the Saint is a coco-nut grove. The tax-gatherer claimed the tax for it, but the owner replied that the trees

[1] Sell, 262 f.

[2] Me tabula sacer
Votiva paries indicat uvida
Suspendisse potenti
Vestimenta maris deo.—Horace, *Odes*, I. v. 13–16.

belonged to the Saint and that they had never been assessed. The other insisted that the tax should be paid, adding that as the coco-nuts had no horns he was not afraid of them. Strange to say, horns grew on the coco-nuts, and they still hang near his blessed shrine, while from that day to this the tax has never been collected. God alone knows whether these things be true or not. I, says Ja'far Sharīf, state only what I have heard. May the guilt of the lie be on the neck of him who invented it !

CHAPTER XX

THE SAINTS RAJAB SĀLĀR AND SAYYID JALĀLU-D-DĪN OF BOKHĀRA; THE ASCENT OF THE PROPHET TO HEAVEN; GŪGĀ

THE festival of the Saint Rajab Sālār is known as 'the table-cloth, or napkin' (*kandūrī*), and it takes place on any Thursday or Friday in the month Rajab, the seventh month. Rajab Sālār, known as Sayyid Mas'ūd Ghāzī, is said to have been the nephew of Sultān Mahmūd of Ghaznī, and was slain in battle with the Hindus at Bahrāich in Oudh, on June 15, 1033 or 1034 A.D. His tomb is a domed building erected two centuries after the death of the martyr on the site of a temple of the Sun. Fīroz Tughlaq of Delhi (A.D. 1351–88) added a well and other buildings.[1] The rite in his honour is done as follows: First, a hole which had been dug on a previous festival and had been filled with the refuse of the food offerings, is reopened for the Kandūrī kī Fātiha, the blessing of the food, Kandūrī meaning 'a table-cloth or napkin'. This is called the fire-pit (*alāwā*), but many people dispense with it. It is only superstitious women, deeming it unlucky to expose the sacred food to the light, who dig these pits to bury in them the refuse of the food. With the exception of fish and eggs they prepare all kinds of meat, bread, cakes, and vegetables, and arrange each person's share on a table-cloth (*dastarkhwān*). Incense is burnt, the Fātiha recited, and the food is shared and eaten. Some make images of little horses of wheat flour boiled in syrup with plates of gram intended for the horses.[2] These are eaten and shared indoors, most people eating a little of it before any other food. Sometimes these horses are known as 'loose' (*khulē ghorē*), and these are eaten and shared out of doors after the Fātiha has been recited over them. Some people, especially those suffering from diseased legs, vow that if they recover health through the favour of His Excellency

[1] *IGI.* vi. 213.

[2] On horse offerings see p. 140 above.

Sālār Mas'ūd Ghāzī, they will make 'loose horses' and recite the Fātiha over them in his name.

Some people on a Thursday or a Friday in this month fill some large pots (*kundā*) to the brim with fruits and food, and after offering the Fātiha in the name of the Saint Jalālu-d-dīn of Bokhāra, eat and share the food.[1] Others, especially Shī'as, offer food in these pots in the name of Maulā 'Alī, son-in-law of the Prophet, a custom not ordained in the Law, but current in Hindostān. This rite is said to be called also Hazārī.[2]

On the fifteenth or sixteenth, or as most of the learned say, on the twenty-seventh of the month Rajab, the seventh month, the Angel Gabriel conveyed His Highness the Prophet Muhammad Mustafā—on whom be the Peace!—to Heaven, mounted on the Burāq.[3] This being regarded as a holy night people keep vigil, read the accounts of it and keep a fast next day. This custom is observed by the pious and learned, while common people neither observe it nor know anything about it.

The cult of the Saint Gūgā, Guggā or Zāhir Pīr, 'the Saint apparent', is common in the Panjāb and in the neighbouring Districts of the United Provinces and Rājputāna. The legends told regarding him are contradictory, but he is usually said to have been a Rājput of the Chauhān sept who died in battle with Sultān Mahmūd of Ghaznī. According to another explanation his title is not Zāhir Pīr, 'the Saint apparent', but Zahriā, 'poisoned' or 'poisonous', because he once sucked the head of a snake. His cult is closely connected with serpent worship, and Hindus regard him as an incarnation of Nāga Rājā, the snake King.[4]

[1] This is apparently Sayyid Jalāl Bukhārī, whose tomb is at Uch in the Bahāwalpur State, a disciple of Shaikh Bahāu-d-dīn Zakarya of Multān. He is sometimes confounded with Shaikh Jalāl Jahāniān Jahāngasht of Multān (Beale, *Oriental Biography*, 193, 371). Another famous Jalālu-d-dīn was author of the *Masnavī*, and Shāh Jalāl has a famous tomb at Sylhet (Rose, i. 544; *IGI*. xxiii. 202; Redhouse, *The Mesnevi*, 132 ff.).

[2] Garcin de Tassy, *op. cit.* 59.

[3] *Korān*, xvii; Muir, *Life*, 117 f.

[4] C. J. Ibbetson, *Punjāb Ethnography*, 115 f.; Rose, i. 172 ff.; *Census Report*, Panjāb, 1911, i. 120 f.; J. Tod, *Annals of Rajasthan*, 1920, ii. 807, 843, 1027; iii. 1452. On his animistic and snake cultus, see Rose, i. 121, 171.

CHAPTER XXI

THE SHAB-I-BARĀT FESTIVAL

THE Shab-i-barāt or barā'at, or Lailatu-l-barāt (*barāt*, or *barā'at* meaning 'a writing conferring immunity'), is so called because on this night it is supposed that the lives and fortunes of mortals for the coming year are registered in Heaven. It is frequently confounded with the Lailatu-l-qadr, 'the Night of Power', or Shab-i-qadr, that mysterious night in the month Ramazān, the actual date of which is said to have been known only to the Prophet and a few of the Companions, when the whole animal and vegetable world bows down in adoration to the Almighty. But there is no connexion between the two festivals. In Egypt the Shab-i-barāt is called Lailatu-l-nisf min Sha'bān, because it is held about the middle of the month Sha'bān, the eighth month of the Musalmān year.[1] In the *Khazāna-jawāhir-jalāliya* of Maulānā Fazlu-llāh, son of Ziyāu-l-'Abbāsī, it is stated that God has in the Korān given four names to this month: Barāt, 'Night of Record', Lailatu-l-mubārak, 'the Blessed Night', Rahmat, 'Night of Mercy', Fāraiqa, 'Night of Discernment'.

Properly speaking, only two nights are celebrated by keeping vigil, the Shab-i-barāt and the Baqar 'Īd. The 'Arafa or vigil of the Shab-i-barāt is kept as follows: On 13th Sha'bān, either during the day or in the evening, which is the evening of the 14th according to the Musalmān calculation, they prepare in the name of as many deceased relations as they can remember—no register of them being kept—stew, curries, sweetmeats (*halwā*), some of which they put on plates, offer the Fātiha over it, and send portions to friends, to those to whom they are under obligations, and to those from whom they hope to receive favours. Learned men never offer the Fātiha over food, probably because the Prophet never did so. In Gujarāt among Sunnīs requiems are sung, sweets and sweet bread are eaten and sent as presents to friends, fireworks are exploded

[1] Lane, *ME.* i. 201.

or sent to relations, especially to those families in which a son or daughter of the house is betrothed.[1]

The regular festival is held on the fourteenth. Those who have not observed the rites on the eve prepare choice food, say the Fātiha over it in the name of the Prophet—on whom be the Peace !—and of their deceased ancestors, and amuse themselves with fireworks. For two or three days before the festival, boys go about beating small drums (*tamkī, tāzā*). Those who have children, if they be boys, make figures of elephants, if girls, of lamps (*pāūtī*) made of clay, and light wicks in them. In front of these figures they lay fruit and sweetmeats, and recite the Fātiha in the name of the Prophet—on whom be the Peace !—, but some recite it in the name of 'Alī Murtazā, the Chosen, and over the lamps in the name of Bībī Fātima, by way of a vow. In front of the elephants and lamps a bamboo framework is erected which is illuminated, and fireworks are let off. After the Fātiha female relations drop silver coins into the lamps. Next morning the person who made the vow sends the fruit and sweets to relations by the boys and girls, who get a money gift in return. With this money and that put overnight in the lamps they make meat cakes (*chakolī*) and distribute them to friends, after which they place the elephants and lamps over the house door or on the walls of the enclosure. They sit up all night reciting a hundred two bow prayers, reading the Korān and the benediction (*durūd*), fasting next day, all this being done according to the commands of the Prophet. But all the other ceremonies are innovations, superfluous and extravagant. The observance of the eve is also an innovation, but it is laudable (*bid'at-i-husna*). On the night of the fifteenth many spend large sums on fireworks ; in fact, more fireworks are let off at this feast than at any other time, and presents to friends on this day invariably take the shape of fireworks. Sometimes they carry on sham battles by letting off fireworks at each other, which occasionally end in clothes being burnt or people being killed or injured. At this time, too, schoolmasters exact presents from the parents of children by sending them pious texts written on paper (*'īdī*), for which they expect a return.

[1] *BG.* ix, part 2, 140.

CHAPTER XXII

THE RAMAZĀN FESTIVAL

THE Ramazān, 'the month of vehement heat', the Musalmān Lent, is the eighth month of the year. According to some authorities, the Musalmāns borrowed the observance from the Christians, but it seems more probable that it was derived from the Harranians or Sabians and the Manichaeans.[1] During the festival the time for breaking the fast (*sahūr, sahargāhī*) is from 2 to 4 a.m., beginning with the morning which succeeds the evening when the new moon of the month Ramazān first becomes visible.[2] It was in the month Ramazān that the Korān descended from Heaven. It is the Divine command that both the beginning and breaking of the fast should be preceded by the making of a vow (*nīyat*, 'intention') to that effect. From the beginning of the fast till sunset it is unlawful to eat, drink, or have commerce with women. Day and night should be spent in meditation on God. In the evening before the sunset prayer (*maghrib*) at 6 p.m. they break the fast (*iftār*), usually eating first a date, or if that is not procurable, by drinking a little water. Young children and idiots are excused from fasting. Sick persons and travellers may postpone (*qazā*) the fast to another and more suitable time, 'but he who is sick or upon a journey shall fast a number of other days. God wisheth you ease, but wisheth not your discomfort, and that you fulfil the number of days, and that you glorify God for his guidance and that you be thankful'.[3]

[1] Hughes, 534; Westermarck, *Origin and Development of the Moral Ideas*, ii. 312. It may, however, have been derived from the old Arabian religion (Margoliouth, *Mohammed*, 248, who says that it was substituted for the Jewish Day of Atonement). Whatever may be its origin, it is evidently a military exercise, intended to train soldiers for endurance and work at night (*ERE*. viii. 875).

[2] *Mishkāt*, i. 466. The apparent new moon or phasis probably served to mark the beginning of the month in all primitive calendars, as it defines the beginning of Ramazān (*ERE*. iii. 61).

[3] *Korān*, ii. 181; Mrs. Meer Hassan Ali, 103 f.

Special prayers are called the 'resting' (*tarāwīh*) because the congregation sit down and rest during the night after each fourth prostration (*rak'ah*) and after every second blessing (*salām*). They take about an hour, consisting of twenty-three or, as some say, twenty prostrations with the blessing (*salām*) of the Prophet after every second prostration.[1] The Prophet commanded his followers to recite these prayers in the company of others with the Imām or leader after the prayer on retiring to rest (*'ishā kī namāz*) and when three bows of the special or voluntary prayers (*wājibu-l-watar*) are still unrepeated. The former being completed the latter are recited. For the purpose of reciting the 'resting' prayers it is necessary to appoint a leader or Imām, or a Hāfiz, one who knows the Korān by rote, as such a person is able to finish them in a couple of days. When the recitation of the whole Korān has been completed, the 'resting' prayers are discontinued. The Hāfiz, or whoever has done this duty, is rewarded by a gift of money or clothes, as may have been arranged. Some people, after the rehearsal of the Korān has ended, continue reciting the 'resting' prayers and the reading of the Korān beginning with chapter 105, 'The Elephant' (*sūratu-l-fīl*), or some succeeding chapter, over and over, till the day before the end of the month. If there be no Hāfiz it is necessary to repeat the 'resting' prayers for thirty days. At the end of every fourth prostration the Imām with uplifted hands offers supplications to God, and the congregation respond 'Āmīn!' and 'Āmīn!' The Shī'as do not recite these prayers, nor do they enter a mosque for this reason, that after every four prostrations the congregation as well as the reader repeat the praises of the Four Companions, which they cannot endure to hear.

Friday, Jum'a, 'the day of the congregation', is the Musalmān Sabbath,[2] the day on which the clay of Father Adam was collected. On that day will be the Resurrection, and during the last three hours (*sā'at*, 'period') there is one in which all requests are granted. On that day the congregation assemble in the mosque with the Qāzī or law officer, the Khatīb or reader, and the Muazzin or caller to prayer. When

[1] Burton, *Pilgrimage*, i. 80. [2] *ERE*. x. 893 f.

the caller is present he first sounds the call to prayer (*azān*), and the others repeat anything that they may remember or are in the habit of saying, after which the reader recites the sermon or bidding prayer (*khutba*), which consists of praises, admonition, and advice. But on the last Friday of the month he gives such a solemn, pathetic discourse on the Ramazān and the excellencies of this night, first in Arabic and then in Persian and Hindostāni, that many of the learned and respectable worshippers are moved to tears.

Most Shī'as observe the night of his Excellency 'Alī—May God reward him!—and that with much pomp, either on the 21st or 20th of this month. They make the representation of a tomb (*zarīh*) like one of the Muharram cenotaphs, and take it round the town, beating their breasts. They then recite the Fātiha over food in the name of 'Alī and distribute it. The reason of this observance is that 'Alī departed this life on one of the days, which of them is uncertain.[1] The Sunnīs likewise, without taking out the cenotaph, cook food and offer the Fātiha over it.

Most people for the whole month, some for fifteen days, others only on the last day or for three days and nights, remain in seclusion (*i'tikāf*) in a corner of the mosque shut in by a curtain or screen, and never go out except for necessary purposes or to perform the legal purifications. They never speak to any one on worldly matters and never cease reading the Korān and praising the Almighty.

It is highly meritorious to perform this recital in a loud, audible voice. By this discipline many have become possessed of merit and penetration, and their blessings and curses are as powerful as a sharp sword. In the case of professional men who have little leisure, the observance of seclusion for a day and night is sufficient. This course of seclusion is an imperative duty (*sunnat al mu'aqqad, farz kifā'ī*), that is, if one man in a town or one member of a congregation fulfils it, it is equivalent to all having obeyed it. In the same way when one man in a town sits in retirement (*goshanishīn*),

[1] 'Alī was wounded by an assassin in the mosque on 17th Ramazān, A.H. 40 (January 22, A.D. 661), and he died on January 25 (Muir, *The Caliphate*, 299).

engaged in contemplation of the Deity, it is the same as if all the inhabitants did it, just as if when one makes a salutation to an assembly, if any member rises and returns it every one's neck is relieved from the obligation.

It has been decided by learned men both in Arabia and in 'Ajam or Persia that the Lailatu-l-qadr or Shab-i-qadr, the 'Night of Power', falls on the 27th night of Ramazān. 'One of these nights at the end of Ramazān, generally believed to be the 27th of that month, not the night supposed by Sale (*Korān*, chap. 97), which is that between the 23rd and 24th days, that is, the night preceding the 27th day, is called the Leylet el Kadr'.[1] On this day they sit up all night burning frankincense pastilles, repeating the voluntary (*nafl*) prayers, reading the Korān, and proclaiming the call to prayer every now and then during the night. On those who remain awake all that night, the Angels shower down from Heaven the peace and blessings of God, even until sunrise next morning, and the excellencies of that night are innumerable. Among Musalmāns there are two mysteries known to none but prophets: first, the Lailatu-l-qadr night on which the whole vegetable world bows in humble adoration to the Almighty; the second, Ismu-l-ā'zam, 'the exalted name of God', which possesses such virtues that he who knows it can effect whatever he willeth, slay the living and raise the dead to life, and transport himself wherever he pleases.

The Ghair-i-mahdī, a small sect who believe that the Imām Mahdī will not appear, erect, each in his own quarter of the town, a meeting-house (*jamā'atkhāna*), where on the night Lailatu-l-qadr they assemble, recite the two bow prayers in the name of the Mahdī, after which they call out these words three times: 'God is Almighty, Muhammad is our Prophet, and the Korān and the Mahdī are both just and true!' They conclude by saying, 'Imām Mahdī has come and gone, and whoever disbelieves this is an infidel!' Hearing this, the Sunnīs become so enraged that they first get boys to pelt these sectarians as if in sport, and then attack them with swords.

[1] Lane, *ME*. ii. 210. According to the *Mishkāt* (i. 279, 491 ff.), it falls on one of the odd numbers during the last nights of Ramazān, generally the 27th.

Their adversaries considering it martyrdom to die on such a night, defend their lives. Hence inveterate hatred exists between these two sects, and many lives are annually lost. 'I have been present', says Ja'far Sharīf, 'at two or three of these bloody encounters, but I have never seen the Ghair-mahdī victorious. I have also remarked in confirmation of a common report that the dead invariably fall on their faces, When people remark this fact to them, alleging that falling in this position arises from their unbelief, they reply, "Not so; our corpses are in the act of prostration in devotion". The real origin of this enmity is this, that both Sunnīs and Shī'as expect the coming of Imām Mahdī, Muhammad the Mahdī, whom the Persians believe to be still alive, and according to their belief he will appear again with Elias the Prophet at the Second Coming of Jesus Christ'. The Ghair-i-mahdī are converted Hindus and foreign Musalmāns, followers of Muhammad Mahdī, a descendant of Husain, grandson of the Prophet, born at Jaunpur in the United Provinces of Agra and Oudh, A.D. 1443. After many adventures he died at Fara in Kurdistān in 1505, and he is venerated as highly as the Prophet—on whom be the Peace!—[1] They say that whoever denies him is undoubtedly destined for Hell. They call themselves Mahdīwālā, 'followers of the Mahdī', or Dā'irawālā, from the circular wall which they adopt in this rite of worship. Others they call Kāfir, 'infidel' or Dastagīrwālā, because they have no belief in the Saint Pīr-i-dastagīr. Their numbers are so small in comparison with Sunnīs and Shī'as that we may apply to them the proverb, 'as salt in wheat flour', when cakes are made.

[1] *BG.* v. 291 f.; ix, part 2, 62 ff.; *ERE.* viii. 336 ff. In 1550, in the Deccan, Sa'īd Muhammad founded the Mahdavī sect, claiming to be the Imām Mahdī (Bayley, *Muhammadan Dynasties of Gujarāt*, 240).

CHAPTER XXIII

THE LAMP FESTIVAL OF BANDA NAWĀZ,[1] GESU DARĀZ

THIS festival is observed on the sixteenth day of the last month of the Musalmān calendar, Zū-l-qa'da, also called the month of Banda Nawāz. His Holiness Banda Nawāz, Sayyid Muhammad Gesū Darāz, 'he of the long locks',—May God sanctify his sepulchre!—was a great Walī or Saint, who came to Gulbarga or Kulbarga in the Nizām's Dominions during the reign of Fīroz Shāh Bahmanī[2] in A. D. 1413, and died there in 1432. He was told in one of his reveries that when, for good reason, people were unable to make the pilgrimage to Mecca, a visit once in their lives to his mausoleum would convey the same merit. On the sixteenth day of the month they perform here his Sandal rite, and on the night following, the seventeenth day or the eighteenth for Musalmāns, they observe the anniversary of his death (*'urs*) with splendour equal to that of the same ceremony in honour of His Excellency Qādirwalī Sāhib at Nāgor-Nāgpatan, as already described. Nay, if possible they observe it with greater splendour. In other parts of the country, however, it is on the fifteenth and sixteenth that they have illuminations in his name, cook cakes or stew, offer the Fātiha over the food, send some to relatives, eat some themselves, and distribute to others. On the night of the sixteenth, or by Musalmān reckoning the seventeenth, some people light sixteen lamps with butter, place them on cakes and offer the Fātiha over them, as previously described.

[1] *Banda-nawāz, banda-parwar,* means 'Cherisher of his servants, patron'.

[2] For the Bahmanī dynasty of the Deccan, see Smith, *Oxford Hist. of India,* 275 ff.

CHAPTER XXIV

THE 'ĪDU-L-FITR FESTIVAL

THE 'Īdu-l-fitr festival, ' the breaking of the fast ', also known as 'Īdu-l-saghīr, ' the minor feast ', by the Turks Ramazān Bairām,[1] is observed on the first day of the month Shawwāl, the tenth month. This month is also known in India as the ' milk month ' (*dūdh kā mahīnā*), because Musalmāns prepare vermicelli (*siwāiyān*), flour boiled in milk, and the ' vacant ' month (*khālī mahīnā*), because it is the only month in which no regular feast occurs, that to be described being supposed to belong to the previous month, Ramazān, and hence it is called Ramazān kī 'Īd, and it is therefore included in it, as it marks the close of the Ramazān festival. In the Panjāb this is the special feast of the Julāha weavers, as the 'Īdu-l-qurbān, 'Īd-i-azhā, Īdu-z-zohā, held on the tenth of the month Zū-l-hijja or Zī-l-hijja, in commemoration of Abraham's sacrifice of Ishmael, is the festival of the Qassāb butchers, the Shab-i-barāt of the Kanghīgars or comb-makers, and the Muharram of the Sayyids.[2]

This is a festival of rejoicing after the tension of the Ramazān or Lent, a carnival after sorrow common in Semitic worship.[3] In southern India before the feast prayers Musalmāns of both sexes and all ages bathe, apply antimony (*surmā*) to their eyes, wear new clothes, which second wives in northern India often present to the image of the first wife of their husbands, known as ' the first wife's crown ' (*saukan maurā*), in order to mollify their ill will towards them.[4] Before they go to the place of worship (*'īdgāh, namāzgāh*) they distribute alms (*sadqa, fitra*), the amount of which is prescribed by the Law,[5] among Faqīrs

[1] Lane, *ME.* ii. 210. [2] *NINQ.* i. 98.

[3] R. Smith, *Religion of the Semites*, 262.

[4] *PNQ.* i. 14. On the danger to widows and widowers from the ghosts of their deceased spouses, see Frazer, *Psyche's Task*, 2nd ed., 142.

[5] *Mishkāt*, i. 421.

and the poor. This usually amounts to 2½ sers or 5 lb. of wheat, dates, grapes, or any grain commonly used for food, and after giving this they are allowed to attend the prayer service. Between 8 a.m. and 12 noon the men form a procession and conduct the Qāzī, or some other Musalmān of learning and rank, to the place of prayer, most of them repeating mentally the glorification of Allāh, or the Takbīr: 'Allāhu akbar! Allāhu akbar! Lā-ilāha illallāh! Allāhu akbar! Allāhu akbar! Allāhu akbar, wa illāhu al hamd!' 'Great is Allāh! Great is Allāh! There is none so great as Allāh! Great is Allāh! Unto Him be praise!' The prayers together with a sermon in Arabic, read by the Qāzī standing on the pulpit, staff in hand in imitation of the Prophet—on whom be the Peace!—last about an hour and a half. When the prayers and sermon are over, the Qāzī is conducted back to his house, and the rest of the day is spent in feasting, making presents, paying and receiving visits. When the men return, their mothers and sisters take some water coloured red and yellow, and while the men are outside the door they wave it over their heads and then throw it away in the hope that the Evil Eye and the influence of any unlucky thing on which they may have trodden may thus be averted. Many, however, dispense with this rite. Should those who fast neglect to give the alms (*fitra*), the fast, the 'resting' prayers and the seclusion practised in the Ramazān will be kept suspended between earth and Heaven.

In the Khutba [1] or bidding prayer or sermon, the prayers are offered in the name of the King whose coin is current in the realm. 'In India the recital of the Khutbah serves to remind every Muhammadan present, at least once a week, that he is in a Dāru-l-harb, "a land of enmity"'. Still the fact that he can recite the Khutbah at all in a country not under Muslim rule must also assure him that he is in Dāru-l-amān, 'a land of protection'.[2] Fīroz Shāh of Delhi (A.D. 1351–88) ordered that the names of all previous kings should be included before his own.[3] If a Nawwāb or nobleman is present as the King's representative he gives a dress of honour to the preacher, or

[1] For the Khutba see Lane, *ME*. i. 107 ff.; *ERE*. x. 221 f.; for translated examples, Sells, 202 ff.

[2] Hughes, 277.

[3] Elliot-Dowson, iii. 292.

some liberal native officer, a Sūbadār or Jam'dār, gives him a piece of muslin. Some people throw gold and silver flowers over the head of the Qāzī, which his servants or relatives pick up for him. After this the preacher again ascends the middle step of the pulpit and offers the supplementary extempore prayers (*munājāt*), praying to the Almighty for the welfare of their faith and remission of sins of all Musalmāns, for the safety of pilgrims and travellers, for the recovery of the sick, for timely rain, preservation from misfortune and freedom from debt. He then comes down from the pulpit, kneels on a praying-carpet, and offers supplications on the part of the people, the congregation at the end of each prayer rising up and ejaculating the word 'Faith' or 'Religion' (*dīn*). Then muskets are discharged. Friends embrace and strangers shake each other's hands, wishing them good health on the occasion of the feast, and after repeating the benediction (*durūd*) they kiss hands (*dastbozī*) with the Qāzī. At such times there is a concourse of Faqīrs and beggars asking alms. If any one has not chanced to meet a friend at the service he calls at his house, where he is welcomed with sandalwood, betel, rose-water, and sometimes he is given food.

CHAPTER XXV

THE BAQAR 'ĪD FESTIVAL

THE Baqar 'Īd festival, the word meaning the 'cow festival', or 'Īdu-z-zohā, 'Īdu-l-azhā, 'Īdu-l-qurbān, Yaumu-l-nahr, the 'festival of sacrifice', is held on the day or evening of the ninth of Zū-l-hijja or Zī-l-hijja, the twelfth month of the Musalmān year. In India it is generally regarded as a substitute for the sacrifice celebrated by pilgrims in the valley of Minā near Mecca. Stew, sweetmeats, and griddle cakes are cooked on the eve (*'arafa*), as is done at the Shab-i-barāt. Fātiha is offered in the name of deceased relations and some keep the fast (*nahr*) which lasts for a watch and a quarter, the watch (*pahar*) being three hours, that is till 9.45 a m. On the morning of the tenth they go to the 'Īdgāh, or place of prayer, repeating the Creed (*takbīr*) all the way thither from their houses, as is done at the Ramazān and 'Īdu-l-fitr.

Rich people after the prayers sacrifice a sheep, carried thither for the purpose, in the name of God, in commemoration of Abraham intending to sacrifice his son Ismāīl, Ishmael, not Ishāq or Isaac.[1] Or seven persons, men, women, and children, jointly sacrifice a cow or a camel, for those who offer such sacrifices will, it is believed, be carried by these animals as quickly as a horse travels over the Pul-i-sirāt or the Bridge of Death. This bridge, finer than a hair and sharper than the edge of a sword, situated between Heaven and Hell, is that over which all mankind must pass at the Day of Resurrection. The righteous will pass over it with ease and with the swiftness of a horse or of the lightning, while the wicked will miss their footing and fall headlong into Hell whose flaming jaws will be gaping beneath them.[2]

[1] By comparison of *Korān*, xi. 74 with xxxvii. 99 ff., it has been urged that the Prophet referred to Isaac, not Ishmael, as the intended victim. But it is held both by Sunnīs and by Shī'as that he intended to sacrifice Ishmael, Hughes, 216, 219.

[2] For the Bridge of Death in comparative religion see [Sir] E. B. Tylor, *Primitive Culture*, 3rd ed., ii. 94; *Researches into the Early History*

In northern India the procedure at the sacrifice is as follows: All Musalmāns except those who possess less than the value of Rs. 40 in cash or jewellery are bound to perform the sacrifice. The dates upon which this is permissible are the 10th, 11th, or 12th of the month Baqar 'Īd or Zū-l-hijja or Zī-l-hijja. One goat suffices for one person, and the bigger animals, cow, camel, or horse, for seven. The sacrifice must be accompanied by the recital of the profession of faith (*takbīr*), 'Bismillāh! Allāhu akbar!', 'God is great!' The knife is held by the person who offers the sacrifice, or with his permission by another Musalmān. The victim is stretched on the ground with its head turned in the direction of Mecca. The sacrificer cuts its throat and leaves the body for a butcher to dress. The meat is divided into three portions, one to be given in charity, one distributed among relatives and friends, and one reserved for the sacrificer. The skin, or its value, is also given in charity, but this charity must be impersonal, such as for the erection of a mosque or school, but it may be given to the mosque crier or to poor students. The conditions regulating the selection of the victim are as follows: Only quadrupeds and only those whose meat is lawful food may be sacrificed, and the animal must be more than a year old, perfect in all its parts. The blood is buried and not scattered over anything, and no sanctity attaches to the blood, meat, or any other part of the carcase.[1] In the time of Aurangzeb the Qāzī, with a slave behind him holding a drawn sword in his hands, received the Emperor and recited the names of the monarchs of his dynasty, ending with a panegyric on the present ruler. As a reward for this duty he received seven sets of ceremonial robes. On the congregation leaving the mosque the camel stood ready for sacrifice at

of Mankind, 349 ff. The Musalmāns borrowed the belief from the Iranian Chinvatperutu (*ERE.* ii. 852). Cf. Burton, *AN.* iii. 340; *Mishkāt*, ii. 609.

[1] From a note by M. Mazharu-l-husain Khān of Bareilly, United Provinces, dated March 18, 1918. See R. Smith, *Religion of the Semites*, 205, 218; Mrs. Meer Hassan Ali, 140 ff. Particularly since the agitation against cow slaughter, serious riots between Hindus and Musalmāns have occurred at this sacrifice (see *Folk-lore*, xxiii (1912), 275 ff.). The ancient Arabs allowed the blood to flow away, giving back to the Deity the element of life, or else they applied it directly to the idol (*ERE.* i. 665).

the foot of the steps. The Emperor, mounting his horse, thrust his lance into the neck of the camel or ordered one of his sons to perform this duty. When his son Shāh 'Ālam was present at Court he usually did this office. 'After this the slaves stretch the camel on the ground and divide its flesh among themselves, as if it were saints' relics '.[1] At Teherān the camel, gaily caparisoned, is led into a square near the Nigāristān, or picture gallery palace, and it is made to kneel. At the auspicious moment a spear in the hand of a relative of the Shāh is struck into a vital spot behind the neck, and scarcely has the blood burst forth before a hundred knives are thrust into the animal by the bystanders, and in a twinkling the carcase is cut up, each quarter of the city striving to get a portion which may be kept for luck during the succeeding year.[2]

The 'Īdu-l-fitr and the 'Īdu-z-zohā or Baqar 'Īd are the two great festivals of the Musalmān year, and both the learned and the illiterate share in them. Besides these there are others, such as the 'Āshūra, Ākhirī-chahār-shamba, Shab-i-barāt, and others which are not properly feasts but are generally regarded as such. The other annual celebrations include merely the recital of the Fātiha in the names of eminent Saints, and these are not true 'Īds or festivals. In many towns and villages there are shrines (*chilla, āstāna*), where throughout the year celebrations (*sandal, 'urs, fātiha*) take place in the names of Saints. For example, at Hyderābād they perform in the name of His Highness Maulā 'Alī his commemoration (*sandal*) on the sixteenth and on his death anniversary (*chirāghan, charāghan, 'urs*) on the seventeenth of the month Rajab, the seventh month, on a hill named after him about five miles north of the cantonment of Secundarābād, where enormous crowds assemble for two days, and even for a day or two before that date. In fact, there is more amusement even than at the 'Āshūrā.

On the eighteenth of the month Zū-l-hijja or Zī-l-hijja Shī'as observe the festival known as the 'Īd-i-ghadīr. It is

[1] Manucci, ii. 349 f.

[2] Benjamin, *Persia and the Persians*, 378. Compare the Arab rite of hacking and devouring the flesh (R. Smith, 338). Cf. Farnell, *Cults of the Greek States*, iii. 211.

celebrated with great pomp at Najaf al Ashraf, and the numbers of pilgrims are increased by crowds who arrive after visiting Karbalā.[1] This is described in the *Bārah Māsā* as a solemnity on which the soul loves to reflect, and the mention of it is heard with delight. All, says this writer, use but one form of language in extolling the excellences of this festival, when the Prophet, in accordance with the divine command, appointed 'Alī Amīru-l-mūminīn, or Commander of the Faithful, and King of Saints, to be his successor. This announcement is said to have been made at a place called Ghadīr Khum, *ghadīr* meaning a place where water stands after rain,[2] a halting-place for the caravans (*kārwān*), half way between Mecca and Medīna. It is said that whoever observes this feast will be entitled to place his foot in the Kingdom of Heaven. There is another 'Īd, the 'Īdu-l-'Umar, held on the third day before the Bārahwafāt festival in the month Safar, to commemorate the assassination of 'Umar ibn al Khattāb, the second Khalīfa, by a Persian slave, Fīroz, familiarly called Lulū, in A.D. 644. As 'Umar was the enemy of 'Alī, this is a day of rejoicing among the Shī'as and of mourning among Sunnīs.[3]

[1] See an account in the *Pioneer Mail*, October 10, 1919, p. 33 f.

[2] Burton, *Pilgrimage*, ii. 59 ; Rose, i. 576.

[3] Muir, *Annals*, 278 ff. ; Rose, i. 576.

CHAPTER XXVI

MAGIC

SĪMIYĀ or white magic is a subordinate branch of spiritualism (*'ilm-i-ruhānī*), and it is divided into two branches: that which is high and related to Deity (*'ulwī, rahmānī*), and that which is low and devilish (*sifla, shaitānī*), with the latter of which is connected the black art proper (*sihr, jādū*). Much Musalmān magic closely agrees with that of Babylonia, which was always regarded as one of the homes of magic.[1] Magic is officially condemned by the Law. 'Whoever obtains a little knowledge of astrology obtains a branch of magic. Whoever goes to a magician and asks about mysteries and believes what he says, verily is displeased with Muhammad and his religion'. 'But there is no fear in making spells which do not associate anything with God'. 'As ye have put faith in Islām, believe not in magic'.[2]

The invocation of spirits is an important part of Musalmān magic, and this (*da'wat*) is used for the following purposes: to command the presence of the Jinn and demons who, when it is required of them, cause anything to take place; to establish friendship or enmity between two persons; to cause the death of an enemy; to increase wealth or salary; to gain income gratuitously or mysteriously; to secure the accomplishment of wishes, temporal or spiritual.

The following account deals with the following subjects: the rules to be observed and the articles required by the magician; the almsgiving, the names, and the recital of spells; the summoning of the Jinn and demons; the casting out of devils.

[1] R. C. Thompson, *The Reports of the Magicians and Astrologers of Nineveh and Babylon*, 1900; *Devils and Evil Spirits of Babylonia*, 1903; *Semitic Magic, its Origin and Development*, 1903; *ERE*. iv. 741 f.

[2] *Korān*, ii. 96; *Mishkāt*, ii. 375, 385; i. 206; ii. 297. But two Sūras in the Korān (cxiii, cxiv) are magical formulae, both disclosed in the earliest teaching of the Prophet.

A Magic Circle.

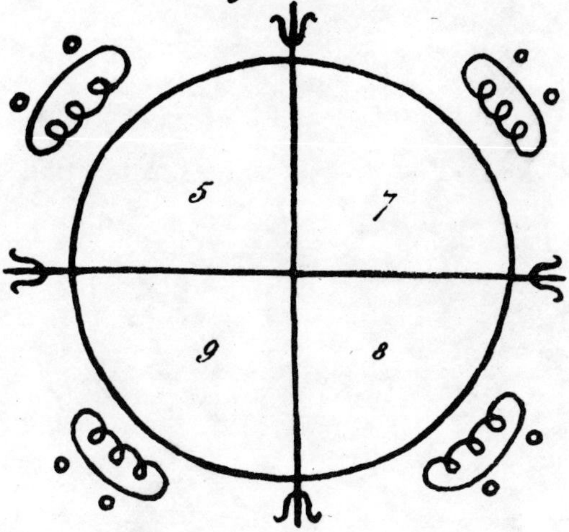

A Magic Square.

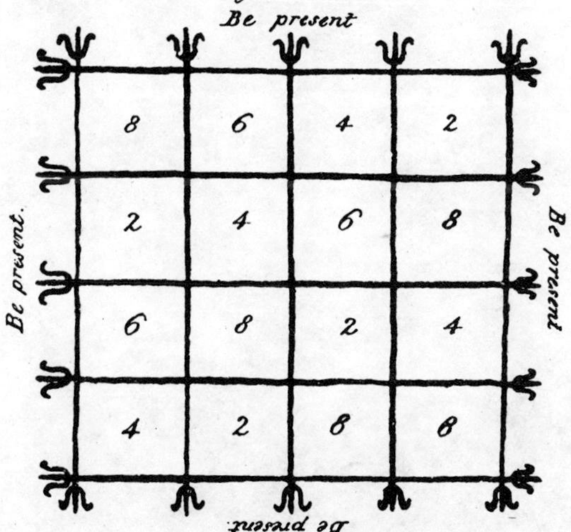

Another kind.

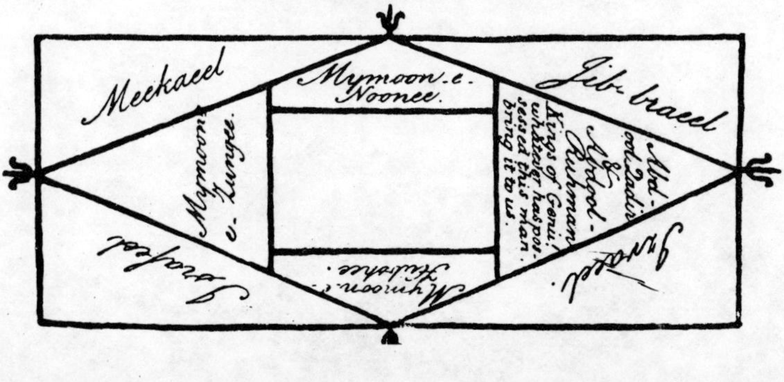

The magician must acquire his knowledge from some learned guide (*murshid*), and he alone is a competent guide who is acquainted with the great names of the Deity (*ism-i-'āzam*). The names describe His attributes, but the great names are short invocations used in this science, and they are of two kinds: the mighty attributes (*ism-i-'āzam*) and the glorious attributes (*asmā'ut-husnā*). These are of two kinds: fiery or terrible (*jalāliya*); watery, airy, amiable (*jamālī*). Besides this, he alone is a true guide (*murshid*) to whom the demons have given information concerning things great and small, and he in whose bosom is the knowledge of all truths. Such a man, however, must not boast of his acquirements and power of working miracles, nor should he be over-anxious to display his powers.

Some guides who are destitute of practical knowledge of the science pretend to teach it to others, but such instruction is of no value. Moreover the student exposes his life to danger, for by such study many have ruined themselves, with the result that they become mad, cover themselves with filth, and wander in deserts and mountains. But with a really learned guide there is no such risk. Even if danger occurs through the ignorance of his pupil, a learned teacher can remedy this. This poor writer, says Ja'far Sharīf, a mere teacher of the alphabet, has long cherished the desire to explore this science and has associated with divines, devotees, magicians, travellers from Arabia and 'Ajam, the lands beyond it, and has gained much knowledge. But the advantage he has derived from the study may be expressed by the proverb, 'to dig up a mountain and find a mouse' (*koh kandan, mūsh giriftan*).[1] Should any one require further information than that given here, there is no better authority that the *Jawāhir-i-khamsa* by His Excellency Muhammad Ghaus Gaulerī—The mercy of God be upon him!

For a student of this science the first requisite is purity.[2] No dog, cat, or stranger may enter his closet, and perfumes such as aloes, benzoin, or gum benjamin should be burnt. If he has

[1] Parturiunt montes, nascetur ridiculus mus. Horace, *De arte poetica*, 139.

[2] In the Deccan the medium must not eat millet, or any food cooked by a menstruous woman (*BG.* xxiv. 418).

to go out for a necessary purpose, he wears on going out of doors a special cap (*tāj*), and a loin-band (*lūng*), leaving his other clothes inside and hanging his impure garments on a clothes line (*alagnī, alganī*). Or he merely performs the minor ablution (*wuzū'*) and then re-enters his closet. The object of changing the clothes is that flies may not be attracted to them and thereby cause defilement. If he experiences a pollution (*ihtilām*) by day or night he must instantly bathe. During the Chilla or forty days preparation he sleeps on a mat, not on a bed. During this time some people fast and bathe twice a day. They talk and sleep little, while some remain indoors and have the entrance of their rooms built up for the time. In performing this forty days' rite they go to a house or place outside the town, or to a mountain, cave, or well, or some place where water is at hand. The noise of a town distracts the attention, and in this work the mind must be concentrated and the thoughts must not wander. Outside a town there are no distractions. Diet depends upon the character of the names to be recited ; if they are terrible (*jalālī*) the use of meat, fish, eggs, honey, musk, quick-lime, oysters, and sexual congress are prohibited. In the use of the amiable (*jamālī*) names butter, curds, vinegar, salt, and ambergris are forbidden. In using both classes of names the following are abominations : garlic, onions, asafoetida, blood-letting and the killing of lice. Failure to obey these rules involves imminent danger to life. Besides these the two chief rules are to eat only things lawful and to speak the truth.

If the magician has to repeat the terrible names, or if the number of them preponderates, he must begin on Saturday, the first day of the week ; for the amiable on a Monday ; for both together, that is, an equal number of both, on a Sunday. If the spell is intended to establish friendship or for some other good purpose he should begin after the new moon, as in the case of other good undertakings.[1] In both cases he should turn his face towards the house of the person who is the object of the undertaking. He should always fast during the three preceding days and commence the recital of the names on the morning of the fourth. If his food is cooked by a servant, he

[1] Frazer, *GB.*, Adonis, Attis, Osiris, ii. 131 ff.

A Magic Figure.

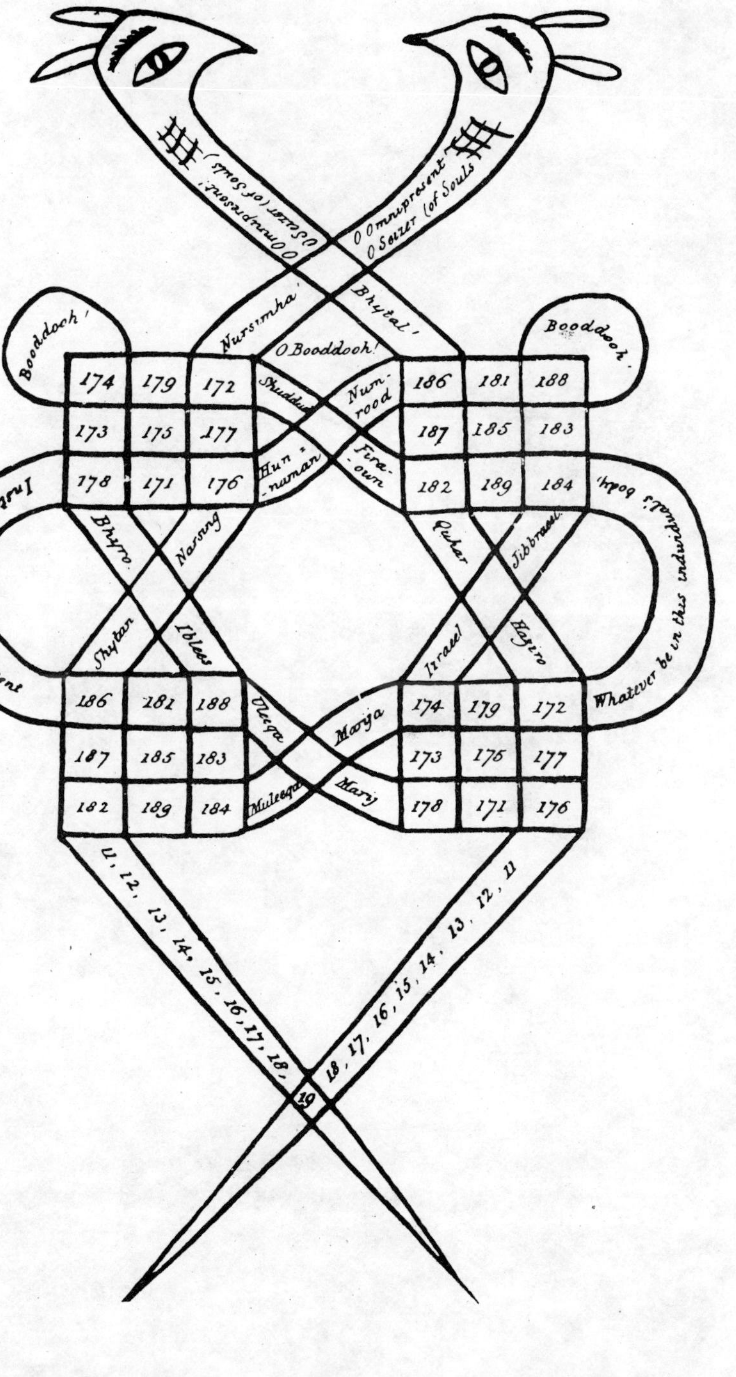

also must observe the same abstinence as his master. If the servant is unable to submit to such privation, the master must cook for himself.

Before beginning the recital of the names in regard to a person, it is necessary to ascertain the initials of his or her name according to the Arabic alphabet (*hurūf-i-tahajjī*). As there are seven letters in other oriental alphabets which are not represented in the Arabic, an equal number of Arabic letters are substituted for them—for *p*, *t*, *ch*, *d*, *r*, *zh*, and *g*, are written *b*, *t*, *j*, *d*, *r*, *z*, *k*. The Arabic alphabet consists of 28 letters, and these are supposed by magicians to be connected with the 12 signs of the zodiac (*burūj*), the 7 planets (*sitārā*), and the 4 elements (*'unsar*). The relation of these to each other will appear from the following table which states the appropriate perfume which should be burnt with each planet, and also the qualities of the planets and the numbers represented by the 28 letters of the alphabet. These form 8 words: *abjad*, *hawwaz*, *hutti*, *kalaman*, *sa'fas*, *qarashat*, *sakhaz*, *zazigh*, the first three of which are said to be those of Kings of Midian, and the others were added by the Arabs.

Hence comes the Abjad or Arabic method of reckoning dates. It derives its name Abjad from the four letters *a*, *b*, *j*, *d*, representing a much older order than the present. In the order each letter has a numerical value: *a* = 1, *b* = 2, *j* = 3, *d* = 4, up to *y* = 10; then come the other tens: *y* = 10, *k* = 20, *l* = 30, *m* = 40, *n* = 50, *s* = 60, *'ain* = 70, *f* = 80, *s* = 90, *q* = 100; then the other hundreds, up to *gh* = 1,000. As an example, *dūd az Khurāsān bar āmad*, 'Smoke (signs) arose from Khurāsān': *d* = 4, *wāw* = 6, *d* = 4, total 14 to be abstracted from '*Khurāsān*'; *kh* = 600, *r* = 200, *a* = 1, *s* = 60, total 912. This gives A.H. 898, A.D. 1492, the date of the death of the Persian poet Jāmī. In the same way the words 'Tāj Sultān ahl-i-jannat' give A.H. 1045, A.D. 1633.[1]

[1] Browne, *A Year amongst the Persians*, 390 f.; Cousens, *Bījāpur*, 75. For other examples see Ferishta, ii. 65, 138; iii. 249, 423; iv. 70, 141; Bayley, *Muhammadan Dynasties of Gujarāt*, 239, 408, 410; Elliot-Dowson, viii. 441 ff.

TABLE. PLANETS AND LETTERS

The Four Elements.				*The Planets with their Influences.*	*The Perfumes of the Planets.*
Water.	*Air.*	*Earth.*	*Fire.*		
Dāl D 4	Jīm J 3	Bē B 2	Alif A 1	Saturn evil	Benzoin coriander seed
Hē H 8	Zē Z 7	Wāw W 6	Hē H 5	Jupiter good	Benzoin Sugar
Lām L 30	Kāf K 20	Yē Y 10	Toē T 9	Mars evil	Benzoin wood Aloes
‘Ain ‘A 70	Sīm S 60	Nūn N 50	Mīm M 40	Sun middling	Benzoin Cinnamon
Khē KH 600	Sē S 500	Tē T 400	Shīn SH 300	Mercury good	Benzoin Sandal- wood
Ghain GH 1,000	Zoē Z 900	Zwād Z 700	Zāl Z 700	Moon middling	Benzoin Camphor
Rē R 200	Qāf Q 100	Swād S 800	Fe F 80	Venus good	Benzoin white Sandal- wood
Crab Scorpion Fish	Twins Scales Watering- pot	Bull Virgin She-goat	Ram Lion Archer	Signs of the Zodiac	

As a further illustration of this table, if a man Ahmad desires intimacy with a woman Rabayā, which he wishes to accomplish by means of magic, it must be ascertained whether the elements, planets, and zodiacal signs agree or do not agree. For example, the initial of Ahmad is *A*, his element is fire, his planet Saturn, his sign of the Zodiac Ram, Lion, Archer. The initial of Rabayā being *R*, her element is water, her planet Venus, her sign of the Zodiac Crab, Scorpion, Fish. Hence the elements are opposed to each other.

Secondly, astrologers have determined the relative dispositions of the planets to be as follows :

TABLE

Venus and Saturn	Venus and Moon	Jupiter and Venus	Jupiter and Sun	Sun and Moon	Jupiter and Moon	Sun and Venus	Friendship
Moon and Mercury	Saturn and Mercury	Jupiter and Mercury	Mars and Mercury	Venus and Mercury	Mars and Venus	Sun and Mercury	Indifferent
Saturn and Sun	Saturn and Moon	Mars and Moon	Mars and Sun	Saturn and Mars	Jupiter and Mars	Jupiter and Saturn	Enmity

Consequently, Ahmad having Saturn for his planet and Rabayā Venus, these being friendly, it appears that the man and woman will live happily together.

Thirdly, with regard to the signs of the Zodiac, they stand as follows : Males, Ram, Lion, Scorpion, Fish, Archer ; Females, Bull, Scales, Crab ; Hermaphrodites, Twins, Virgin, He-goat, Watering-pot. Between males and females friendship exists, between males and hermaphrodites sometimes friendship, sometimes enmity, between females and hermaphrodites the most inveterate enmity. In this instance, part of one corresponding with the other, it is so far favourable. From these various considerations it may be concluded that some degree of harmony and some of discord may be expected as the results of the union.

For each name there are what are technically known as the 'repeating of the Divine attributes' (*nisāb*), 'Divine attributes' (*zakāt*), 'tithes' (*'ushr*), 'locks' (*qufūl*), 'repetition' (*daur, mudawwar*), 'gifts to avoid calamity' (*bazl*), 'seal' or 'conclusion' (*khatm*), 'speedy answer' (*sariu-l-mujāvabat*) appointed for each Ism or name. In the *Jawāhir-i-khamsa* there are in all forty-one names of the 'Mighty attributes' (*ism-i-'uzām*), the first of which runs as follows : 'Subhānaka la ilāha illa anta, Yā Rabba kulli shay'in, wa wārithuha wa rāziguha, wa rahimuha', 'Glory be to thee, the Lord of all, the Inheritor thereof, the Provider thereof, the Compassionate thereof !' [1]

[1] Prof. E. G. Browne, who has kindly examined this incantation, is doubtful about the word *wārithuha*, which is unusual.

By way of example we offer the Nisāb &c. of the above Ism. To find out the Nisāb &c. of this Ism, the number of letters composing the Ism, which is 45, as noted below,[1] is to be considered as so many hundreds, which makes its Nisāb 4,500, half of which, 2,250, added to it gives its Zakāt 6,750 ; adding to this its half, 1,125, we get its 'Ushr 7,875 ; half of the above half, 1,125, or 563, gives its Qufl. Add the Qufl, 563, to its 'Ushr, 7,875, we get 8,438 ; doubling this we get 16,876, which is its Daur and Mudawwar. There is no rule for the following, they being always the same for every name : its Bazl 7,000, its Khatm 200 ; its Sariu-l-mujāvabat 12,000.

The Nisāb consists in repeating it 4,500 times ; its Zakāt 6,750 ; its 'Ushr 7,875 ; its Qufl 563 ; its Daur, Mudawwar, 16,876 ; its Bazl 7,000 ; its Sariu-l-mujāvabat 12,000. Total 56,764. The giving of the 'alms' and 'tithes' (*zakāt*, *'ushr*) to the Ism or names is considered to be the giving of offerings requisite for ensuring success in the undertaking, that the labours of the suppliant may not return to him in vain.

This name has for its demons Hūmrāīl and Hamwakīl, and for its Jinn Shatkīsa.[2] In beginning the recital of the name these demons are addressed by prefixing to their names 'O' (*Yā*), and to that of the Jinn 'Bahaqq, Nidā, Madad, Kumak', meaning 'by the aid of'. As a specimen, in the above name the formula is : 'Yā Hūmrāīl ! Yā Hamwakīl ! Bahaqq-i-Shatkīsa, Subhāna-llāh' &c. Thus, whether it be this name, or any of the forty-one named above, or any other which a person may have received from his tutor—for there are innumerable others current—it is necessary that its Nisāb &c. be given in order to command the presence of the Jinn. Previous to reciting the name he must each time address the demon or

[1] According to the former Table, *s*= 60, *b*= 2, *h*= 8, *a*= 1, *n*= 50, *k*= 200, *l*= 30, *a*= 1, *L*= 30, *h*= 25, *a*= 1, *l* doubled= 60, *a*= 1, *a*= 1, *n*= 50, *t*= 400, *fa*= 11 (omitted), *r*= 200, *b* doubled= 4, *k*= 20, *l* doubled = 60, *sh*= 300, *y*= 10, *hamza*= 1, *wāw* doubled= 12, *a*= 1, *r*= 200, *s*= 500, *h*= 5, *wāw*= 6, *r*= 200, *a*= 1, *z*= 7, *q*= 100, *h*= 5, *wāw*= 6, *r*= 200, *a*= 1, *h*= 8, *m*= 40, *h*= 5. Total 2,613.

[2] For Musalmān demons and spirits see *ERE.* iv 615 ff. The beliefs in South India described in this chapter seem to be largely derived from Hindu sources (Rose, i. 413, 561 ; Burnell, *Devil Worship of the Tulavas*, *Indian Antiquary*, vol. xxiii, xxiv).

Jinn by name. Should the name have no Jinn, the demon alone must be invoked, and after that the name should be recited. For example, if a name is to be repeated a hundred times, the names of the demon and Jinn must be as often repeated. Among the forty-one great names, some have two demons and one Jinn, and vice versa ; each name has a separate Jinn, but the same demons are common to several names.

After reciting the Divine attributes the magician, in order to familiarize himself with it, or to cause the presence of the Jinn, must within 40 days repeat the name 137,613 times. This number in the case already given is thus calculated The total number of the letters forming the name is 45, which is to be considered as so many thousands, and when 45,000 is multiplied by 3 the result is 135,000. Add to this the combined number 2,613 which the letters of the name denote, and the total is 137,613, called in Persian Da'wat and in Hindostānī Sūjnā. The magician divides this number 137,613 into as many nearly equal parts as can possibly be gone through in one day's recital. By thus reciting it the mind of the inquirer becomes enlightened, he sometimes falls into an ecstasy and fancies himself, whether asleep or awake, carried and accompanied by demons and Jinn to distant realms, to the highest Heaven, or into the bowels of the earth. There they reveal to him not only all hidden mysteries and render the whole human race obedient to his will, but they cause all his desires, temporal as well as spiritual, to be accomplished. Most magicians have by experience proved the power of these names, and whoever strictly follows the rules laid down invariably obtains his heart's desire. The uses and beneficial effects of the name are many, but, as they are noticed later on, we may leave them for the present.

We now pass to the second variety of names, the 'Glorious Attributes' (*asmāu-l-husnā*), as connected with the 28 letters of the Arabic alphabet, the knowledge of which my late father, says Ja'far Sharīf, bestowed upon me as a secret inheritance. These will be exhibited, with the demons attached to each, in the following table.

Alif A Yā Allāhu ! O Allāh ! Kalkāilu	Bē B Yā Rahmānu ! The Merciful ! Amwakīlu	Jīm J Yā Rahīmu ! The Compassionate ! Rūiāilu	Dāl D Yā Māliku ! The King ! Rūdāilu
Hē H Yā Quddūsu ! The Holy One ! Ittrāilu	Wāw W Yā Salāmu ! The Peace ! Hamwakīlu	Zē Z Yā Mu'mīn ! The Faithful ! Rūiāilu	Hē H Yā Muhaiminu ! The Protector ! Samkāilu
Toē T Yā 'azīzu ! The Mighty ! Lūmāilu	Yē Y Yā Basīru ! The Seer ! Jarjāilu	Kāf K Yā Jabbāru ! The Repairer ! Kamlāilu	Lām L Yā Mutakabbiru ! The Great ! Lūqāilu
Mīm M Yā Khāliqu ! The Creator ! Ittrāilu	Nūn N Yā Bārīu ! The Maker ! Jibrāilu	Sīn S Yā Mussawwiru ! The Fashioner ! Shamsāilu	'Ain 'A Yā Ghaffāru ! The Forgiver ! Sarkasāilu
Fē F Yā Qahhāru ! The Dominant ! Raftāmāilu	Swād S Yā Wahhābu ! The Bestower ! Isrāfīlu	Qāf Q Yā Razzāqu ! The Provider ! Kalkāilu	Rē R Yā Fattāhu ! The Opener ! Sarhamākīlu
Shīn SH Yā 'Alīmu ! The Knower ! Mīkāilu	Tē T Yā Qābizu ! The Restrainer ! Jibrāilu	Sē S Yā Bāsitu ! The Spreader ! Hamwakīlu	Khē KH Ya Khāfizu ! The Abaser ! Tankāilu
Zāl Z Yā Rāfi'u ! The Exalter ! Ittrāilu	Zwād Z Yā Mu'izzu ! The Honourer ! Ruqāilu	Zoē Z Yā Muzīlu ! The Destroyer ! Lūqāilu	Ghain GH Yā Sāmi'u ! The Hearer ! Isrāfīlu

If a man desires the accomplishment of his wishes he may either recite one of the above-named 'Mighty Attributes' or one of the 'Glorious Attributes', both of which will equally answer his purpose. But the beneficial effects of the former are greater, though they are seldom recited owing to the trouble involved in it.

Other Species

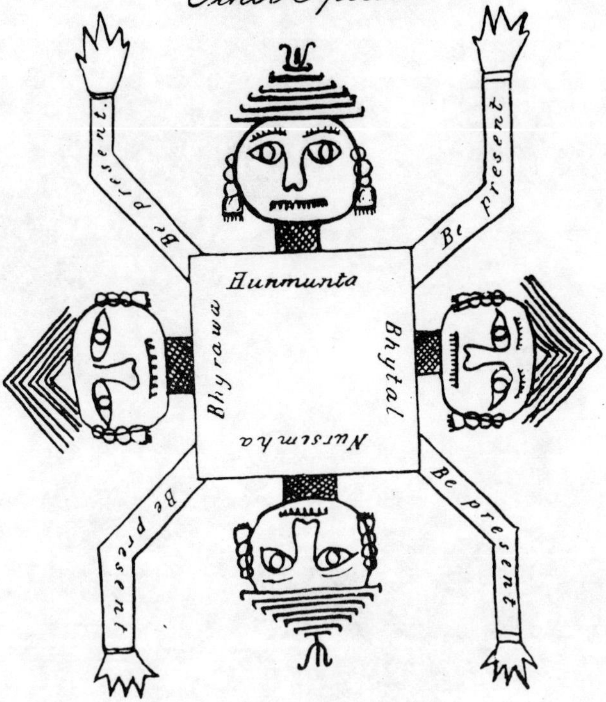

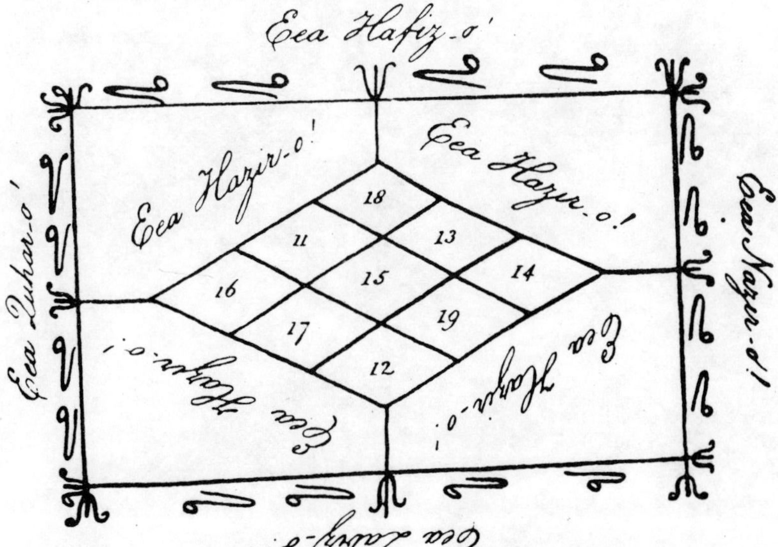

The manner of reciting the invocation (*da'wat*) is as follows : For instance, if an inquirer (*tālibu-l-'ilm*) desires to make another subject to his will he will act as follows. Suppose the object desired (*matlūb*) to be a man named Burhān, whose name is composed of five letters, *b*, *r*, *h*, *a*, *n*—after the magician by reference to the table ascertains the different Attributes of the Deity attached to each letter, together with the names of their corresponding demons, by first repeating the names of the demons and then those of the Deity, as detailed already in the case of the first of the names contained in the *Jawāhir-i-khamsa*, a certain number of times, as will presently be more particularly stated, the object will become subject to his will. Whether the wisher does the recital himself, or employs another to do it for him, the substance of the following, in any language, must be recited daily four times, twice at the beginning of the Blessing, 'O God have mercy upon Muhammad and upon his descendants, Thou didst bestow Mercy and Peace and Blessing and Compassion and Great Kindness upon Abraham and his descendants !' After the invocation is to be recited, 'O Lord ! Grant that the object, Shaikh Burhān, may be so distracted by love with such a one (the seeker) as to be day and night forgetful of his natural wants !'

I may here mention a point essential to be known in order to be able to recite the name—that the reckoning of the Abjad is divided into four parts, units, tens, hundreds, thousands. If the numeral representing the letters falls on the units it is to be considered so many hundreds, on the tens thousands, on the hundreds tens of thousands, on the thousands hundreds of thousands. By this rule the letter of the name Burhān are as follows : $b = 2$; 200 ; $r = 200$; 20,000 ; $h = 5$; 500 ; $a = 1$; 100 ; $n = 50$; 5,000 ; total 25,800.

The magician having previously divided the sum total into any number of equal parts, and having fixed upon the number of days in which the recital may be finished, say a week or so, he must finish it within the time appointed, or his labour will have been in vain. He burns aloes or some other sweet perfume, turns his face towards the house of, or directly at the object, and recites these words, 'Amwakīlu, Yā Rahmānu ! Sarhamakīlu ! Yā Fattāhu ! Itrāilu ! Yā Quddūsu ! Kalkāilu ! Yā

Allāhu! Jabrāīlu! Yā Bārīu!' Before reciting these five names it is necessary to give their Attributes (*nisāb*, *zakāt*). But in reciting this kind of spell, instead of repeating it for the Attribute &c. the number of times as laid down for the other names, it is sufficient if it be recited in the above way a thousand times for each name with its demon, and there is no need to recite the 'Speedy Answer'.

This invocation of the Jinn is known as Tashkīr-i-Jinn.[1] When a magician has once commanded the presence of the demon and Jinn, he may by their means cause whatever he pleases to be done. He can acquire by mysterious means his daily food and money sufficient for his expenses by demanding it from them. I have heard, says Ja'far Sharīf, that a man never asks for more than he needs because the Jinn would not provide it. Before commanding the presence of the demons and Jinn, the seeker must shut himself up in his closet, which should be smeared with red ochre. He spreads a prayer-carpet, red if possible, sits on it, and observing the utmost purity, he goes through the ritual in the course of a week, the sooner the better. After that, in order to secure the presence of these beings, he must shut himself up for forty days and repeat the invocation 137,613 times, dividing it into forty parts, one for each day. The best place for the Chilla, or forty days' abstinence, is some secluded spot near the sea, in a cave, garden, or place outside the town where nothing is likely to disturb him.

After he has begun the recital of the spell every night or week, some new phenomenon will appear, and in the last week the demons and Jinn, attended by their legions, will arrive. A demon, a Jinn, or one of their band will present himself and say respectfully, 'Sir magician! Why dost thou require our presence? We are here with our forces'.[2] At this crisis the magician must call up all his courage. He must

[1] Browne, *A Year amongst the Persians*, 444. *Taskhīr* means 'subduing, subjecting'. In Chaldean magic the conjurations 'begin by commemorating the various kinds of demons whom they are to subdue by their power, and then describe the effects of the charm' (Lenormant, *Chaldean Magic*, 15; cf. 19).

[2] Compare the tale of 'Alaeddin and the Wonderful Lamp' (Burton, *AN*. x. 33 ff.).

not address his visitors at once, but by moving his hand or finger he should ask them to be seated. When he has finished his daily task he should ask their names, demand of them a sign or token, and learn how often it will be necessary to repeat the invocation to ensure their presence. They will instruct him on these points and he should strictly obey their orders. If he speaks to them before he has finished his daily task they will cause some misfortune to befall him, or they will suddenly disappear and all the pains he has taken will become of no avail.

He should adjure them by a mighty oath, in the name of Almighty God or of Solomon, son of David [1]—on whom be the Peace !—and then dismiss them. He should on no account disclose the meeting to any one, he should never dismiss them while he is in a state of impurity, and he must never delay bathing after coition or nocturnal pollution. All his life he must refrain from committing adultery. In short, he should do nothing but what is lawful. A beginner in the art should never undertake it for the first two or three times except in the presence of his instructor, otherwise he may lose his life. Many by not attending to this have become mad or idiotical. It is much better to abstain from the practice altogether.

For the information of Europeans, says Ja'far Sharīf—May their wealth ever increase—I here relate some of the well-known virtues of the invocation recorded in the *Jawāhir-i-khamsa.* First, when any one waits on a king, noble, or his own gracious master, he need only repeat the Great Invocation seventeen times with his open hands spread towards Heaven. Then he blows on them and draws his hands once over his face, and then as the great man beholds him he will become so attached to him that however angry he may have been he will now be pleased. Secondly, if any one repeats this invocation forty or seventy times after morning and evening prayer his mind will become clear and enlightened,

[1] On the mighty oath on the seal-ring of Solomon, see Burton, *AN.* vi. 104 ; and on the magical control of the Jinn, *Korān,* xxviii. 17 ; *ERE.* iv. 811 f. In the Panjāb dust-storms are repelled by invoking Hazrat Sulaimān, the Lord Solomon, and pointing with the finger in the direction you wish the storm to take. (*PNQ.* iii. 167 ; Crooke, *Popular Religion,* i. 151, 266 ; ii. 19, 39, 75.)

and in his heart there will be naught but love towards God. No worldly concerns will disturb his peace of mind, and the future will be revealed to him in dreams. Thirdly, if he desires that any event, temporal or spiritual, may occur, he should repeat the invocation twenty-four times on a Sunday morning before sunrise, and then, by the Grace of God, his desires will be realized that very day. Fourthly, if he wishes to make a person subject to him, on a Wednesday after bathing he should put on new clothes, burn incense, and repeat the invocation a hundred and eleven times over some food and drink. He should then blow on this and get the person to partake of it, and then he or she will become desirous (*tālib*) of him. Fifthly, if a man has many secret enemies who slander him and treat him with haughtiness, after his usual prayers he should repeat the invocation forty-one times morning and evening, and then his ill-wishers will become his dearest friends. Sixthly, if any one desires to make princes or nobles obedient to his will he must procure a silver ring with a square tablet engraved on it, and write on the tablet the letters of the invocation, 2,613 in number. This number, or the numbers of the demons and Jinn added to it, should be formed into a magic square of the Sulsī or Rubā'ī type, as described below, which should be inscribed on the tablet. The total number of the letters is thus calculated : add to 2,613 the letters of the name of the demon Hūmrāīl (*h*=5, *m*=40, *r*=200, *a*=1, *i*=10, *l*=30) or the total 286 ; of the demon Shatkīsa (*sh*=300, *t*=400, *kh*=600, *i*=10, *s*=500, *a*=1), total 1,811. So 2,613 plus 286 plus 112 for Hamwakīl plus 1,811 make the total 4,822. When the ring is finished he must place it before him for a week, daily morning and evening, recite the invocation 5,000 times and blow on it. When all this is done he must wear the ring on his little finger, known as Kānunglī, because it is used for cleaning the ear. In short, to command the attendance of the demons and the Jinn is no easy matter. At the present day if any one is able to secure their obedience he is regarded as a Walī or Saint, and a worker of miracles. This humble worker, says Ja'far Sharīf, this mere teacher of the alphabet, has tried to prove the effects of reciting two or three of these invocations. But he found it a difficult task to finish them, and he experienced such awful sights that he was unable to complete any of them. Finding his labour lost he abandoned the design.

Besides these mighty names there are many Attributes of the Deity and verses of the Korān which one may recite without much trouble, and their effects are well established. But in order to gain knowledge of them you must humbly supplicate the great adepts in the art, and they communicate them only privately, breast to breast, hand to hand, ear to ear. If they are described in books it is never with sufficient minuteness to make them intelligible. To this humble inquirer, Ja'far Sharīf, through the grace of God and the kindness of his teachers, many powerful spells and select sentences of the Korān have descended. But as they were given under the pledge of secrecy it would be improper to disclose them. However, one verse is so well known that I may as well mention it—the Āyatu-l-fath, the 'verse of victory'. If a man constantly recites this verse for a time God will undoubtedly within forty days grant his desires and make him prosper. The men of old constantly proved this by experiment. The Āyatu-l-fath, which should be repeated forty times after the five appointed times of prayer, is as follows: 'And with Him are the keys of the secret things; none knoweth them but He; He knoweth whatever is on the land or in the sea; and no leaf falleth but He knoweth it; neither is there a grain in the darkness of the earth, nor a thing green or sere, but it is not noted in a distinct writing'.[1] To secure increase of subsistence and wealth, a man should after the morning and evening prayers repeat a thousand times the two following Attributes of the Almighty. If he derives any benefit from the repetition in two or three months he may go on reciting them a thousand or five hundred times. The names are Yā Ghanī, 'the Independent', Yā Mughnī, the 'Enricher'.

In the *Shar'-i-Bukhārī* Abū Huraira, 'the father of the kitten', so nicknamed by Muhammad because of his fondness

[1] *Korān*, vi. 59, Rodwell's version. In the last clause Sale gives: 'perspicuous book', and comments: 'the preserved table, the register of God's decrees.'

for a cat[1]—May God have mercy upon him!—states that Adam was created out of clay (*tīn*), that is, of two of the elements, water and earth, and the Jinn of flame without smoke (*mārij*), that is, of air and fire: 'We created man of dried clay, of dark loam moulded, and the Jinn we had before created of subtle fire'.[2] Jinn are spirits and constantly abide in the lowest or first firmament. Some sages declare that they have bodies, but from the circumstance of their being internal, that which is not seen, the term Jinn has been applied to them.[3] The extent of their knowledge is likewise hidden from us, and a madman is frequently nicknamed Majnūn or Jinūnī in Arabic, because he is possessed by the Jinn. Sometimes they are regarded as the offspring of Jann, or Iblīs, Shaitān or Satan, and their mother Mārija, the smokeless fire of the Samūm wind, as Adam and Eve were parents of mankind. Jinn differ from mankind in three particulars, in their spirits, form, and speech. Those among them who perform good actions are called Jinn, those who do evil Shaitān. When the former do evil, such as causing the death of any one or causing separation between two persons, it is not that such is their nature, but they do such actions through the means used by the magician and by the influence of the names of the Deity. The name of the Jinn most beloved of the Deity was al-Hāris.[4]

In the commentary on the Korān known as *Tafsīr-i-baizawī* and the *Tawārīkh-i-rauzatu-s-safā* it is said that Shaitān or Satan was the offspring of the Jinn, and that God of His

[1] He was Qāzī of Mecca under 'Usmān, died A.D. 679 (Muir, *Life*, Introd. xvi.; note, 512; *Annals*, 426).

[2] *Korān*, xv. 26–7, with Sale's commentary on ii. 28–31.

[3] *Jann*, 'covering, veiling (darkness), lying hid in the womb (embryo)': *Jinn*, 'an angel, spirit, genius'. (F. Johnson, *Persian, Arabic Dictionary*, s.v.; *ERE*. i. 669.) In the Panjāb they are said to have no bones in their arms, possess only four fingers, and no thumb (*NINQ*. i. 103).

[4] In the original text 'Hoorras', possibly referring to Hāris, which was a name of Iblīs (Hughes, 135). On the Jinn, see R. Smith, *Religion of the Semites*, 119 ff.; Sale, *Korān*, Preliminary Discourse, 52; Lane, *AN*. i. 26 ff.; *JRAI*. xxix. 252 ff.; xxx. App. 11 f.; Westermarck, *Origin and Development of the Moral Ideas*, ii. 589 f.; Rose, i. 516; *ERE*. x. 135 f. On their names, Burton, *AN*. v. 13, 278.

Different Varieties

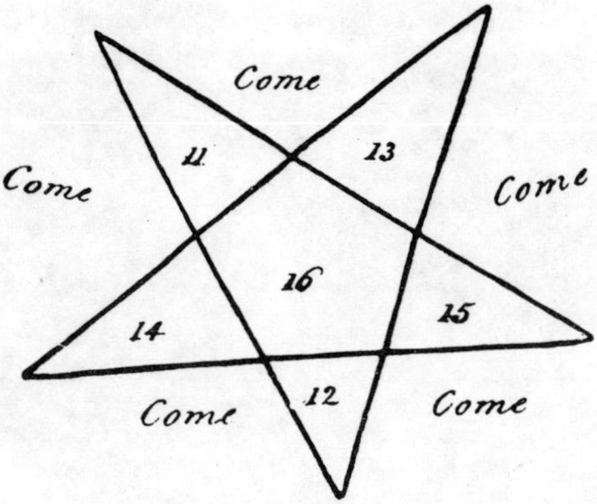

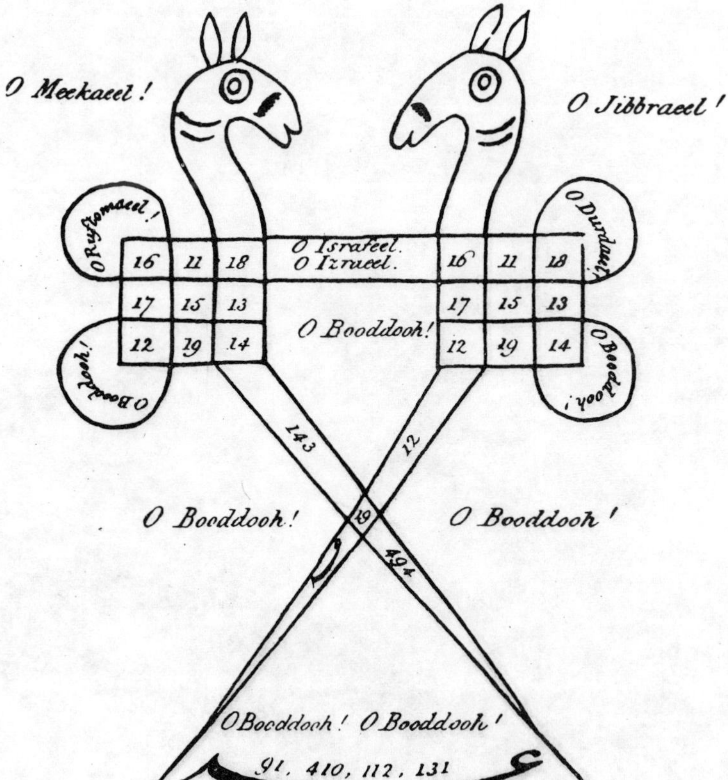

infinite mercy honoured him with the title of 'Azāzīl, a fallen Angel, their names having all a similar termination, as Jabrāīl, Mīkāīl, Isrāfīl, 'Izrāīl, and others. Imām Zāhid has recorded that it was owing to his disobedience that Satan received the name of Iblīs, 'he who despairs of the mercy of God',[1] because he refused to prostrate himself before Adam, and because in his malignity he tempted Adam and Eve to eat wheat.[2] And when he caused their separation, Adam being banished to Ceylon and Eve to the neighbourhood of Mecca, he was called Shaitān, 'he who opposes'. Thus he ruined not only himself but all the race of Adam. He was the son of Hūlīānūs, who was the son of Tārnūs, the son of Sūmās, the son of Jānn. Satan has four deputies or Khalīfa: Malīqa, son of 'Alīqa; Hāmūs, son of Janūs; Mablūt, son of Balabat; Yūsuf, son of Yāsif. And as Cain was the vilest of the sons of Adam, so is Satan in the race of the Jinn. As the name of the wife of Adam was Hawwā' or Eve—the Peace be upon her!—so Satan's wife was Awwā'. And as Adam's surname was Abū-l-bashar, 'father of mankind', so that of Satan was Abū-l-marrat, 'father of bitterness'. As Adam had three sons, Hābīl or Abel, Qābil or Qābīl Cain, and Shīs or Seth, so Satan had nine: Zū-l-baisun, who with his host occupies bazars, and all the wickedness done there is his work; Wassīn, ruler over grief and anxiety; Awān, the companion of kings; Haffān, patron of wine-bibbers; Marra, superintendent of music and dancing; Laqīs, lord of the worshippers of fire; Mazbūt, master of news, who causes people to circulate malicious and false reports; Dāsim, lord of mansions, who causes hatred between man and wife. When people return from their journeys he prevents them from thanking God for their safety, and causes wars and contentions. Some say that he is the lord of the table-cloth (*dastarkhwān*), and does not allow people to say the Bismillāh or grace when they sit down to meals, and after eating he causes them to forget to return thanks (*shukr*, *ihsān*). Last of the nine is Dalhān, whose

[1] Iblīs, διάβολος, with which Burton (*AN.* vii. 360) suggests a connexion; *balas*, 'a wicked or profligate person' (Hughes, 84).

[2] Some say that the forbidden food was an ear of wheat, a fig, or the grape (Sale, *Korān*, 5 note).

abode is in places of ablution and prayer, where he defeats the object of the pious by throwing difficulties in the way of the performance of their duties. These nine sons of the undaunted, the infernal Satan, are the mortal enemies of the race of Adam. They never allow them to do a good action, but exert all their influence in causing them to sin.[1] He has nine children added to his family for every one born among men.

In the *Shar'-i-Bukhārī* Jābir, son of 'Abdu-llāh Ansārī—May God bless him!—states that the Almighty divided all created beings into four classes: Angels, Devils, Jinn, and mankind. But Abū Dardā, a companion of the Prophet[2]—May God bless him!—has given a different account, stating that first came snakes and scorpions, then insects, then spirits, then the sons of Adam, all quadrupeds, birds, and the like.

Malik Gatshān is king of all the Jinn, and he lives in Mount Qāf, the mountain which surrounds the world, resting on the stone Sakhrat, a great emerald which gives its colour to the sky. To the east he has 300,000 servants and to the west reigns his son-in-law, 'Abdu-l-rahmān, with 30,000 servants. To both of them His Holiness Muhammad Mustafā himself—on whom be the Peace!—gave these Musalmān names. Kings of the Musalmān Jinn have their names terminating in *nūs*, such as Tārnūs, Hūlīānūs, Dakhīānūs. Kings of Tarsā, the Ātishparast, or fire-worshippers, have their names ending in *nās*, as Jatūnās; kings of the Hindu Jinn in *tās*, as Naqtās. This Naqtās when he entered the service of His Excellency the Prophet Shīs, or Seth—Peace be unto him!—was converted to Islām. Among the Musalmān Jinn there is a class of Imām or leaders, like Abūfardā, Masūr, Darbāg, Qalīs, and Abū-mālik. In the *Tafsīr-i-kabīr* it is stated that the Jinn are of four kinds: Falakīya, who inhabit the firmament; Qutbīya, who reside about the north pole; Wahmīya, who haunt the imaginations of men; Firdausīya, who dwell in Paradise. In the *Tafsīr-i-niyābīya* it is said that there are twelve troops of the Jinn, six occupying Rūm or Turkey,

[1] See Burton, *AN.* iii. 17. [2] *Mishkāt*, i. 38.

[3] *Encyclopaedia Biblica*, ii. 1747.

Farang or Europe, Yūnān or Greece, Rūs or Russia, Bābil or Babylon, and Sahbatan. The other six are in the region of Yājūj and Mājūj, Gog and Magog, the latter perhaps Armenia, Nūbat or Nubia, Zanzibar, Zangbār 'black land', Hind or Hindostān and Sind. Among these three legions are Musalmān and their king is Bakhtānūs. As to the real nature of the Jinn, they are nine-tenths spirits and one-tenth flesh.

Ja'far Sharīf gives his experiences as follows: I have always been accustomed from my youth up to study the practice of exorcism or incantations (*da'wat*), the writing of amulets and charms, the consulting of horoscopes and the prognostication of the future. Many a time have persons possessed by the devil consulted this humble student, and either by the recital of supplications (*du'ā*), or by some wise contrivance of my own, they have been cured. I used to feel much doubt regarding the effects produced, and I frequently said to myself, 'O God! What relation or connexion can possibly exist between the Jinn and men, that the former should possess such powerful influence over the latter, or that by the recital of incantations they should be cast out?' With these doubts in my mind I continued studying the subject, consulting learned men and divines and reading standard works on the subject, like the *Tafsīr*, or Commentary on the Korān, the Hadīs, or Traditions of the Prophet, and others, in order that I might acquire knowledge of these matters. I have related what I have seen.

When persons suffer from demon possession the symptoms are: some are struck dumb, others shake their heads, some go mad and walk about naked, they feel no inclination to do their usual business, but lie down and become inactive. In such cases, if it be required to make the demoniacs speak, or to cast the devil out, various devices are employed which will now be described.

The use of the magic circle or geometrical figure to control the Jinn is very like the Tantrik methods used in India, or the Yantrams of the Madras Presidency.[1] Magic circles, squares,

[1] Browne, *A Year amongst the Persians*, 148 f.; A. L. Anantha Krishna Iyer, *Cochin Tribes and Castes*, i. 306, 317; ii. 229 ff.; Thurston, *Castes*, iii. 193 f.

and figures are drawn on the ground, or on a plank with various coloured powders, cowdung ashes (*bhabhūt*), ashes, charcoal, or sandalwood, and when the demoniac is seated in the centre of the figure, the incantation (*afsūn*) is recited. Round these diagrams fruits, flowers, betel, sweets, and sometimes spirituous liquors are placed. Some people sacrifice a sheep before the circle, sprinkle the blood round it, and place a lamp lighted with a charmed wick (*palītā*) upon it. Or they merely kill a fowl and sprinkle the blood round it. Some give a rupee or two to a person possessed by the devil, who has to place it within the diagram. Then the Arabic incantation given below is recited over some cowdung ashes, or over five kinds of corn, the exorcist each time blowing on the object and throwing it at the head and shoulders of the demoniac. Or he breathes on flowers and throws them at him. He burns some perfumes such as powder (*abīr*), aloes (*'ūd*), benzoin or gum benjamin, coriander (*dhaniyā*), wood aloes (*agar*), or sandalwood near the patient,[1] and recites the invocation twenty-one times, directing the patient to sit with his eyes shut, and to smell the fumes well while he repeats the supplication. During the recital of the incantation, if any motion of the body be observed the exorcist should say, 'If thou be a male devil bow thy head to the right, if a female to the left, if a hermaphrodite forward'. Some demons violently shake the head and body of the demoniac. When the recital is finished, the exorcist asks the patient whether he feels any intoxication, lassitude, sense of weight in his head, any fear in his mind, or if he believes that some one behind him is shaking his head. If any such symptoms appear, the case is one of demon possession, otherwise not. The idea of a demon catching the patient is nonsense, derived merely from the fancies of the common folk. The incantation (*afsūn*) is an appeal to various demons, Fathūna, Habībeka, Almīn, Saqīka, Akesan, Balīsan, Talīsan, Sūradan, Kahalan, Mahalan, Sakhīan, Sadīdan, Nabiān, and it invokes them by the seal (*khātim*) of Solomon, son of David, to come from the east and west, right and left.

Incantations to cause a devil to enter a person's body in Arabic, Persian, and Hindostānī are very numerous, but I have

[1] On the use of perfumes to affect the vision in magic, see *ERE*. ix. 739.

A Magic Figure.

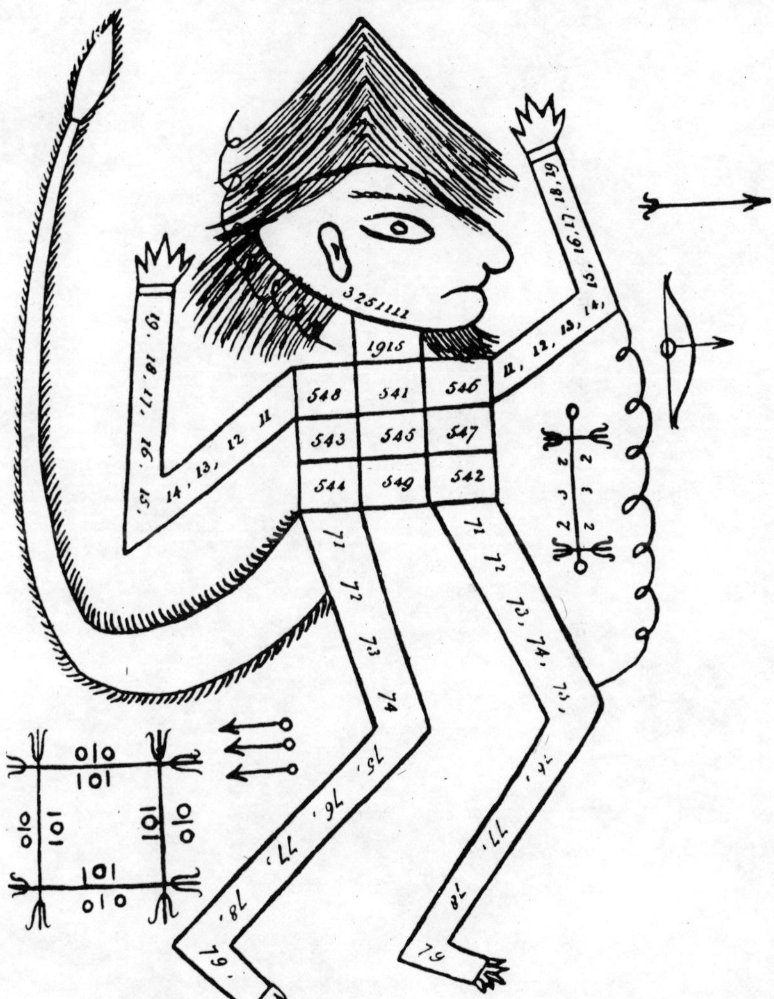

omitted them as they can be learnt from those who practise the art. Some devils when they seize a person do not let him go for two or three weeks, nay, for as many months. The demoniac then never speaks, and though the devil may be present in him he does not move or walk. To prevent certain devils from escaping, the exorcist ties a knot in the hair [1] of the demoniac after reciting in Arabic the following verse of the Korān three times and blowing upon it: 'His command when he willeth aught is but to say to it "Be", and it is. So glory be to Him in whose hand is the sway over all things! And to this shall ye be brought back'.[2] Some read the following verse eleven times over some sweet-smelling oil and blow it into the ear of the patient: 'We also made trial of Solomon, and placed a phantom [one of the Jinn] on his throne, whereupon he turned to Us in penitence'.[3] Sometimes they recite the following invocation to God Most High, and blow it into one or both ears of the patient: 'O Hearer! Thou knowest with thine ears, thine ears are within hearing, O Thou Hearer!'

After the demoniac is fully possessed by the devil he screams, takes a lighted wick (*kākrā*), and goes on lighting and extinguishing it by putting the lighted end in his mouth, or he bites a fowl and sucks its blood. When he begins to speak with some degree of sense, the exorcist asks the name of the demon, his sign, whence he came and whither he is bound, what he was doing or causing to be done while he was in the body of the patient. If he answers, well and good. If he is silent the exorcist recites an incantation over a rattan, and gives the demoniac a sound flogging which makes him tell everything.[4] For some devils are so wicked that they will not reveal their names, nor say when they intend to depart. The strange thing is that the flogging leaves no marks on the body of the demoniac. Then the exorcist asks what he desires in the way of food. He must get whatever he asks for—a pound or two of millet

[1] On the hair as the seat of strength, see Frazer, *GB.*, The Magic Art, i. 102, 344.

[2] *Korān*, xxxvi. 82–3.

[3] *Korān*, xxxviii. 33; Sale *in loco* gives the Talmudic fable.

[4] On flagellation as a means of expelling spirit influence, see Frazer, *GB.*, The Scapegoat, 259 ff.; *ERE.* ii. 228 f.; Crooke, *Popular Religion*, i. 99.

or fried rice, dumplings (*matkulā*), curdled milk, boiled rice, curries of meat, fish or fowl, eggs, a sheep, liquor, sweets, fruits, flowers, lamps made of flour lit by wicks soaked in butter, two images, male and female, made of flour, and anything else the demon wants. These things are arranged on a large potsherd, or on a winnowing or common basket, which the exorcist waves three times from the head to the feet of the demoniac, first in front, then behind. The contents he afterwards distributes among beggars, or he places the whole under a tree or on a river bank. This is to be given in alms on the day when the demon says he will depart.

When this time comes the exorcist asks the demon in what place he purposes to throw down the demoniac when making his exit, and what he intends doing with him. He answers, 'On this very spot', or 'Under such and such a tree', and 'I wish to take with me meat, offal, and so on', or 'nothing at all'. If the exorcist does not approve of this he says, 'Nay, but thou must throw him down here, or in the yard of the house, and thou must take a shoe or a sandal in thy mouth, or carry a grindstone on thy head'. When the demon departs he runs with such speed and makes such a noise that people flee from him in terror. The demoniac frequently runs away with stones so large that two or three men could hardly lift them. Sometimes he runs away without taking anything. The exorcist must continue holding him by his hair, either at the back or side of his head, and he must let him lie wherever he falls. Then he recites the incantation or the Throne Verse, Āyatu-l-kursī of the Korān: 'God! There is no God but He, the Living, the Eternal! No slumber seizeth Him nor sleep! His, whatsoever is in the Heavens and whatsoever is in the Earth! Who is he that can intercede with Him but by His own permission? He knoweth what hath been before them and what will be after them. Yet naught of His knowledge shall they grasp save what He willeth. His Throne reacheth over the Heavens and the Earth, and the upholding of both burdeneth Him not; and He is the High, the Great!'[1] This is recited over an iron nail, or a wooden peg, which he strikes into the ground. The moment the demoniac falls down, the exorcist

[1] *Korān*, ii. 256.

A Puleeta, (or Lamp Charm.)
for commanding the Devil's presence

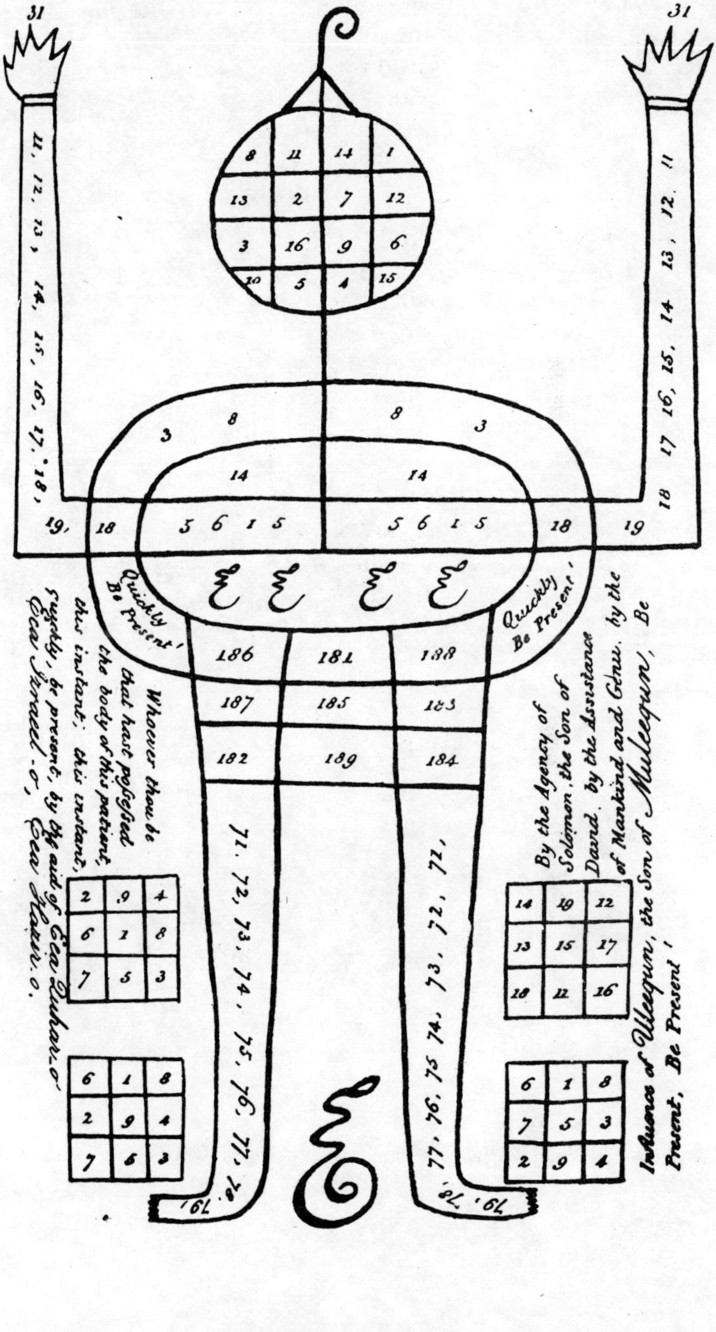

instantly plucks out one or two hairs from amongst those which he holds in his hand, recites some recognized spell over them, puts them in a bottle and corks it up, whereupon the demon which beset the patient is supposed to be imprisoned therein.[1] Then he either buries the bottle in the ground or burns it, after which the demon never returns.

Some practitioners known as Syānā, ‘ wise, cunning ’, make a small wax doll, fasten one hair to the crown of its head and another in the bottom of the cork, fill the bottle with smoke, put the doll into it and cork it up. They put it in the smoke to prevent people from distinguishing the doll which remains hanging in the middle of the bottle. The Syānā then pulls out a hair or two from the head of the demoniac as he falls to the ground, and contrives to insert them in the bottle. Then he holds it up to public view and says, ‘ Behold ! I have cast the devil out of this demoniac and shut him up in the bottle. Now, if you pay so much well and good, if not I will let him loose again ’. These fools, seeing the doll in the bottle, believe that it is the devil himself, and out of fear giving the Syānā as much as he asks, get the bottle buried or burnt.

The instant the demon leaves the demoniac the latter regains his senses, and staring round amazed asks, ‘ Where am I and why is this crowd assembled round me ? ’ After this a supplication should be said three times over a handful of water, and this should be dashed on the patient’s face. Afterwards they repeat, ‘ Lā haula wa lā quvvata illā bi-llāhi-l-Aliyyi-l-Azīm ! ’, ‘ There is no Majesty and no Might save in Allāh, the Glorious and the Great ! ’ Then they take the patient home, wash his face, hands, and feet, and either on this or on the following day an amulet (*ta‘wīz*), of a special kind used for this purpose, is tied on his neck or arm in order that the demon may not seize him again.

When a person has long suffered from disease, in order to ascertain whether this is due to a devil or to enchantment, the following figure is drawn on the ground or on a board. Some flowers are put in the sick man’s hand, and he is told to grasp them firmly, and to put his closed fist near the

[1] Cf. ‘ The Fisherman and the Jinni ’ (Burton, *AN.* i. 37 ff. ; Frazer, *GB.*, Balder the Beautiful, ii. 138).

diagram. Then the exorcist takes some more flowers, and having read the following incantation over each and blowing upon it, he dashes it against the hands of the patient, when in a few minutes his hands will begin to move into one of the compartments. The diagram and the incantation are as follows :

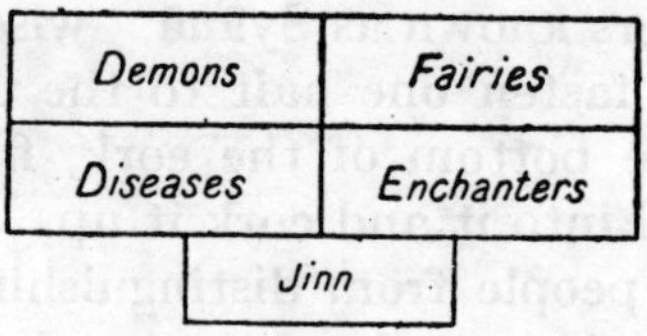

'It is from Solomon, and it is this : In the Name of God, the Compassionate, the Merciful ! Set not yourselves against me, but come to me submitting yourselves as Muslims. K, H, I, 'A, S, H, M, 'A, S, Q.[1] [Then follow some unintelligible words.] By the blessing of Solomon, son of David, warn, warn me ! May both his hands go, and by the command of God reach this figure !' After reciting this spell he says now and again, 'In these five compartments are inserted the names of the five afflictions. God grant that the hands of the patient may enter the compartment containing the name of the malady with which he is afflicted !'

Some devils usually attack people in their sleep and harass them not a little. Some do not enter his body as soon as their presence is required. In this case the demoniac is made to sleep, and to continue sitting night and day in one of the compartments marked on the ground as already described. At night, either for the purpose of commanding the presence of the demons or for casting them out, a charmed wick (*palītā*), made of paper inscribed with mystic characters, by the inhaling of the smoke of which demons are expelled, is lighted with three kinds of oil and one of balsam for three, five, or seven

[1] *Korān*, xxvii, 30–1 ; xix. 1 ; xliii. 1 ; lxviii. 1. These letters at the beginning of these chapters are supposed to conceal several profound mysteries (Sale, *Korān*, Preliminary Discourse, 42 f.). The meaning of them was probably unknown to the Musalmāns themselves, even in the first century. They may have been private marks, or initial letters, attached by their owner to the copies received when the text of the *Korān* was fixed (Rodwell note on *Korān*, lxviii).

A Puleeta, (or Lamp-Charm:) for Casting out Devils.

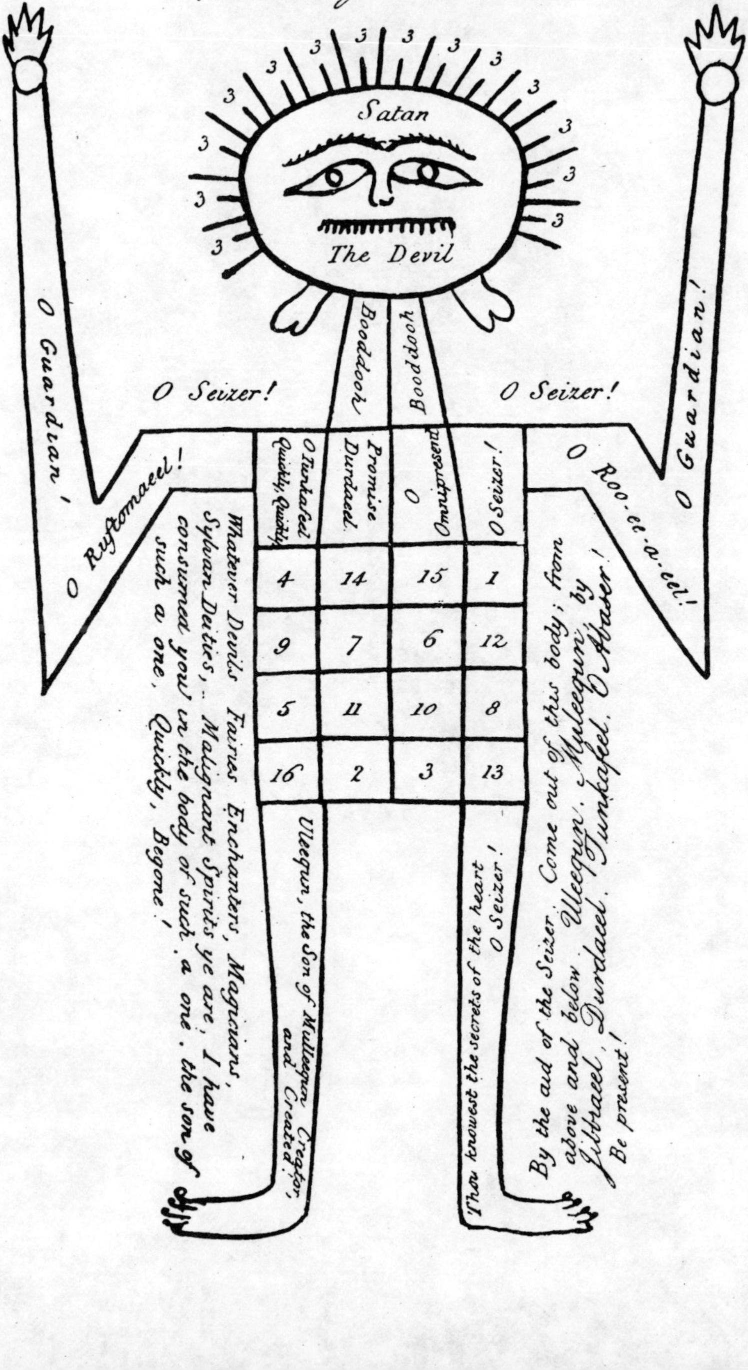

(*mohanī, mohinī kā kājal*), which women rub on their foreheads or eyebrows to cause their husbands to love them, or they rub a little of it on the man's hair or the soles of his feet. Ja'far Sharīf remarks that if a married woman wishes to keep her husband true to her there is no harm in reciting a verse of the Korān, because writing on or reciting over anything a verse of the Korān, and afterwards drinking or eating it, is highly meritorious, particularly if it keeps her husband from committing sin. In Sind when a man wishes to attract a woman's love he selects seven large cloves on the seventeenth day of the month and recites the following charm over each of them : 'O Cloves ! O Cloves ! Ye are truly good. She that is bound by the cloves can never remain away from me. If I give these cloves to any woman she will eagerly [rising and falling] come to me ! ' He then contrives that the woman may eat the cloves. Or on the first day of the month he recites this charm over a handful of salt : 'O Salt ! O thou salt one ! Thou essence of the seven seas ! O certain person ! [naming the woman]. Eat my salt and kiss my feet ! ' The reciter then dissolves the salt in water and drinks it, on which the woman falls violently in love with him. The charm known as the 'breaking of the trouser-string' is done by reciting a charm over seven or nine threads of raw cotton spun by a girl who has not yet been betrothed. The bits are rolled up and knotted seven times, after which the lady is warned of the danger. Should she persevere in her cruelty one of the knots is opened, and forthwith her trouser-string breaks.[1]

When disputes come before the council of a caste, charms are used to induce the members to come to a favourable verdict. Some have a charm engraved on an amulet (*ta'wīz*) or on a ring (*karā*) which they wear on finger, wrist, or upper arm. Others write charms on paper and bind them up in a bit of brocade or silk and cotton cloth (*kamkhwāb, mashrū'*), and wear them on the hair, turban, arm, wrist, or neck. Others, again, use for this purpose various kinds of roots or herbs, the gathering of which is done according to a special ritual. They go to the tree or plant and say, 'We intend to come to-morrow at such a time to take you away for such a purpose '. These

[1] Burton, *Sindh*, 178 f.

fumigated with the smoke. These are much more generally used than the more elaborate charms already described. 'How to write a charm to cure fevers: Take some olive leaves and on a Saturday, being yourself in a state of purity, write on one of the leaves, "Hell is hungry", on another "Hell is refreshed", and on the third, "Hell is thirsty". Put these in a rag and bind them on the left arm of the patient.'[1] Make two intersecting triangles on a sheet of paper with one continuous motion of the hand, sew this up in a sheet of cloth and tie it round the patient's neck. When the fever has left, throw the cloth into a well or river.[2]

It is common among Musalmān women, when their husbands ill-treat or neglect them, or take a fancy for other women, to procure something in the way of a philtre or embrocation which will cause the renewal of love. Some of these are of such a filthy kind that it is impossible to reproduce them.[3]

Betel leaves, or betel nuts, are often given for this purpose, so that when a man comes under the dominion of a woman and overlooks her misconduct it is said that she must have given him betel nuts to eat. The flesh of the chameleon and various wild roots and herbs are also used in this way. Owl's flesh is a powerful charm, the eating of which causes a man to become a fool and lose his memory, and women give it to their husbands to make them ignore their misdoings.[4] Some women procure the ashes of the dead from a Hindu cremation ground, recite incantations over it, and sprinkle it at night on a man's bed or over him when he is asleep. In the Panjāb burglars carry with them such ashes and sprinkle it over the inmates of a house to prevent them from waking.[5] Another well-known charm is the 'magic lampblack' or the 'lampblack of the enchantress'

[1] Ibn Khallikān, iii 62.

[2] *NINQ.* ii. 10. For a number of charms and folk remedies used in S. India, see *Man*, vi. 182 ff. Many Hindu charms of the same kind will be found in the *Atharvaveda*, vi. 8, 9, 89, 135; ed. Whitney, i. 287, 347, 382; ed. Bloomfield, Sacred Books of the East, 99 ff., 103 ff., and other references in the index.

[3] For Hindu love charms, see *Atharvaveda*, vi. 89, 102, 130, 131, 132, 139; Whitney, i. 347, 355, 379, 384 f.

[4] Crooke, *Popular Religion*, i. 279.

[5] *NINQ.* i. 103. Hindu cremation grounds are naturally a haunt of demons and witches (Tawney, *Kathā-sarit-sāgara*, i. 159).

A Puleeta — (or Lamp-Charm,) for Casting out Devils.

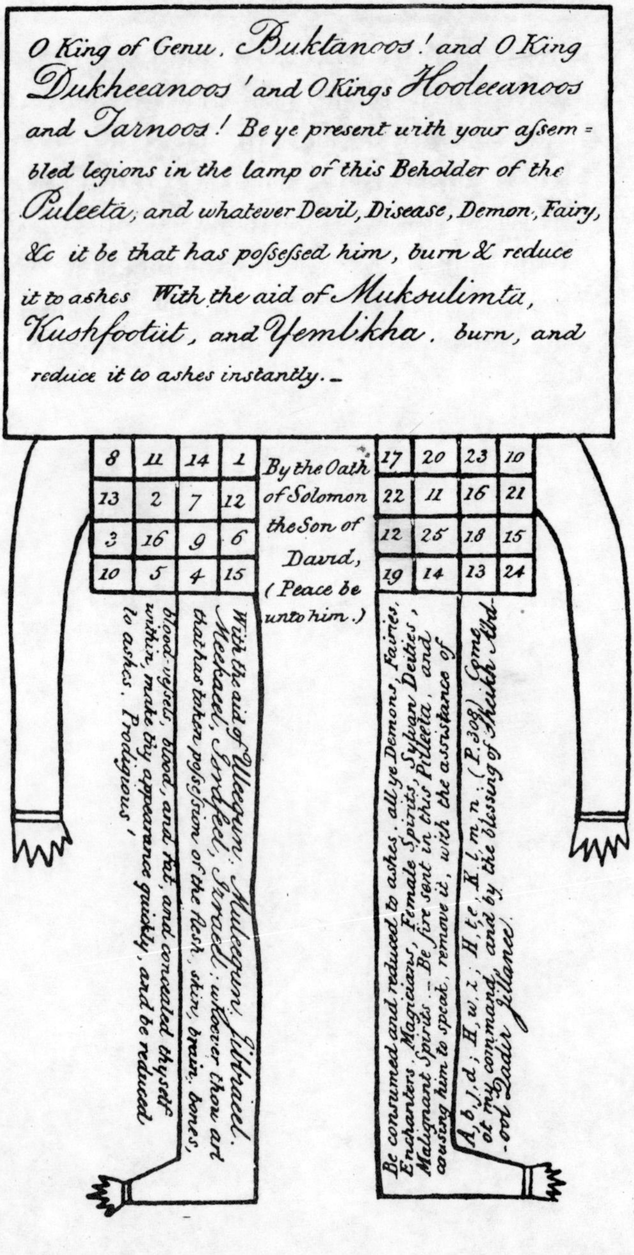

recites a spell over it, and throws it in the direction from which it came. If it be really the work of a devil he returns the same stone, by which people know that it is his work. Otherwise they conclude that it is an enemy who has done this, and they take measures accordingly.

Some exorcists who are tricksters practise devices to gain money. Thus, when a man is rich and timid they secretly throw, or cause to be thrown, stones or bones into his house by day or night. The householder sends for one of these rogues to find out the cause and desires him to cast his horoscope. The trickster, to frighten him, tells him that it is the work of a devil, whom he describes as a monster of the air with four heads, of an elephant, buffalo, dog, or horse, and tells him that the monster wants to eat his liver, that this is the reason why he flings the stones, and that he will strangle him unawares. This makes him so alarmed that his very liver melts like water. 'I will prove what I say', says the rogue. So he takes up a stone or a bone, paints it as has been already described, and flings it away, taking good care that it is thrown back. This frightens the dupe still more, and he offers anything to avoid the danger. The rogue then recites some spells and goes off with his booty. I myself, says Ja'far Sharīf, have been a witness of such tricks.

If the Jinn occupy a house, steal food, and frighten people, so that they are never free from sickness and worry, the following incantation should be recited twenty-one times for three days running, morning and evening, over some water which is blown upon and poured on the floor. Or it is recited over four iron nails or wooden pegs twenty-one times, and blown upon, the nails or pegs being driven into the four corners of the house. The incantation runs: 'They plot a plot against me, and I will plot a plot against them. Deal calmly therefore with the infidels and leave them a while alone'.[1] Some write the names of the Ashābu-l-kahf, the Companions of the Cave, with that of their dog, and paste it on the house walls.

The following are smoke charms, used for removing tertian ague, demons, fairies, fear, and false imaginations. They are thrown into the fire and the patient is covered with a sheet and

[1] *Korān*, lxxxvi. 15, 17.

consecutive nights. Within this time if the wick has been lighted to command the presence of, or disappearance of, the demon, he comes or retreats.

The charmed wick is made in this way. Take a red or black earthen pot, fill it with all kinds of fruits, some money, half a rupee or a rupee, as the fee of the exorcist, and fix on it a cover coloured like the pot, the outer surface of both being marked with sandalwood paste. Besmear the place where the patient sleeps with cowdung or red earth, stroke him from head to foot with a piece of blank paper, and on this write the lamp charm. Roll it up obliquely, round or flat, to make it burn well, and to prevent it from unfolding, wind a piece of thin muslin with some cotton or thread round it. Then use the cover of the pot as a lamp and light it with three kinds of oil, or that of the *karanj* tree (*pongamia glabra*).[1] When the lamp is lighted in the evening, perfumes should be burnt, and the patient is directed to sit by the lamp and stare into it. It must continue burning till he falls asleep. When the charmed wick is set alight, two or three flames of various colours, black, green, or yellow, will appear both to the patient and to the bystanders. Some demoniacs cannot sleep in a light like this, some get up and walk about, or do not feel sleepy, while others, though they do not object to look at it, seem evidently excited. At all events, by the burning of this charmed wick the devil is cast out. Should he be present he is warned to depart, which he does under the influence of the charm, and if the patient suffers from any bodily disease it will be removed.

If devils annoy any one by throwing stones, which is a common habit of devils,[2] the exorcist takes one from among those that are flung, paints it over with turmeric and quicklime,

[1] A tall erect tree or climber, the seeds of which yield oil, used for illuminating and medicinal purposes (Watt, *Econ. Dict.* vi, part 1, 322 ff.).

[2] 'In E. Africa it is believed that sacrilegious trespassers in a sacred grove are assailed by showers of missiles: cases of this are often alleged to occur in India, and the writer has heard of two cases in E. Africa where colonists who had no knowledge of these beliefs, and had built their houses in the vicinity of sacred fig-trees, asserted that they were periodically disturbed at night by stones thrown on their roofs' (C. W. Hobley, *JRAI.* xli. 432 f.).

A Lamp-Charm
for Causing the Devil's presence.

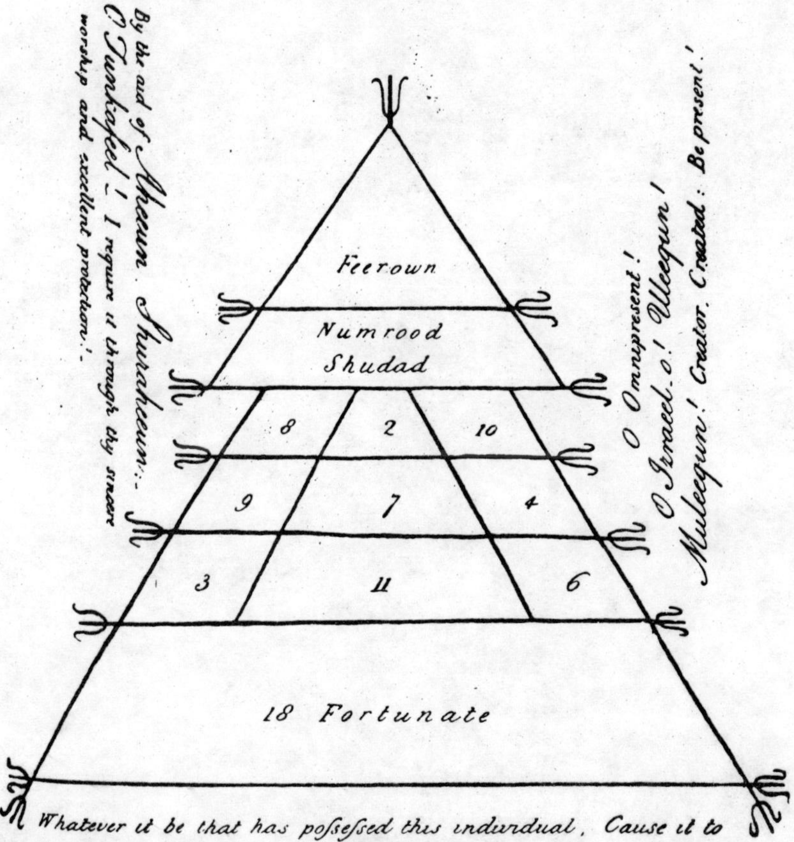

Whatever it be that has possessed this individual, Cause it to be present - and burn and consume it to ashes this instant, Ye Demons ! with your Hosts, Rooaeel!

substances are known to few, and when they go to fetch them they take with them a chicken, fruits, and liquor, which they put near the tree or plant, kill the chicken and rub some of the blood on the tree or plant, and then take what they require.[1] It is by reciting incantations which can be learned from those skilled in the art and from Sannyāsīs and other Hindu ascetics that their purpose is effected. In fact, many of these charms are borrowed from Hindus.[2]

In order to cause enmity between two persons it is common to recite chapter 105 of the Korān, 'The Elephant': 'Hast thou not seen how thy Lord dealt with the army of the Elephant [Abyssinia]? Did He not cause their stratagem to miscarry? And he sent against them birds in flocks. Clay stones did He hurl down upon them, and He made them like stubble beaten down'.[3] This should be recited at noon, or some other time, forty-one times over some earth taken from a grave, which should then be thrown on the persons whom it is desired to embroil, or on the roads leading to their houses. Or they take forty black pepper-corns, and for a week morning and evening recite this charm in the persons' names. Then the pepper is burnt and enmity is produced. Or a man, bareheaded in a cemetery or mosque, with his face turned to his enemy's house at noon, recites the following verse forty-one times for forty-one days, and then a quarrel is sure to arise between them. 'And we have put envy and hatred between them that shall last till the Day of Resurrection'.[4] To this the invocation is added: 'Yā Qahhārhu! Yā Jabbārhu! Yā 'Izrāīlhu!' 'The Dominant! The Omnipotent! The Angel of Death!'

If a man wishes to be revenged on a powerful enemy the following methods are used. But it is not every one who succeeds, and practitioners undertake the charm only for those in need of relief, and the Almighty will hear only the supplica-

[1] This is apparently a way of apologizing to the tree-spirit for disturbing it. Cf. Frazer, *GB.*, The Magic Art, ii. 18 f., 36 f.

[2] Russell, ii. 521; iv. 34 f.; *PNQ.* i. 89; ii. 5; Crooke, *Popular Religion*, ii. 46; A. K. Iyer, *Cochin Tribes*, i. 348; *JRAI.* xxxviii. 157, 159.

[3] This refers to the attack by Abraha, Abyssinian viceroy of Yemen, on Mecca, A.D. 570 (Muir, *Life*, Introd. c ff.).

[4] *Korān*, v. 69.

tions of those who are really distressed. He should recite the Tabat, Abū Lahab, the 111th chapter of the Korān backwards (*ma'kūs*),[1] or the 50th chapter, Chihal Qāf, the Forty Qs, morning and evening daily for twenty-one days, forty-one times at each period. Or he makes a doll about a span high, more or less, out of earth taken from a grave, or from a Hindu cremation ground, recites the 105th chapter or the 111th backwards, or the 50th over twenty-one small thin wooden pegs, three times over each peg, and drives them into different parts of the doll, on the crown of the head, forehead, both eyes upper arms, armpits, palms, nipples, both sides of the body, navel, thighs, knees, and soles of the feet. The doll is then shrouded like a human corpse and buried in the name of the enemy, who, it is believed, will soon die.[2] Another method is to draw a human figure on the ground, on an unburnt brick, or on an image made of clay. The following incantation is recited over it : 'Thou, the Dominant ! Full of wrath, terrible art Thou ! whose vengeance none can endure !'

[1] On charms recited backwards, Crooke, *Popular Religion*, ii. 276 f. The heterodox Bōn-pa of Tibet recite the Om Mani formula backwards (Waddell, *Buddhism of Tibet*, 150).

[2] This is the well-known Corp chre of Scotland. For other examples see *ERE.* v. 295 ; viii. 319 ; x. 447 ; Russell, i. 334 ; ii. 231, 248 ; iii. 241, 562 ; A. K. L. Iyer, i. 348 ; ii. 473 ; for a figure of this kind see Thurston, *Tribes*, vi. 124 ff. with a photograph ; Crooke, *Popular Religion*, ii. 278 f. ; Waddell, *Buddhism of Tibet*, 408 ; Rose, i. 229, 237 ; *JRAI.* xxxviii. 160 ff. ; Frazer, *GB.*, The Magic Art, i. 55 ff.

A Puleeta (or Lamp Charm,)
to cast out the Devil

8	11	14	1
13	2	7	12
3	16	9	6
10	5	4	15

Whoever ye are, Demons, Fairies, Genii, Malignant Spirits, Devils, Nursoo,* Chooraeel,† Sheikh Suddo,‡ (by the aid of Uheeun Shuraheein,) that have taken possession of the flesh, skin brain, bone, blood-vessels, blood! Be present instantly this very hour, in this body and be burnt and reduced to ashes. – Uleequn, the Son of Muleequn. Numrood, Murdood, Shuddad, Haman, Feeraown; Qaroon; Aheeun; Shuraheein; O Quhar-o, O Izraeel-o. Moosuhur Mumee Allah See Meg Meg, Yemmay, Yemmay

* Nursoo (alias Narsinga,) 4th Aöö-tar of Vishnoo.

† Chooraeel, the Ghost of a woman who died while pregnant

‡ Sheikh Suddo: (P. 278) a Moosulman, who became a Demon

CHAPTER XXVII

AMULETS AND CHARMS

MAGIC squares are sometimes so large as to include as many as a hundred compartments in a line, but here only those having up to ten compartments will be described. Magic squares include the following varieties: Dupayā, Sulsī, Rubā'ī, Murabba, Khamsī, Musaddas, Musabba', Musamman, Mustassa, Ma'shshar. That is to say, they are binary or 'two-legged', ternary, quaternary, and so on.[1] In the Dupayā or 'two-legged' square nothing is to be subtracted, but the number is to be divided by 12, and with the quotient the compartments are to be filled up, increasing one in every square as you proceed, in the manner following:

3	8	1
2	4	6
7		5

Should anything remain it is to be added to the number in the sixth or fractional compartments (*kasar kē ghar*). For example, the numerical quantity of the word *Bismillāh*, 786, divided by 12 gives 65, and 6 over. With this fill up, adding

[1] For the mathematical rules for making magic squares, see *EB.* xvii. 310 ff. For examples, *ERE.* iii. 445, 449. On Musalmān charms and amulets, ibid., iii. 457 ff.

65 in each compartment and 6 more in the sixth compartment :

195	526	65
130	260	396
461		325

To form a Sulsī square—from a given number subtract 12, and with one-third of the remainder fill up the compartments as follows :

4	9	2
3	5	7
8	1	6

This is the magic square of Hawwā' or Eve, whose number is 15. Deduct 1, leaving 3 remain, a third being 1 ; with this unit fill up the square, adding 1 to each compartment until the whole is filled up. In whatever way the numbers are added up they will form the same total. In thus subtracting and dividing, if 1 remains over and above, it should be added to the original number in the seventh compartment, if 2 in the fourth, and then the numbers will correspond. In forming Sulsī magic squares, the compartment in which to begin is likewise varied according to the elements, whether they be earth, water, air, or fire ; thus :

Smoke-Charms.

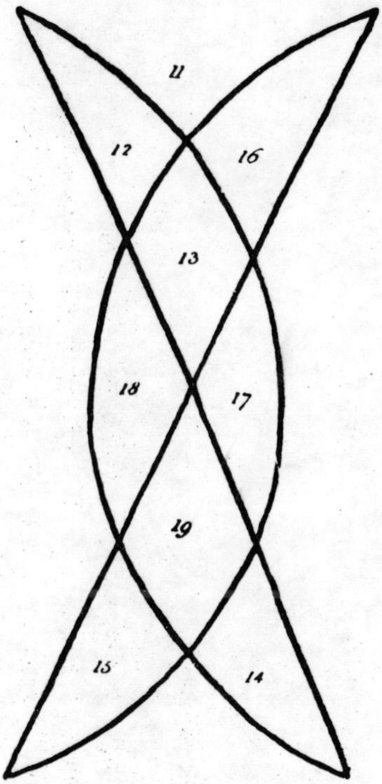

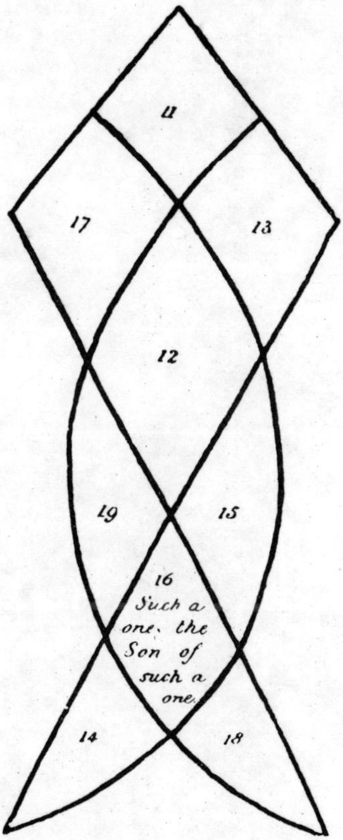

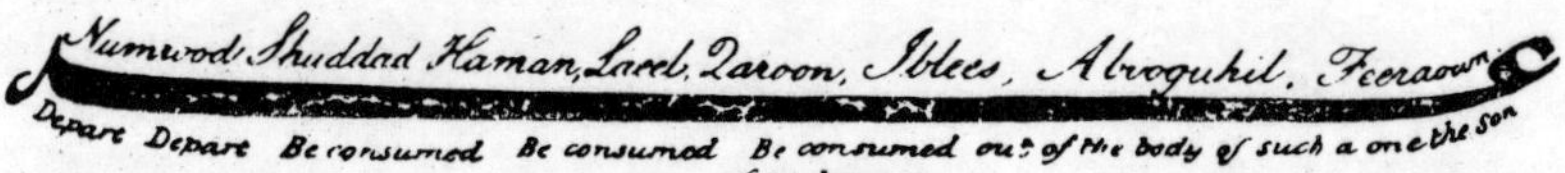

AIR

2	7	6
9	5	1
4	3	8

FIRE

4	9	2
3	5	7
8	1	6

EARTH

6	7	2
1	5	9
8	3	4

WATER

6	1	8
7	5	3
2	9	4

To form the Rubā'ī square, deduct 30 from the given number, divide the remainder by 4, and with a quarter fill up 16 compartments, thus :

8	11	14	1
13	2	7	12
3	16	9	6
10	5	4	15

This magic square is that of Ajal or Death ; its number is 34, deduct 30, 4 remains ; divide by 4, 1 remains, and with the latter fill up. If 1 remains over, add 1 to the thirteenth compartment ; if 2, add 1 to the ninth ; if 3, 1 to the fifth.

Besides this method there is another by which Rubā'ī squares are formed : Subtract 21 from the given number, begin the remainder from the thirteenth compartment and fill up the sixteenth ; having previously filled up from 1 to 12 as above directed, fill up the other four ; e.g. Maryam or Mary's name is 290, deduct 21, 269 remains, and with it fill up as follows :

8	11	270	1
269	2	7	12
3	272	9	6
10	5	4	271

Murabba' squares, like the Sulsī, are of four kinds depending on the elements, thus :

EARTH

8	11	14	1
13	2	7	12
3	16	9	6
10	5	4	15

WATER

14	4	1	15
7	9	12	6
11	5	8	10
2	16	13	3

AIR

15	1	4	14
10	8	5	11
6	12	9	7
3	13	16	2

FIRE

1	14	15	4
8	11	10	5
12	7	6	9
13	2	3	16

Khamsī squares are formed by subtracting 60 from the number, dividing the remainder by 5, and with one-fifth filling up 25 compartments, by increasing 1 in each, thus :

A Puleeta, (or Lamp Charm,) for Casting out the Devil.

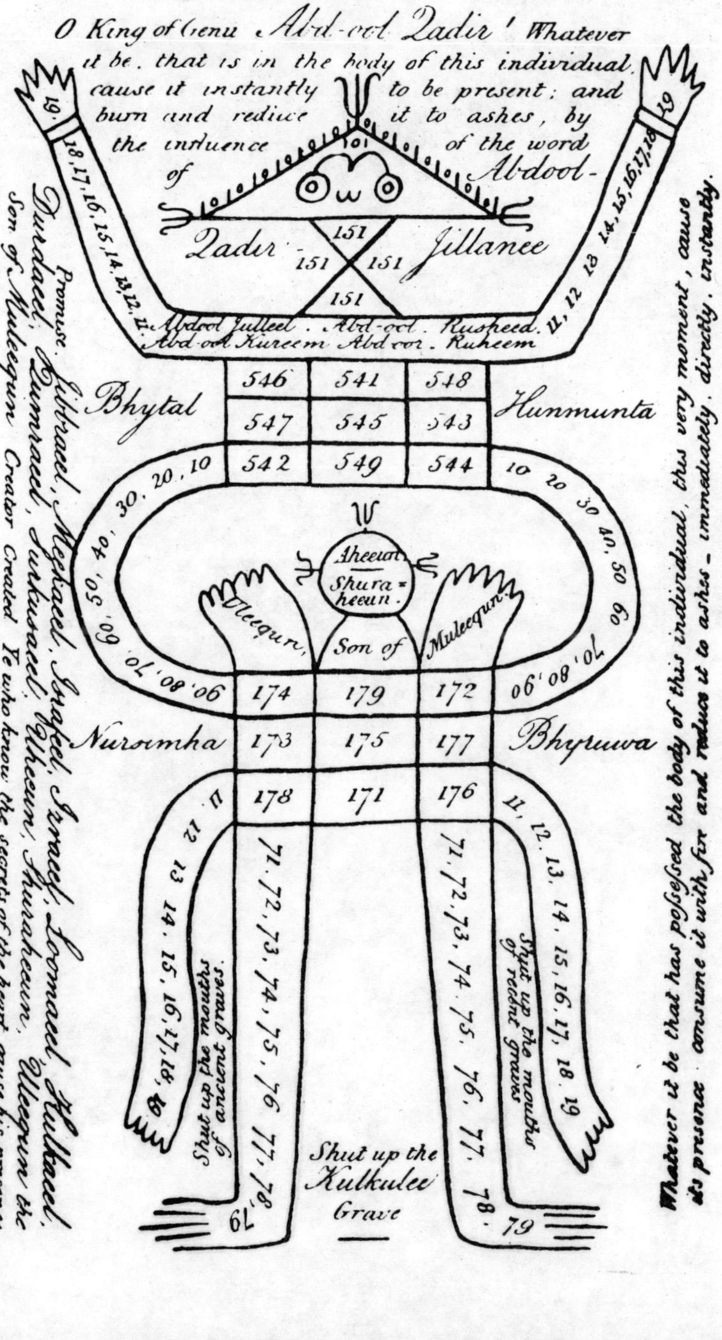

7	13	19	25	1
20	21	2	8	14
3	9	15	16	22
11	17	23	4	10
24	5	6	12	18

If in making the division for forming this square 1 remain, 1 is to be added to the twenty-first compartment ; if 2, to the sixteenth ; if 5, to the eleventh ; if 4, to the sixth.

To form a Musaddas magic square, deduct 105 from any given number, divide by 6, and with one-sixth fill it up, thus :

36	18	30	19	7	1
13	26	2	34	24	12
5	9	22	29	15	31
25	6	14	8	35	23
21	32	10	17	3	28
11	20	33	4	27	16

In forming this square, if 1 remain, add 1 to the thirty-first compartment ; if 2, to the thirty-fifth ; if 3, to the nineteenth ; if 4, to the thirteenth ; if 5, to the seventh.

To make a Musabba' square, you must deduct 160, divide by 7, and with one-seventh fill up as follows :

40	23	13	45	35	18	1
32	15	5	37	27	10	49
24	14	46	29	19	2	41
16	6	38	28	11	43	33
8	47	30	20	3	42	25
7	39	22	12	44	34	17
48	31	21	4	36	26	9

In forming the above, if from 1 to 5 remain, add 1 in the forty-third compartment.

To make a Musamman square, subtract 252, divide by 8, and with the quotient fill up as follows :

36	43	35	32	27	60	26	1
41	4	49	59	21	17	45	24
37	15	11	10	58	51	50	28
23	47	57	52	12	9	18	42
3	46	8	13	53	56	19	62
25	63	54	55	7	14	2	40
31	20	16	6	44	48	61	34
64	22	30	33	38	5	39	29

In forming this square, if from 1 to 7 remain, add 1 to the number in the seventy-fifth compartment.

In a Mustassa square, subtract 360 from the given number, divide by 9, and with one-ninth fill up as follows :

70	59	27	16	76	55	43	22	1
50	39	28	6	66	54	33	12	81
40	18	7	67	56	34	13	73	61
60	29	17	77	46	44	23	2	71
20	19	78	57	45	24	3	72	51
30	8	68	47	25	14	74	62	41
9	79	58	37	35	4	64	52	31
10	69	48	36	15	75	53	42	21
80	49	38	26	5	65	63	32	11

If in this from 1 to 8 remain, add 1 in the seventy-third compartment.

In a Ma'ashshar square, subtract 495 from any given number, divide the remainder by 10, and with one-tenth fill up as follows :

28	60	42	61	39	70	98	72	34	1
33	4	26	74	76	95	84	24	21	68
69	83	13	92	10	90	86	12	18	32
2	79	14	50	53	56	43	87	22	99
71	96	85	55	44	49	54	16	5	30
66	19	8	45	58	51	48	93	82	35
36	20	94	52	47	46	57	7	81	65
37	23	89	9	91	11	15	88	78	64
63	80	75	27	25	6	17	77	97	38
100	41	59	40	62	31	3	29	67	73

In this, if from 1 to 9 remain, add 1 in the ninety-first compartment.

Magic squares of these varieties are used as love charms, to create enmity, to cause men to be silent regarding another, to prevent dreaming, and to cast out devils. In northern India they are used to cure various diseases, to cause butter to increase in the churn, or milk in a woman or in a cow, to remove cattle disease, to make fruit-trees give their fruit, to make a husband obey his wife.[1] In southern India, when used as love charms they are written about the time of the new moon, the best days being Fridays, Mondays, Wednesdays, and Thursdays, and the best hours those during which Jupiter, Mercury, and Venus are dominant. For all purposes magic squares are written on a porcelain plate or on paper, the inscription being washed off and drunk. Among the Memans of Gujarāt, in a case of spirit possession, the Sayyid asks the patient to send him daily a white china plate, on which he writes with saffron magic squares, figures, or chapter 113 of the Korān, the writing being dissolved in water and drunk.[2] Or they are worn about the person or burnt, and the patient is fumigated with the smoke, or they are bound up in cotton soaked in perfumed oil and burnt in a lamp, or they are engraved on rings which are worn on the fingers. Some people write the charm on birch bark (*bhojpattar*, *betula utilis*), or have it engraved on a thin metallic plate covered with wax, protected by brocade, and worn as an amulet, or it is sealed up in a hollow metal case,[3] hung on the neck, worn on the upper arm, on the loins, or in the turban, or tied in the corner of a handkerchief.

They often have an amulet-case made to hold a stone

[1] *PNQ.* i. 83, 88, 136; ii. 167; *NINQ.* i. 102; iv. 36; v. 17.

[2] *BG.* ix, part 2, 57. For other examples of drinking charms, see Frazer, *Folklore in the O.T.* iii. 413 f.; Thurston, *Castes*, iv. 489; Rose, i. 211. On the acquirement of magical sanctity by drinking, see Halliday, *Greek Divination*, 124 ff. The favourite passages of the Korān used in amulets are 'The Daybreak' and 'The Men' (cxiii, cxiv), and 'The Throne' verse (ii. 256).

[3] Some of these amulet-cases are highly ornamental (Baden-Powell, *Handbook of the Manufactures and Arts of the Punjāb*, 177 f., with an illustration).

engraved with verses of the Korān (*nād-i-'Ali*, 'a call to 'Alī ')[1] with some tiger's claws (*bāghnakh*) set in silver. When they get an amulet from a Mashāikh, Mullā, or other learned man, or if they can procure any part of an offering made at a shrine, such as flowers or sandalwood, they put it into the case. Some people kill a 'double-headed' snake, or amphisbaena[2] on a new-moon night (*amāvas*) which falls on a Sunday, recite a charm over it, put it in an earthen pot, and bury it in the ground. After the flesh has disappeared they take the bones, thread them, and wear them round the neck as a cure for scrofula. Besides such things they use the feathers, hair, or bones of various animals and birds as protectives to ward off apparitions, the Jinn, and misfortunes. When a man is making an amulet he should turn his face towards the house of the person for whom it is intended. When sentences of the Korān are used in charms and amulets, the numerical values of the letters, as already described, are added together, and with the sum total the magic square is filled up.

Abu Huraira reports that Muhammad said, ' Verily there are ninety-nine names of God, and whoever recites them shall enter Paradise '.[3] The Emperor Humāyūn's respect for the names of God was so great that once when he sent for one Mīr'Abdu-l-haiy, whose name means ' Slave of the Eternal ', he merely called him 'Abdu-l, leaving out the last word because he had not yet bathed that morning.[4] Hence many people make magic squares containing one of these names. The following is a list of these names, with their meaning, the numerical value of their letters, and their uses.[5]

Allāh,[6] ' the Supreme ', 66, for all purposes. Ar-Rahmān,

[1] For a complete version of the ' call ' see *Āīn*, i. 507.

[2] The so-called 'double-headed' snake (*eryx Johnii*) is called *dutondī*, ' two heads ', by the Marāthas, and *domunhā*, with the same meaning, in N. India (*BG.* xviii, part 1, 80 ; *PNQ.* iii. 61 f., 98). The true amphisbaena is a worm-shaped lizard (*EB.* i. 891).

[3] *Mishkāt*, i. 542. On the magical value of the name, see Farnell, *The Evolution of Religion*, 184 ff. ; Frazer, *GB.*, Taboo and Perils of the Soul, 318 ff.

[4] Ferishta, ii. 178.

[5] On the ninety-nine names of Allāh, see E. H. Palmer, *The Qurān*, Sacred Books of the East, vi, Introd., 67 f.

[6] Allāh, a male deity, of whom Al-lāt was the female partner, was the patron of the Quraish tribe (Margoliouth, *Mohammed*, 109, and see *ERE.* i. 664).

'the Compassionate', 258, for enlightening the mind. Ar-Rahīm, 'the Compassionate', 258, for increase of rank. Al-Malik, 'the King', 91, for obtaining wealth. Al-Quddūs, 'the Holy', 170, to remove fear. As-Salām, 'the Peace', 131, for health. Al-Mu'min, 'the Faithful', 136, for security from enemies. Al-Muhaimin, 'the Protector', 145, for personal protection. Al-'Azīz, 'the Mighty', 94, for increase of honour and dignity. Al-Jabbār, 'the Omnipotent', 206, in order to become independent of princes. Al-Mutakabbir, 'the Great,' 662, for increase of wealth and dignity. Al-Khāliq, 'the Creator', 731, for obtaining an easy labour. Al-Musawwir, 'the Fashioner', 336, for cancelment of debts. Al-Ghaffār, 'the Forgiver', 1281, for pardon of sins. Al-Qahhār, 'the Dominant', 306, for preservation from tyranny. Al-Wahhāb, 'the Bestower', 'the Recoverer', 14, for finding things lost. Ar-Razzāq, 'the Provider', 308, for increase of subsistence. Al-Fattāh, 'the Opener, Accomplisher', 489, for victory. Al-'Alīm, 'the Knower, Omniscient', 489, for acquiring knowledge. Al-Qābiz, 'the Restrainer', 905, for destroying enemies. Al-Bāsit, 'the Spreader, Provider of Bread', 72, for the increase of daily bread. Al-Khāfiz, 'the Abaser', 1481, for the subjection of enemies. Ar-Rāfi', 'the Exalter', 351, for increase of dignity. Al-Mu'izz, 'the Honourer', 117, for honour. Al-Muzīl, 'the Destroyer', 770, for the ruin of enemies. As-Sāmi', 'the Hearer', 180, to cure ear-ache and deafness. Al-Basīr, 'the Seer', 302, for knowing the secrets of the heart. Al-Hākim, 'the Ruler', 68, for sovereignty. Al-'Adl, 'the Just', 104, for justice. Al-Latīf, 'the Penetrating', 129, for obtaining good fortune. Al-Khabīr, 'He that knows', 812, for ascertaining mysteries. Al-Halīm, 'the Long-suffering', 88, for the relief of trouble. Al-'Azīm, 'the Great', 1020, for gaining greatness. Al-Ghafūr, 'the Pardoner', 1286, for forgiveness of sins. Ash-Shakūr, 'the Requiter, Rewarder', 526, for the removal of sorrow. Al-Kabīr, 'the Great', 232, to secure the grant of desires. Al-Hafīz, 'the Guardian', 998, to relieve fear. Al-Muqīt, 'the Giver of Strength', 550, for success in undertakings. Al-Hasīb, 'the Reckoner', 80, for release from imprisonment. Al-Jalīl, 'the Glorious', 73, for terrifying an enemy. Al-Karīm, 'the Munificent', 270, for accomplishment of spiritual and temporal desires. Ar-Raqīb, 'the Guardian', 312, for protection. Al-Mujīb, 'the Answerer of prayer', 55, to secure answers to prayer. Al-Wāsi', 'the Liberal', 137, for prosperity in trade. Al-Wadūd, 'the Loving', 20, for affection. Al-Majīd, 'the Lord of Glory', 57, for recovery from sickness. Al-Bāis, 'the Raiser', 573, to relieve the dead. Ash-Shahīd, 'the Witness', 319, to cause children to be obedient. Al-Haqq, 'the Truth', 108, to acquire knowledge. Al-Wakīl, 'the Advocate', 66, for protection from lightning and fire. Al-Qawī, 'the Strong', 116, to overcome an enemy. Al-Matīn, 'the Firm', 500, for increase of a woman's milk and of water. Al-Walī, 'the Patron', 46, to make a master subservient to one's will. Al-Hamīd, 'the Praised', 62, to remove the habit of evil-speaking. Al-Muhsī, 'the Numberer, Comprehender', 148, for curing forgetfulness. Al-Mubdī, 'He who makes manifest', 'the Beginner', 56, to cause easy labour. Al-Mu'īd, the Restorer', 124, for knowledge of mysteries. Al-Mumīt, 'the Destroyer', 490, for the death of an enemy. Al-Muhyī, 'the Quickener', 60, to ward off demons and fairies. Al-Haiy, 'the Living', 62, to remove insects which attack fruit trees. Al-Qaiyūm, 'the Subsisting', 156, for long life. Al-Wājid, 'the Finder', 14, to recover lost property. Al-Majīd, 'the Glorious', 48, to gain wealth. Al-Wāhid, 'the One', 19, to acquire knowledge of literature. Al-Samad, 'the Eternal', 'the Perpetual', 134, to avert poverty. Al-Qādir, 'Lord of Power', 305, to remove distress and anxiety. Al-Muqtadir, 'the All Powerful', 744, to obtain dignity and wealth. Al-Muqaddim, 'He who gives the preference', 184, for warding off distress. Al-Mu'akhkhir, 'He who puts whatsoever He wills last', 846, to fulfil desires. Al-Awwal, 'the First', 37, for victory in battle. Al-Ākhir, 'the Last', 801, to remove fears. Az-Zāhir, 'the Evident', 1106, to preserve from blindness. Al-Bātin, 'the Hidden', 62, to become a friend of mankind. Al-Wālī, 'the Governor', 47, to save from family trouble. Al-Muta'ālī, 'the Sublime', 551, to secure accomplishment of wishes. Al-Barr, 'the Righteous', 202, to remove evil. Al-Tauwāb, 'the Hearer of the penitent', 409, for forgiveness of sins. Al-Muntaqim, 'the Avenger of sin', 630, for rest in the grave. Al-'Afūw, 'the Pardoner of sin', 156, for pardon of sins. Ar-Ra'uf, 'the Merciful', 286, for freedom of the oppressed.

Māliku-l-mulk, ‘ Master of the Kingdom ’, 212, for wealth. Zū-l-Jalālī wa-l-Ikrām, ‘ the Lord of Greatness and Liberality ’, 1100, for answer to prayer. Al-Muqsit, ‘ the Just ’, 209, to repress evil thoughts. Al-Jāmī‘, ‘ the Assembler ’, 114, for unity with the separated. Al-Ghanī, ‘ the Independent ’, ‘ the Opulent ’, 1060, for wealth. Al-Mughnī, ‘ the Enricher ’, 1100, to become independent of men. Al-Mu‘tī, ‘ the Giver ’, 129, to preserve from ignominy. Al-Māni‘, ‘ the Protector ’, 161, to give protection from the enemy. Az-Zārr, ‘ the Spoiler ’, 1001, to ward off the Devil. An-Nāfī‘, ‘ the Bestower of gain ’, 201, for success in farming and trade. An-Nūr, ‘ the Light ’, 256, to illuminate the mind. Al-Hādī, ‘ the Guide ’, 20, for accumulating wealth. Al-‘Badī‘, ‘ the Incomparable ’, 86, for comprehension of the abstruse. Al-Bāqī, ‘the Permanent’, 113, to secure approval of one’s actions. Al-Wāris, ‘ the Inheritor ’, 707, for peace. Ar-Rashīd, ‘ the Director ’, 514, to secure fulfilment of desires. As-Sabūr, ‘the Patient’, 298, for delivery from enemies. The enumeration of the names varies in different lists.

Among miscellaneous charms the following may be noted. To prevent voiding urine at night hang the following amulet round the neck of the patient :

Marmusallah "armed" III	5 Musallah, 5 III "armed"	11 5 30
D H H H H	d n A a III Rijālu L-ghaib Regents of the World	Yam-mal 115

By keeping the following talisman at hand, demons, fairies, and sorcerers will be baffled :

8	1490	1493	1
1492	2	7	1491
3	1495	1488	6
1489	5	4	1494

If a man is afflicted with strain of the muscles near the navel (*naf talna*), caused by lifting weights, or from some internal artery, which Indian physicians say occasionally shifts its place and causes various morbid symptoms, a couple of copies of the following verse should be made, one washed off and drunk, the other tied with a thread over the navel: 'God is the Lord! But His purpose most men do not understand.' Write this in Arabic in twenty-five compartments, making up the incantation.

The following cures itch. Two or three copies are to be made, washed off, and drunk now and then:

15	35	92	6
bh	w r z	w r	w d a
a'a	18	23	5
2	88	23	L
5'a	39	9	2

To cure piles—Repeat the following charm over water, blow upon it, and make the patient drink it off: 'Departest thou? Depart! Depart! Depart! Running water, dry up! Such is the order of the Saint Jalāl Jahāniyā Sāhib Jahāngasht! Quickly begone!'

The following magic square, tied on the back, renders an attack of small-pox mild:

8888	12221	15554	1111
14443	2222	7777	13332
3333	17776	9999	6666
11110	5555	4444	16665

The following magic square, formed out of the numbers of the Korān, is good for all purposes :

2, 911, 536, 642	7,764,097,710	970, 512, 213
1, 941,024, 426	3,882,048,855	5,823,073,284
6, 793,585, 497		4,852,561 068

When a house is haunted by the Jinn or by demons the following amulet should be hung over the door and they will vanish : 'O Muhammad ! O Allāh ! The faithful He regards ; to the faithful is success from God ! Verily, verily, victory He regards ! The Best of Helpers, the Elect, the Best for us, verily ! Towards men the most patient of Helpers, the Best !' On the left side write : 'O Mikāīl ! O 'Alī ! O 'Izrāīl !' On the right : 'O Jabrāīl ! O 'Alī ! O 'Izrāīl !' When a man is beset by a devil, the following diagram should be hung on a wall, so that the sight of the patient may daily fall upon it. This scares the devil. 'In the name of Solomon ! In the name of the Merciful, the Compassionate ! Do not rise against me, but come and surrender to Musalmāns !'

A horoscope (*zāicha, janampattrī*) is a slip of paper illuminated with sketches and aspects of the planets, eclipses, and other important events, and describing the duration of life, habits, tastes, dispositions, and the future fate of the person for whom it is constructed. The system in use by Musalmāns closely corresponds with that of the Hindu Joshī or astrologer. The manner of consulting it in sickness is as follows : Learn the name of the patient and that of his mother and ascertain their numerical value by the rules of Abjad ; add them together and divide by 12. If 1 remain, the destiny of the patient is in the sign of the Ram (*hamal*) ; if 2, in that of the Bull (*saur*) ; 3, in the Twins (*jauzā*); 4, in the Crab (*saratān*) ; 5, in the Lion (*asad*) ; 6, in the Virgin (*sumbula*) ; 7, in the Scales (*mīzān*) ; 8, in the Scorpion ('*aqrab*) ; 9, in the Archer (*qaus*) ; 10, in the He-goat (*jadī*) ; 11, in the Watering-pot (*dalv*) ; 12, in the Fishes (*hūt*). When the sign of the Zodiac has been ascertained, find his planet and his qualities from the table already given. But the immediate object is to ascertain the danger-point of life which, if he survives, he will reach his full span, 125 years. The following table gives the details. If death is portended it can be warded off only by the use of amulets and charms.

Signs of the Zodiac	Ram	Bull	Twins	Crab	Lion	Virgin	Scales	Scorpion	Archer	He-Goat	Watering-Pot	Fishes
Woman	7, 13, 20	12, 30	4, 12, 20, 30, 40, 50	7, 19, 30	8, 16, 20, 40, 50	2	18	30, 39	2	7, 15	30	7
Man	1, 9, 20, 50	5, 30	2, 4, 10, 15	4, 19, 30, 40	5	16, 20, 40	17	4, 12, 3	2	3	1	2, 56, 30, 40

When it is desired to predict the future progress of a sick person, it is necessary, first, to ascertain the time when he was taken ill. When this is known from the statement given below for each day of the week, his prospects can be foretold. If the date has been forgotten, the number of letters in the names of the patient and of his mother should be added together and divided by 7. If 1 remains, he must have been taken ill on Saturday ; 2, on Sunday ; 3, on Monday ; 4, on Tuesday ; 5, on Wednesday ; 6, on Thursday ; 0, on Friday.

Before dealing with the week-days we must explain the use of propitiatory offerings (*sadqa*, *sadaqa*), which are used to overcome an unfavourable forecast. These consist of money, an animal, clothes, grain, food, &c., which are waved over the patient or merely shown to him, and are given away to Faqīrs in his name ; or they are laid under a tree, near water, or at a place where four roads meet.[1] Mullās and Syānās, that is, learned men and exorcists, have their own special kinds of offerings. Thus, they make an image of pulse (*māsh*) flour, a span and a half or two spans long, in the shape of a man or of Hanumān, the Hindu monkey god. In the mouth of this figure they put a stick about a span long with rags wound round both ends, and set them alight, as well as lamps made of paste put on the head of the figure. On its forehead they make a Hindu sectarial mark (*nāmam*). Then they pierce the figure all over with nails and set it up in a large basin (*kundā*), or on a potsherd (*thīkrā*). In front of it they lay balls of boiled rice coloured black, yellow, and red, eggs coloured in the same way, and a sheep's liver, which they occasionally pierce with thorns, some sheep's blood, two or three uncooked fishes, and then scatter flowers and greenery round the offering. They then light a lamp made of flour paste with four wicks made out of the clothes worn by the patient, soaked in various kinds of oil, and place the lamps on the blood. When all the lamps are lit, the figure looks as hideous as the Devil himself. They then wave the basin or potsherd over the patient and put it away, after which they wash the patient's hands and feet, and tie on his neck an amulet or charmed cord, such as may be found necessary. Such charmed cords are commonly used in this way, and the Korān speaks of women who blow on knots to do mischief to those whom they dislike.[2]

In northern India a thread of five colours, wound three times round the thumb and then put on the great toe at night for a fortnight, cures piles, while for quartan ague they tie a cord seven times round an *acacia arabica* tree (*kīkar*), and let the patient embrace the tree.[3]

In this respect the days of the week are important. Saturday, Saturn's day, is unlucky, and if a person be taken ill on that day the origin of the disease may be attributed to grief, heat of blood, to the Evil Eye, the symptoms being headache, palpita-

[1] On the cross-roads as a place where dangerous influences can be dispersed, see Westermarck, *Origin and Development of the Moral Ideas*, ii. 256 f.

[2] Chap. cxiii, with Sale's note.

[3] *PNQ*. i. 125 ; ii. 205 ; cf. Elworthy, *The Evil Eye*, 413 ; Hastings *Dict. Bible*, v. 552.

tion of the heart, extreme thirst, restlessness, sleeplessness bleeding from the nose or bowels. It may be inferred that the illness will last seven days, will be at its height for one day and seven hours, and that the patient will recover. The remedies are to make propitiatory offerings and to use amulets and charms. Illness on Sunday, the Sun's day, is due to the Evil Eye of a woman of a green complexion, in whose presence he has eaten some rich savoury food. The symptoms are lassitude followed by rigours, heat, headache, pains in the bones, eyes suffused with blood, countenance yellow, sleeplessness at night. The disease will last fourteen days and will then cease, and the treatment is that usually given in such symptoms. Illness on Monday, the Moon's day, is due to a chill after bathing or to over-exertion, the symptoms being pain in the loins and calves, palpitation in the liver, retching, giddiness, extreme drowsiness. It will last a fortnight, when the patient after the usual treatment will recover. Sickness on Tuesday, Mars' day, is due to the fairies or demons, the symptoms being pain in the chest and abdomen, specially round the navel, shivering, want of sleep and of appetite, great thirst, incoherence of speech, eyes bloodshot. It will last a week, followed by recovery under the usual treatment. Illness on Wednesday, Mercury's day, is due to non-fulfilment of a vow made for the dead, grief over something lost or dread of an enemy, the symptoms being pain in the head, neck, wrists, or feet, and it will last nine days and be at its worst for a day and a watch, or fifteen hours. Illness on Thursday, Jupiter's day, is due to being overshadowed by a fairy, with symptoms of pain in the neck and umbilicus, broken sleep, distaste for food and drink, the patient lying quiet with his eyes shut. It will last ten days, and then recovery will follow the usual treatment. Illness on Friday, the day of Venus, is due to some corporeal affection, the symptoms great drowsiness and lassitude. It will last twelve days, and be at its worst for two days, followed by recovery.

CHAPTER XXVIII

MAGICAL METHODS

In order to ascertain where stolen goods are concealed, the condition of a patient possessed by the Devil, or where treasure has been buried, it is the custom to rub collyrium (*anjan*) on the palms of the hands of a child or adult, and to make him stare hard at it. In the Panjāb charms are written by a sorcerer on a piece of paper, and over it a large drop of ink is poured. Flowers are put in the hands of a young child who is told to look into the ink and say, 'Summon the Four Guardians!' The child when asked if he or she can see anything, answers, 'I see four persons'. Then he is told to ask them to clean the place, lay carpets, and summon their King. When he appears, questions are put to him through the child, and appropriate answers are received. No one hears or sees the spirits except the child.[1] Ja'far Sharīf remarks that he has heard it generally said that the Hindu Orders of Jogīs and Sannyāsīs practise these arts, and that in this way they have discovered hidden treasure. Some foolish people say that buried treasure shows like sparks of fire at night, and that sometimes a ball of fire rolls about near the place where it is concealed. In northern India it, or rather the snake which

[1] *NINQ.* i. 85. On Lekanomancy, or magic by staring into a vessel filled with some fluid, see Halliday, *Greek Divination*, 145 ff.; Lane, *ME.* i. 337 ff.; Burton, *Pilgrimage*, i. 387 f.; *ERE.* iv. 351 ff., 807, 817. Compare the Magic Mirror, Lane, *ME.* i. 337. In the time of Mahmūd Shāh of Gujarāt (A. D. 1511–26) the king of the fairies appeared to a girl in a magic mirror (Bayley, *Muhammadan Dynasties of Gujarāt*, 323 f.). The holy stone of John Dee used for a similar purpose is now in the British Museum (*EB.* vii. 920 f.; Brand, *Observations on Popular Antiquities*, iii. 60 f.). His magic mirror is in private hands (10 *Notes and Queries*, i. 16).

guards it, is said to speak from the place where it is hidden.[1] From such appearances, and by the aid of the collyrium, its position may be ascertained. The person to whose palm the collyrium has been applied often utters ridiculous nonsense. For instance, he says, 'At such and such a place there is a metal pot full of rupees, pagodas, or gold mohurs'. If he is asked about a patient his answer is, 'The disease is bodily, or produced by sorcery, or the demon of such and such a place wants food'.

The collyrium (*anjan*) is of five kinds: for the discovery of stolen property (*arth*, 'object, purpose'); for inquiries about devils, evil spirits, and the condition of the sick; for discovering where treasure is concealed; that which is applic-cable to all purposes; and that which when rubbed on a person's eyes or forehead renders him invisible, while he himself is able to see. I myself, says Ja'far Sharīf, place no faith in these collyriums and invocations of spirits (*hāzirāt*). Though I was born in Hindostān and educated among Musalmāns, by the grace of God and the study of good books, and by good counsel, the belief in such things has been effaced from my mind. Let no one say that I wish to flatter Europeans—May their good fortune continue!—God preserve me from any false assertions!

To prepare the collyrium, in the case of the first and second varieties, take the root of the prickly chaff-flower (*aghādā kī jar, achyranthes aspera*), Indian or white liquorice root (*safed ghungchī kī jar, abrus precatorius*), or merely *trianthema decandra*, called *bishkaprā* or *bishkoprā*,[2] grind them well with water and rub the powder on the inside of a new earthen jar. Place this inverted over a lamp lighted with castor oil and collect the lampblack. This is then applied to the hand of a footling child or one born by the foot presentation,[3] who will be able to describe the place where stolen property is

[1] Crooke, *Popular Religion*, ii. 135.

[2] Watt, *Econ. Dict.* i. 81, 10; vi, part 4, 77.

[3] In Great Britain special powers are attributed to a child born in this way (*County Folklore, Fife*, 396; Gregor, *Folklore of N. Scotland*, 45 f.). In the Panjāb, to cure lumbago, the part is touched with the foot of such a child (*PNQ*. i. 112). Also see Rendel Harris, *Boanerges*, 56, 64, 110, 125, 133, 139.

hidden, and the condition of the sick, whether the patient is attacked by a bodily disease, or has been possessed by the Devil.

In the third type, take a piece of white cloth and soak it in the blood of one of the following animals or birds : a cat, a drongo shrike (*kolsā, dicrurus macroccreus*), an owl (*ghuggū*), the larger owl (*chugd*). Then roll up in it their eyes, livers, and gall-bladders, and use the cloth thus prepared as a wick for a lamp fed with castor oil. If the hand be rubbed with this lampblack, hidden treasure will become visible.

In the fourth type, a handful of country beans (*sīm, balar, dolichos lablab*) is burnt in a new earthen pot so as to prevent the smoke from escaping, and the charcoal is well pounded and made into a smooth paste with castor oil. This is put on a person's hand, and he is told to stare at it. In half an hour or so he will say, 'I see that the carpet-spreader (*farrāsh*) has come and has swept the place. Then comes the water-carrier who has sprinkled it with water. Then the host of the Jinn, demons, and fairies arrives followed by their commander, who takes his seat on a throne'. So he goes on telling all he sees. Then the Jinn leader is told the purpose for which he has been summoned, and he never fails to do what he is required to do. This collyrium applied to any one's hand makes him see, whereas the other varieties must be used on a boy or girl born by the foot presentation, one who has grey or cat's eyes, who has never been bitten by a dog, and has no scar of a burn on the body. To such a person the use of the collyrium and the control of spirits will be vouchsafed, but probably not to others.

The fifth variety (*alop anjan*) will make the person using it invisible.

Certain well-known kinds of wicks are used for the control of spirits (*hāzirāt*). When such a wick (*palītā*) is to be used, they take a new earthen pot with its cover, wash them well in water, daub a few patches of sandalwood paste on the pot, tie wreaths of flowers round its neck, place near it all sorts of fruit and flowers, and burn benjamin or benzoin pastilles. Then they pour some perfumed oil into the hollow of the cover, light a wick, and repeat the appropriate spell in Arabic. The boy or girl is bathed, dressed in clean clothes, adorned with flowers, and he or she is told to stare at the flame and tell everything which is seen. As in the case of the collyrium already described, the child will tell everything about stolen property, diseases, and the like.

Some write the following charm, paste it on the back of a looking-glass, and make the child stare into the glass :

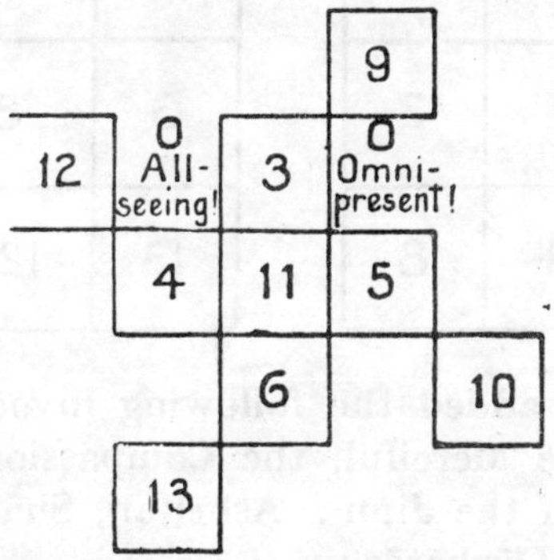

Some people write the following magic square on a porcelain or copper plate, fill the latter with water, and make the child look into it :

4	9	2
3	5	7
8	1	6

Some people, in addition to these methods, write the following charm on the child's forehead : 'We have removed the veil from off thy face, and thy sight is become new this day. Come, Ja'far, the Jinn, son of Taiyār—"the flying one"!'

Other magic squares are used for this purpose, and they

are written, with the purpose for which they are designed, on the magic wick. The following are examples :

9	3	7	1
6	2	8	4
3	9	1	7
2	6	4	8

11	14	1	8
4	5	10	15
6	3	16	9
13	12	7	2

To these may be added the following invocation : 'In the Name of God, the Merciful, the Compassionate !' with the following names of the Jinn : Ashtītan, Shatītan, Kabūshin, Shālīsha, Shīshin, Qūrbatāshin.

The Fairy Bath is used by men and women in the following cases : when a person suffers from chronic disease ; if he be married and have no issue for four or five years ; if a virgin becomes pregnant, or, through the influence of the fairies, suffers from haemorrhage or abortion ; if a child dies immediately after birth, or remains weak and puny ; if a man and his wife cannot agree ; if a man fails to obtain employment, or if he finds service and it turns out unprofitable. When such misfortunes occur it is wise to perform the rite of the Fairy Bath (*Parī kā nahān*). Here the word 'bathing' includes the recital of incantations and other similar rites. The methods of using collyrium (*anjan*) and the invocation of spirits (*hāzirāt*), already described, are employed to ascertain things unknown. But the Bath is used to remove known evils, such as the influence of demons. The Bath rite is done by a Syānā or sorcerer, by a Mullā or learned man, or by the Parīwālī or Fairy Women. The method is as follows. They bring water from seven or nine different sources, wells, rivers, the sea, and so on, and put it into an earthen pot with leaves of different trees or plants, such as the pomegranate, guava, lime, orange, jasmine, Spanish jasmine, sweet basil, and henna privet. If the object of the rite be the removal of the influence of a demon, the 36th or 73rd chapter of the Korān is read over the pot; if the object be to change the luck (*bahkt kholnā*), the 48th chapter is read. Then they make out of pulse flour the figure of a man or of the Hindu monkey god, Hanumān, between a span and a cubit long, tie to its neck a cord made of three kinds of coloured thread, while the other end is attached to the waist or neck of the patient, and lay before it the liver of a sheep, coco-nuts, flowers, parched rice, glass bangles, a piece of yellow cloth, a sheep, and a fowl. They then take nine limes and repeat over them the Āyatu-l-kursī or Throne verse of the Korān (ii. 256), and place the limes on the head, shoulders, loins, back, knees, and feet of the sick person. Then they bathe him with water from the pot already described. They dig a hole to contain the bath water, because if any one happens to tread on it the patient's disease will be communicated to him. For this reason the rite is usually done near some water, or in a garden. This bathing is done on the three first Saturdays, Sundays, Mondays, Tuesdays, or Thursdays of the month. At the last bathing they pour over him three times water from a clean earthen pot, once on his head, then on his right shoulder, then on his left, and then dash the pot to pieces before him. Immediately after the bath they tie to his neck, upper arm, or wrists a special magic square intended to cast out the demon, or remove the trouble from which he is suffering. The Fairy Bath is well known among women, and the rite is carried out by one of the women who have control of the fairies, but these are few in number.

Another device is that of the Fairy Tray. The assemblage of the fairies (*pariān kā akhārā*) usually meets on Thursdays or Fridays, either by day or night. The ritual is as follows: They hang a canopy (*chāndnī*) to the ceiling of the room and spread a carpet on the floor. The Fairy Woman puts on a clean rich dress, red or white, smears sandalwood paste on her neck and henna on her hands, the latter being washed off when it colours her fingers, adorns herself with flowers, puts rose essence (*'itr*) on her dress, lampblack or antimony on her eyes, and blackening powder (*missī*) on her teeth. Those possessed by demons and the spectators dress in their best and assemble in a room where women singers of the Dom caste perform. Then the Fairy Woman causes her who is possessed by the fairies (*asebwālī*) to seat herself in front on a metal tray (*tabaq*). There are two kinds of Fairy Trays (*parī kā tabaq*), one called the Flower Tray (*phūl kā tabaq*), consisting of a white cloth spread on the ground on which are arranged in a circle sandalwood, aloes wood, coloured powder, betel leaves, betel nuts and fruits of all kinds, in the centre of which the Fairy Woman sits. The other Tray, to be described later on, is called the Fruit Tray (*phūl kā tabaq*). After she has sat there a while the fairies descend upon her. She becomes distracted and in response to the music she lets her hair loose and sits on her knees (*duzānū*) or cross-legged (*chārzānū*). This sitting on the knees is different from the European mode of kneeling. The woman rests her body or sits upon the left foot placed horizontally with the sole turned upwards, while the right foot is held perpendicular, with the great toe touching the ground and the heel up, the hands resting on the thighs. In repeating prayers in this position the eyes are diverted to the region of the heart, the right foot is never moved from its original position, while the left is turned vertically in the act of prostration (*sijda*), when the forehead touches the ground, and then placed again in its original position and the worshipper sits on the sole of it.[1] Then the fairy woman whirls her head round and round, and taking hold of her hair brushes the patient two or three times with it. The latter is then affected, and rolls her head in the same way. At this crisis either she or the fairy woman, or the fairies occupying her body, speaking through her, appoint the number of Baths or Trays which the patient requires, the place where, and the dates and times when, they are to take place. These injunctions are obeyed. They go on in this way,

[1] The Mughal Emperors used to sit on the throne with crossed legs (*chahārzānū*), a position of comfort which Orientals allow to persons of rank. This position, however, is called Pharaoh's mode of sitting (*Firā'ūnī nishast*), if assumed in the presence of strangers, Pharaoh being proverbial for vain-glory. The position suitable in society is the *duzānū*, the person first kneeling down with the body straight; he then lets his body gradually sink till he sits on his heels, the arms being kept extended, and the hands resting on the knees (*Āīn*, i. 160).

singing and playing all or most part of the night. The moment a fairy besets the fairy woman she whirls her head round and round, and when it leaves her she lies down and rests.

There are in all fourteen fairy assemblages (*pariān kē akhārē*), and the fairy woman acts according to the particular kind of fairy which possesses her. For instance, if the shadow of a fairy belonging to the troupe of Rājā Indra (he being the Hindu god of the firmament and his heaven is well supplied with fairies)[1] falls upon her, she ties bells (*ghunghrū*) to her ankles and begins to dance. If the fairy belongs to the court of Gend Bādshāh or to that of Sikandar or Alexander Bādshāh, she puts on men's clothes, which were previously laid on the Tray, and dagger in hand, stroking and twirling her moustaches, she pretends to be angry and calls out to the possessed woman, 'Thou fool! Thou coquette! Hast thou forgotten me and created another?' To this the other answers humbly, 'Sir (*Miyān*)! I am your selfsame devoted slave, and I have often stated my case to your wife. Probably she has forgotten to tell you'. To this the reply is, 'No one has told me of it, but since you say so I forgive you'. Then with a laugh she pelts the other with a flower or with the refuse (*ugāl*) of the betel which she has been chewing. As these women go on whirling their heads round and round those who want anything state it. Thus, they ask whether certain friends are well or ill and when they intend to return; if they are ill, whether this is a bodily ailment, or because the shadow of a demon has fallen upon them. The remedies prescribed by the fairy woman are employed with a firm faith in their efficacy. As they whirl their heads round and round, women who venerate them fan them with a fly-whisk or with a handkerchief. In return the Fairy Women give them some refuse food, and when they partake of it they, too, become excited, swing their heads, lie down to rest, and in a few minutes recover their senses. The fairy women exhibit their powers to impress other women, never in the presence of men. Sensible, respectable women never sanction such rites, and do not take part in them. Some women who want something and who are possessed by demons,

[1] For the fairies of Indra's court, see W. J. Wilkins, *Hindu Mythology, Vedic and Puranic*, 52.

instead of attending these séances, send for one of the women to their houses, where the rite is performed.

The Fruit Tray rite is done as follows : Place on a carpet all kinds of fruits, fresh and dry, sixteen dishes of sweet stew, sixteen jars of sugar sherbet, seventeen earthen plates full of rice milk, and other kinds of food, such as cakes, sesamum, and rice soaked in syrup, coco-nut kernels, almonds and dates sliced, with clothes, such as drawers made of mixed silk and cotton, a skirt, a red veil, a bodice, bangles, a pair of shoes and some money. Then the visitors sit up all night while the fairy woman becomes affected as already described. Early on the following morning the fairy woman repeats the names of all the fairies, the red, the green, the yellow, the earthy, the fiery, the Hūr or damsels of Paradise,[1] the emerald, the diamond, and so forth. Then she makes a prostration (*sijda*), and taking some of the fruits, bangles, and other things wrapped up in a red or saffron coloured cloth, carries them to the bank of a river or tank, and throws them in, as the share of the fairies. The remainder she distributes as relics to those present, and takes the clothes as her own share.

The Fairy Woman's Bath (*nahān*) is done as follows : Take seven new earthen pots, fill them with water from seven or nine wells, spread a red handkerchief over them, put in a few leaves taken from seven or nine trees, and lay them aside. Then seat the woman who is possessed by the fairies on a stool, while four women hold a saffron-coloured handkerchief over her head as a canopy. The fairy woman pours the water over her head through the handkerchief, and divides some limes, as already described. When this is done, she takes the woman to a river or tank and bathes her. While this is going on, one of the fairies descends on the Fairy Woman, and she swings her head as she stands. The other women keep filling pots of water and pour them over the woman who is possessed, and while doing so call out, ' Catch hold of the foul shadow that is upon her, bind it, banish it to Mount Qāf, imprison it there and burn it to ashes ! ' At this crisis, if the other women are

[1] For the Hūr or damsels of Paradise, see Korān (lv. 56–78) : ' Therein shall be the damsels with retiring glances, whom nor man nor Jinn hath touched before them ' ; Burton, *AN*. iii. 20.

slow in handing the water to her, she cries, 'Wretches! What evil has come upon you? I will destroy you! Give me water quickly, that I may beat with a shoe the foul creature that is on her and destroy it!' The women, in terror, hasten to hand the water to her. She then repeats the names of some demons and fairies, blows upon the patient, dresses her in dry clothes, waves a black cock or hen over her, and gives it away as a propitiatory offering. She then takes three different kinds of coloured thread (*gandā*), of silk or cotton, plain or twisted, and makes twenty-one or twenty-two knots in them. Mullās and Syānās, in making each knot, recite an incantation over it, blow upon it, and when it is ready bind it on the neck or upper arm of the patient. But these Fairy Women are usually illiterate, and do not even know the names of God. So they merely make a knot in the thread. The use of these magic cords is illustrated in a story told of the Prophet. The Jews bribed the sorcerer Labīd and his daughters to bewitch Muhammad. They got some hairs from his beard, tied eleven knots with them on a palm branch, and threw it into a well which they covered with a large stone. This caused the Prophet to lose his appetite, to pine away, and neglect his wives. Gabriel told him the secret, the well was emptied and the knots untied, whereupon the spell was broken and the Prophet was relieved.[1]

During these rites the Fairy Woman holds in her hand a cane, either plain or ornamented with stripes of silver leaf. On the Tray day she places this before her, and every now and again fumigates it with the smoke of benzoin, telling the bystanders that the cane belongs to the fairies. Of late years men have begun to pretend that fairies beset them, and they whirl their heads and thus make money. I have heard, says Ja'far Sharīf, that they use these disreputable means to debauch other men's wives.

[1] Muir, *Life*, 371; Margoliouth, *Mohammed*, 231; *Korān*, cxiii. 4. On the use of knotted threads in magic, see Enthoven, *Folklore Notes*, Gujarāt, 125, Konkan, 33, 63; Russell, iii. 252; iv. 110, 386; Rose, i. 253; Thurston, *Castes*, vi. 70.

CHAPTER XXIX

THE MAGICAL DETECTION OF THIEVES

THERE are many excellent means by which thieves may be compelled to restore stolen property.[1]

The owner of the stolen goods sends for a thief-catcher, and if he suspects any one he calls a few of his neighbours to attend. The thief-catcher daubs the floor of the room with yellow or red ochre, and draws on it a hideous figure like one of those already described. He then rubs some assafoetida near the centre of the two stones of a handmill, and places it in the centre of the figure. He binds some flax cloth round the middle pin of the mill, so that the upper stone seems to be suspended in the air. Near the mill he lays some fruit or food, burns frankincense and lights a lamp with oil in a human skull-cap. He then tells every man and woman present to touch the centre of the mill and come back to him, saying that no innocent person need fear to do so, because the stone is suspended in the air by magic, and that it will fall on the hand of the thief, so that he will be caught between the two stones. After they have undergone this test, the thief-catcher smells the hand of each of them, and when he finds that some one's hand has no smell of the assafoetida, because he was afraid to touch the mill, he takes him aside and says, 'I will not expose you if you promise to restore the goods'. If he really is the thief he accepts the offer.

Another method is the following: The thief-catcher, having arranged the room as before, places there two human skull-caps, one full of milk, the other of sherbet, makes an image of flour paste, puts a lamp on its head, lays flowers and fruit before

[1] These methods are common in countries beside India. For the Malay Peninsula, see Skeat, *Malay Magic*, 537 f. In Persia diviners of stolen goods are known as Rammāl (*raml*, 'to make a mat of palm-leaves'), and their methods resemble those described in the text (Wills, 120). It was used in Buddhist times (*Jātaka*, Cambridge trans., i. 224).

it, and drives into the image as many wooden pegs as there are persons present. He pretends to go on praying, and as each person comes before him he draws out one of the pegs and hands it to him, telling him that the peg belonging to the thief will certainly increase in size. When the business is over he measures the pegs and often finds that the culprit, in order to save himself, has cut a piece off his peg.

An effectual method is to make a diagram as follows containing the name of each person present, with that of his father :

So and So	43	43
Son of So and So	43	43

The thief-catcher folds up each of the papers in a pill made of wheat flour. He puts fresh water into a brass water-vessel (*lotā*) and throws all the pills into it. The pill containing the thief's ticket will rise and float on the surface of the water.

If the following diagram is drawn on an egg, which is then buried in a grave, the belly of the thief will swell and remain so until the egg is dug up.

The Eternal One

421, 822, 318.6

O Buddhū! Grant that the belly of him who has stolen the goods may swell by the influence of this Charm!

God hid 8.161.89

4 4 12 882

The following verses of the Korān,[1] written on a green lime fruit and burnt in the fire, or buried in the earth, will cause the ruin of the thief : 'Of what thing did God create man? Out of moist germs. He created and fashioned him, then made an easy passage from the womb, then causeth him to die and burieth him ; then, when He pleaseth, He will raise him again to life. Aye, but man hath not yet fulfilled the bidding of his Lord. Let man look at his food. It was He rained down the copious rain, then cleft the earth with clefts, and caused the up-growth

[1] lxxx. 31–7.

of the grain.' When the thief delivers the goods to the owner, if the same verse be recited over some water which is breathed upon and given him to drink, all his trouble will disappear. Or two persons are made to hold up a water-vessel on the points of their right forefingers, pressed against the ring round the neck, on which the names of the persons concerned have been inscribed. Then the thirty-sixth chapter of the Korān is recited over it from the beginning up to the part where it saith, 'But he said, O that my people knew how gracious God hath been to me, and that He hath made me one of the honoured ones!'[1] When the names written on the jar are called out, the jar will rock from side to side when it comes to the name of the thief.

A certain method, says Ja'far Sharīf, which I have seen with my own eyes, is this: Apply lampblack to the bottom of a bell-metal cup, collect a number of boys and get them to place their hands, one by one, upon it. As the cup begins to move, when any boy puts his hands on it, the thief-catcher presses his hands on those of the boy and says, 'May the cup move towards the thief!' or, 'May it go where the property is hidden!' and it will certainly do as he wishes.[2] Ja'far Sharīf tried this experiment when a girl stole his sister's nose-ring (*nath*), and covered it with a small tray (*khwāncha*). By this means the girl was detected and the jewel recovered. People may believe it or not as they please.

A similar charm is said to have been practised in the reign of Aurangzeb. Sorcerers 'take a brass bowl and put in it some grains of uncooked rice and some flowers, over which an incantation has been recited. Then they take another bowl of the same metal and beating it with a short stick they say some words softly, and the first bowl with the flowers begins to move of itself very slowly. At last it arrives at the place where the thing is lying. The thief, seeing the crowd and hearing the sound of the basin, runs off, abandoning everything'.[3]

[1] xxxvi. 24–8.

[2] In Persia a cup, engraved with verses of the Korān, is rolled by the diviner, and it moves to the place where the stolen goods are concealed (Morier, *Hajji Baba*, 311).

[3] Manucci, iii. 213.

The charm of 'turning the Korān' (*Qu'rān gardan*) is done by placing a key in the book, so that the handle and part of the shaft may project, and it is fastened by a piece of cord tied round the volume. Two persons put their forefingers under the handle and so support the book, which hangs down lightly between their hands. A certain verse is recited for every suspected person, and at the name of the thief the volume turns round of itself, so that the handle slips off the forefingers of the two persons that hold it.[1] A similar charm is done by giving new rice to the suspected person, whose saliva dries up in his terror and he is unable to chew or swallow the rice.

[1] Burton, *Sindh*, 182. This is the key and Bible charm practised in Great Britain (Brand, *Observations on Popular Antiquities*, iii. 353 f.).

CHAPTER XXX

TRAVELLING ; LUCKY AND UNLUCKY DAYS

MUSALMĀNS, in consequence of the difficulties and danger of travel, and the isolation due to localized village life and caste prejudices, take careful precautions, as Hindus do, to avoid the risk attending journeys. Certain spirits of the air, known as Rijālu-l-ghaib, or Mardānu-l-ghaib, 'the hidden, concealed men', are supposed to be invisible, and to move in a circular orbit round the world, their stations varying on certain days. Their influence is specially exercised for three and a half hours at the close of each lunar day, during which interval it is unlucky to undertake a journey. These spirits correspond to the Yoginī or Lokapāla, 'regents of the quarter of the heaven', of the Hindus, and the Chihal Abdāl, or 'forty holy men' of the Persians.[1] When a man is starting on a journey the Rijālu-l-ghaib should not be in his front, but behind, or on his left. If this is not the case, he will meet with distress and hardship and his property will be in danger. Some astrologers say that there is a planet named Shukūr-i-yulduz which is so dangerous, that if a traveller finds it on his front or right he will suffer distress. In 1806 when the Persian ambassador was starting for India, astrologers decided that a fortunate conjunction of stars existed which, if missed, could not recur for some months. At the same time he was told that he could not pass either through the door of his own house or the gate of the fort, as an invisible but baneful constellation was exactly opposite. To avoid this difficulty an opening was made in the walls of his house to enable him to reach the shore in safety.[2]

The Rijālu-l-ghaib abide in different places on different days of the month. To ascertain their position, tables, couplets,

[1] Lane, *AN.* iii. 669 ; Burton, *AN.* ii. 111 ; viii. 13 ; Rose, i. 225 ff., 243 ff. ; Manu, Laws, v. 96 ; *PNQ.* i. 136 ; ii. 44 ; cf. W. W. Fowler *Religious Experiences of the Roman People*, 251.

[2] Malcolm, *Hist. of Persia*, i. 417.

and hemistiches are used, of which a few are given below, the first table being that generally followed :

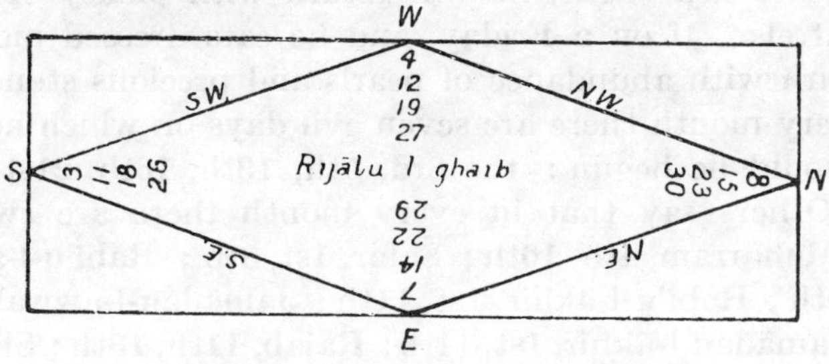

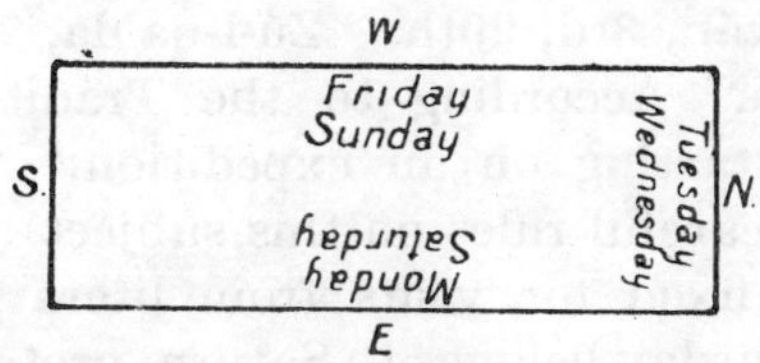

There is also a mnemonic couplet, as follows :

East, on Saturday and Monday ; on Friday and Sunday, west ; on Tuesday and Wednesday, north ; on Thursday, south addrest.

To ascertain the stations of the Rijālu-l-ghaib some have recourse to a hemistich (*misra*'). The letters which compose it stand for the different quarters of the globe. They are K N J G B M sh, K N J G B M sh, repeated twice, so as to form words which are pronounced

Kanajgin bāmshin, kanajgin bimash
Kanajgin bāmshin, kanajgin bimash.

K stands for SE. ; N, SW. ; J, S. ; G, W. ; B, NW. ; A, NE. ; M, E. ; sh, N. ; K, SE. ; N, SW. ; J, S. ; G, W. ; B, NW. ; M, NE. ; sh, E. ; K, N. ; N, SE. ; J, SW. ; G, S. ; B, W. ; A, NW. ; M, NE. ; sh, E. ; K, N. ; N, SE. ; J, SW. ; G, S. ; B, W. ; M, NW. ; sh, NE.

If a person wish to go on a journey on a Saturday, he should eat fish before starting, for in that case his wishes will soon be accomplished. If on a Sunday, he should eat betel leaf and he will prosper. If on a Monday, and he looks in a mirror, he will speedily gain wealth. If on a Tuesday, and he eats coriander seed, everything will happen as he wishes.

If on a Wednesday, and he eats curdled milk, he will return in good health and with a large fortune. If on a Thursday, and he eats raw sugar, he will return with plenty of goods and chattels. If on a Friday, and he eats dressed meat, he will return with abundance of pearls and precious stones.

In every month there are seven evil days on which no good work should be begun: the 3rd, 5th, 13th, 16th, 21st, 24th, 25th. Others say that in every month there are two evil days: Muharram, 4th, 10th; Safar, 1st, 8th; Rabī'u-l-awwal, 10th, 20th; Rabī'u-l-ākhir, 1st, 11th; Jamādau-l-awwal, 10th, 11th; Jamādau-l-ākhir, 1st, 11th; Rajab, 11th, 13th; Sha'bān, 4th, 6th; Ramazān, 3rd, 20th; Zū-l-qa'da, 2nd, 3rd; Zū-l-hijja, 6th, 25th. According to the Traditions, Thursday is the best for starting on an expedition.[1] Humāyūn, the Emperor, issued careful rules on this subject. Saturdays and Thursdays were fixed for visits from literary and religious men, because Saturday belongs to Saturn, protector of religious men and respectable families, and Thursday to Jupiter, protector of Sayyids, learned men and teachers of the Law. Sundays and Tuesdays were fixed for State officers and government business, because Sunday belongs to the Sun, which rules the fates of rulers and kings, and Tuesday is that of Mars, patron of warriors and brave men. Mondays and Wednesdays were allotted to pleasure parties, as Monday is the day of the Moon and Wednesday of Mercury, 'and it was therefore reasonable that on those days he should keep company with young men, beautiful as the Moon, and hear sweet songs and delightful music. On Fridays, as the name Jum' imports, he called to prayer all the assemblies, and sat with them as long as he found leisure from other duties'.[2]

Some people dispense with the above tables and count the days of the month on their fingers, beginning with the little finger, counting it as 1, the ring finger 2, the middle 3, the forefinger 4, the thumb 5, the little 6, and so on. The dates which happen to fall on the middle finger are unlucky, 3rd, 8th, 13th, 18th, 23rd, 28th.

[1] *Mishkāt*, ii. 254. For similar rules, see Enthoven, *Folklore Notes*, Gujarāt, 128 ff.; Rose, i. 239 ff.

[2] Elliot-Dowson, v. 121.

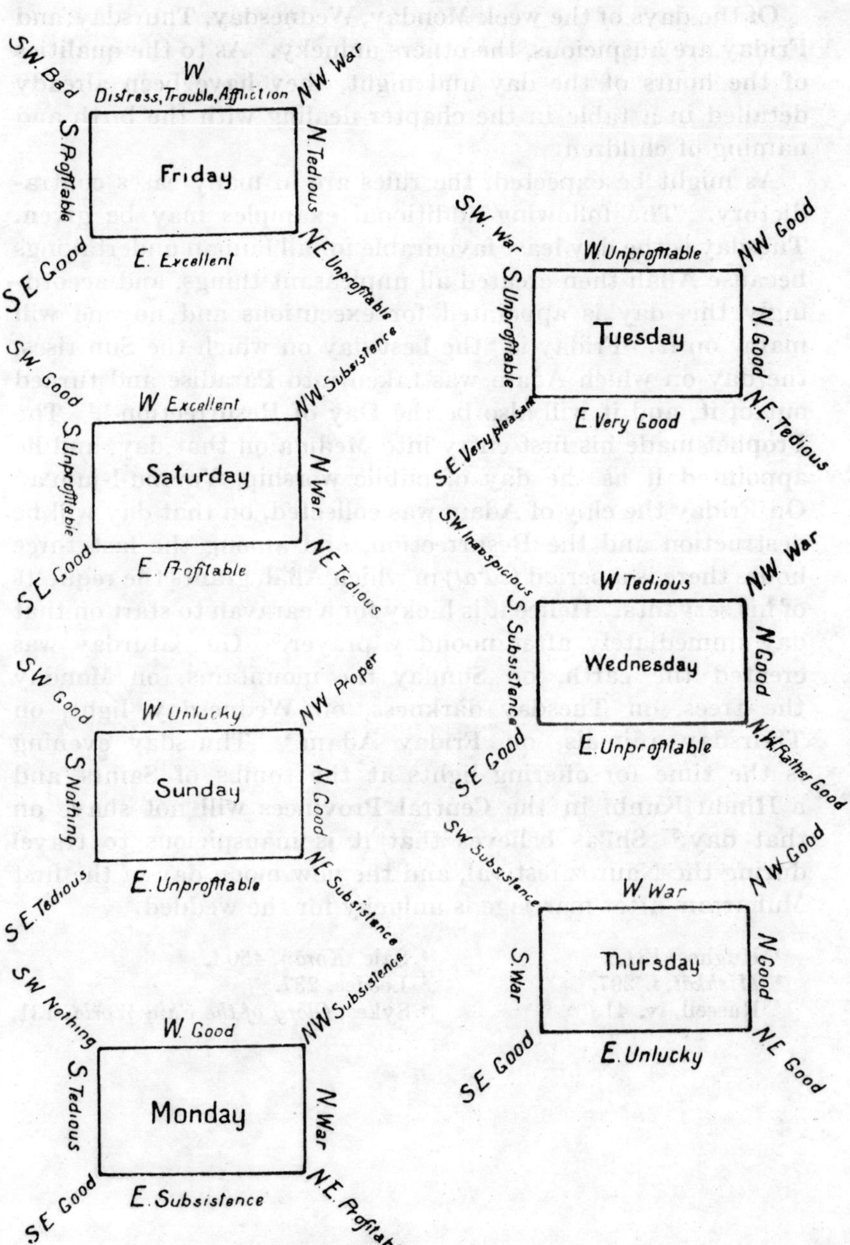
Friday
W
Distress, Trouble, Affliction
NW. War
N. Tedious
NE Unprofitable
E. Excellent
SE Good
S. Profitable
SW. Bad
Saturday
W Excellent
NW Subsistence
N War
NE Tedious
E. Profitable
SE Good
S Unprofitable
SW. Good
Sunday
W Unlucky
NW Proper
N. Good
NE Subsistence
E. Unprofitable
SE Tedious
S Nothing
SW Good
Monday
W. Good
NW Subsistence
N. War
N.E. Profitable
E. Subsistence
SE Good
S. Tedious
SW Nothing
Tuesday
W Unprofitable
NW Good
N. Good
N.E. Tedious
E. Very Good
S.E. Very pleasant
S. Unprofitable
SW. War
Wednesday
W Tedious
NW. War
N Good
N.W. Rather Good
E. Unprofitable
SE Good
S. Subsistence
SW Inauspicious
Thursday
W War
NW Good
N Good
NE Good
E. Unlucky
SE Good
S. War
SW Subsistence

Of the days of the week Monday, Wednesday, Thursday, and Friday are auspicious, the others unlucky. As to the qualities of the hours of the day and night, they have been already detailed in a table in the chapter dealing with the birth and naming of children.

As might be expected, the rules are in many cases contradictory. The following additional examples may be given. Tuesday is the day least favourable for all human undertakings because Allāh then created all unpleasant things, and accordingly this day is appointed for executions and no one will marry on it. Friday is 'the best day on which the Sun rises, the day on which Adam was taken into Paradise and turned out of it, and it will also be the Day of Resurrection '.[1] The Prophet made his first entry into Medīna on that day, and he appointed it as the day of public worship, Yaumu-l-jum'a.[2] On Friday the clay of Adam was collected, on that day will be destruction and the Resurrection, and among the last three hours there is a period (*sā'at*) in which Allāh grants the requests of his servants. Hence it is lucky for a caravan to start on that day immediately after noonday prayer.[3] On Saturday was created the earth, on Sunday the mountains, on Monday the trees, on Tuesday darkness, on Wednesday light, on Thursday animals, on Friday Adam.[4] Thursday evening is the time for offering lights at the tombs of Saints, and a Hindu Kunbī in the Central Provinces will not shave on that day.[5] Shī'as believes that it is inauspicious to travel during the Nauroz festival, and the new moon day of the first Muharram after marriage is unlucky for the wedded.[6]

[1] Hughes, 131.
[2] Sale, *Korān*, 450 f.
[3] *Mishkāt*, i. 297.
[4] Leedes, 237.
[5] Russell, iv. 41.
[6] Sykes, *Glory of the Shia World*, 131.

CHAPTER XXXI

SŪFĪ MYSTICISM

THE term Sūfī is derived from *sūf*, 'wool', in allusion to the woollen garment often, but not universally, worn by people who follow this rule of life. The suggestions that the term is derived from *safā*, *sāf*, 'clean', or from σοφός are now generally rejected. Generally speaking, the Sūfīs are men and women who adopt the ascetic or quietistic mode of life. The system is believed to have arisen among the Persian Musalmāns in the ninth century as a reaction against the rigid monotheism and formalism of Islām.[1]

The custom of initiating (*talqīn*, *bayāt*) of disciples (*murīd*) had its origin with our ancestors, and this duty is entrusted to wise, reverend persons (*mashāikh*). When a man or woman wishes to become a disciple they go to the sages belonging to the household of the particular Pīr or Saint who is recognized as such by family descent (*silsila*), or the candidate invites the Pīr and other friends and relations to his own house, where he entertains them. Either before or after dinner, in the presence of the company, or in a closet, the spiritual guide (*murshid*), after doing the minor ablution (*wuzū'*), with his face turned eastward, seats the candidate before and facing him, so that the latter may look in the direction of the Qibla or Mecca. Some, however, allow him to face in any direction. Then he takes hold of the right hand of the candidate, so that their thumbs touch. In the case of a woman who is not secluded she holds one end of a handkerchief or sash (*patkā*), and the guide the other. But if she be a veiled woman (*pardanishīn*),[2] she sits behind a screen or curtain, because the Pīr, though he be

[1] See, with bibliographies, *ERE.* ii. 99 ff.; *EB.* xix. 123 f.; xxvi. 30 f.; Hughes, 608 f.; Macdonald, *passim.* For the Panjāb Sūfīs, Rose, i. 517 ff.; in Persia, Browne, *A Year amongst the Persians*, 122 ff. On Christian influence on these beliefs, *ERE.* ix. 482.

[2] Among Musalmāns the seclusion and veiling of women are the direct consequence of polygamy and the facility for divorce in the early age of Islām (Margoliouth, *Mohammed*, 460). But it was prescribed by the Prophet, though it is not justified, as usually supposed, by the Korān (xxxiii. 53–4). See *ERE.* iii. 495.

a Murshid, is not regarded as a relation, and from where she sits she takes hold of the scarf as already described. The fee to the Murshid consists of a suit of clothes (*khil'at*), money, parched rice, sweetmeats, sandalwood, miniature flower gardens (*chaman*), and lighted pastilles. The Murshid sees that the rite of initiation is duly performed, that the candidate is shaved and bathed, that he learns the names of the heads of the Order, that he promises to revere them, that he receives certain articles of dress, that he gets a new name, learns a new form of salutation, swears not to lie, steal, or commit adultery, that he promises to work hard as a beggar, or in some other calling, that he eats only things lawful, and, finally, that the initiation feast is duly given.

First, the Murshid directs the candidate to repeat the formula of asking forgiveness from God (*istighfār*), the five sections of the Creed (*kalima*), and other supplications, after which the candidate says to his Pīr, 'Whatsoever sins I have intentionally or unintentionally committed I now repent, and I sincerely promise before my Pīr, and in the presence of God and his Minister, never to commit them again'. Then the Murshid repeats the names of all the Saints of the Order according to the genealogy (*shajara*) which goes back to the time of the Prophet—on whom be the Peace!—and asks 'Do you consent to acknowledge these Pīrs?' Some Pīrs, merely naming their own Murshid, ask, 'As I have accepted him, do you accept me as your Murshid?' The candidate in either case replies, 'I do'. When he has repeated all their names, the Pīr lets go the hand of the candidate, takes a cup of sherbet, offers certain prayers over it, blows upon it, drinks two or three sips himself, and hands it to the candidate, who rises from his seat, and with profound reverence drinks all of it. Some Murshids also require candidates to recite two bow prayers (*rukū'*) of thanksgiving (*shukrīyā*). After this the gifts are presented to the Murshid.

The candidate having thus become a disciple (*murīd*), salutes all present and they return the salutation, adding, 'Be thou blessed!' Next day or the day after the Murshid furnishes the disciple with a list (*shajara*) of the Pīrs of the Order, so that he may remember them. Some foolish people consider these lists sacred, venerate them even more than the Korān, make amulets out of them, hang them round their necks, and when they die they are placed on their corpses at burial. The Murshid then whispers to his disciple the mysteries of godliness. Disciples esteem their Murshid as one of their four fathers: the natural father, the preceptor, the father-in-law, and the Murshid.

When a Murshid intends to initiate a Faqīr, either in his own line (*silsila*) or in any other, the candidate prepares a feast (*melā*, properly 'a fair, religious assemblage'). Some forty or fifty Faqīrs, more or less, of various Orders, with their friends and beggars, assemble by invitation, being summoned by a herald (*iznī*). Flowers, sandalwood, sweets, hemp (*gānjā*, *bhang*), dry tobacco (*sūkhā*) for chewing, and tobacco mixed with treacle for smoking (*gurākū*) are provided. The Murshid causes the candidate to shave the 'four beauties of his face' (*ābrū*), his beard, moustache, eyebrows, and body hair, or instead of a complete shaving a few hairs from each part are removed with a pair of scissors. While he is being shaved and his nails cut, the Murshid repeats sentences from the Korān or prayers in Arabic. Then after the candidate has been bathed, he makes him stand or sit before him and repeat the five clauses of the Creed, the two clauses of the Confession, the assertion of the Unity of the Godhead, the rejection of infidelity, and the appeal for forgiveness, as well as the other Creeds in use among Faqīrs. Having thus given the disciple such admonition and advice as he deems necessary, he repeats again all the names of his Murshids and asks, 'Have you consented to acknowledge each and all of these?' The disciple answers, 'I have'. When he has made him repeat this three times, he places with his own hands a cap (*tāj*) on his head, or gets another to do so. He then ties a small cloth turban, eight or ten cubits in length, round it, and puts on him the dress called 'the shroud' (*kafanī*), the sleeveless shirt (*alfā*), the rosary (*tasbīh*), the bead necklace (*kanthā*), the thread or hair necklace (*selī*), a leathern belt (*tasma*), a loin-cloth (*lūng*, *langotī*), and a waistband (*kamarband*).[1] On his foot he hangs a small circular piece of mother-of-

[1] The dress thus assumed is, or is supposed to be, that of the Murshid, who thus confers his afflatus on his disciple, on the analogy of the dress

pearl (*dāl*), and hands him a stick (*chharī*) with a handkerchief (*rūmāl*) wound round the upper end, and a wallet or cup (*kachkol, kishtī*) usually consisting of a shell of the double sea coco-nut (cocos de mer, *loidoicea sechellarum*).[1] He then gives him to drink some of the leavings (*jhūthā*) of his own sherbet. As he puts on each article of dress he repeats some verses of the Korān, or Arabic prayers. When he is decked out in his new dress, the Pīr gives his disciple a new name, such as Bismillāh Shāh, 'Amru-llāh Shāh, Hasanu-llāh Shāh, Latīf Shāh, or Gulzār Shāh. In all cases Faqīrs assume the title of Shāh or 'King' to signify that they are lords of their own wills and that they have renounced the world. Then the assembled Faqīrs cry out, 'He is made! He is made!', and from that time he is known by his new name. Then the Murshid tells him to turn his face to the Qibla or Mecca and to make prostration (*sijda*) to God. After this, instead of using the common salutation, 'Salāmu 'alaikum'! 'With you be the Peace!' he addresses to his Murshid and others of the fraternity the words, 'Ishq Allāh wa Murshid Allāh!' 'To the Elect of God and Spiritual Guide to God!' or 'Ishq Allāh, jam' Fuqarā Allāh!' 'To the favourites of God, to all the Faqīrs of God!' To this the Murshid, instead of replying, 'Wa 'alai-kum Salām!' 'With thee be the Peace!' answers, 'Sadāra 'ishq jamāl Allāh!' 'Always beloved, thou beauty of Allāh!' These ceremonies practised by Faqīrs are not in accordance with the Shar', or law, the word of God, or the traditional sayings of the Prophet—on whom be the Peace!—Like many other irregular customs they have become established in Hindostān. At the end of these rites the Murshid gives the newly-elected Faqīr the following precepts: 'What stands do not touch, what lies down do not move', that is to say, do not steal; 'Let your tongue observe truth', that is, do not lie; 'Keep your loin-band tight', that is, do not commit adultery; 'Treasure these things in your mind. Child! Beware!

of honour (*khil'at*), 'that which is put off', originally the actual robes worn by the royal personage, who thus confers with it a portion of his own dignity and sanctity: cf. Bayley, *Muhammadan Dynasties of Gujarāt*, 231.

[1] For an account of this remarkable nut, see Watt, *Econ. Dict.* v. 87 ff.; Yule, *Hobson-Jobson*, 229 ff.

Exert yourself; gain your living by begging or working, it matters not which; eat only what is lawful'. Food is then distributed to the Faqīrs, his own proper share to each. The leaders, the Murshid and the Khalīfa, and the resident or non-wandering members of the Order (*makāndār*, 'householders') receive a double portion as compared with that of the wandering Faqīrs. When all this is done the candidate becomes a real Faqīr, and no one reproaches him for associating with them.

It is the rule with Faqīrs that, whether they do or do not say the prayers at the appointed times, they must say something on their beds and make prostration (*sijda*) to Almighty God. This, to use their phrase, is being 'friends with one's bed' (*bistar kē āshnāyān rahnā*). When they have occasion to salute any one they say, 'God is Great, Sir! Be you happy!' ('Allāh, Allāh hai barā, Bābū, khush raho!') or, 'May the shadow of 'Alī and the Prophet be upon you!' ('Sāya 'Alī o Nabī kā rahē'). In like manner when people of the world salute a Faqīr they say, 'My service to you, Sir!' ('Bandagī hai, Shāh Sāhib!') or, 'I salute you, Master!' ('Salām hai, Shāh Sāhib!'). By such means they show their respect for the Order.

Musalmān Saints are supposed to form a corporation of a certain number always subsisting. In this corporation the highest is the chief (*ghaus*), the four 'pegs' (*autād*), the third seven 'who abound in good gifts' (*akhyār*), the fourth forty 'lieutenants' (*abdāl*), the fifth seventy 'the excellent' (*nujabā*), sixth, three hundred 'leaders' (*nuqabā*).[1]

All Faqīrs originated from four spiritual guides (*Chār Pīr*), and there are fourteen households (*Chaudah Khanwāda*). The following are the details: The first Pīr was Hazrat Murtazā 'Alī, 'Alī, the Chosen, son-in-law of the Prophet. He initiated as his Khalīfa or deputy Khwāja Hasan Basrī, who died October 11, A.D. 728.[2] He constituted as his deputies Khwāja Habīb 'Ajamī, who died on August 28, 738, and the fourth Pīr, 'Abdu-l-wāhid bin Zaid Kūfī. From the third Pīr have descended nine households: i. Habībiyān, from Khwāja

[1] Lane, *ME.* i. 223; Ibn Khallikān, iii. 98; Husain R. Sayani, *The Saints of Islām*; S. Lea, *Travels of Ibn Batuta*, 153; *Encyclopaedia Islām*, i. 69.

[2] Rose, iii. 431 f.

Habīb 'Ajamī; ii. Taifūriyān, from Bāyazīd Bastāmī, surnamed Taifūr;[1] iii. Karkhiyān, from Shaikh Ma'rūf Karkhī; iv. Junaidiyān, from Junaid Baghdādī, to which the Tabaqātī Faqīrs trace their origin; v. Saqtiyān, from Sirī Saqtī; vi. Gāzrūniyān, from 'Abdu-llāh Haqīqī, also known as Hanīf Gāzrūnī; vii. Tartūsiyān from 'Abu-l-farra Tartūsī; viii. Sahrwardiyān or Suhrwardiyān, from Shaikh Ziyāu-d-dīn Abū Najīb Suhrawardī;[2] ix. Firdausiyān, from Najmu-d-din Kubrā Firdausī. From the fourth Pīr have sprung five groups: x. Zaidiyān, from 'Abū-l-wāhid bin Zaid; xi. 'Ayāziyān, from Fuzail bin 'Ayāz; xii. Adhamiyān, from Ibrāhīm Adham Balkhī; xiii. Hubairiyān, from Amīnu-d-dīn Hubairatu-l-Basrī; xiv. Chishtiyān, from Shaikh Abū Ishāq Chishtī. From these have descended the Chishtī Faqīrs.

Besides these there are a few other groups among Faqīrs, but these fourteen are the principal, from which the rest have branched off. The origin of most of them may be traced to His Holiness 'Aliu-l-Murtazā, and of one or two others to Abū Bakr Siddīq, and from them to His Holiness Muhammad Mustafā—on whom be the Peace![3]

The following are some of the more important Orders of Faqīrs in India descended from the above.

The Qādiriyā Order was instituted A.D. 1165 by Sayyid 'Abdu-l-Qādir-al-Jīlānī, Pīr Dastagīr, whose tomb is at Baghdād. They practise both the silent and the audible form of service (*zikr-i-khafī, jalī*), reject music and singing, wear green turbans, and one of their garments must be ochre-coloured. The recital of the blessing of the Prophet (*durūd*) is a conspicuous part of their rites.[4] Sir R. Burton was initiated into the Order and gives his diploma.[5]

The Chishtī trace their origin to Abū Ishāq, ninth in succession from 'Alī, son-in-law of the Prophet, settled at Chisht in Khurāsān. One of his disciples, Khwāja Mu'īnu-d-dīn settled at Ajmer (A.D. 1142–1236). His successor was Qutbu-d-dīn

[1] *ERE.* vi. 525 f.; Rose, i. 538.

[2] *Āīn*, ii. 356; Rose, i. 544; iii. 344, 387; Temple, *Legends of the Panjāb*, ii. 307; *Census Report*, Panjāb, 1891, i. 195.

[3] For Musalmān Religious Orders, see *ERE.* x. 719 ff.

[4] Hughes, 478; *Āīn*, iii. 357; *Mishkāt*, i. 37; *ERE.* i. 11 f.

[5] *Pilgrimage*, ii. 327.

Bakhtyār Kākī, buried near the Qutb Minār in Old Delhi, and to him succeeded Bābā Farīdu-d-dīn Shakarganj of Pākpattan. The Dargāh at Ajmer was constantly visited by the Emperor Akbar.[1] Members of this Order are partial to vocal music, as was the Khwāja, their Pīr, who in one of his religious reveries said that singing was the food and support of the soul. We should, therefore, he said, sing and listen to singing. They have no special dress. In repeating the Confession of Faith they lay peculiar stress on the words 'illā-llāhu', repeating these with great vigour and shaking at the same time their heads and the upper part of their bodies. The Order is said to be specially favoured by Shī'as. The congregation is worked up to a high pitch of devotion by their religious songs, and often sink down exhausted. They frequently wear coloured clothes, especially those dyed with ochre or acacia bark. Their chief shrines are the tombs of Nizāmu-d-dīn Auliya at Delhi, of Mīrān Bhīk at Ambāla, Bābā Farīd at Pākpattan, Hazrat Sulaimān at Taunsā in the Derā Ghāzī Khān District, and the Dargāh at Ajmer. They tie the cloths used to drape the Muharram standards to their necks, upper arms, and sticks, and keep a long lock (*kākul*) on their heads, that is, they shave half their heads and let the hair grow on the other half. They constantly repeat the name of 'Alī whom they consider equal to God and the Prophet.[2]

The Shattāriyās are disciples of 'Abdu-llāh Shattārī, a descendant of Shihābu-d-dīn Suhrawardī, who came from Persia to India and died in Mālwā A.D. 1406.[3] Their garb is like that of the Qādiriyā, and they with the Chishtī and Qādiriyā are known as Benawā, 'without provisions, destitute'. Those who have their hair shaved are called Mulhidnumā, 'those who do not conform to the Law', and are hence regarded as infidels. Those who do not shave their hair except over the right temple, from which the Murshid at the time of initiation has clipped a few hairs, are called Rasūlnumā, 'resembling the Prophet'.

The Madāriyā or Tabaqūtiyā are followers of the Saint Zinda Shāh Madār. They generally wear dark clothes, and fasten to

[1] Smith, *Akbar*, 181.
[2] *Āīn*, iii. 361; *Census Report*, Panjāb, 1891, i. 193 f. Rose, i. 531 ff.
[3] *JASB* 1874, part 1, 216.

one of their ankles a chain which they throw out and drag back as they beg at shops. Or they bully the shopkeeper to give them alms and use obscene abuse till they are bought off. Some keep tame tigers, bears, and monkeys, the two last being taught to dance and perform tricks. Some of them are jugglers, and make a figure of a man or animal to dance without any apparent mechanical means. Others place an earthen pot without a bottom on their heads and put fire in it, on which they lay a frying-pan and cook cakes. They are one of the disreputable Orders of begging Faqīrs.[1]

The Malang or 'robust' are usually said to be followers of Jamanjatī, a disciple of Zinda Shāh Madār, and form a branch of the Madāriyā. But the term is applied in a general way to any unattached religious beggar who drinks and smokes hemp to excess, wears nothing save a loin-cloth, and keeps fire always near him. They are said to wear their hair long and tied into a knot behind.[2] In the Deccan their dress is like that of the Muharram Malang Faqīrs. Some wear round the waist a chain or rope as a waist-band (*kardalā, kardhanī*), or the perineal band is so narrow that it hardly covers their nakedness. They resemble in many ways the Hindu Gosāīn ascetics, wander through deserts and mountains, visit shrines of Saints, and wherever they sit down they light a fire (*dhunī*) and sometimes rub ashes on their bodies.

The Rafā'ī or Rifā'ī form an Order founded at Baghdād, A.D. 1180, by Ahmad ar Rifā'a, and correspond to the Howling Dervishes of Turkey and Egypt.[3] According to another account the founder was Ahmad Sa'īd Rifā'ī. Another, and in India a more common, name for them is Gurzmār, because they strike their bodies with a sort of mace (*gurz*). All sorts of marvels are told and believed about them. They strike the points of their mace against their breasts and eyes, aim sword blows at their backs, thrust a spit through their sides or into their eyes, which they are said to be able to take out and replace. Or they cut out

[1] *BG.* ix, part 2, 23, 82 f.; Rose, i. 551; iii. 43; Crooke, *Castes*, iii. 397.

[2] *Census Report*, Panjāb, 1891, i. 197.

[3] Macdonald, 267 f.; Brown, *Dervishes*, 113 ff.; Rose, i. 588 f.; Lane, *ME.* i. 305; ii. 93, 216.

their tongues, which on being put back in their mouths reunite. It is even said that they are able to cut off their heads, and fix them again on their necks with saliva, and what is equally strange, there is no haemorrhage, or if it does occur the performer is said to be inexpert. The wound, it is said, is healed by the application of saliva, for when they are being initiated the Murshid rubs a little of his own saliva on their tongues and says, 'Wield the mace on yourselves without fear, and if you are cut apply your own spittle to the wound and it will quickly heal by the influence of your Pīr, Ahmad Sa'īd'. Sometimes they scar their tongues with a red-hot iron, put a live scorpion into their mouths, make a chain red-hot, pour oil upon it, and when a sudden blaze is produced draw their hands through it. I have heard, says Ja'far Sharīf, who gives these details, that they can cut a living being into two parts and reunite them by means of spittle. They are also said to eat arsenic, glass, and other poisons. They rattle their maces in front of shops till they receive alms, but sometimes they throw away the money they receive, as it is unlawful to take money by extortion. While many of these accounts are exaggerated and absurd, due to trickery or auto-suggestion, the Gurzmār certainly inflict tortures on themselves. There are similar allied Orders such as the Rasūlshāhīs of Gujarāt known as Mastān, or 'madmen', who carry a long club and beg for money to purchase drink. In northern India the Chhalapdār (*chhalap*, the cymbal on which they play) are said to walk on blazing charcoal.[1]

The Jalāliyā take their name from that of their founder, Sayyid Jalāl Bukhārī (A.D. 1307–74) of Uch in the Bahāwalpur State. They wear a necklace of fine wool (*pashm*), or of thread of various colours, a neckband (*gulūband*), and a small loincloth (*lūng*, *langotī*), and carry a club (*sontā*). They have a scar on the right upper arm made by cautery with a lighted cloth match at initiation. They beg in bazars, and if they do not receive alms brand themselves with a match of this kind, while others gain their ends by noise and uproar. In the Panjāb, their head-quarters, they give little heed to prayer, smoke quantities of hemp (*bhang*), eat snakes and scorpions, shave their heads, moustaches, and eyebrows, leaving only

[1] Mrs. Meer Hassan Ali, 370 f.

a scalp-lock (*chontī*) on the right side. They are branded with a special mark on the right shoulder, wear glass armlets, a woollen cord round their necks, a cloth on their heads, and are vagabonds with no fixed dwelling-place. One section of the Order is called Chihaltan, the 'forty bodies', who are said to be sprung from a luckless woman who, wishing to be a mother, swallowed forty philtres instead of one and produced forty children.[1]

The Mūsā Sohāgiyā take their name from Mūsā Sohāg, a Saint who lived at the close of the fifteenth century. His prayers for rain once saved the land from famine, and in order to protect himself from the crowds who followed him he used to wear women's clothes. His tomb is at Ahmadābād, now the head-quarters of the Order. His followers dress like women and wear a cap with bangles and other female ornaments. They accept alms from the Kanchanī or dancing-girls and the Bangrīhār or bangle-makers. When alms are refused they break their bangles and chew the fragments. They play on the mandoline (*tanbūrā*) and various kinds of fiddles and guitars (*sitār*, *sārangī*), and dance before their Murshid in the presence of the Jam' Allāh or Order, or perform for hire. They are good musicians, and say that their singing causes the rain to fall uot of season, melts the rocks, and, as in the case of Orpheus, brings the wild beasts round them to listen.[2]

The Naqshbandī are followers of Khwāja Pīr Muhammad Naqshband, whose tomb is at Bokhāra. He and his father were makers of brocade, hence the name Naqshband, 'pattern-maker'. The Order was introduced into India by Shaikh Ahmad Sirbandī, a descendant of the Khalīfa Abū Bakr. They worship by the silent method, sitting perfectly calm and quiet, and repeating the Creed under their breath, often sitting in meditation (*murāqaba*), quite motionless with the head bent and eyes closed or fixed on the ground. They forbid all singing and music, and are extremely strict adherents of the institutes and traditions of orthodox Islām.[3] In the Deccan they go

[1] *Census Report*, Panjāb, 1891, i. 195 f.; Rose, i. 552 f.; ii. 350; Dabistan, ii. 226.

[2] *BG*. ix, part 2, 23.

[3] *Census Report*, Panjāb, 1891, i. 196; Rose, i. 547.

Musical Instruments.

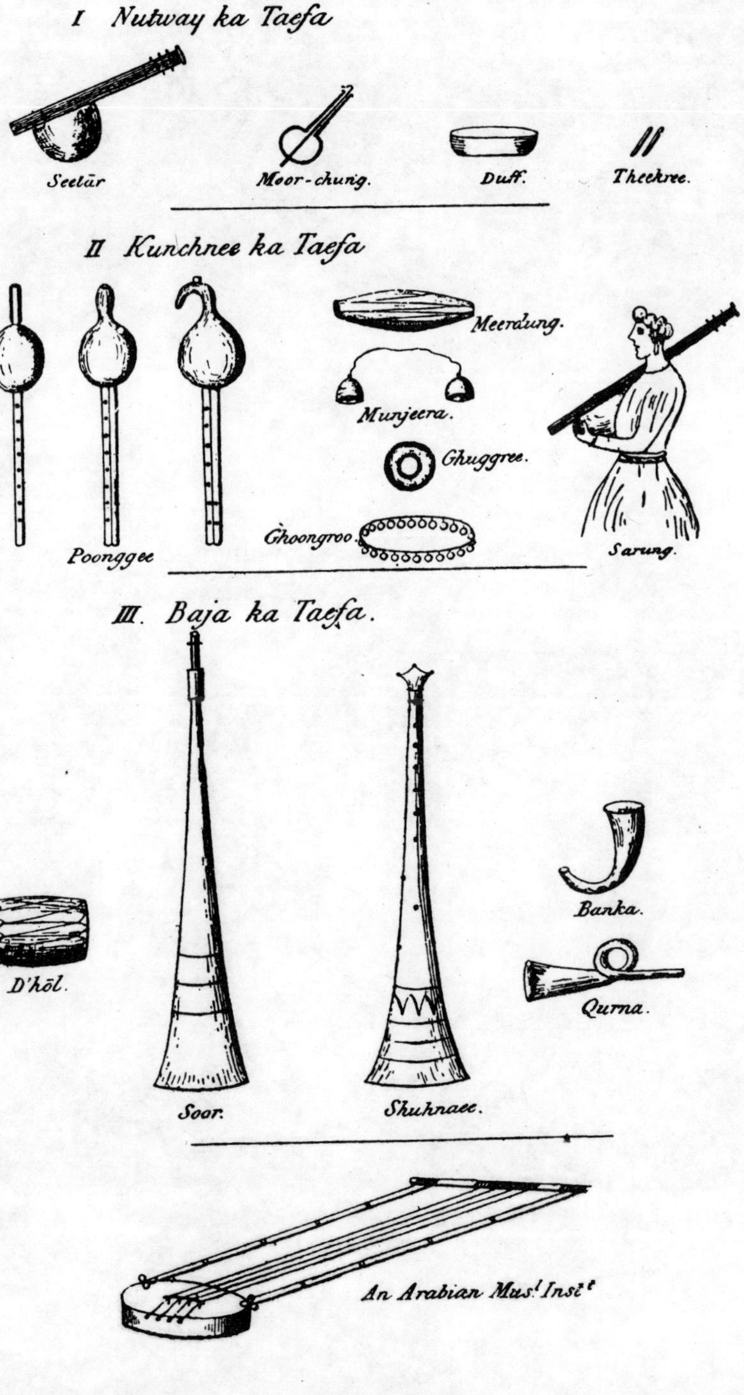

about carrying a lighted lamp, singing verses in honour of their Murshids, in glory to God and praises of the Prophet. In Sind the novice begins with the three 'works' (*shagl, shugl*) of the Qādiriyā Order. After the morning ablution and prayers he begins the ecstatic devotion (*zikr*),[1] repeating the formula a thousand times. In the same way he repeats 'Ill-Allāh, Allāh, Hū', the total number of repetitions being four thousand, after each hundred saying 'Muhammadun Rasūlu-llāh' 'Muhammad is God's Apostle' When vain thoughts intrude on his mind, he says 'Yā Fā'il', 'The True Agent', God. After this comes the meditation (*tasawwur*), when the pupil is directed to think of his Pīr or teacher's form, and to suppress his breath and suppose in his heart to express the word 'Allāh'. In the second phase the words 'Yā Allāh' and 'Yā-hū' are repeated for forty days. In the third stage he thinks of his Shaikh, breathing 'Allāh' through his nose when inspiring, and 'Hū' when expiring. This is repeated five hundred times after the morning, and a thousand times after evening prayer.[2]

The Bāwā Piyārē kē Faqīrān wear a loin-band (*tahband*), a quilt dyed in red ochre (*bhagwī*), on which are sewn triangular or square patches of white cloth, the whole hanging to the feet. On their heads is a tall cap (*tāj*), and over it a small turban (*phentā*). They carry two sticks, and when they beg they cry 'Allāhu ghanī!', 'God the self-supporting!', make supplication and ask for alms, going generally in parties of two or three, sometimes offering fruit and receiving a gift in return.

Most Faqīrs never carry with them anything save a crooked stick or a piece of iron (*chharī, chhathī*), sometimes painted, a wooden club (*sontā*), an iron prong (*zafar-takyā, bairāgan*) crooked in form, sometimes of wood, like that which Hindu Jogīs place under their arm-pits to support them when sitting,

[1] The word *zikr*, 'recollection', implies 'the fixing in the mind of some object of thought. It is accomplished by concentrating the attention upon the conception and its name, or upon some religious idea and its corresponding formula of expression. To assist in fixing the notion the mental effort is accompanied by vocal repetition of the name or formula with varying tone, pitch, and force of voice' (*ERE*. x. 42; Lane, *ME*. ii. 151 f.; Rose, i. 539 f.).

[2] Burton, *Sindh*, 214 f.

a back-scratcher (*pushtkhār*), like an artificial hand, made of some metal with a handle, with which they scratch themselves, a bag of lamb skin (*hīmācha*), a wallet (*kachkol*, *kishtī*), a fan (*mirwaha*, *bādkash*, *pankhā*), a sort of puzzle consisting of a number of pins put through holes in a board, the pins having knobs at one and at the other end rings through which a long compressed ring is passed (*gorakhdhandhā*). Some carry a lance (*barchhī*), a dagger worn in front (*peshqabz*), a dirk (*katār*), a knife (*chhurī*), and a weapon formed of two antelope horns joined at their bases (*mārū*). When they visit any one they carry some fruit or a sweet-scented flower or leaf, and offering it they say, ' The green leaf is the delight of the Darwesh '.

Faqīrs may be divided into two classes, Beshar', ' without the Law ', and Bashar', ' within the Law '. A large proportion belongs to the former class, and are debauchees, using intoxicants like hemp, opium, wine, or spirits, all of which they consider lawful. These do not follow the precepts of the Prophet as regards fasting, praying, and controlling their passions. But those ' within the Law ' pray, fast, and follow the rules of Islām. Among these are many varieties. The Sālik, ' pilgrims on the way to salvation ' (*tarīqa*), have wives and families, live by farming or trade, or by begging. The Majzūb, or ' abstracted ', are supposed to lead an ascetic life. But ' some Sāliks are termed Sālik-i-majzūb, and continue to observe all the external forms and ordinances of the Faith. Others are called Majzūb-i-sālik, as being so affected by their mystical affection for the Deity and Gnosticism that they are dead to excitement, hope, and fear. This class is, of course, rare, and requires a peculiar conformation of mind. The pretenders to it are common, as the pretence is easy and its advantages great. The Majzūb is usually a professed debauchee and a successful beggar. He is a staunch free-thinker and explains away the necessity of all such rules as ablution, praying, fasting, and fighting for the Faith. He believes not in the miracles of the Prophet, or the doctrine of a future state. When a man of education arrives at this point he resembles the Hukamā, or metaphysicians, who think nothing so unfashionable as belief in the Korān. The religious fanatics usually hold the tenet of Wahādīyat al Wujūd, or the unity of existence (in kind),

Musical Instruments.

utter Pantheism, as the very phrase denotes that God is all things and all things God '.[1] In the Deccan the Majzūb are ' outside the Law ', and have no wives, families, or property; in fact, the bazar is their home. Their dress consists solely of a loin-cloth and their hair is dishevelled. If any one offers them food they accept it and eat, if not they fast and rarely beg. They are so absorbed in religious reveries that they do not distinguish between things lawful and unlawful, and pay regard to no sect or religion. Sometimes they speak, at other times remain mute. Sometimes they go about in a state of nudity,[2] and lie down where they can, regardless of filth. Some are said to be such powerful miracle-workers that they can instantly effect what they please. Ja'far Sharīf remarks that it is strange that though they neglect sanitation there is no offensive smell about them. They fear, he says, neither fire nor water, for when they please they stand on hot embers, or sit in a large frying-pan or a boiling cauldron for hours at a time, and they dive and remain under water for two or three hours.

Another class is known as Āzād, ' free, unrestricted ', who are also ' outside the Law '. They shave their beards, whiskers, moustaches, eyebrows, and eyelashes, and all the body hair, and live celibate lives. Whatever they receive, good or bad, they eat, and they have no fixed abode, generally travelling and living on alms.

The Qalandar, the ' Calendar ' of the Arabian Nights, are not really an Order, but a class of begging monks. Some have wives, some not; some are ' within ', others ' without ' the Law. They occupy straw huts outside, or retired spots, within towns where they pass their time in solitude, trusting to Providence, laymen providing their food and drink. The places where they resort are called Takya or ' pillow '. In the Panjāb they lead about bears and monkeys, and they are said to make excellent pipe bowls. They have a secret argot, and settle their own disputes with order and dignity. Their chief shrine is that of Bū 'Alī Qalandar at Pānīpat.[3]

The Rasūlshāhī, Rasūl being the title of the Prophet, shave

[1] Burton, *Sindh*, 218 f.

[2] This is now prevented by municipal regulations in British territory.

[3] Rose, i. 543 f., 619 f.; iii. 257; *BG.* ix, part 2, 22.

all the face hair, wear a cap and a loin-cloth with a sheet to use in cold, wet, or hot weather. They drink spirits, do not marry, and live by begging. Those in Gujarāt are dissipated, Sunnīs 'without the Law', without settled homes.[1]

The Imāmshāhī shave their face hair, wear a sleeveless shirt (*alfā*), a waist-band (*tahband*), and a thread or hair necklace (*selī*). Their distinguishing mark is a narrow perpendicular line extending from the tip of the nose to the top of the forehead. They are celibates, living by alms and claiming miraculous powers. It is therefore well to court their blessing and avoid their curses. The Hindostānī couplet runs:

'View not with scorn the humble sons of earth,
Beneath a clod a flower may have birth',

alluding to their habit of smearing themselves with ashes.

The Nikalsenī are a curious sect in the Panjāb who are said to worship the famous General John Nicholson, who was killed at Delhi in 1857. He is reported to have flogged some of them because they worshipped him, and they are said to be in some way connected with the Margala Pass near Rāwalpindī. They have disappeared from recent Census returns.[2]

Many other Orders might be described, but to understand Darweshes, says Ja'far Sharīf, to learn about their ecstatic services (*zikr*), and how to obtain the accomplishment of one's wishes, are things which can be attained only by unwearied perseverance, by associating with holy men, and by the study of the Tasawwuf or Sūfī mysticism.

Spiritual guides, known as Mashāikh, Pīr, or Murshid, are of two kinds, ancestral (*jaddī*) and successors (*khalafāī*). The ancestral guides are those in whose families the rights of initiating (*bayāt*) of disciples have descended from their grandparents on either side, or for two or three generations. The successors are those whose fathers and mothers belonged to trades differing from theirs, or were learned men among whom the custom was established by some Murshid of either kind. The dress of both classes consists of a cap (*tāj*), a turban ('*imāma*), a mantle (*pairāhan*, *qamīs*), a shirt (*kurtā*), double sheet (*dopattā*), a shawl (*shāl*), a double shawl (*doshālā*), a hand-

[1] *BG.* ix, part 2, 24. [2] *PNQ.* ii. 181; Rose, iii. 199 f.

kerchief (*rūmal*), drawers (*izār*), a waist-cloth (*lūng*), out of which they select such articles as they please. Some wear round their necks a string of beads (*tasbīh*) or a necklet made of hair or thread (*selī*), round their waists a strap (*tasma*), on their wrists a thread bracelet known as 'remembrance' (*sumaran*), and they carry in their hands a stick (*chharī*) or other weapon used by Faqīrs. They are 'outside the Law' (*beshar*'), and have families. They subsist on the services, as they are called, of their Murīds or disciples. The disciple once or oftener in the year visits his Pīr and offers a present to him, sometimes in the course of conversation slipping it under the seat or bed on which his teacher happens to be sitting, and saying nothing. Or he hands it to him with an apology that he is unable to give more. They also receive alms or tithes (*zakāt*) from men of substance (*sāhib-i-nisāb*), or kings or nobles give them a daily, monthly, or annual allowance in the form of a plot of rent-free land (*jāgīr*) or a gift (*in'ām*). Some of them, besides initiating disciples, live by fortune-telling, by making amulets or charms, practising medicine and pronouncing incantations or blessings. Sometimes every year or so they go on circuit to visit their disciples, and if they are offered money accept it and perform initiations.

The procedure in appointing a deputy (*khalīfa*) is as follows: The Pīr seats the person to be invested with the post of a deputy (*khilāfat*) before him, as in the case of initiating a disciple, and after reciting certain prayers he makes over to him the succession lists (*shajaranāma*) of the former Pīrs of the Order, and the forms of ecstatic devotion (*zikr*), which have succeeded to him from his predecessors. Then he says, 'I have now constituted thee my deputy or successor, and I have given thee authority in such and such a group (*silsila*), in which thou art authorized to make disciples, Faqīrs or deputies, as it pleaseth thee'. Then with his own hands he invests him with his own robe (*jubba*) and other garments, either those which he has worn himself or a new suit, and reads to him the list of the successors (*shajara-i-khilāfat*). Pīrs grant this right of succession for the love of God, that is to say gratis, but if their successors, as an act of merit, offer gifts of money or clothes, there is no objection to receiving them. If the successor be a wealthy man, on the occasion of his installation he invites learned men, Faqīrs, and friends, and has the Fātiha recited over stews and sweets on which he entertains them. After this he has the power of initiating others. Faqīrs who have reached the dignity of Mashāikh ordinarily add at the beginning or middle of their names the title Shāh, or ' King ', and to the end the designation of the Order, such as Chishtī, Tabaqātī, Qādirī or Shattārī ; thus, 'Abdullāh Qādir Qādiri, Hamīdu-llāh Shāh Chishtī, but the terms Tabaqātī or Shattārī are uncommon.

Next to the dignity of a Prophet is that of a Walī or Saint, for it will last till the Day of Judgement. Though prophecy has ceased, the office of Walī continues. In order to gain the rank of Walī the grace of God is indispensable. Verily, as the Eternal Registrar has decreed, so it must happen in this world. In short, there are certain acts and austerities incumbent on holy men which it is necessary to know and practise. It is forbidden to Murshids to publish these in books or to reveal them. They are disclosed only to those Murīds or disciples who become inquirers (*tālibu-l-'ilmī*), who are members of the Faith of Islām, and mean to make a study of the subject. It must suffice at present merely to name them, and should any one wish to study the ' works ' (*shagl, shugl*) or the ecstatic devotion (*zikr*) or the ' acquirements ' (*kasb*), he must apply to learned men for a knowledge of the discipline or penances (*riyāsat*), the devotional exercises (*aurād*), the ' viewings ' or ' beholdings ' (*dīd*), and the devotions (*zikr*). Two precepts are to be specially observed—to eat only things lawful, and to speak the truth. Mashāikhs and Darveshes have also enjoined the repression of the following five vices or noxious things (*mūzī*) : the ' ears ' or the ' snake ', that is the taking of revenge without inquiry and consideration ; the ' kite ' or the ' eagle ', that is, the eye or covetousness ; the ' large black bee ', which dwells in the nostrils and craves for anything which smells sweet or savoury ; the ' dog ', whose seat is in the tongue, the longing for what is savoury ; and the ' scorpion ', the sensual appetite, which must be repressed.

In order to derive benefit from these devotions (*zikr*) a man must be careful to do only what is good, to remove from his mind envy and covetousness, to keep his thoughts pure and undefiled, to depend on, reflect on, think of God alone, to be ever engaged in contemplation of Him, to retain no love for relations or for the world, to consider everything comprehended in Him, to take no delight in troubling or annoying others, to perform with zeal such occupations as the Murshid prescribed. Then the Almighty will raise him who does such things to the dignity of a Walī. There are also many things which must be said and repeated aloud, and it is easy to do this with the mouth. But it is most difficult to endure the hardships which the performance of these duties entails.

CHAPTER XXXII

DRESS, THE TOILET

As regards the materials of dress, the Prophet forbade the wearing of silk, satin, sitting on quilted red saddle-cloths, wearing silk and cotton mixed (*mashrū*‘, ‘ what is ordained by the Law ’), but this last is now permitted, and a Musalmān who may not wear silk in his lifetime may be shrouded in it.[1]

The fashion of dress varies throughout the country, particularly among converts from Hinduism to Islām. The following account from Gujarāt may be taken as an example.[2] A rich Musalmān wears indoors a cap of velvet or embroidered cloth, or, if he be of simpler tastes, of plain muslin or cotton cloth. The upper body is covered with a short shirt (*pirāhan*) of fine muslin, and his lower limbs in trousers made of cotton, cotton and silk (*ilāchā*, ‘ cardamom-like ’) or chintz. In the cold season a waistcoat (*kabcha*) of velvet, brocade, or broadcloth is sometimes worn. In the house his feet are bare, but in the cold season well-to-do people put on socks. When he goes out the rich man changes his cap for a turban or scarf (*dopattā*) wound loosely on the head, and over his shirt he draws a coat (*angarkhā*), tight round the chest and rather full in the skirts, which hang to the knee, it being usually made of muslin, embroidered broadcloth, or velvet. Sometimes, if he affects the Hindostānī or north Indian fashion of dress, he puts on light red leather or green shagreen shoes which come from Delhi. The ceremonial dress differs from the ordinary dress only in being richer, the turban of gold cloth, the coat richly embroidered on the shoulders and breast, the shoulder scarf bordered with silk, and the trousers made of brocade or Chinese silk cotton. Fashions, too, vary under the influence of large cities like Delhi, Lucknow, or Hyderābād. Fashions, again,

[1] *Mishkāt*, i. 340 ; Burton, *AN*. ix. 21 ; A Yusuf Ali, *Monograph on Silk*, 121 f.

[2] *BG*. ix, part 2, 100 ff.

Miscellaneous.

Varieties of Shoes. Fig 1.

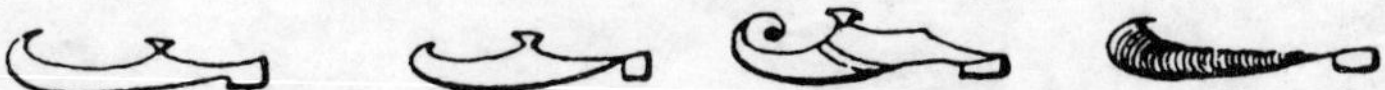

Appashaes. Chanddoree. Nowkdar. Chuppul.

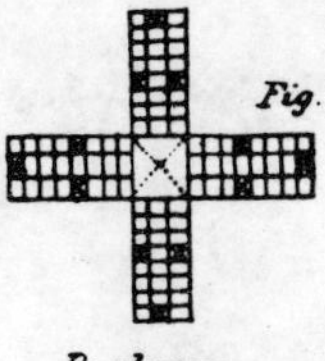

Fig. 2.

Pucheesee.

Fig. 3.

Mogol-Putthan.

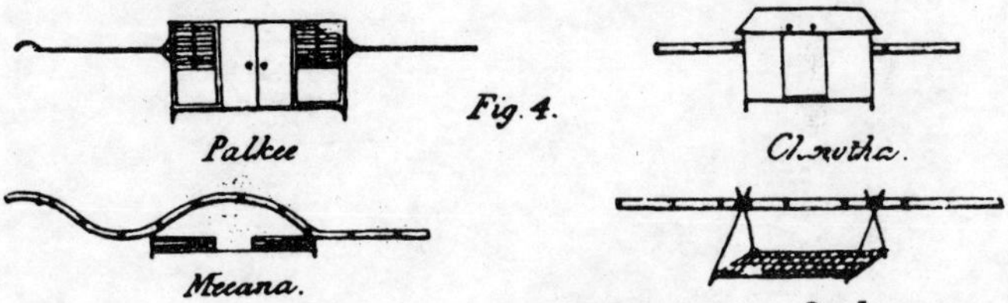

Fig. 4.

Fig. 5. Miswak.

Positions in Prayer.

Qeeam. Rookoo. Do-zano bythna. Sijdah.

Fig. 6.

Different Modes of Salutation.

Sulam. Bunduges. Koornish Tusleem Qudum-bosee, or Zumeen-bosee Gullay milna

Ushtung (vulg: Sashtung)

are rapidly changing, and there is a tendency among younger men to abandon the graceful flowing draperies of a former generation, and to replace the older dress by trousers of European cut, an imitation of the European frock coat, or a woollen coat buttoned to the neck, to wear patent leather shoes, and instead of the cap or turban to wear the Turkish or Egyptian dark red fez.

The dress of the middle-class Musalmān is like that of the higher class, but the materials are less costly. The poor man wears drawers of coarse cotton cloth, a coloured turban, a coat of cheap broadcloth and thick-soled shoes. He keeps a suit of a better kind for important occasions. Among the peasantry of northern India it is sometimes difficult to distinguish the Musalmān peasant or labourer from a Hindu merely by his dress, except that the jacket of the Hindu is fastened to the right, that of the Musalmān on the left, a distinction which in Central Asia marks off the Musalmān from the Buddhist.[1] The enormous drawers are characteristic of the Panjābī and Afghān, one set worn by a chief being six yards across.[2]

A rich woman wears a scarf or head-shawl (*orhnī*), a bodice (*angiyā*), a gown (*peshwāz*, 'open in front'), and trousers (*izār*). The closely fitting drawers or trousers made of chintz or coloured cloth worn by the lower-class Musalmān women in northern India are perhaps the most unbecoming dress in the country. The rich woman's skirt is of red or light tints for maidens and married women, of dark blue, bronze colour, or white for old ladies, and bronze and black for widows. The trousers are usually made of some kind of chintz or coloured cloth, and they are rather tighter than those worn by men. Though rich women are not in the habit of often leaving the house, they are careful to wear shoes or slippers. Except that it is of costlier materials, the ceremonial dress does not differ much from that worn at ordinary times. In Gujarāt, except among the more advanced classes, European fashions have not made much way. But the half-Turkish, half-European chemise is in favour as well as other Persian, Turkish, or Arabian models, and the use of English shoes and stockings

[1] Ratzel, *History of Mankind*, iii. 326.

[2] Crooke, *Things Indian*, 163.

is extending.[1] But the fashions both of male and female dress are so varied in different parts that space does not allow of a catalogue of fashions and materials.[2]

The wearing of new clothes is a serious matter. If a man has his measure taken for new clothes on Sunday he will suffer trouble; on Monday, he will have ample food; on Tuesday, his clothes will be burnt; on Wednesday, he will enjoy happiness and tranquillity; on Thursday, the wearing of them will be propitious; on Friday, it will be well; on Saturday, he will suffer many misfortunes. If he puts on new clothes on Sunday he will enjoy happiness and ease; on Monday, his clothes will be torn; on Tuesday, even if he stands in water, his clothes will be burnt; on Wednesday, he will easily obtain a new suit; on Thursday, he will appear neatly dressed; on Friday, as long as the suit is new he will be happy; on Saturday, he will fall ill. If he puts on new clothes in the morning he will be wealthy and fortunate; at noon, he will look elegant; at sunset, he will be wretched; in the evening, he will fall ill. Akbar ordered that all clothes received in the Imperial wardrobe in Farwardīn, the first month of the Persian year, provided they were of good quality, should have higher rank assigned to them than those arriving at other times.[3] It may be noted that the shoe of the right foot should be put on and taken off before that of the left.

The shape of the turban is infinitely varied. A man's drawers should not reach below the ankle joint, and the coat (*jāma*) should be a little above the bottom of the drawers. The turban (*pagrī*) should be tied, and the ends (*shamla*) left waving behind. Some, however, let them dangle on the right and left sides of the head. Red is the colour of the infidel, perhaps from its association with blood sacrifice, and should not be worn by men, though it is permitted to women. The wearing of red by a king was a sign of wrath.[4] The screens surrounding the encampment of the Mughal Emperors were of scarlet, and

[1] *BG.* ix, part 2, 101; Edwardes, *Gazetteer, Bombay City*, i. 256 f.

[2] See Watson, *Textile Manufactures*; M. F. Billington, *Woman in India*; *EB.* xiv. 417; Industrial Monographs on Textiles, published by the Governments of the Panjāb and United Provinces.

[3] *Āīn*, i. 91.

[4] Burton, *AN.* iii. 197; v. 156.

a scarlet umbrella was carried over the Musalmān Kings of the Deccan.[1] Bahādur Shāh, King of Gujarāt, was in wrath, but when his fury was abated by a song of a minstrel he put off his red dress and donned one of green.[2] The family of 'Abbās wore black in opposition to the Ummayads, whose family colour was green. The green worn by Sayyids, who hence are sometimes called Sabzposh, ' wearers of green ', was borrowed from the old Nabatheans.[3]

According to the Traditions all the hair should be allowed to grow, or the whole head should be shaved. The retention of the scalp-lock (*shūsha, chotī, chontī*) is sometimes explained on the ground that it furnishes a handle to draw the wearer into Paradise, and it is said to prevent the pollution of the mouth of a decapitated Musalmān from an impure hand, but it seems to have been used as a protection for the head adopted by the Arabs of the desert.[4] The growing of the sidelocks (*zulf*) is regarded by some as a vain innovation (*bid'at*) and unseemly (*makrūh*), that is, neither lawful nor unlawful. When boys are first shaved, a tuft is often left on the crown and forehead, but this is not the fashion among adults. Some of the frontier tribes wear the hair in ringlets on each side of the head, but this is not the rule among Indian Musalmāns. Women generally wear the hair in a long plait hanging behind or twisted into a knot.

The Sunnat or practice of the Prophet was to wear the beard not longer than one hand and two fingers' breadth, and that the moustaches should be either cropped or shaven close. In the Hadīs or Traditions it is laid down that if a man does not preserve his beard, he will rise on the Day of Judgement with a black face like that of a hog ; and that if he grows his moustache to such a length that he wets them in the act of drinking water, the water of the Hauzu-l-kausar, or Fountain of Paradise,[5] will be denied to him, and the hairs at the Last Day will become like so many spits, so that when he tries to make the prostration (*sijda*) they will prevent him from bowing, and if notwithstanding he bends his head his forehead will not reach

[1] Ferishta, iii. 198.
[2] Bayley, *Muhammadan Dynasties*, 389.
[3] Burton, *AN*. ix. 113.
[4] Ibid. i. 284 ; *Pilgrimage*, i. 163.
[5] Sale, *Korān*, Preliminary Discourse, 68.

the ground. The beard (*rīsh, dārhī*) is the sign of manhood, and hence highly respected, so that to seize a man by his beard or to pull a hair from it is considered a deadly insult. But a tale is told of Muhammad Shāh Fārūqī, King of Gujarāt, that he spared the life of a child and provided for him because his hand accidentally touched the beard of the Sultān.[1] A popular saying is 'Dārhī Khudā kā nūr', 'The beard is the light of God'. The order of the Prophet was, 'Do the opposite to the polytheists and let your beards grow long'.[2]

In order to avoid pollution it is well to pare the hair over the lips. In Egypt it is the custom to shave portions of the hair above and below the lower jaw, leaving, according to the example of the Prophet, the hairs that grow in the middle below the mouth. Or instead of shaving those parts they pull out the hair. Very few shave the rest of the beard and none the moustache. The former they suffer to grow to the length of about a hand's breadth below the chin, and, in imitation of the Prophet, they do not allow the moustache to become so long as to hide completely the skin under it, or to extend in the least over the upper lip and thus incommode them in eating and drinking.[3] Some of the Indian frontier tribes, like the Bangash Pathāns, shave the head and eradicate most of the hair on the chin and cheeks, leaving little but the ends of the moustache, and the local Mullās consider the wearing of a fringe to be improper.[4] A pilgrim told Akbar that the Prophet, seeing a man with his beard cut off, said that he resembled the inmates of Paradise, and probably in imitation of Hindu practice, which the Emperor favoured, it was ordered that beards were to be shaven, but this innovation was soon withdrawn.[5] To remove the hair from under the arm-pits and below the navel, to circumcise and to pare the nails are five things enjoined by Ibrāhīm or Abraham—May God reward him!—but which the Prophet has not ordained. In Sind Musalmāns usually shave their heads for the sake of cleanliness and coolness. But the Baloch let their hair grow long, and those in the hills wear it falling over their shoulders like the Pathāns and other

[1] Bayley, *Muhammadan Dynasties*, 403. [2] Hughes, 40.
[3] Lane, *ME.* i. 34 f. [4] Rose, ii. 59.
[5] *Āīn*, i. 189 207, 208 ; Smith, *Akbar*, 257 ; Elliot-Dowson, v. 536.

hill tribes around them. No Musalmān ought to cut his beard, but many Pathāns grow a military moustache and shave their chins, while the Khwājas have generally retained their Hindu customs in this matter.[1] For shaving the best days are Monday, Wednesday, Thursday, and Friday, the other days of the week being considered inauspicious.

The habit of dyeing the beard is common. In Arabia it is dyed with henna, gall-nuts, and other preparations, especially sulphate of iron one part, ammoniate of iron one part, gall-nuts infused in eight parts of pure water, but this process is not permanent. In northern India the hair dye (*khizāb, wasma*) is made of oxide of iron (*lohchan*) ½ ounce, salt 6 grains, wheat flour ½ ounce, mixed with 2 ounces of water, boiled and stirred till the mixture becomes like a paint. When cool it is applied to the beard, and this is bound up with castor-oil leaves in a cloth. After an hour it is washed off with an infusion of emblic myrobalan (*āonlā*). Another method prescribes gall-nuts, sulphate of copper and salammoniac, or henna and indigo leaves are ground up in water and applied to the hair for half an hour.[2]

Village women converted from Hinduism sometimes follow the Hindu practice of using vermilion to mark the parting of the hair as a mark of coverture, but this practice is forbidden by the orthodox. In the Central Provinces and Bombay a powder (*kunkū*) made of turmeric, borax, and lime-juice is substituted, this having the advantage of not injuring the hair or skin.[3] Musalmān women usually remove all body hair, except that of the head and eyebrows. Some use for this purpose quicklime or a depilatory (*nūrā*) consisting of yellow arsenic one ounce, pounded and mixed with quicklime till the compound assumes a yellowish tinge. It is applied to the skin in a paste made with hot water, and it must be washed off after a minute or two, as it burns, as well as stains. This admirable invention is ascribed to the learned Sulaimān or

[1] Aitken, *Gazetteer of Sind*, 196 f. ; *Census Report*, Balūchistān, 1901, i. 40. The cutting or shaving of a woman's hair is equivalent to a curse against the life of her husband, or the implication that she is a slave, the phrase ' tress-shorn ' (*chotīkat*) meaning a slave.

[2] Saiyid Muhammad Hadi, *Monograph on Dyes and Dyeing in the North-west Provinces and Oudh*, 70 f.

[3] Russell, ii. 44 ; iv. 109.

Solomon, who could not endure the sight of the hairy legs of Bilqīs, queen of Sheba.[1] Some remove the body hair with a pledget of fir gum (*lūbān shāmī*).

Certain days are prescribed for bathing. If a person bathes on a Sunday he will suffer affliction ; on Monday, his goods will be increased ; on Tuesday, he will suffer from anxiety of mind ; on Wednesday, his property will increase ; on Thursday, his property will increase ; on Friday, all his sins will be forgiven ; and on Saturday, all his ailments will be removed.

The teeth are cleaned with a twig (*dāntan, miswāk*), tooth-brushes which may be made from the hair of the hog being forbidden.[2] The trees commonly used for this purpose are the Nīm (*melia azadirachta*) in north India, and the Pīlū (*salvadora persica*) in the south. Others used for this purpose are the Agarā (*acquillaria agallocha*), Kālē madh kā jhar (*phyllanthus multiflorus*), Khajūr (*phoenix dactilifera*), and the Maulsirī, Baulsirī, Bakal or Bakul (*mimusops elengi*). The twig is about a span long, split at one end and chewed to make it softer, the end not used being held between the ring and middle finger with the thumb pressing against the other extremity. Dentifrice (*manjan*) is often made of burnt almond shells, or of the residue tobacco of the pipe (*gul*), mixed with black pepper and salt. But common people often merely use charcoal, which is made by burning the wood of the Chebulic myrobalan (*harrā, terminalia chebula*) or betel-nut (*supārī, supyārī, areca catechu*) into cinders and pounding it fine. Missī (*mis*, 'copper'), a powder composed of yellow myrobalan, gall-nut, iron filings, and vitriol, much used in India to strengthen the teeth and reduce their whiteness, is seldom applied by modest women in Sind.[3] But Indian Musalmān women plead that it is lawful because Fātima, daughter of the Prophet, used it. The following is the best prescription : gall-nut (*māphal, mājūphal, quercus infectoria*) 2 oz. ; bluestone, blue vitriol (*nīlā tūtiyā*) 2 drachms ; steel filings (in the Deccan, *bīr*) 1 oz. ; chebulic or black myrobalan (*hardā, harrā, harlā, terminalia chebula*) ½ oz. ; acacia flowers (*kīkar kī phalī, acacia arabica*) ½ oz. ; some

[1] Burton, *Sind Revisited*, 278 ; *AN*. ii. 62 ; Lane, *ME*. i. 51 ; *Korān*, xxvii. 44, with Sale's note.

[2] *Mishkāt*, i. 88 ff.

[3] Burton, *Sindh*, 266.

lime juice. Pound and sift the vitriol, mix it with the steel filings, add the lime juice, and put the compound into the sun to dry, that is, until the mixture turns black, which will be in about two hours; then pound this as well as the other ingredients, sift and keep for use.

The eyes are painted with Surmā and Kājal. Surmā, Ismid, Kohl, Kuhl, is properly antimony, but much of the so-called antimony sold in the Indian bazars is really galena, imported from Kābul and Bokhāra. It has been used from time immemorial in India and other parts of the East.[1] It is applied with a probe (*mikhal*) in a very fine powder to the eye, or on the inside of the eyelids, to improve the brightness of the eyes not, as commonly supposed, on the eyelashes or outside lids, for which Kājal is used. It is said to give the eye the shape of an almond (*bādām chashm*).[2] It is the eye-paint of Scripture,[3] and it is said to be a great preservative of sight in the glare of the desert and checks ophthalmia. A legend tells that when God commanded Moses to ascend the Koh-at-Tur (Mount Sinai) to show him His countenance, he exhibited it through an opening the size of a needle's eye, at the sight of which Moses fell into a trance, and on waking saw the mountain on fire. The mountain thus addressed the Almighty, 'Why hast thou set me on fire, who am the least among mountains?' Then the Lord commanded Moses, 'Henceforth thou and thy posterity shall grind the earth of this mountain and apply it to your eyes'. Hence Surmā is supposed to be the miraculous substance thus created. The tale current in the Panjāb is that a Faqīr from Kashmīr came to Mount Karanglī in the Jhīlam District and turned it into gold. The people fearing that in time of war it would be plundered, by means of a spell turned the gold into antimony, which is now washed down by the rain from the mountain. It is said that if it is used for eight days it will restore the sight of those who have become blind by disease or by accident, but not of those born blind.[4] It was recommended by the Prophet to strengthen the sight and to

[1] Rajendralala Mitra, *The Indo-Aryans*, ii. 146.
[2] Sir A. Burnes, *Cabool*, 95.
[3] 2 Kings ix. 30; Jer. iv. 30; Ezek. xxiii. 40; Burton, *AN*. i. 54.
[4] *PNQ*. iv. 9.

make the eyelashes grow.[1] Kājal, or lampblack, is collected on an earthen plate held over an oil lamp and kept in a box (*kajlautī*). It is applied to the outer lids and eyelashes of women and children as a protection against sun glare and to ward off the Evil Eye. For this latter purpose it is applied to the eyes of a bridegroom by his brother's wife as he starts to etch his bride.

Henna (*menhdī*) is a preparation of the leaves of *Lawsonia ılba*, cultivated throughout India for this purpose and also tound as a hedge plant. Its effects on the skin are those of an astringent or dye, and it improves the hair. The dry leaves are pounded in water or rice gruel ten or twelve hours before use, and then it should be exposed to the sun or to gentle heat. It is applied to the roots of the hair with a brush, after the hair has been cleaned with soap or pearl ash. In five or six hours a deep brick-dust hue is produced, which is converted by the use of a paste of indigo into a bottle-green, and finally into a jetty, lustrous, crow's wing colour. Women often tinge with it only the tips of their fingers and the toe nails, while others make a stripe across the knuckles. The shade varies from light orange to deep scarlet, and to olive when long applied. It is extensively used in the marriage rites. The use of it by women is not mere caprice, as it checks perspiration in the hands and feet, and produces an agreeable and healthful coolness.[2]

Safflower (*kusum*, *carthamus tinctorius*) produces a beautiful red dye which is prepared as follows. Take of the dried flowers 2 lb., put them in a towel suspended by its four corners on sticks fixed in the ground, pour cold water on them and rub the flowers in it as long as the stained water remains yellow. When it begins to get red, squeeze the water out of the flowers and spread them out. After sprinkling them with 2 oz. barilla (*sajjīkhār*), mix them well together. Put the flowers again on the suspended cloth, and pour on them three jars of cold water, keeping the strained liquid from each jar separate.

[1] *Mishkāt*, i. 371 ; ii. 364.

[2] Burton, *Sind Revisited*, i. 324 ; *Mishkāt*, ii. 363. The 'camphire' of the Song of Solomon, i. 14 ; iv. 13 A.V. is rightly translated 'henna' in R.V.

Add to these the juice of 20 or 25 lemons, which will change the liquid into a beautiful colour. In dyeing cloth it is first soaked in the liquor of the faintest colour, then in that which is darker, and lastly in the darkest, leaving it in each only a few seconds or minutes. The colour is fugitive, and so far no method has been discovered to make it permanent.[1] Safflower has a mystic significance, and cloths of this shade are used at marriages and in various magical rites.

Various kinds of perfumed powders are in common use. 'The perfumes for men shall have smell, but not colour; the things that women rub on must have colour but not smell'.[2] Chiksā is a perfumed powder composed of a variety of odoriferous substances. Take of mustard seed, aloe seed, cotton seed, 8 oz. of each; wheat or gram flour, 8 oz.; fenugreek seed, 8 oz.; turmeric coloured zedoary, 4 oz.; rush-leaved cyperus, 1½ oz.; poppy seed, sandalwood, leaves of sandal, of each 6 drachms, and various other aromatic substances. The fenugreek seed is toasted and mixed with the other ingredients. In using this powder it is generally mixed with sweet-scented oil (*phulel*) instead of water. Poorer people use much fewer ingredients in preparing it.

Abū-l-fazl mentions three varieties of sandalwood (*sandal, chandan, santalum album*): white, yellow, and red. The best is the Macassar (*magāsarī*), which is yellow and oily.[3] The references throughout this work are not to the sandalwood itself but to a perfumed embrocation made by rubbing a piece of the wood on a stone (*sandalāsā, sandlāsā*). There are special rules for applying it. This is done with the right hand, and invariably to the right side of the neck first, drawing the fingers held apart from behind forwards, so as to leave four distinct streaks. Then the same is done to the left side, and afterwards the abdomen is merely touched with the forefinger dipped in the paste, meaning, 'May your offspring enjoy good health!' Lastly, the back is touched in the same way, meaning, 'May all your relations continue well!' Its use for

[1] Saiyid Muhammad Hadi, *Monograph on Dyes and Dyeing in the North-west Provinces and Oudh*, 9 ff.

[2] *Mishkāt*, ii. 361.

[3] *Āīn*, i. 80; Watt, *Comm. Prod.* 72 ff.

ceremonial purposes is much more common in southern than in northern India.

Agar, agarā, calambac, aloe or eagle wood is the aloes or lignum aloes (*aquillaria agallocha*) of the Scriptures. When thrown into fire it smokes and gives a pleasant perfume. It is prepared in pastilles, which are sometimes confounded with those made of benzoin or styrax. They are composed of aloe wood, sandalwood, benzoin, patchouli, liquidambar, storax, yew leaves, mastic, with sugar-candy or gum. These are pounded fine, mixed up with rose-water and made into pastilles. The best come from Bījāpur in the Deccan.

Argajā is a yellowish coloured perfume, of which the common variety is a mixture of sandalwood, wood aloes, and some odoriferous oil. The following is good receipt : Grind sandalwood and wood aloes with rose-water, add oil of aloes wood, civet, of each 2 māshās or 34 grains ; '*itr* or otto of roses, jasmine oil, of each ¼ rupee weight ; mix all together and rub the perfume over the body.

Otto, or '*itr* of roses, is said to have been invented by the mother of the Empress Nūrjahān on her marriage with Jahāngīr.[1] In India it is chiefly produced by the distillation of *Rosa damascena.* It is made by allowing the distilled rose-water (*gulāb*) to rest for the night, the thin film of otto being skimmed off in the morning. It is offered to guests on a little cotton, twisted on the end of a short stick. At entertainments rose-water is served in a long-necked silver bottle (*gulābpāsh*), perforated with holes at the top like a muffineer, out of which it is sprinkled over the guests.[2]

Abīr is a grateful perfumed powder, the simplest and most common variety of which is made of rice flour or powdered mango or deodār cyperus mixed with camphor and aniseed. A superior variety is made of powdered sandalwood, zedoary, rose flowers, camphor, and civet, all pounded, sifted, and mixed. The dry powder is rubbed on the face and body and sprinkled on clothes to scent them. A powder of the same name, used by Hindus to fling about at the Holī festival, was formerly made of the rhizome of *Curcuma zedoaria,* powdered, purified, dried, and mixed with a decoction of sappan wood. A similar powder

[1] Elliot-Dowson, vi. 338. [2] Watt, *Econ. Dict.*, vi, part 1, 561.

was found in a casket recovered from a Buddhist Stūpa at Sopārā.[1] The flowers are laid in eight or ten layers, each separated by a layer of sesamum seed, which after being left all night is then put out to dry. This process is repeated for ten days when the scented sesamum is put in bags or jars and finally ground in a press (*kolhū*), from which the oil drops into a vessel. It is finally stored in leather bottles. That used by Hindus at the Holī is usually made of barley, rice flour or that of the *Singhārā* nut (*traba bispinosa*), mixed with a red dye.

The term Ispand or Sipand is incorrectly applied in southern India to the seeds of henna (*menhdī*, *Lawsonia alba*). It is properly *Peganum harmala*, the seeds of which are often burnt near the sick with the object of repelling evil spirits and the Evil Eye. It has been suggested that this action may exercise some useful effect as an antiseptic.[2] It is presumably from its connexion with spirits that in northern India Hindus of high caste will not touch it, and leave it to the sweepers. Akbar used to keep an official called Sipandsoz to protect his horses from spirits, and seeds of Indian colza (*sarson*, *sinapis glauca*) were used in the same way.[3] It is also burnt during the forty days after parturition, particularly at the door of the house whenever a visitor departs, as well as when the infant is taken out of the room to be bathed and when it is brought back. It is generally thrown into the fire with some benzoin or benjamin, or with mustard seed and patchouli. The use of incense is unknown in Musalmān religious worship, but it is permissible to fumigate the corpse, to burn it at the tombs of Saints and in certain rites of exorcism and magic. The best kind is frankincense, derived from varieties of the *Boswellia*, but cheaper substitutes are also used. Foul-smelling substances, like leather, are burnt to repel evil spirits.

Whenever the use of flowers is mentioned in these pages the reference is generally to garlands, nosegays, and the like, not to single flowers. The forms in which they are used are carefully distinguished : Baddhī, a long flower chain or garland worn by bride and bridegroom round the neck, hanging to the waist and crossing behind and before ; Gajrā, a flower bracelet shaped like

[1] *BG.* xiv. 411 f.
[2] Watt, *Econ. Dict.*, vi, part 1, 126, 135.
[3] *Āīn*, i. 139.

a carrot (*gājar*) ; Gend gahvārā, flowers formed like the scale of a balance, and offered in discharge of a vow ; Hār, a string of flowers worn as a necklace and hanging down the breast ; Jālīmuīband, flowers forming a sort of network veil tied to the forehead and covering the front part of the head, worn only by women ; Pākhar, ' iron armour such as that worn by men and horses ', an ornament of flowers intended to represent armour, thrown over the head and body of a horse ; Phūl kā chādar, flowers arranged in the form of a sheet, spread on graves ; Sarpech, sarposh, a string of flowers worn round the head by women ; Sehrā, seharā, an arrangement of flowers tied on the forehead, covering the eyes like a veil, worn by bride and bridegroom to protect them from the Evil Eye ; Turra, a nosegay or bouquet, sometimes used as a flower ornament for the hair.

CHAPTER XXXIII

JEWELLERY

The jewellery worn by Musalmāns presents great differences of type and fashion, but there is little that is really distinctive, both men and women often wearing patterns closely resembling those of the Hindus, this being particularly the case among the many converts from Hinduism to Islām, though, of course, the use of symbols or figures of Hindu deities are avoided. Musalmāns as compared with Hindus do not invest so much of their savings in jewellery to be sold in times of need. In some parts of the country there is a prejudice against wearing gold on the feet. Some classes forbid their women to wear anything save gold above the feet, but silver may be used in the form of anklets or toe-rings, and if this is not procurable some cheaper substance like pewter or bell-metal is used.[1] In the time of the Prophet, when the type of daily life was simpler, the wearing of gold rings was prohibited.[2] Among Musalmāns, as among Hindus, the primary intention in wearing jewellery is not for ornament, but to secure protection against the Evil Eye and the attacks of spirits. Hence comes the use of things supposed to possess spirit power, such as the wood or leaves of certain trees and plants, the hair or claws of tigers or parts of other animals.[3] Men, as a rule, wear little jewellery except as amulets, but among the rich trading classes in western India, like the Bohrās or Memans, the wearing of necklaces, wristlets, ear-rings, bangles, finger rings, collarettes, or gold chains is common.

According to a Rabbinical legend adopted by Islām, Sarah,

[1] *Census Report*, Central India, 1901, i. 208.

[2] *Mishkāt*, ii. 348, 353. According to Ferishta (iii. 244), Husain Nizām Shāh, King of Ahmadnagar (A.D. 1553–65), on one occasion, after prayers, observing that he was wearing a girdle of gold, recollected that it was unlawful to pray while wearing it, cast it off and repeated his prayers.

[3] *BG.* xviii, part 1, 106, 547 ff.

when she was jealous of Hagar, declared that she could not rest till her hands were stained with the blood of her rival. So Abraham pierced Hagar's ears and Sarah was thus able to stain her hands with the blood. Hence came the use of ear-rings. Musalmān women usually wear these rings fixed all along the outer border of the ear, often four to eleven in each, the left having invariably one less than the right. The Traditions declare, 'Whoever likes to put into the nose or ear of his friend a ring of hell fire, let it be a gold ring ; wherefore be it on you to make your ornaments of silver '.[1] But this law is now generally ignored, and many Musalmān women wear a gold nose ring (*nath*) in the left nostril, and another (*bulāq*) in the central cartilage. Many women wear round their necks, strung with black thread, silver cases containing a verse from the Korān, some charm, or some animal or vegetable substance. 'Verily spells and tying round the necks of children the nails of tearing animals, and the thread which is tied round a woman's neck to make her husband love her, all these are of the polytheists '.[2] Among Musalmān women in southern India the ear is often dilated widely by the use of pegs or pledgets of cloth, each of a size larger than the last. Among Hindus and some Musalmāns in the Central Provinces, if the flesh of the ear thus dilated happens to be torn by accident or in a scuffle, the woman is regarded as defiled and has to undergo special purification. In north India young children, otherwise naked, wear some protective hung from the waist to repel the Evil Eye. In the south little girls wear a 'fig-leaf' of silver with the same object, while little boys wear a conical, elongated object, both amulets having a phallic significance.[3]

[1] *Mishkāt*, ii. 355. [2] Ibid. ii. 376, 377.

[3] *JRAI.* xxxviii. 194 ; Thurston, *Castes*, vi. 113. On Musalmān jewellery, see Sir E. Maclagan, *Monograph on Gold and Silver work in the Punjab* ; T. C. Hendley, *Journal of Indian Art*, 1906–7 ; B. H. Baden-Powell, *Handbook of the Manufactures and Arts of the Punjab*, 175 ff. ; T. N. Mukarji, *Art Manufactures of India*, 97 ff.

CHAPTER XXXIV

FOOD AND DRINK

MUSALMĀNS submit to few of the vexatious restrictions which the rules of caste impose upon Hindus, but their association with this people suggests taboos in the use of certain foods, some of which are of foreign origin and come down from the early days of Islām. According to the *Kansu-l-daqāiq* and the *Shar'-i-wāqiāt*, the flesh of certain animals is unlawful, that of others prohibited. The flesh of those that are cloven-footed, those that chew the cud, and are not beasts of prey, is lawful food, such as that of sheep and goats, deer, antelopes, the hare, the rabbit, the cow, bull, female and male buffalo, &c. Those that are neither cloven-footed nor chew the cud, like the jackass, &c., are unlawful. Others which though cloven-footed do not chew the cud, or those which have merely canine teeth, are unlawful, such as the hog, wolf, jackal, tiger, bear, hyaena, and the like. 'That which dieth of itself, and blood and swine's flesh, and that over which any other name than that of God hath been invoked, is forbidden to you. But he that shall partake of them by constraint, without lust or wilfulness, no sin shall be upon him. Verily God is Indulgent, Merciful '.[1] Although the Imām 'Azam, Abū Hanīfa of Kūfa, has pronounced horseflesh unlawful, his disciples contradict this, and, therefore, some considering it improper (*makrūh*), that is to say, things from which the Prophet abstained yet did not forbid to others, eat of it. But most people regard it as unlawful food. Of birds, all those that catch prey with their claws or tear it with their teeth, are unlawful, such as the sparrow-hawk (*shikrā, micronisus badius*), the peregrine falcon (*bahrī, falco peregrinus*), and the goshawk (*bāz, astur palumbarius*), the kite, crow, vulture, bat, kingcrow,

[1] *Korān*, ii. 167.

owl, and others of a like kind. Such as do not seize their prey with their talons, but pick up food with their bills are lawful, such as the paddy-bird (*bagulā, baglā, ardea torra*), duck, peacock, partridge, quail, goose, snipe, dove, pigeon, and the like. Locusts may be eaten, but all creeping things, like scorpions, snakes, earthworms, and so on, are unlawful. Those that live in water are all unlawful except those with scales and the eel (*bām*), the lamprey (*tanbū*), the Katarnā, a little-valued fish, which are improper but not prohibited, and those that do not weigh less than a Dirham or drachm or more than 1½ Man, 120 lb. Others which do not answer these conditions are unlawful, such as alligators, turtles, frogs, crabs, and the like. Shrimps, however, are only prohibited (*makrūh*) and may be eaten. Fish found dead in water are unlawful food, but if they be taken out and die afterwards, this is held to be equivalent to ritual slaughter (*zabh*).

The use of wine or spirits (*sharāb*),[1] hemp (*gānjā, bhang*), fermented palm juice (*tārī*), opium (*afīm, afyūn*), preparations of opium (*madad, madak, madat*), opium extract (*kusumbhā*) and the electuary (*ma'jūn*), with other intoxicating liquors, are forbidden. Under the general head of intoxicants (*khamr*) alcohol and narcotics are generally included. If, however, prohibited substances, like hog's lard, are prescribed by a physician, when in his opinion they are needed to save the life of the patient it is lawful to use them, but not otherwise. Water should not be drunk while standing, except in three cases : the water of the holy well Zamzam, water and other drinks distributed on the road to those engaged in processions (*sabīl*), and water used for the lesser ablution (*wuzū'*).

Among the more learned and enlightened Musalmāns it is now generally admitted that there are no grounds for their refusal to eat with the 'people of the Book' (*ahl-i-kitāb*), that is to say, with Jews and Christians. This feeling which prevails among the less advanced Indian Musalmāns is mainly due to race jealousy, and restrictions borrowed from the Hindus, and in some parts of the country it shows signs of abating.

Among Musalmāns, as the term for ritual slaughter (*zabh*) implies, the killing of animals for food is in the nature of

[1] *Korān*, ii. 216.

a sacrifice, a feeling which also prevails among Hindus.[1] An animal becomes legally fit for food when it is killed by any 'man of the Book', Musalmān, Jew, or Christian, by drawing the knife across the windpipe, gullet, and carotid artery, but if only two of these are divided the meat is unlawful (*harām*). Low-class Musalmāns are not always careful to see that the throat is cut before life has actually ceased. The formula used is 'Bismi'llāhi Allāhi Akbar', 'In the name of God, the Most Great!'

A rich Musalmān in Gujarāt takes three meals a day: seven o'clock breakfast of tea and coffee with sweets; a midday meal of unleavened bread, soup, minced savoury meat, cream, vegetables, and sometimes rice; about 7 p.m. a meal of rice and pulse or rice boiled with meat, with clarified butter or ghī, and some kind of meat and fish and a dish made of curds, mangoes, lemons, or plantains. Middle-class people eat three less elaborate meals. The poor generally have two meals: breakfast about 11 a.m. of millet cakes; at 7 p.m. rice and pulse with a little clarified butter, and as a relish onions or chillies with water to drink.[2]

Hindus use vessels made of brass and other alloys, Musalmāns only those of copper, which they are supposed to keep carefully tinned. Instead of the Hindu water-pot (*lotā*) they use a vessel with a spout (*badhnā*),[3] a pot (*katorā*) for cooking vegetables, another (*degchī*, *patelī*) for cooking meat, a kind of tray (*lagan*), and a glass (*gilās*) of tinned copper.

In Gujarāt 'in a rich or middle-class household, for the ordinary day meal the whole family meet in one of the rooms of the ladies' apartments, and with a servant to bring in the dishes, men and women eat together. In poor families where the woman has to work, the men generally eat first and the

[1] The Desasht Brāhmans of the Deccan eat only the meat of a sacrificed goat (*BG.* xvii. 51), and the priests of the Kālī temple at Calcutta sell the flesh of the victims, the sanctity of the place and rite removing the taboo, to Hindus (Ward, *The Hindoos*, ii. 127); cf. Manu, *Laws*, v. 7. This was also the custom of the Achaemenian Kings of Persia (Maspero, *Passing of the Nations*, 593 f.).

[2] *BG.* ix, part 2, 109; cf. Lane, *ME.* i. 169 f.; Hughes, 103 f.

[3] This is believed to be due to the belief in the necessity of using flowing water for ablution.

women after they have dined. As a rule, only very near relations are allowed to dine with the family. But as a mark of special trust well-tried friends are sometimes allowed to share the privilege. The room is made ready for dinner by laying a white-coloured or printed cloth (*dastarkhwān*)[1] over a part of the carpet, and by setting a china or earthenware cup and plate, with one or two spoons, a metal bowl or glass tumbler to drink from, and a napkin for each person. Fruit is laid beside the cups and plates. When dinner is ready the party sit down on cushions ranged round the cloth or on the carpeted floor. The host first seats himself at the head of the cloth, the rest of the family taking their places according to choice. Before eating, a brass or silver ewer (*āftāba*) with a basin is handed round by a servant, each person holding his hands over the basin on which water is poured and flows into the basin. After this the more religious before each mouthful say 'Bismillāh', 'In the name of God!' Then the dishes are handed round by a servant or passed round, each guest helping himself. A water jar stands by the cloth and the guests fill their cups from it as they need. At the close the servant again brings round the ewer and basin and the hands are washed. The children are generally the first to leave, and the elders, both men and women, if they have no special business, sit smoking or chewing betel leaf. Among many families meals, especially dinner, are merry, with much talk and laughter.[2]

The staple dishes of Musalmāns are Pulāo or stew, Khicharī or rice boiled with pulse, and Kabāb or roast meat.

There are many varieties of Pulāo. The terms Yakhnī, 'cooked', or Khārā, 'saltish', are applied to the complicated stew or broth made of rice and meat. The common kind is made of rice, clarified butter, curds, and spices, such as cummin,

[1] This represents the Arab Sufra, or skin receptacle for holding food, on which the meal is spread, a relic of nomadic life (Burton, *Pilgrimage*, i. 76; *AN*. i. 164).

[2] *BG*. ix, part 2, 111 f.; Lane, *ME*. i. 179 ff. There is a good account of a feast at the house of a Musalmān noble in E. Terry, *Voyage to East India*, ed. 1777, p. 195 ff. Compare a painting of a feast in Smith, *HFA*, plate cxviii, p. 472. The entertainments in gardens, which form such pleasing incidents in the life of the higher classes in Persia, are hardly known to Indo-Musalmāns (Wills, 311 ff.).

cardamoms, cloves, cinnamon, coriander, coriander leaves, black pepper, green ginger, onions, garlic, and salt. Take half a ser or about 1 lb. mutton, four or five whole onions, a piece of green ginger, two dried cassia leaves, eight corns of black pepper, six quarts of water ; boil together in an earthen vessel until 1½ or 2 quarts remain ; mash the meat with the liquor and strain the broth (*yakhnī*). Put ½ lb. butter into a tinned copper vessel and melt, frying in it the onions cut into long slices until they become reddish. In the butter which remains fry a fowl which has been already boiled, take it out and fry the dry rice in the butter. As the butter evaporates add the broth and boil the rice in it. Then put in 10 or 12 cloves, 10 or 12 peppercorns, 4 pieces of mace, 10 or 12 small cardamoms, all whole, one dessertspoonful of salt, a piece of sliced ginger, and 2 dried cassia leaves. When the rice is done, remove all the fire from below the pot except a very little, and place it on the cover of the pot. If the rice is hard add a little water and put in the fowl, so that it may imbibe the flavour. When serving, put the fowl on a dish and cover it with the rice, garnishing the latter with a few hard-boiled eggs cut in two and the fried onions. The difference between a Pulāo and a Chulāo is that in the former the mixture is done by the cook, in the latter by the guest, who takes with the plain rice whatever delicacy he pleases.

Other varieties of Pulāo are Bābūnē, flavoured with camomile ; Qorma, made like ordinary Pulāo except that the meat is cut into very thin slices ; Mīthā or ' sweet ', made of rice, sugar, butter, spices, and aniseed instead of ginger ; Muza'far sholā, ' saffroned ', made with rice, saffron, milk, rose-water, and sugar, thin and cooling ; Muza'far Pulāo or Shahsranga, ' six-coloured ', like the last, but not so watery ; Tarī Pulāo, made of rice, meat, turmeric, and butter ; Soyā or dill (*peucedanum graveolens*) Pulāo is made with dill added ; Machchhī, Māhī, ' fish ', Pulāo has fish instead of meat ; Imlī, ' tamarind ' Pulāo contains tamarind ; Dampukht, ' steamed ' Pulāo is made by adding the butter when nearly cooked and steaming ; Zarda, ' yellow ' Pulāo has saffron added ; Kūkū Pulāo is made with fried eggs ; Dogoshta, ' two meats ', is made of rice, meat, butter and spices, excessively hot ; Pulāo maghzīāt, ' brain, marrow', is Mīthā Pulāo with the addition of almonds, pistachio nuts, or other fruits; Biryānī, 'fry', is made with marrow, plenty of spices, limes, cream, and milk: Take 2 lb. raw meat, cover with curds, ginger, garlic, and salt, lay aside for three hours, fry 2 oz. of sliced onions and 12 oz. butter in an earthen pot, take out the onions and three-quarters of the butter and remove it from the fire. Then boil 2 lb. meat in water, scatter half the boiled rice on the fried meat, sprinkle it with spices and onions, pour a little butter on it, repeat the layers of meat, rice, spices, onions, and butter as before. Then pour a little milk over the whole sufficient to soften the rice. Make the earthen pot air-tight with pulse flour and cook on a charcoal fire; Mutanjan (*mutajjan*, 'fried in a pan') Pulāo has meat, rice, butter, and sometimes pineapples and nuts; Kash, Halīm, Būnt or Chanē kī dāl Pulāo is made of gram, wheat, meat, and spices; Labnī Pulāo is made of cream in a silver dish, with nut kernels, sugar-candy, butter, rice, and spices, particularly aniseed; Jāman Pulāo is made of the Jāman fruit (*eugenia jambolana*); Tītar, 'partridge', Pulāo is like Yakhnī, but partridges are used instead of meat; Bater Pulāo, as its name implies, is made of quails; Kofta of forced meat balls highly spiced; Khārī thalī of meat with wheat flour or pulse: Khārī chakolī of meat, vermicelli, and green pulse.

Khicharī, the Anglo-Indian Kedgeree, is thus made: 4 oz. mūng pulse (*phaseolus radiatus*) fried slightly in a little butter, a process called *baghārna*. Sprinkle a little water on it while it is on the fire and then boil it in ¾ pint water in a tinned copper vessel. When it is soft take it off the fire, put 4 oz. butter into another smaller vessel and when it is melted throw into it a handful of sliced onions. Fry till they become reddish and then remove from the fire. To the remaining butter add 8oz. washed rice and fry a little. Then add the pulse with the water in which it was boiled and two pieces of sliced ginger. When the water has nearly evaporated reduce the fire below and put the rice on a pot cover and shake it (*dam dena*, 'to give it breath'), but before doing so add 10 or 12 cloves, a couple of pieces of mace, 10 or 12 peppercorns, 2 dried cassia leaves, a dessertspoonful of salt and cover up. This is Safed or 'white' Khicharī. When a yellow colour is desired add pounded turmeric about the size of a pea with the pulse. When served up, decorate with four hard-boiled eggs and the fried onions. Ubālī or 'boiled' Khicharī is made of rice, pulse, hot and cold spices, the former being pepper, cloves, mace, cinnamon, cardamoms, cubebs ; the latter chillies, onions, garlic, ginger, coriander, cummin seed, tamarind, &c. Kash Khicharī is the same as the last with the addition of meat. Bagharī or Qabūlī Khicharī is like Ubālī, but made with butter, and Bhūnī, or 'roasted' Khicharī, has still more butter. Khichrā is made of rice and wheat with as many kinds of pulse as possible : *tor* (*cajanus indicus*), *chanā*, gram (*cicer arietinum*), *mūng* (*phaseolus radiatus*), *lobiā* (*vigna catjang*), *balar* (*dolichos lablab*), *masūr* (*lens esculentus*). Sholā is Khicharī with meat, Shartāwā, without meat, made thin.

Rice (*chāwal*). Rice is prepared in various ways : Khushkā or Bhāt, boiled ; Ubālā, parboiled and dried in the sun, a form in which it is much used and preferred, as it has a richer flavour ; Kānjī, in the Deccan *gānjī*, is rice gruel ; Turānā, Bāsī khānā is boiled rice kept in cold water over-night, and used by the poor next morning when it has become sour ; Chalāū or Baghārā khushkā is fried rice ; Gulathī, rice boiled to a pap to which butter is added, recommended as easy of digestion to those suffering from bowel complaints.

Bread (*rotī*) is leavened or unleavened. Nān or Rotī ma'talan is leavened bread baked in an oven, leaven instead of yeast being used, and the cakes pressed against the inner heated sides of the oven (*tannūr*) ; Bāqirkhānī, which is said to take its name from that of its inventor, one Bāqir Khān, differs from the last only in name ; Gāodīdā, 'ox eyed', is so called from its round shape ; Gāozabān, 'ox tongue', is of a long shape ; Shīrmāl is sweet, the flour being kneaded in milk ; Girdā or Nān dākhilā is large and round shaped ; Qurs, round, like the sun's disk ; Phulkā, 'swollen', Khamīr phulkā, or Nān pāo is made with yeast in small flat cakes ; Khamīrī rotī, or leavened bread, is that used by Europeans. Unleavened bread is of many kinds : Rotī, unleavened wheaten cakes baked on an earthen or iron plate (*tawā*) of which the common Chapātī is a smaller and thinner kind ; Samosā or Sambusā, a three-cornered piece of pastry made of mincemeat ; Mīthī Pūrī, thin sweet cakes fried in butter or oil ; Parātā, a roll made of flour and butter ; Phīkī Pūrī is plain, insipid fried cakes ; Khajūrī, 'like a date', is sweet bread shaped like a date, made of wheat flour, poppy seed, coco-nut kernel, mixed with water, cut in small pieces and fried ; Satparātī Rotī, 'seven crusted', is made of layers of thin cakes, every alternate one buttered and sprinkled with sugar, the whole fried in butter or toasted on an earthen or iron plate ; Phenī, 'foam like', is made like the last, but smaller in size and without sugar ; Matkulā is wheat flour paste, sweetened and formed into a long shape by hand-pressing, steamed like a boiled dumpling ; Baldār, 'twisted', is a wheaten cake with butter in separate layers, like our pastry; Pūrī are cakes fried in butter, made of three kinds with fruit, meat, and pulse, like patties ; Laungchirā, 'clove-like', or Besan kī Rotī, are cakes of gram flour, fried or plain ; Matthī Rotī or Qīmāq is made of flour, white of eggs and onions, fried in butter ; Chalpak, a thin cake fried in oil or butter ; Chīlā, a thin cake of pulse meal ; Khātā or Mīthī rotī, saltish or sweet bread ; Andon kī rotī, bread in which eggs are mixed ; Gulgulā, made of wheat flour, sugar, curds, with anise and cardamom seeds, made into balls or dumplings and fried in butter ; Dahī Barī, Māsh Dahī, flour of pulse (*phaseolus radiatus*) cooked with buttermilk ; Roghandār, bread with plenty of butter.

Roasts. Kabāb is meat cut into thin long pieces, dried in the sun and roasted by placing them on a spit over live coals or frying in butter. In North India Sīkh Kabāb consists of bits of meat with alternate slices of onion or other condiments, fixed on a spit and roasted over a bright charcoal fire. The Kabāb-farosh, or seller of such dainties, sells also Golā or balls of meat and Prasandā, a small cutlet-like delicacy prepared in a frying-pan. Koftē Kabāb is meat hashed with hot and cold spices, tamarind excepted, pounded in a wooden mortar, made into flat cakes and fried in butter ; Tikkī kā Kabāb is a South Indian name for similar meat balls, with spices and without tamarind, fried in butter ; Husainī Kabāb consists of pieces of meat with salt and lime juice and toasted over a fire. Shāmī, 'Syrian', Kabāb is chopped meat with all the aromatic and cold spices, except chillies and tamarind, green ginger, and lime juice, made about a finger thick and fried in butter. Kalejē kā Kabāb consists of the liver, heart, and kidneys, cut into small pieces fixed on a skewer and roasted with salt. Laddū Kabāb, which is shaped like the sweet balls of that name, is made of chopped meat with all hot and cold spices and aromatics, green ginger, and lime juice, formed into balls and roasted over a fire, the balls being tied up with string to prevent them from falling asunder. Patthar kā Kabāb, or 'stone-roast', is used on a journey, slices of meat being roasted on a stone which is heated by fire lighted on it. Machchhī kā Kabāb is roasted fish, Qaliyā, broiled meat dressed with any condiment and usually eaten with Pulāo.

Curries are of many kinds. To make Sālan, 'saltish, spicy', wash some meat in water, put it into an earthen or metal vessel and either let it boil in its own juice, which will be sufficient if the meat is tender, or add a little water. Then add butter and spices and stir it well. The following is a more common receipt for good curries: 4 oz. butter, or half that quantity if the meat is fat; or if a dry curry is desired, 2 oz. onions, 2 or 3 cloves of garlic, 3 drachms of turmeric, cummin, and coriander seed, 3 red chillies, 4 or 5 corns of black pepper, ½ oz. green ginger and a teaspoonful of salt. The spices are all to be ground separately on a stone (*sil*), adding a little water when the substance is dry, the coriander seed being previously toasted to improve its perfume. Put the butter into an earthen pot or tinned copper saucepan; fry half the quantity of onions cut in long slices in it, and when they have become yellow-brown in colour take them off and set them aside. Then add the remaining butter to the meat, mix it up with all the spices and cover it up; remove it occasionally, and before the meat is sufficiently done sprinkle a teaspoonful of water over it. If much gravy is required a proportionate quantity of water is added, but the drier a curry is the nicer it tastes. Dopiyāzā, so called because it contains a double quantity of onions (*piyāz*), and others have no gravy. The following ingredients are sometimes added to improve the flavour: dried cassia leaves, dried coco-nut kernels, or essence of coco-nut, made by rubbing rasped coco-nut with water through a coarse towel, tamarind water, green or dried mangoes, and other fruits, lemon grass (*cymbopogon nardus*), fenugreek, the leaves of which greatly improve a curry.

The varieties of materials used in curries is very great: various kinds of meat, flour of different kinds of grain, and vegetables which it is unnecessary to describe in detail.

Curry powder. The following is an excellent receipt for curry powder: Take of powdered turmeric 20 teaspoonfuls, red dried chillies or cayenne pepper 8 teaspoonfuls, coriander seed, cummin, dried cassia leaves, of each 12 teaspoonfuls, and mix them together.

Sweetmeats. The varieties of sweetmeats (*shīrīn, mithāī*) are innumerable. One of the favourite kinds, Halwā, is made as follows: Fine wheat flour (*sūjī*) 2 lb., fried in 1 lb. butter, to which add 4 to 6 lb. syrup, 3 rupees' weight of coco-nut kernel, $\frac{1}{3}$ rupee weight of spices, 1 stick cinnamon, 10 cloves, 10 cardamoms and a little aniseed, and mix over a fire. In Akbar's time Halwā was made of flour, sugar-candy, butter, 20 lb. of each, the whole providing 15 dishes.[1]

Sherbet (sharbat) is a solution of sugar in water or of sugar-candy in rose-water. If lime juice is added it is called Ābshorā. Another variety is made of the best Damascus plums in water, with lemon or orange juice and sugar. Other kinds are made from violets, honey, raisin juice, &c.

Pickles (*āchār*). To make mango pickle, take 300 green mangoes, split them in two, take out the stones and dry them in the sun for three days. Then take $4\frac{1}{2}$ oz. of turmeric, $3\frac{3}{16}$ oz. garlic, 6 lb. salt, $1\frac{1}{2}$ oz. mustard seed, and the same quantity of coriander seed toasted. Mix the spices together and lay the mixture in alternate layers with the mangoes. Add 9 oz. gingeli or sesamum oil, or as much as will cover them.

Curds, curdled milk (*dahī*). 'Dahī differs from curd as prepared in Europe in being practically sour boiled milk, the fermenting agent being added when it is nearly cold. And the milk being boiled immediately as obtained from the cow contains all its fat or butter. In this form it is called Sārā, and if kept hot may be accumulated for some days till sufficient has been collected to make Dahī. Whole-milk Dahī contains too much fat to be made into cheese. It is, in fact, cream cheese'.[2] The ferment used is a little stale Dahī, tamarind or lime juice.

[1] *Āīn*, i. 59.

[2] Watt, *Comm. Prod.* 474 f.

CHAPTER XXXV

INTOXICANTS, STIMULANTS

Opium (*afyūn, afīm*) is the inspissated juice of the opium poppy (*papaver somniferum*). It is used in various forms by Musalmāns, particularly by those living in cities, but in rural districts the habitual opium-eater, known as Afyūnchī, Afīmchī, Pīnak, 'drinker', or Shahdmakkhī, 'honey bee', from his fondness for sweets, is rarely seen. Opium is taken in the form of pills, followed by a little sugar or sweetmeats, or dissolved in water, and, if it is impure, strained or mixed with saffron. This last, the liquid form, is called Kusumbhā, 'saffron', and is commonly used by Rājputs.[1] It is often taken in moderate quantities to flavour tobacco and as a febrifuge and stimulant. Though much evil results from the excessive use of the drug, the demoralization said to be due to it has been much exaggerated. Very moderate consumers take about 1 Tolā, 180 grains Troy, 11·662 grammes per month, and the average consumption by an habitual opium-eater is believed to be about 5 Tolā per mensem. In some cases it has been reported that as much as a Tolā a day is taken boiled in milk. The worst forms of the drug are Chandū and Madak or Madad. Chandū is made by steeping opium in water till it becomes soft, when it is boiled and strained. It is thus reduced to syrup (*qiwām, qimām*), which is kept for use. The pipe (*bambū*) is cleaned with a wire (*girmit*) and the Chandū is heated in the flame of a lamp till it becomes soft, when a little is placed in the pipe-bowl (*dawāt*), lighted and inhaled. Madak or Madad is made from the syrup of opium as above described, or more usually from the inspissated juice (*pasewā*) of the opium, which separates as it dries after being collected from the capsules, and this juice when collected on rags is known in northern India as Kafā. This syrup is mixed with chopped betel leaves, paper, acacia leaves, cardamoms or chopped coco fibre, and it is sold in balls. Chandū is smoked in a

[1] Tod, *Annals of Rajasthān* (ed. 1920), i. 341, 541.

special pipe (*nigālī*), but Madak in the ordinary tobacco bowl (*chilam, mahrū*). A form of opium constantly mentioned by the older travellers is Post or Koknār, a decoction of opium capsules, which was administered by the Mughal Emperors to princes or other men of rank whom it was desired to reduce to idiocy or remove without scandal.[1]

Among the preparations of hemp, Bhang, also known as Siddhī, 'accomplishment',[2] Sabzī, 'green leaves', Thandāī, 'a cooling drink', Bijayā or Vijayā, 'conquering', Būtī, 'sprig, flower', is the dried larger leaves of either or both the male and female plants, whether wild or cultivated, of *Cannabis sativa.* Charas is the resinous substance that appears spontaneously on the leaves, stems, inflorescence, and fruits of the hemp plant when cultivated in cold and dry regions. Gānjā is the dried flowering tops of the cultivated female plants, which become coated with a resinous exudation from glandular hairs, very largely in consequence of their being deprived of the opportunity of forming seed.[3] Bhang is prepared by mixing black pepper with the hemp and crushing the mixture on a stone slab (*sil*) with a roller (*battā*). This is infused in water, strained and drunk. Bhang butter (*bhang ghī*) is made by boiling Bhang in milk, skimming off the cream and turning it into butter; it is used as an anaesthetic by native surgeons. In the Deccan the hemp leaves (*siddhī*) are washed in water to the amount of 3 drachms, to which are added 45 grains black pepper, cloves, nutmeg, and mace, of each 11¼ grains. This is triturated with 8 oz. water, milk, juice of water-melons, or cucumber seed, strained and drunk. It is often drunk without the spices, which are believed to make it more intoxicating.

In the case of Charas the exudation is collected by a man who covers himself with a blanket and runs through a hemp field, thus absorbing the gum with the dew adhering to the leaves. The blanket is then scraped, washed, and wrung. The products are made into an electuary of which five grains mixed

[1] J. Fryer, *A New Account of East India and Persia*, Hakluyt Society, i. 92; iii. 169; Bernier, *Travels*, 106 f.; Elliot-Dowson, vii. 131.

[2] The Siddhas, in Hindu belief, are semi-divine beings who dwell in the upper air.

[3] Watt, *Comm. Prod.* 258 ff.

with tobacco is smoked and proves speedily intoxicating. In Sind it is never eaten raw either for intoxication or as a medicine, but it is either smoked or eaten in the form of an electuary known as Ma'jūn. Bhang is said to terrify the consumer, to make him speak in an animated way, and to keep him armed against any efforts to make him reveal confidential matters.[1] Gānjā is used by rubbing the leaves between the hands and smoking it with tobacco, but it is also smoked by itself. Ma'jūn is an electuary taken internally by Musalmāns, particularly by the most dissolute, as a nerve stimulant, intoxicant, and for the relief of pain. An overdose not infrequently causes mental derangement. In the popular belief it gives intoxication (*kaifa*), vigour (*quwwat*), and it is used as an aphrodisiac. The chief ingredients of this electuary are Gānjā, milk, butter, poppy seeds, flowers of the Dhatūrā or thorn-apple, powder of Nux vomica and sugar. Another receipt is as follows: Take 2 quarts milk, put into it 2 lb. Gānjā leaves and boil till the liquid is reduced to 3 lb. Take out the leaves and coagulate the milk by adding a little sour milk (*dahī*). Next day churn it and separate the butter, adding wild cloves, nutmeg, cloves, mace, saffron, of each 3 drachms, sugar-candy 15 drachms, and boil till it forms an electuary. Or, more simply, the leaves of the hemp are fried in butter and strained and the residue is drunk with some sugar, or the liquor is boiled with sugar until it acquires a consistence sufficiently thick to form cakes when it cools. In the north of India 6 lb. of Bhang are added to 4 lb. clarified butter and 70 lb. sugar. The Bhang is soaked for a night in water and next day the water is drained off. A little butter is melted in a pan, and the Bhang is mixed with it. Water is then added, and the mixture is boiled until the Bhang becomes soft, when it is strained and pounded into a paste. This is then boiled with the rest of the sugar and milk. It is allowed to harden by drying and cut into small pieces. Two squares are enough to cause intoxication to an ordinary person. People seldom become used to taking Ma'jūn, and it is usually employed as a sexual stimulant and as an excitant to debauch.[2]

[1] Burton, *Sindh*, 169 f.; Balfour, *Cyclopaedia of India*, i. 337.
[2] Atkinson, *Himalayan Gazetteer*, i. 765 f.

Tobacco is known in northern India as Tambākū, the Indian form of the Spanish tobacco, from the American name of the plant, thus showing its foreign origin.[1] In the Deccan it is called Gudākū or Gurākū (*gur*, 'raw sugar', Telugu, *āku*, 'leaf'). Most Musalmāns smoke or chew tobacco, or use snuff, and women smoke and sometimes chew. In the Panjāb Shī'as smoke tobacco in a clay bowl (*chilam*), but the Mullās of the Sunnī Pathāns discourage smoking and the use of Charas.[2] Musalmāns very generally use the Huqqa or pipe with a stand, while Hindus often prefer the small hand pipe made of a coconut bowl, which can be handed from one man to another and carried while travelling. But the use of cigarettes is rapidly increasing. The right to use the caste or tribal pipe is carefully restricted, and exclusion from its use is a common form of social boycott (*huqqa pānī band karnā*, 'refusal to allow a man to smoke or drink water with his fellows'). In Lucknow, which is famous for its tobacco, it is made plain (*sādā*) or fermented (*khamīrā*). In the former the dried leaf is pounded and mixed with its own weight of coarse sugar (*shīrā*). Khamīrā tobacco is made by adding to the leaves musk and spices. Chewing tobacco (*khainī*, *sūrati*, 'from Surat') is steeped when green in red ochre and dried. The following are approved receipts for pipe tobacco in the Deccan: 8 lb. tobacco leaves, 8 lb. treacle, 1 lb. preserved apples, or, as a substitute, preserved pine-apple or jujube (*ber*, *zizyphus jujuba*), 1 lb. raisins, 1 lb. conserve of roses (*gulqand*). These are well pounded together in a wooden mortar, put into an earthen pot, the mouth of which is made air-tight, and it is buried underground for three months before being used. If spiced tobacco be desired, they add Pegu cardamoms, cubebs, sandalwood, patchouli, and spikenard, 8 oz. of each, and mix them well together before the

[1] Tobacco was introduced into northern India in 1604–5, and the historian, Asad Beg, gives a curious account of the first experiment of its use in Akbar's court. His Majesty, however, was advised not to use it (Elliot-Dowson, vi. 165 ff.; Smith, *Akbar*, 407 ff.). Doubtless to the Portuguese is due the credit of having conveyed both the plant and the knowledge of its properties to India and China (Watt, *Econ. Prod.* 796).

[2] Rose, iii. 184. On the prohibition of the use by Wahhābīs, see Palgrave, *Personal Narrative*, 283 f.

pot is buried. In the Panjāb the spices comprise preserved apple, conserve of roses, dried betel leaves, a kind of scented wood (*mushkbālā*), sandalwood, wild jujube, and the pulp of the Amaltās (*cassia fistula*). Tobacco without spices is considered the most wholesome, and if it is duly fermented underground it becomes mellow and agreeable. A mild tobacco (*halkā, phīkā*) is distinguished from the strong (*kaurā*) by placing a little on the tongue and seeing if it causes irritation. If a mild tobacco is desired, wash the leaves a few times in cold water and then dry in the sun, then pound. Another receipt is as follows: Take of good tobacco 40 lb., raw palmyra sugar 40 lb., *nagarmothā* (*cyperus rotundus*) 6 drachms, twenty ripe plantains, 10 wood apples, 6 drachms cloves. Pound all separately, except the tobacco and sugar. Then mix with them 4 lb. tobacco and sugar; make eight divisions of the remaining tobacco and sugar, grind one at a time well with the mass, add them all together and knead them well with the hands. Then bury the compound for a month in a dunghill.

The common tobacco pipe (*huqqā, qaliyūn*) consists of three parts: the bowl (*chilam*) containing the fire and the tobacco; the stem with the 'snake' (*naichā*) on which the pipe-head is fixed; the bowl containing water or rose-water. The pipe used by rich people is often a work of art. That used by middle and low-class people is of the same shape, but the bowl is of clay, the stem of wood, and a coco-nut shell serves as the water bowl.

Snuff (*sūnghnī, nās*) is dry tobacco powdered and perfumed. In eastern Bengal it is rarely used except medicinally, being said to cure headaches by eliminating morbid humours from the brain.[1] The best comes from Benares and Masulipatam.

For lighting the tobacco specially prepared balls of charcoal (*gul*) are used. They are made of tamarind or Pīpal (*ficus religiosa*) charcoal, mixed with acacia gum, molasses, and rice gruel.

The use of Betel (*pān*) is habitual among Indian Musalmāns of both sexes. Betel leaf is the produce of a perennial creeper (*piper betle*), probably introduced into India from Java. It has been used from very early times and is chewed generally in a packet (*bīrā*), among the lower classes the leaf being generally

[1] Wise, *Notes on Races, Castes, and Trades*, 113.

mixed with areca nut (*areca catechu*), known as Supārī, lime and Kath, a crystalline substance produced from the tree *Acacia catechu,* and by richer people with cardamoms, camphor, and other spices. 'It is somewhat astonishing that a narcotic stimulant so much used by all natives of India should have attracted so little attention in writings on medicine. . . . But no European physician in India seems to have experimented on the value of the drug as a tonic, stomachic, and slight stimulant. Acting on the great reputation enjoyed by Pān all over the East, and on the remarks made on the drug by such early travellers as Marco Polo, Dutch botanists and physicians have used it experimentally, and have come to the conclusion that the chewing of betel leaves does promote health in the damp and miasmatic climate of that country '.[1] The juice stains the teeth and mouth, and in popular belief it is an indispensable adjunct to a woman's beauty, and it is said to distinguish a man from a dog. The distribution of betel is a prominent act in the reception of visitors, when it is recognized as a sign of closing an interview, and at Darbārs or public levees. The usual etiquette is that when given from the hand it implies the superiority of the donor, when presented in a silver or gold box it implies equality. The giving of betel, probably owing to its supposed spirit power as a stimulant, assumes a sacramental form. Among the Rājputs it was given before going into battle or on dangerous service.[2]

[1] Watt, *Econ. Dict.* vi, part i, 255. On the popular view of the value of betel, see Elliot-Dowson, iii. 114 ; *Āīn*, i. 72.

[2] Tod, *Annals of Rajasthān*, i. 346, 381, 481, 552, 570 ; ii. 969, 1040.

CHAPTER XXXVI

GAMES

CHESS, one of the most universal games, known as Shatranj (*chaturanga*, 'an army arranged in four divisions'), is the only game allowed to be lawful by Musalmān doctors, because it depends wholly on skill and not on chance, but the Prophet is said to have denounced it.[1] The difference between European or Frankish (*farangī*) and Indian chess is thus stated by Sir R. Burton [2]: The queen is always placed to the right of the king; pawns never move two squares, and when one reaches the end of the board it is changed for the piece belonging to the particular square attained; a checkmate wins the game, but when the antagonist loses all his pieces, except the king of course, only half a game is reckoned. Finally, what we do in one move by castling with them takes three: the rook must be moved to the next square to the king; the king makes one move like a knight beyond the castle; the king takes the square next to the castle. The game called Turkish (*rūmī*) is puzzling to Europeans owing to the peculiar use of the queen and bishop. It invariably begins with the queen's pawn two squares and queen one square, after which the latter piece can move only one square obliquely, and must take other pieces and give check in the same way. The bishop moves obliquely like the queen, but passes over one square even when it is occupied by another piece. Another modification, originally derived from India, is called Band. Its chief peculiarity is that when any piece is defended by a second, provided the latter be not the king, the former cannot be taken. This, of course, protracts the game considerably, so that two or three days may elapse before checkmate can be given. Again, in

[1] Sale, *Korān*, 89, 93 note; *Mishkāt*, ii. 373. There is much dispute regarding the origin of the game (*EB.* vi. 100 ff.; H. J. R. Murray, *Hist. of Chess*, Oxford, 1913).

[2] *Sindh*, 292.

Indian chess the king makes a knight's move, and may only do so if he has not been checked. When making this move the king may not cross any square commanded by an opposing piece, nor may he move into check. In the first game either player may make the first move, but for the second game the winner of the first has the move.[1] Another very curious rule is that onlookers and visitors may express their opinions regarding the moves, and the players may not object. The onlookers have also the privilege of pointing out an illegal move.

In Ceylon the only variations from the English game are the absence of castling ; the additional power of the king to jump at any time as a knight until he has been once in check ; the limitation of the first move of the pawn to a single square ; when any pawns reach any of the last squares they can become only the piece that was in the same colour or line of squares originally, provided such piece has been originally captured by the enemy, so as to be available for replacing on the board.[2]

In Bombay 'as ordinarily played, chess differs from the European game only in one or two points. These are that only the pawns of the king, queen, and castles can at starting move two squares ; that the first move of the king when not under check may be the same as a knight's move ; that only the king's and queen's pawns can become queen ; and that, if it goes on till only five pieces are left, the game is drawn. As played it is noisier than the English game ; each player has several friends to back him, and every move is the subject of stormy discussion. Two other varieties of the game, the Persian and the Hindu, differ much from ordinary chess. The Persian game is called Zarāfa, 'beauty, ingenuity', played with more squares and pieces. The Zorībāzī, or Hindu game, uses the ordinary board and men, but with the rule that no covered piece can be taken '.[3]

Nard or backgammon is played by men who have been in Persia, or who have learned it from natives of that country or

[1] G. A. L. Sinha, *The Chess Amateur*, July, 1909.
[2] H. Parker, *Ancient Ceylon*, 586 : for chess in Persia, see Wills, 97.
[3] *BG.* ix, part 2, 173.

from Englishmen. Persians call it **Takht-ī-Nādir Shāh**, 'Nādir Shāh's throne'.[1]

Pachīsī is the most popular Indian game. The board consists of four triangles with their various sides so placed as to form a square in the centre. Each rectangle is divided into 24 small squares, each consisting of 3 rows of 8 squares each. It is usually played by four persons, each of whom is furnished with four ivory or wooden cones (*got*, *gotī*) of a peculiar colour for distinction, and takes his station opposite one of the rectangles. His pieces start one by one from the middle row of one of his own rectangles, beginning at the division next to the large central space. They then proceed round the outside rows of the board, passing, of course, through that of the adversaries' rectangles, travelling from right to left, i. e. contrary to the course of the sun, until they get back to the central row from which they started. Any piece, however, is liable to be taken up and thrown back to the beginning, as in backgammon, by any of the adversaries' pieces happening to fall upon its square, except in the case of the twelve privileged squares which are marked with a cross. In that case the overtaking piece cannot move from its position. Their motion is determined by the throwing of six or seven cowry shells used as dice, which count according as the apertures fall uppermost or not. One aperture up counts 10; two 6; three 3; four 4; five 25; six 30; seven 12; and if none be turned up it counts 6. A throw of 25 or 30 gives an additional move of 1. At the last step the throw must amount to exactly 1 more than the number of squares left to make the piece go into the central space, that is, as we should say, off the board. If it happens to stop in the last square, therefore, it cannot get off till the player throws 25 or 30. The players throw in turns, and each goes on till he throws a 2, 3, or 4, when he loses the lead. If the same number be thrown twice consecutively it does not count. The game is generally played with six cowries, making the highest throw 25, the six apertures up then counting 12. Hence it is termed Pachīsī from *pachīs*, 25.

[1] Nādir Shāh, King of Persia, sacked Delhi in A.D. 1739. For the game, see Burton, *Sindh*, 292; *AN.* x. 132. According to Ferishta (i. 150), it was invented by Būzrūj Mihr, minister of the Persian King, Nūshīrwān.

The board is used as a carpet, ornamented and marked with different colours of cloth sewn on it. It is sometimes played by two persons, each taking the two opposite rectangles with eight pieces, and playing them all from the rectangle next to him. The game continues till three of the players get out, and it is never played for money.[1]

Pachīsī is an ancient Hindu game, represented in a painting in the caves of Ajanta, and boards marked out in marble squares in a quadrangle in the Agra fort and at Fathpur Sīkrī were, it is said, the places where Akbar used to play the game, using slave girls as the pieces.[2] In Sind Chanarpisī is simpler than Pachīsī. The board is divided into twenty-five squares, and each player has four pieces with the same number of cowries. The latter are used like dice at backgammon to decide the number of squares to be moved over. The name is derived from *chanar*, the technical term when all four cowries fall to the ground with the slit upwards, and *pisī* when only one is in this position. The game may be played by either two or four persons, and he wins who first reaches the central square. Whenever a piece is in one of the crossed squares it cannot be taken by the adversary.[3]

Chausar, 'four-limbed', takes its name from the cross-like shape of the board. It is played chiefly by men, Pachīsī by women and the poor. The game is played either by four players with four counters each, or by two players with eight counters each. In shape the board is like a cross of four rectangles, the narrow sides placed so as to enclose a central space square in shape. Each rectangle is marked like a chess-board eight squares long and three broad. Starting one by one from the middle line of his own rectangle and from the square next the central space, the player sends his four cowries round the outer line of squares till they work back to the starting-point. The difficulty is that, as at backgammon, the pieces, unless protected, may be taken up by the other player, and have to begin again. The game goes on till three

[1] Sir E. B. Tylor, *JRAI.* viii. 116; Murray, *op. cit.* 31; Temple, *Legends of the Panjāb*, i. 244 f.; *BG.* ix, part 2, 173. On the Burmese form of the game, Shway Yoe, *The Burman*, ii. 83 f.

[2] *BG.* xii. 528; Syad Muhammad Latif, *Agra, Historical and Descriptive*, 86, 142.

[3] Burton, *Sindh*, 294.

of the players succeed in working their men round the board.[1]

Chaupar is played on a cloth board in the form of a cross. Each arm of the cross is divided into twenty-four squares in three rows of eight each, twelve red and twelve black. In the centre where the arms meet is a large black square. The cross is called Chaupar, the arms Phānsā, the squares Khāna. On this board are played two games called Chaupar, but technically one that is played with dice is called Phānsā and that played with cowries Pachīsī. Another variety is Chandal-mandal, a favourite game of Akbar.[2]

Dice are known as Pāsā or Dhārā, and the game Qimārbāzī or Jūābāzī. It is played with four-sided pieces of ivory, about two inches long and one-third inch in diameter. The sides are marked with an ace (*pāon*), deuce (*duo*), cinque (*panjo*), and sice (*chakko*).[3] A set of three dice is generally used, and when not combined with any other game, playing with these is called Jūā. No skill is required and the highest number wins. The game is prohibited by British law and forbidden in the Korān.[4]

Cards (*ganjīfa, tās*) are played with two kinds of cards: Angrezī or English, a pack containing 52 cards; Mughalī 96, the latter divided into eight suits, each of twelve cards: Bādshāh, 'king', Wazīr, 'prime-minister', and ten from 10 to ace. In Gujarāt in the common game three players use eight suits of round cards, twelve cards to each suit, i. e. 32 cards to each player. Of the eight suits four are major and four minor. The major are: Tāj, 'crown', Safed, 'white', with a mark representing the Moon, Ghulām, 'slave', Shamsher, 'sword'. The minor are Chang, 'bell', Surkh, 'red', with a mark representing the Sun, Barat, a 'Banker's bill', Kumāj, Kumāch, Kumāsh, 'an unleavened cake'. In the major suits the value of the cards runs: Bādshāh, 'king', Wazīr, 'prime-minister', 10, 9, and so on to ace; in the minor, Bādshāh, Wazīr, ace, 1, 2, and so on to 10, the lowest. The major cards of a suit are trumps. By day the Sun set, by night the Moon set is the superior. The person playing the Sun may

[1] *BG.* ix, part 2, 173.

[2] Temple, op. cit., i. 243 f.; *Āīn* i. 303 f. Plate xvii.

[3] Burton, op. cit., 293.

[4] ii. 216; v. 93.

be paid in cards of either description, discarding the lowest. Cards are shuffled before being dealt. He who holds the Sun starts the game in the day, and the holder of the Moon by night.[1] The game played by Akbar was more elaborate.[2] In north India the suits are : hearts (*pān,* ‘ betel ’), diamonds (*īnt,* ‘ brick ’), spades (*hukm,* ‘ order ’), clubs (*chiriyā,* ‘ bird ’). The cards from 1 to 10 are *ekkā, duggī, tiggī, chaukā, panjā, chakkā, satthā, atthā, nahlā, dahlā, Ghulām,* ‘ slave ’, knave, Bībiā, queen, and Bādshāh, king. The ace is the highest card of each suit. Three persons only play, and the two of diamonds (*īnt kī duggī*) is discarded, thus leaving 51 cards, of which 17 are dealt to each player. No trump is turned up, because spades are always trumps, and the holder of the ace of spades leads. There is no partnership, each player playing for himself. The play and deal pass to the right. To deal a card is *tās bāntnā,* to play a card *pattā phenknā,* to play winning cards *sar karnā.* Thus *tās* is the pack, *pattā* a single card. To lose is *khilāl* : *kis ke ūpar khilāl huā,* ‘ Who has lost ? ’ [3]

Miscellaneous games are very numerous. Odd and even (*tāq-juft, nakhā-mutth, bharmutth, Mughal-Pathān*) is played like draughts on a diagram sketched upon the ground, or on a board or paper, using sixteen cowries or ‘ men ’. A variety of this in the Deccan is Madrangam, played with four tigers and sixteen sheep. To fly kites is Patang or Kankawwā urānā. The game is played with great enthusiasm not only by boys, but by elderly men, the kite being square, without a tail, and the string strengthened with starch and covered with pounded glass to help in cutting the kite-string of an adversary.[4] Pigeon-flying is most favoured in cities, the owners frantically whistling and waving flags from the house-tops to recall their own or to entice the birds of a rival sportsman.[5] Akbar called it ‘Ishqbāzī, ‘ love-play ’, and delighted in it.[6] Chaugān or polo was a Mughal game and it was played by the earlier Sultāns of Delhi. About 1864 it was revived by Europeans, being copied from that played at Manipur on the eastern frontier, and Balti

[1] *BG.* ix, part 2, 173.
[2] *Āīn,* i. 306 ff.
[3] Hoey, *Monograph on Trade and Manufactures,* 188.
[4] Mrs. Meer Hassan Ali, 216 f.
[5] Manucci, i. 108.
[6] *Āīn,* i. 298 ff.

and Chitrāl on the north-west. Athletics include cricket, football, wrestling (*chatpat* in the Deccan, *kushtī* in north India), the use of heavy dumb-bells or clubs (*mugdar*), and raising and stretching the body on the feet and hands (*dand*). Games with fencing swords and quarterstaves form part of the Muharram celebrations. Cockfighting is still practised in out-of-the-way places, and Muhammadans keep fighting quails, amadavats (*lāl*), or partridges, but the keeping of such birds is generally confined to ne'er-do-wells.

The games of children[1] are like those played by Hindus. Among them may be mentioned : Aghūlzap, marbles, of which Ekparī-sabsarī, throwing marbles into a hole, is a variety ; Akalkhwājā is played with marbles and two holes, the player counting one each time his marble strikes another or goes into a hole ; Andhlā Bādshāh, ' the blind king ', is a kind of blind man's buff ; Ānkh michaulī, michhāwal, mundawwāl is blind man's buff, known in Bengal as Kānī makkhī, ' the one-eyed fly ' ; Bāgh bakrī is the game of tiger and goats, sometimes thirteen of each ; Baro-chhapjā, ektārā, dotārā is another kind of blind man's buff ; in Būjhā-būjhī a child's eyes are bound up and he is asked to tell who touched him, and until he succeeds in guessing he is not released ; of Būntī-chandū there are two varieties, one Urān-chandū, in which a cap is thrown into the air, and whoever catches it pelts the others with it as they run away, and Bamā-chandū, in which a stone is set up against a wall at which each boy aims his cap (*chandū*) three times, and whoever succeeds in knocking it down flings it at the others ; Chakrī, Chakkī is a bandalore, a small reel with a cord fixed in its centre which winds and unwinds itself alternately by the motion of the hand ; Chīl jhapattā, ' falling on one like a kite ', in which, if a boy raises his hands at the word ' *gadhā-pharphar* ', which he should not do, he is tickled by all the party ; in Ghirkā a stick is fixed in the ground with another across resting on a pivot, and a boy sitting at each end with their feet touching the ground whirl it round, the joint making a creaking noise ; Ghūm, ' turning ', is another game of the same kind in which boys hold a rope fastened to a pole fixed in

[1] For children's games in south India, see F. R. Hemingway, *Tanjore Gazetteer*, i. 65.

the ground and run round it ; Gillī-dandā is tip-cat, the gillī being a short stick struck by the other and longer one ; Gophiyā, guphnā, gophan is a sling used to discharge clay balls at birds ; Gulel is a pellet-bow used in the same way to protect the crops ; Hardo, Kabaddī, Phalā, or Torā is prisoners' base, in which boys divide into two parties, one of which takes its station on one side of a line or ridge (*pālā*) and their rivals on the other ; one boy shouting 'Kabbaddī ! Kabbaddī !' tries to touch one of those on the other side ; if he is able to do so and return in safety to his party the boy touched is said to be 'killed' and falls out of the game, but if the assailant is caught and cannot return he 'dies' and falls out in the same way ; the attack is made alternately and that side is victorious in which some remain after all their rivals are 'dead' ; in Jhārbandar, 'tree monkey', or Dab-dabolī, one boy climbs a tree and defends his position against the others ; in Kānchitī or Sawārī a boy is held by the ears by another boy who strikes a piece of wood supported by two stones and tries to knock it down. Lattū is the game of tops, and Phisal-bandā sliding down the steep banks of a tank, river, sloping stone, or hill. In Qāzī-Mullā one boy acts as the chief law officer and another as a learned divine. Sātkudī, 'seven steps', is like our hop, step, and a jump. Thikrīmār, 'throwing a potsherd (*thikrī*)' is like our Ducks and Drakes.

EPILOGUE

By the grace and blessing of God the *Qānūn-i-Islām* has been completed with great diligence and perseverance, and at the particular request of a just appreciator of the merits of the worthy, a man of rank, of great liberality and munificence, Dr. Herklots—May his good fortune, age, and wealth ever increase! Amen! and Amen!—for the benefit of the honourable English gentlemen—May their empire be exalted!

Nothing relative to the customs of Musalmāns in Hindostān will be found to have been concealed.

The only thing I have now to hope for from my readers is that they will wish the author and translator well, for which they will receive blessings from God and thanks from mankind.

> This is my hope from every liberal mind,
> That all my faults indulgence meet may find;
> Those who through spite or envy criticize,
> Are witless wights, and the reverse of wise.

Finished at Ellore.

INDEX-VOCABULARY